Jumping

— over —

the wheel

Jumping

over

the wheel

by

GEOFFREY BLAINEY

A Rathdowne Book
ALLEN & UNWIN

First published in 1993

A Rathdowne Book
Allen & Unwin Pty Ltd
9 Atchison Street, St Leonards NSW 2065, Australia

National Library of Australia
cataloguing-in-publication data:

    Blainey, Geoffrey, 1930-
    Jumping over the wheel.

    Includes index.
    ISBN 1 86373 564 X

    1. Pacific Dunlop - History. 2. Rubber industry and trade - Australia - History. I. Title.

    338.7678

Designed by text-art
Printed in Australia by Southwood

Contents

John Boyd Dunlop, riding on his own invention, the pneumatic tyre.

Preface

PACIFIC DUNLOP began as a small firm making the new Dunlop bicycle tyre in a Melbourne lane in 1893. When the first motor cars appeared on the roads it began to make the pneumatic tyre for cars, trucks and motor bikes. Branching into scores of other rubber products, ranging from hot-water bottles to shoes, it was one of the main manufacturing firms in Australia by the 1920s. Then it moved in a big way into clothes and textiles — the waterproof coat was a launching point — in the late 1960s, eventually becoming the main Australian seller of clothes and footwear. Then came other products, either using rubber as a raw material or serving the automobile industry. Some of the developments were unexpected. Rubber led the firm into latex products, including surgical gloves and condoms which, in the growing fears of AIDS in the 1980s, were very much health products. They in turn guided the company towards sophisticated medical products such as pace-makers and implanted bionic ears. Car tyres led into car batteries, and that led to making the huge batteries for American nuclear submarines and the new fleet of Australian submarines. Likewise, rubber cables led to plastic cables and then to optic fibres. The company really began with the wheel and was almost imprisoned by it: the later expansion came by learning to jump over the wheel.

Set up simply as an Australian and New Zealand rubber firm, with strict limits on where it could operate, it went overseas in the 1970s, becoming the world's largest manufacturer of various products. Founded as an offshoot of an overseas company, it became independent in 1899, lost some of its independence nearly thirty years later, finally regaining it completely in the early 1980s. In the course of expansion it bought out firm after firm. One firm — a dogged maker of rubber goods with the tantalising name of Barnet Glass — it had to buy out twice in the course of a quarter of a century.

An astonishingly large piece of Australia's industrial history is connected to Pacific Dunlop, partly because it took over, directly or indirectly, such well–known Australian names as Perdriau, Beaurepaire and Olympic, Repco, Slazenger, Prestige, Berlei, Grosby, 'Chesty' Bond, Ansell, Peters, Edgell-Birds Eye, Robur, Herbert Adams, Olex and Telectronics and literally a hundred other names. No Australian company has ever controlled so many household names. Pacific Dunlop also bought out GNB Batteries and other large businesses in North America and Europe. These names are part of the history of Pacific Dunlop. Some deserve a book in their own right.

I had no idea the firm was becoming so wide-ranging when I was invited to write its history in time for the centenary in 1993. The book is longer than I intended, but so much had to be omitted. I was encouraged to write the history as I saw it. I thank Sir Leslie Froggatt who was the chairman when I began the work, and today's chairman, John Gough, for their fairness and unfailing co–operation. A succession of three managing directors — Leith Jarman, John Gough and Philip Brass — I thank for their willingness to discuss issues and events. They will probably not always agree with some of the points I make or the shades of meaning I give. I thank John Rennie, the secretary, for organising the project with an experienced eye for what would be needed. Many others who gave me specific information I thank at the end of the book under the heading of Notes on sources of information.

John McLean, who came from Dundee via Hong Kong to Australia and first worked for Dunlop at head office in 1958, began to gather reminiscences from old employees and useful historical items long before this project formally began. He continued to gather and delve. I thank him and all others who helped to make this book more accurate and comprehensive than it would otherwise be. All faults and misunderstandings in the book — and no doubt they exist — are mine.

Geoffrey Blainey
June 1993

A Belfast toy

JOHN DUNLOP did as much as anyone to inaugurate the modern era of transport on land and air, but he himself made much of his living from the simple horse. Born in 1840, the son of an Ayrshire farmer, he went to Edinburgh to become a veterinarian at a time when in the cities the working horses and riding horses were that profession's main clients. Earning his diploma just before he was twenty-one, he crossed the narrow seas to Ireland where he practised in County Down for five or six years. It was in Belfast that he eventually settled. The demand for his services was so large that he employed a variety of staff. Even then, when he ran perhaps the largest business of its kind in all Ireland, he could not cope with all the requests to inspect lame horses and sick cows, sheep and dogs.

'He always seemed happy', recalled his daughter. In looks and manner he was described by one journalist as simple and unostentatious, a 'plain' Scot; but his approach to his work was far from plain. Though he rarely boasted he once said of his veterinary work: 'My style of treatment was quite original and unique.' He displayed his originality — and thereby reshaped the whole world — when in his late forties he became interested in the workings of the common wheel.

In 1887 his son John received a tricycle which he rode around the corridor-shaped yard of the Dunlop stables and stalls. The sight of his son riding over the rough gravel and cobblestones on wheels capped with a solid but thin strip of rubber made him think that there might be a faster and smoother kind of wheel. When exactly he had the brainwave of filling a rubber tyre with air is not clear, but in October 1887 he set to work to make one for his son. Already he knew how to make rubber articles. As an ingenious vet, he had made rubber gloves with which he could place remedies in a horse's mouth, and rubber tubes through which to pour medicine for cows which were paralysed after

John Boyd Dunlop, whose face appeared in Dunlop advertisements long after he had severed all links with the Dunlop companies.

giving birth to calves. Taking a thin strip of rubber and fitting it in the shape of a tube on top of a wooden hoop, he filled the rubber with air from a pump 'just in the way one would inflate a football'. In short he used the kind of light hand-pump which in the space of a few years would — as a result of his experiments — be henceforth called a bicycle pump.

John Boyd Dunlop's yard, Belfast, where he first tested his new tyre in 1887.

On a cold day in December 1887, Dunlop went into his work yard in Belfast to conduct his first experiment. Standing at one end of the long yard walled by two-storey buildings he held in his hand the front wheel which he had temporarily taken from his son's tricycle. Vigorously he threw it along the yard, but it did not go the full length. He then bowled an air-filled tyre fixed crudely to a wooden disc of the same size as his son's wheel. As he hoped, the air-filled tyre sped along the yard with wonderful momentum, hitting the back gate and bouncing off. Dunlop's veterinary assistant, watching the experiment, was a little suspicious. Suspecting that Dunlop had put more force into bowling the air-filled wheel, he himself tested the two wheels. The result was the same: the pneumatic tyre proved to be much faster. With one simple experiment Dunlop had come to a momentous conclusion. An air-filled tyre was capable of remarkable speed. Alternatively, it could travel with the expending of much less energy.

It was the speed as much as the comfort of an air-filled tyre which impressed Dunlop. A horse-drawn cart or a bicycle shod with such tyres would presumably go faster with the expending of less energy, and such an invention might create a revolution both in work and in leisure. He could not guess that the pneumatic tyre — the phrase he always used — would become so useful and versatile that it would make possible a form of transport which virtually displaced the working horse on which he had so far based his own career.

John Dunlop did not try his idea immediately. A very busy man, he could not easily find the time for this diversion. It was not until 28 February 1888 that he completed the making of two hollow wooden hoops, each shod with a pneumatic tyre and so shaped that they could be fitted over the existing rear wheels of his son's tricycle. He had hoped to fit a similar hoop to the front wheel but the shape of the forks of that wheel prevented him. The rear wheels of the tricycle must have seemed strange and cumbersome, almost resembling shoes that were covered with large and ill-fitting galoshes.

There was a full moon that night, and an eclipse of the moon had been predicted for about eleven. The Dunlop children were allowed to stay up and watch the spectacle. It was also an opportunity to test the new tyres on the rough stones of the neighbouring streets. As Dunlop recalled, the moon was full and the sky clear, when Johnny rode his tricycle out of the yard and into the street. Johnny rode for nearly an hour and was 'perfectly delighted'. After watching the eclipse he was allowed to ride again. Next morning the father inspected the new rubber tyres and to his delight found they had stood up well, not a single scratch being detected where the rubber had met the surface of the streets.

In no hurry to perfect or to patent his promising invention, John Dunlop made his next experiment five months later. He decided that an adult-sized 'Quadrant' tricycle should be shod with air-filled tyres. The tube, of thin sheet rubber, was larger than his pioneer tubes but held the air well. This heavier tricycle provided a more demanding test of the air-filled tyre. Ridden again and again on a pebbly road of 'newly laid macadam', it passed the test. Again its speed was breath-taking. All these trials had been conducted in relative privacy, usually in Dunlop's spacious yard in Belfast, and so news of the invention was slow to spread. The few who did hear of it were not inclined to believe that it was successful. Even Edlin and Sinclair, who had made the new Quadrant tricycle, expressed their doubts when Dunlop explained that he himself had made his own wooden rims and rubber tyres rather than rely on the orthodox tyres of solid rubber. Explaining that the tricycle was now much faster than any other made in Belfast — faster even when ridden by a child — he invited them to ride their bicycles over to his house and inspect the new machine. The only way to show off the new machine was to race it along the public street, and Dunlop told his young son to be ready to demonstrate his skills as soon as the two cycle-makers arrived:

> The following week both partners of the firm came over to my place. My son darted out of the yard on his tricycle, and the two gentlemen followed him on their machines. One of them was a good rider and overtook my son, who then put on a sprint and neither could catch up on him. Both gentlemen were thoroughly surprised at the speed of the machine, especially as it was ridden by a very young lad.

A Belfast toy

It was now time to protect his invention. On 23 July 1888, in his full name of John Boyd Dunlop, he took out a patent for what he called his device or 'improvement in tyres of wheels for bicycles, tricycles, or other road cars'. The choice of the phrase 'road cars' gives just a hint that it was not yet envisaged that an inflated tyre could sustain the heavy loads carried by carts and wagons. The carrying capacity of a rubber air-inflated tyre was still a matter for speculation and legitimate doubt. To carry the weight of a boy or a grown man was a very different burden from the weight of a heavy, wheeled wagon loaded with five tons of iron girders. Would Dunlop's invention carry a heavy weight? He was far from certain of the answer to that question.

He did not yet know that at least one other inventor had worked at this same idea, patenting it as long ago as 1846. His earlier rival was also a Scot, Robert William Thomson, who in his early twenties had invented a similar tyre. Made either of the guttapercha used to coat telegraphic cables or of native rubber, his tyres were designed to 'present a cushion of air to the ground'. He described them as aerial wheels. He tested and improved them, and tried them on the wheels of a horse-drawn brougham or carriage in Regent's Park in London. His invention found no market and was eventually forgotten.

In the history of mechanical invention the same machine is often invented by different people working in isolation and unaware that others are tackling the same problem. Sometimes the same thing is separately invented three or four times in the space of a couple of years. An inventor who ultimately wins fame and just occasionally a fortune is more than a person who initially thinks of a new idea. Success lies in turning the idea from theory into practice. It is not easy to make an invention: it is even harder to make that invention useful and practical. Dunlop was more successful than his predecessor, Robert Thomson of Kincardineshire, not only because he tackled the problem at a later time when knowledge of rubber and other raw materials was more advanced, but because, by the 1880s, hundreds of thousands of bicycles and tricycles were being ridden in Europe, America, Australia and other lands. And the bicycle, being light in weight, was far more suitable than a horse-drawn wagon or a steam traction engine for experiments involving a delicate air-filled tyre.

Dunlop not only worked in a more favourable environment than any inventor of the 1840s, he was also willing to keep on experimenting. Without that quality his invention, dynamic as it was, would have been buried in the big bound books of the patent office. He must have realised that a worthwhile invention consists not only of the original idea but of a chain of little subsidiary ideas, each mastering the obstacles thrown up by a new invention. Even when he had sprung a surprise on the two Belfast cycle-manufacturers by showing them his son astride a fast-travelling cycle, he knew that he had surprised them rather than convinced them. Many questions were still not answered. Would a new air-filled tyre last long or would its short life make it too expensive for all but the wealthy cyclists? Would the tyre be likely to puncture, thus proving itself too unreliable? Would it be hazardous on slippery roads? Would it lose its air too quickly to be practicable? Would the weight of a heavy cyclist rather than a schoolboy be such that the walls of the tyre were soon cracked or unsafe? Would it be useful only on a tricycle where two rear wheels shared the weight and not on a bicycle? Dunlop could not yet provide answers to those questions. Without a confident answer his invention would remain promising rather than important.

His two acquaintances, the Belfast cycle-makers, now built him a vehicle which could thoroughly test the merits of the air-filled tyre. They built a bicycle — not a tricycle — and so the tyre on the only rear wheel would have to support more weight. Dunlop wondered whether this flimsiest of tyres would quickly fall to pieces under all that weight: 'having some doubts as to the rear tyre wearing satisfactorily, the rear wheel was made large in diameter'. For the raw materials for the tyres on the big back wheel and the small front wheel, Dunlop sent a special order to Scotland. From Arbroath came the cloth that formed the cover or casing of the tyre. It was simply the best sailcloth used for yachts. With a pair of scissors and an adhesive, Dunlop personally turned the cloth and rubber into two tyres, each with an inner tube of rubber, an outer casing of finest sailcloth and a layer of rubber to prevent the cloth from being worn too quickly on the roads. At his own house he pumped each tyre high so that the bicycle could gain maximum speed. To those who watched his boy race along the Belfast streets the tyres were a joke. Whereas the typical machine had a thin strip of rubber on the rim of the wheel, the Dunlop bicycle had a fat sausage of a tyre. Even Dunlop confessed that the tyres were 'rather clumsy looking'.

The bicycle race was a popular entertainment at sports meetings, and in Belfast in May 1889 the captain of a local cycling club, Willie Hume, entered a racing bicycle equipped with Dunlop's inflated tyres. There was merriment when he appeared on the course. The smiles of the cynics vanished. Competing against the penny farthing machines, Hume's bicycle, with fat Dunlop tyres, won each of the four races. In August of that year the new tyres were first seen in an English race. Most of the Lancashire spectators, both at Liverpool and Bury, were amused at the sight of such tyres, until they showed their speed.

The Belfast cycle-makers, Edlin and Sinclair, made a few dozen bicycles with pneumatic tyres, selling them locally. Dunlop believed, however, that the invention deserved a stronger organisation. As he did not have the skill to market the new tyre, he finally entrusted the task to a minor Dublin businessman, William Harvey du Cros. Descended on his father's side from Protestants who had migrated from France to Ireland, du Cros was aged about forty-three, and a skilled organiser in the relatively humble post of assistant secretary of the Irish Commercial Travellers' Association. Infatuated with

A Belfast toy

Arthur du Cros, crack racing cyclist and managing director of the original Dunlop company in Dublin.

sport, a former fencing champion of Ireland and middle-weight boxing champion, he was already a keen cyclist. Once, with his son Arthur, he rode all the way from Dublin to Belfast and back, a return journey of more than two hundred miles.

William du Cros — his name was normally pronounced as Doo-croe — was President of the Irish Cyclists Association, and that gave him useful contacts and a potential influence. He also believed in the importance of Dunlop's invention. Quickly, du Cros began to organise a small company to promote

I have been carefully considering wheels and types for some time past and I would not be very much surprised if the pneumatic be superseded in the course of 2 or 3 years It is a question whether we should not try and be first in the field I dont think the pneumatic will ever be beaten on track however ..

Yours truly
J.B. Dunlop

Dunlop knew the value of his invention but was not over-confident in the late 1880s.

the new tyre. As a sales outlet, he enlisted a well-known Dublin cycle shop. Thus it was that the new company, formed on 18 November 1889, was given the cumbersome name of the Pneumatic Tyre Company and Booth's Cycle Agency of Dublin. The name of the firm was soon shortened and the more important name of Dunlop added.

In its new office and factory in Dublin, the Dunlop Pneumatic Tyre Company was a shining success. Under the driving leadership of du Cros, the Chairman of Directors, the company made and sold tyres at a high profit. Above all it was alert for ideas that would make the tyres more practical and durable. From Charles Welch of London and W. E. Bartlett of Edinburgh it bought new inventions which helped to fix the tyre to the wheel or detach it with relative ease. Anything that made a puncture more easily repaired was a windfall for the Dunlop company. In addition the Dunlop company bought the rights to a new air valve invented by Charles Wood. These patents were compensation for the fact that John Dunlop's original invention could not be securely patented and protected because of the earlier invention back in the 1840s. In England in 1892 a court declared Dunlop's major patent to be invalid. In France four years later another court came to the same conclusion.

John Dunlop, who had retired to live in Dublin, originally held 3000 of the 25 000 shares in the company. He did not rely on its dividends, for he held other business interests, including a large share in a sheep station in Australia. He did not dominate the discussions when he sat on the board of the Dunlop company; indeed in 1895, after a quarrel with du Cros, he ceased even to sit on the board of the company that carried his name. A few months later the head office and the main activities of the firm were removed from Ireland to England.

In spirit and ownership it was becoming the du Cros, not the Dunlop company. The father of the du Cros family had competence and flair, and flair was vital in launching a new product that had many critics. He was also aggressive and proprietorial. His six sons and various relations were soon prominent on the payroll. When a branch had to be opened, a son or nephew was likely to be assigned the task and the high salary too. The sons did their tasks with some of the father's skill and drive. Dunlop expanded quickly, opening factories in France, Germany and North America in the early 1890s. Another early conquest was Australia, where the terrain and long distances and climate seemed to be waiting for the Dunlop invention.

The cycling craze

I N 1886, at seven o'clock in the morning, two cyclists set out from Melbourne to cross the plains to Geelong. They were riding penny farthings, bicycles so named because the front wheel was much bigger than the rear wheel so that the wheels appeared to be like a big penny and a little farthing. The tyres were made of solid rubber, giving their riders a sense of perpetual vibration on the little-used road. Gaining a little from a side wind, they spent over four hours to reach a point just past Geelong. Their speed of eleven miles an hour, slow as it seems, was fast for cyclists travelling along a typical country road. After eating a steak, they began the return journey. All their strength seemed to be needed to pedal 'those terrible big wheels'. A cold northerly wind bit into their skin. 'It seemed to laugh at us on our high perches', wrote one of the cyclists. By nightfall, feeling exhausted, he flopped beside the road. At least he felt strong enough to continue to the nearest hotel, the Guiding Star, where he spent the night. He imagined that his friend, who pressed ahead, must have reached Melbourne, but the friend too had decided to call it a day. Eleven years later one of the cyclists, writing 'the wheel notes' for a leading weekly newspaper, recounted the long ride because it belonged, like the lofty penny farthing bicycle, to a vanished era. Cycling, he said, had been revolutionised. The main causes of the revolution were the present style of safety bicycle and the pneumatic tyre, two British inventions which were first seen on Australian cycling tracks within the same twelve months.

In New South Wales the safety bicycle was first used in the racing season in the summer of 1889–90. Many riders disliked the new machine, complaining that they were too close to the ground. The New South Wales Cyclists' Union initially banned safety cycles from competing with the penny farthing or 'ordinary', partly because the nimble new cycles dodged amongst the 'towering ordinaries', causing accidents. In Melbourne, as in Sydney, the shock at seeing the nimble newcomer gave way to attraction, and in 1892 the Austral Wheel Race was run for the last time on the high bicycles. Soon the small safety bicycle was normal.

The first pneumatic tyres probably reached Australia early in 1890. Fitted to safety cycles, they caused amusement. Much fatter than the solid tyres, they reminded some journalists of fire hoses wrapped round the wheels. A traveller named Malcolmson brought out from Belfast one of the first cycles to be fitted with Dunlop's new tyres and apparently lent the machine to a young bicycle dealer, E. W. Rudd. He rode it at a sports meeting held at the Melbourne Cricket Ground. Already cycling was so popular that the Melbourne Cricket Club allowed cyclists to race, before large crowds, on a rolled, mown track that circled the grassy outfield and consisted of four laps to the mile. Rudd realised that the new tyre was speedy. It was also fragile. One of the tyres on Rudd's bike was soon punctured on the grassy arena. To make matters worse, Rudd was not told how he could repair a puncture. Eventually, Malcolmson released the secret, and Rudd recalled that he was 'locked in his bedroom for a whole afternoon to learn how to repair a puncture'.

As a rider, Rudd was sufficiently impressed to import a few similar machines equipped with the new Dunlop tyres. He tried to sell them in Melbourne but most customers resisted his sales talk. 'It was a terrible job to sell machines with pneumatic tyres', he recalled. One of the disadvantages was that a cyclist stranded on the side of the road might take many hours to mend a puncture. These bicycles were usually half as dear again as a typical bicycle running on solid or cushion tyres. Fortunately Rudd's firm, trading in a shop in Elizabeth Street under the name of Rudd and Rand, was importing a variety of other bicycles and so could make a reasonable living during the many months in which customers eschewed the latest tyre.

Slowly the pneumatic tyre began to win the heated arguments in Australian towns. Disparagingly called sausage rolls, because they were much fatter than the normal tyre, they were seen as a fad that could not last. In races they were soon the winners. In Sydney the handicappers in some cycling races demanded that the cyclists who sent in their applications as starters must name the type of tyre they were riding on so that they could be handicapped accordingly. On several of the longest rides attempted, the successful cyclists rode on the new tyres. In the small town of Perth in 1892 several of the men who raced on pneumatic tyres were so fast in track races over a set distance that officials tried to ban them: such cyclists were taking an unfair advantage over rivals on the old-fashioned tyres. The handicappers 'were thrown into disarray', wrote Jim Fitzpatrick in *The Bicycle and the Bush*, one of the finest books written on sport in Australia. It was as futile to try to ban the new tyre as it was to ban the new motor car that began to appear on Australian roads a few years later.

From their Melbourne shop Rudd and Rand sold more and more pneumatic tyres, especially on the English bicycles of the Humber brand. They encouraged riders to bring in their bikes so that the old-fashioned tyres could be replaced with new Dunlop pneumatics. Rand claimed that his firm at that time 'produced the first pneumatic tyre that ever was made in Australia'. Presumably it was made from English raw materials by a skilled worker who had recently migrated to Australia with the practical knowledge acquired in an early Dunlop plant. In any case the wheels of the cycles of that era were of such diverse measurements that the fitting of a British-made pneumatic tyre to an unorthodox rim of a cycle wheel often must have required drastic reshaping of the rubber and cotton — even to the extent of virtually manufacturing a tyre and tube from the imported strips of cotton fabric and rubber.

Back in Ireland, the Dunlop company was eager to meet the growing Australian demand. Though Australia held only three million people compared to the thirty-nine million people in the British Isles, it formed an unusual and attractive market. Australian men were more likely to buy a bicycle, partly because they earned higher wages. Furthermore, they could ride a cycle the whole year round in most climatic regions of their land. In Australia a machine without a roof, and without protection against extremes of cold and rain, was not such a liability.

Early in 1893 Rudd was 'called home', to borrow his phrase, in order to discuss ways in which sales of Dunlop pneumatic tyres could be promoted in Australia. In the end his firm, to be known as the Austral Cycle Agency, was granted the monopoly of selling Dunlop products in Australia. Details of the arrangement — and how exactly the profits were to be divided between the Australian and British firms — have disappeared. One detail, however, was of profound importance for Australia's industrial history. The British firm agreed that pneumatic tyres should henceforth be made in Australia rather than shipped out from the British Isles.

While negotiations were being clinched, economic troubles became serious in Australia. Between the signing of the contract and Rudd's return to Melbourne, about half of the banks in Australia temporarily shut their doors as the result of a public financial panic. A severe depression settled on most cities. The cycle trade could not escape it. The consolation was that the new bicycles with their fast-improving tyres might still turn an army of walkers into cyclists, despite the depression.

Now that Dunlop was eager to assemble bicycle tubes and tyres in Australia, the remaining task was to decide where to assemble them. Melbourne was the favoured place, not merely because Rudd lived there. With nearly half a million people it was still the largest city in Australia, though it was fast being overtaken by Sydney. More than Sydney it was the home of cycling and was to remain so. Melbourne had one other advantage that no intending manufacturer could ignore. It was the home of protectionism. Unlike London or

Dublin or any city in the British Isles, Melbourne's politics revolved around the principle that the government must protect local factories from foreign imports and that manufacturing was ultimately the economic hope of Victoria. The Australian newspaper with the biggest daily circulation, the *Age* of Melbourne, was the pulpit of protectionism, and its editor, David Syme, was to become one of the prominent investors in the infant rubber industry in Melbourne. Even in 1893 the Victorian government collected an import duty of about thirty per cent on foreign-made bicycles and spare parts. Here was an incentive for Dunlop to avoid the import duty by shipping the raw materials to Melbourne and assembling them there.

It was easy to find a vacant factory in 1893. The city was studded with them, along with vacant offices and warehouses. In the heart of the city, within sound of the chimes of the post-office clock and the bells of the Swanston Street cable trams, a three-storey building of brick was cheaply rented by the Dunlop company. It stood in a narrow lane that ran between Lonsdale Street and Little Bourke Street, in a part of the city that is now lined with Chinese cafes and even then was favoured by a few Chinese shops and factories. Only five minutes' walk from the cycle shop of Rand and Rudd, the factory in Tattersall's Lane seemed large enough to accommodate at least fifty workers if the demand for tyres continued to grow.

The new factory manager, J. M. Peers-Smith, was about nineteen years of age. The *Australian Cyclist*, reporting his arrival from England, made no comment on his age. It was normal to be young in the cycling trade. On 19 October 1893 the journal simply informed readers that in England Peers-Smith had worked as a traveller or itinerant salesman for Dunlop. Normally the manager of a new factory would be expected to be experienced in manufacturing processes but the work at the new building in Melbourne was simple and called for no machinery of complexity. It was primarily the cutting and joining of the raw materials of rubber and cloth imported from Coventry in England, thus producing the outer covers and inner tubes. Few, if any, of the factory workers had experience in rubber. All they needed were dextrous hands, careful workmanship, and stamina to work the long hours required.

Peers-Smith encouraged racing cyclists to ride along the cobblestones of Tattersall's Lane and consult him about their difficulties. Occasionally he announced in the cycling newspapers that 'racing men' were welcome to call on certain days, between ten and twelve in the morning or three and five in the afternoon, when he would give their tyres a 'thorough overhaul'. Presumably he inspected the tyres and tubes on their bicycles, alert for any weakness that might force the rider to drop out of a cycling race or to lose valuable time making repairs. Such an inspection was wise because the rubber tube was fragile and the outer cover could easily slip off the rim. If in a major race the cyclist holding a winning position was to lose due to a puncture, the publicity was damaging for the manufacturer of his tyres. Already competitors were

Tattersall's Lane, Dunlop's first factory and sales branch in Australia, stood in the narrow streets of Melbourne's Chinese quarter.

making Dunlop-type tyres in England and shipping them to Australia, sometimes displaying them in shops alongside signs implying or even claiming that the tyres had been made by Dunlop.

One record of the first years of the factory has survived. A large leather-bound volume inscribed 'Private Ledger', it records in large handwriting a variety of payments. On 29 June 1893 the sum of £400 in cash was received from the head office in Dublin. While the sum seems small, it was probably enough to pay all salaries and wages at the factory for several months. Other pages of the ledger report that a wire advertising sign — presumably displaying the name of Dunlop — had been bought for the city shop of Rudd and Rand, electrical fittings had been paid for, and a typewriter had been purchased for the office inside the factory door. Eventually the telephone was connected to the office so that bicycle shops in Melbourne could ring through their order: the long-distance phone belonged to the future. The tyre business was still on a small scale. On 1 March 1894 the plant and machinery, fittings and fixtures were valued at only £121, while the stock of raw materials and tyres in the factory was worth just over £2000.

That year the Dunlop agents in Melbourne spent £40 on a horse-drawn dogcart, with two seats back to back. Another £21 was spent on a bicycle, presumably so that the manager could ride in style to appointments. Before long a handcart worth £1 19s, and presumably used for delivering materials, was added to the vehicles. There must already have been a horse to pull the dogcart, but horsefeed does not appear often in the ledger.

Mr Peers-Smith and his assistant, Mr H. Tuson, were often away from Melbourne, and in the ledger were listed the expenses of their visits to promote sales and give advice to cyclists in Bendigo, Sydney, Adelaide, Tasmania and New Zealand. It was on this last visit that Peers-Smith rescued a woman from drowning in the sea at Wellington. When he returned to England in 1894, showered with praise for his goodwill and courtesy, he was entitled to feel pride that the factory was running profitably and giving work to eighteen operatives.

E. W. Rudd, assisted by T. Rand, guided the venture in the first years. A dapper man with his tidy moustache and striped bow-tie and his white handkerchief peeping just the right distance from the top pocket of his coat, he was systematic and amiable in his business dealings. In 1894 he went to Europe by steamship with balance sheets that testified to his success. A year later he stepped down, the business of tyre-making now thriving.

The Irish family running the parent Dunlop company in the British Isles liked to place its relatives in the main overseas posts. A young member of the family was already in Melbourne and experienced enough to take over the management of Dunlop in Australia and New Zealand. The new manager, William John Proctor, was a nephew of Harvey du Cros, the chairman of the home company. He was a native of Lucan, near Dublin, but in telling people the year of his birth he was not always consistent; when he first came to Australia he gave his birth year as 1872, though later he gave it as 1874. As it is probable that he was only nineteen years of age when he arrived in Melbourne, he might well have decided that he would gain more respect in business if he pretended to be older. Later he had a tendency to claim more than he should have claimed; and after the departure of Rudd he was inclined in his talkative moments to tell the cycling press that he had founded the Dunlop business in Australia back in 1893. In fact he was at first an

William 'Jack' Proctor, Charles Proctor, Jimmy Carpenter (winner of the 1897 'Austral'), and F. Roche who was the agent for Raleigh cycles.

accountant for Rudd and Rand in the Austral Cycle Agency, where he showed plenty of ability. Possibly he was being groomed by his uncle for the top job in Australia; early in 1895 he went to England in the mail steamship and apparently asked for and was granted the top post in Australia. As a preliminary he was escorted through the Dunlop tyre works in Coventry where six hundred were employed, and shown also the Humber and Swift bicycle factories. His special treat was to be allowed to ride, with the three other cyclists, the new Swift 'quadruplet' — a machine built for four — all the way to Stratford-upon-Avon and back. Sweeping down one hill, the long bike travelled at thirty-five or forty miles an hour.

Proctor returned to Australia with two Humber machines in his voluminous luggage. Leaving the ship in Adelaide, he came by train to Spencer Street station in Melbourne where he was welcomed by a group of cyclists. Rudd was not quite so welcoming because he was no longer the manager. He remained the co-proprietor in Elizabeth Street of probably the largest cycle showroom in Australia, while Proctor set up his office in the tyre factory .

Proctor was then aged twenty-one (so far as can be ascertained) but in appearance and manner he was older. Genial and dashing, popular with the young brotherhood of cyclists in Melbourne, he undoubtedly worked hard in the factory. When he was visited by a reporter of The *Australian Cyclist* in August 1895, he was wearing an apron and doing the manual task of fitting tyres to a vehicle — perhaps the solid tyres for a cart — in readiness for the Agricultural Show. The reporter commented on his popularity and his pleasing Irish brogue. 'Jack' Proctor soon showed himself to be a fine leader of a small business. Feeling sure that sales of tyres could be increased dramatically, he began to advertise on a bold scale. His Dunlop Pneumatic Tyre Co. hired a publicity man — a rare post in those days. The eager publicity man was to remain with Dunlop for more than half a century and to influence the development of cycling and later of motoring throughout the land. His name was Harry James. He was in his early twenties, and his face was clean-shaven at a time when most young men sported a moustache. He had enthusiasm and, for his age, commonsense. He showed an ability to think up schemes that were sky-high and then drag them down to manageable levels. A cyclist himself, he appeared often on the sporting pages, and along the Sydney road he broke the world cycling record for twenty-five miles with a time of one hour and one minute.

The pneumatic tyre must have been one of the first products to be launched in Australia with strenuous advertising. Soon the word Dunlop appeared in newspapers, hoardings, and painted messages on the brick walls of city buildings. In the eyes of cyclists, Dunlop and the pneumatic tyre were the same. The word DUNLOP began to pop up on the trunks of trees, the outer walls of shops, the back page of magazines, and the walls of tramcars in Melbourne and Adelaide. Dunlop advertised not only in the specialist cycling magazines but in a cluster of smaller journals ranging from the *Bankers' Magazine* and *Punch* to the *Coachbuilder* and *Jewish Herald*. Women opening a cookery book found an advertisement for Dunlop at the back. Patrons at the opera saw a sketch of a Dunlop tyre as they turned the pages of their programme. Country travellers who bought a copy of that essential booklet, the *Victorian Railways Time Table*, were advised that they should think of cycling as well as travelling by train. Indeed they could combine both, taking their bicycle in the guard's van of a train to a rural station and then setting out for a day's cycling in the countryside.

As cycling grew in popularity — and much of that popularity stemmed from the new pneumatic tyre — the small Dunlop office and factory expanded. So many tyres were sold in Sydney that in 1896 a small office was needed there. The office must have opened in July or August, judging by the Sydney purchases listed in the private ledger for those months — a safe, a set of scales, a typewriter, gas fittings, linoleum for the floor and blinds for the windows, advertising signs for the front of the office or shop, and an office desk which cost £1 17s 6d. By 1898 additional offices had been opened in Adelaide and in Christchurch, New Zealand. When in June 1898 the London directors of what was now called the Dunlop Pneumatic Tyre Co. issued their annual report, they listed eight British cities where they had opened factories and offices, four cities in Australia and New Zealand, two in North America, one in South Africa, and seven European cities extending from Paris, Brussels and Copenhagen to Milan, Vienna and even Moscow.

In Melbourne the young men running Dunlop had to face fierce competition from rival brands of pneumatic tyres that were displayed in the cycle shops. Some of the rival tyres were cheaper; sometimes they were advertised with flair. More important, some of the rival tyres could be legitimately proclaimed as outstanding after they had proved their strength in a long journey. Increasingly the ability of a particular make of tyre and cycle to carry the rider long distances became the basis of publicity in the tyre industry. The heroic era of Australian cycling had arrived.

One of the first rides to capture the people's imagination was begun in 1893. Percy Armstrong and R. Craig set out from the new goldfield of Croydon, not far from the Gulf of Carpentaria, with the aim of riding to Sydney. No similar feat had been attempted on a bicycle in Australia. Perhaps nowhere in the world had cyclists attempted such a bold expedition, for most inland roads were primitive, no adequate road map could be bought even for the main roads, and along the way their chance of buying spare parts or repairing a major break was small. The climate was trying, the winds could be hot and blustery and dust-laden, and drinking water could be scarce. The two cyclists sensibly began their journey of nearly two thousand miles in the coolness of August. They made their way to the port of Townsville and then rode south, following stock routes rather than coastal roads.

The tyres on their safety bicycles were the popular cushion tyres which, two years later, would be almost completely supplanted by the pneumatic tyres. Cushion tyres consisted of an inner tube of solid rubber, providing a padding that was of some comfort. Though Armstrong and Craig had to bind their tyres with strips of green hide when the rubber began to deteriorate, they at least proved the worth of cushion tyres.

Reaching Sydney after some forty days on the track, Armstrong was persuaded to continue his journey to Melbourne. In Sydney a cycle shop gave him a new bicycle complete with Dunlop pneumatic tyres. As those tyres gave a speed unattainable with the cushion tyres, Armstrong resolved to make an eye-catching time for the journey. Unfortunately for him, there was no Hume Highway, only a series of primitive roads connecting the main towns. Wherever the road was softened by steady rain and churned up by loaded farm wagons, Armstrong had to dismount and carry his bike, sometimes walking in mud for several miles. At the end of his second day he reached the village of Jugiong, snug in the valley through which the heavy motor-transports now

Dunlop advertised on a large scale in the first years of the new Commonwealth of Australia.

roar at night. On his third day he reached Albury. At the close of his fourth day he was sitting on the edge of the bush, and using the light of his camp-fire to repair wheel-spokes he had accidentally broken. He reached Melbourne at noon on the fifth day, having spent four days and four hours on the 578 miles.

A record time for the road journey between the two cities, it was talked about wherever cyclists met. In Tattersall's Lane, the Dunlop staff made the most of the good news. Their only regret was that the two riders had not used Dunlop pneumatic tyres on the first and longer leg of the ride. And yet who could tell whether a set of two pneumatic tyres, with their vulnerability to punctures from sharp stones and thorns on outback roads, were fully capable of carrying riders safely across Australia?

In the south-east corner of the continent a procession of riders tried to make new records on the long overland routes. Hardly a month passed without an acclaimed rider setting out from the general post office in a capital city with the aim of breaking a record. Thus in February 1894, J. E. Snell rode from Adelaide to Melbourne, wisely choosing the solid surface of a route through Mount Gambier and Hamilton and Colac rather than the dangerous ride across the Ninety Mile Desert to Bordertown. When he reached a town, a local reporter eagerly noted his physical condition and sought his comments on the state of the road and telegraphed the news of his progress to the cities. Readers of the morning newspapers in Adelaide and Melbourne eagerly read how far he had travelled on the previous day. His ride aroused such enthusiasm that five thousand people were waiting at the General Post Office in Melbourne to cheer him. Several Dunlop officials were with the bystanders, for he rode on their pneumatic tyres. He told them — and they told the press whenever the opportunity came — that he had had to pump air into his tyres only three times in the course of a ride of 589 miles. Moreover his tyres suffered only one puncture.

In 1896 and 1897 the cycling heroes came riding from the far west. The flat country of the Western Australian goldfields was ideal for cycling. Most of the gold towns had no railway, and as high fares were demanded by the stage-coaches, the incentive to use a bicycle was high. Fast messenger services were established between the main gold towns, and the couriers travelled on bikes. A few of the cyclists decided that it was practicable to travel overland to Adelaide and Melbourne, across a desert traversed by nothing that could be called a road. The prevailing westerlies favoured an west–east ride though the absence of made roads and even of townships along the Nullarbor deterred all but the brave. The first of the brave was Arthur Richardson who, in November 1896, set out from the gold town of Coolgardie. He rode into Adelaide thirty-one days later. Early in the new year William Snell left the busy gold town of Menzies, north of Kalgoorlie, with the aim of riding all the way to Melbourne. That it was the height of summer did not deter him. Riding home to marry a Victorian girl, he went like the wind. Dunlop assisted him on the last leg from

Repairing a puncture, using a 'Dunlop midget outfit'.

Adelaide, providing a cyclist to pace him. He covered the distance from the goldfields to Melbourne in the sensational time of twenty-eight days.

The cyclist whose feat pleased the largest public was little William Virgin. His height was five feet three and a half inches (161 centimetres), his occupation a cycle messenger on the goldfields, and his ambition was to ride all the way from Perth to Brisbane, the longest ride so far attempted in Australia. Loading his Dux bicycle with provisions and water, he was farewelled in Perth. Along the track one of his pedals hit a stump and snapped: fortunately he found a bush blacksmith who repaired the pedal. By now the bikes of long-distance riders carried cyclometers to count precisely the miles they travelled, and by the time he reached Melbourne his tally was already 2394 miles. Virgin surprised reporters when he revealed that so far he had suffered no puncture. Dunlop's pneumatic tyre had really arrived. Virgin rode on towards Brisbane, losing a day or two when a dog bit him, but completing the Perth–Brisbane journey in the remarkable time of sixty days. Small boys, hoping one day to own a cycle, imagined that they too were Billy Virgin, riding their way into the headlines.

Harry James, seeking new ways of publicising Dunlop, was alert for riders who could bring prestige. He feared that a couple of brilliant but unknown riders might break records, using the tyres of a rival manufacturer, and so give endless publicity to the rival. James tried to sign up, in advance, as many as possible of the potential record-breakers. One of the speedsters who eluded him was Pat O'Dea. Across the Nullarbor he smashed the record, averaging a remarkable 103 miles a day. In the illustrated weekly and monthly magazines — the daily papers did not normally carry sketches or photographs — the moustachioed O'Dea could be seen sitting on his bicycle, his trousers tucked into his long socks, a hat conspicuously missing from his head. Attention was diverted from his own face and physique by the huge white letters on his black jumper. They proclaimed that O'Dea rode on B and B Tyres — a little-known pneumatic tyre made in Perth.

Harry James of Dunlop spent much time as a talent scout, searching for riders about to break into the record book. In April 1897 he opened his morning *Argus* and read, to his astonishment, that for the first time a cyclist had ridden from Adelaide to the centre of Australia and was planning to continue north to Darwin. Alice Springs was then the armpit of Australia, isolated, small and rarely visited. It was on the road to nowhere. Another thirty years would pass before the train line approached Alice Springs.

The name of the cyclist was Jerome Murif. In cycling circles his name appeared to be unknown. James immediately wondered what kind of tyres were on his wheels because if Murif succeeded in crossing the dry lands of the centre and if he was thereafter promoted he would become the most celebrated cyclist in Australia. Alice Springs was a tiny town, and a telegram arriving there was sure to find him. James at once wrote out this message:

Congratulations on amazing achievement and best wishes for successful termination of pioneering ride across Australia. Stop. Would like to know what machine and tyres you are riding. Stop. Reply paid. Dunlop Tyre Co., Melbourne.

Murif received the telegram but thought lightly of the good wishes. As for disclosing the brand of tyres on his bike, he preferred to be silent. 'Thanks', he replied in the briefest of telegrams: 'good wishes not negotiable up here — Jerome Murif.'

Harry James was even more determined to learn what kind of tyre had carried the cyclist into territory which was previously believed to be within the reach of camels rather than bicycles. Hoping that Murif was riding those tough new Dunlop tyres called 'Bushman', and guessing that he had bought them in Adelaide, the starting point of his journey, James made urgent enquiries to Dunlop agents asking to whom they had recently sold such tyres. Eventually he was told that a dealer had sold a German bike called the Electra to Murif who had then asked that it be fitted with 'Bushman' tyres.

The lonely cyclist was clearly a world apart from the normal record-maker. Shunning publicity and the money that often followed it, Murif had set out without even hinting to the bicycle dealer that he intended to ride across Australia. He had not told the newspapers in Adelaide. He had simply hopped on his new bicycle and with a little equipment — a felt hat on his head, a water bag over his shoulder, a revolver, and a small swag tied to his handle bar — had pedalled out of Adelaide. He was not foolhardy: he knew the bush. He was simply anonymous, and even to this day the stories of him are ambiguous, some saying he was Australian-born and others speaking of his Irish brogue. While he did not seek publicity he could not escape it. Anyone who rode from the staidest city of Australia wearing a pair of pyjamas and passed the isolated cattle stations wearing dusty once–white pyjamas was easily traced. Harry James continued to send telegrams of congratulations to the little overland telegraph stations which he rode past. Murif, however, was not interested in publicising Dunlop tyres. When he reached the tropical port of Darwin after a ride of eighty-three days he was surprised to learn that he was a hero. Returning by steamship to Adelaide he could not understand the fuss when he landed. He shunned the offer of a testimonial to which Dunlop was to be a major subscriber, and simply vanished.

Dunlop imagined that an attempt — this time from Darwin to Adelaide — to improve on Murif's record would earn a mountain of publicity. Moreover the new riders might achieve a tally of punctures even fewer than Murif's four. Accordingly, two cyclists were sent by sea to Darwin. Their journey southwards, however, was a chain of mishaps. The man in the white pyjamas now seemed all the more remarkable.

As cycling feats attracted louder volleys of publicity, and as the top cyclists provided ever-glowing advertisements for the brand of tyres they rode on,

Dunlop tyres carry 'half a ton' along St Kilda Road, Melbourne, about 1907.

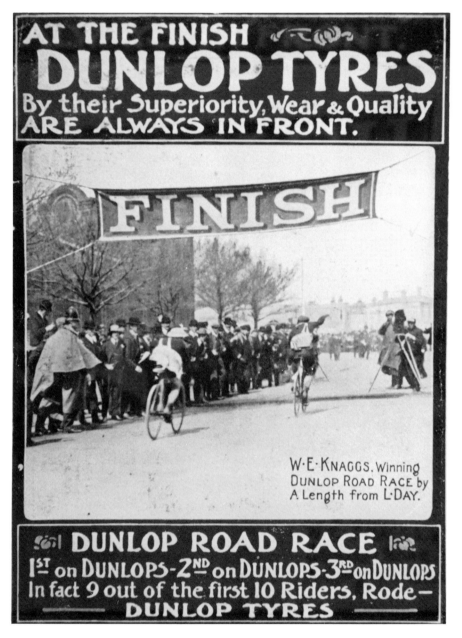

Around 1900, Dunlop was one of the few companies to use photography in its advertising. The finishing line of many cycling races, at the Haymarket corner in Melbourne, featured in many advertisements.

Dunlop decided to become a promoter of cycle racing. The main long-distance race in Australia was ridden along the 165-mile road from the western Victorian port of Warrnambool to Melbourne. The race's first sponsor was a bicycle shop in Elizabeth Street, Melbourne. From their own shop and a chain of agencies in country towns, 'Tom' Scott and R. Moreton sold an English bicycle called 'Raleigh' and an American model called 'Yellow Fellow'. A new Raleigh cycle was offered as first prize in the first Warrnambool–Melbourne race in 1895. Unfortunately the handicapping was a mixture of hit and miss, with the riders being sent away in only three groups — the first with a two hour start, the second group with a one hour start, and finally the scratch riders. The winner came from the group which had been given the luxury of a start of two hours. His riding time of 11 hours and 44 minutes, slow — very slow — by today's standards, was much faster than the press and spectators had predicted; and when he reached the busy haymarket at the top end of Elizabeth Street most of the intending spectators had not yet arrived.

In the following year a wider variety of handicaps was introduced but that improvement was nullified by the decision to allow riders to bring along their own pace-makers. A sour taste was in some mouths when the winner came into sight riding a Raleigh, having been assisted by Raleigh pace-makers on a swift ride that sliced nearly three hours from the previous best time. By 1897 the rules of the race were sufficiently straightened out for Dunlop to risk its name as an assistant sponsor. It agreed to provide the refreshments for the racing cyclists by setting up food stations at several points along the dusty road. It also went out of its way to ensure that many of the best riders favoured Dunlop tyres.

The riders assembled at Warrnambool just before dawn on a cool morning in late September. One of the favoured riders, George Carpenter of East Melbourne, was pottering about near the starting line when he was dismayed to hear his back tyre blow out. Dunlop was ready with a spare wheel fitted with a Dunlop racing tyre. Quickly it replaced the old wheel and its punctured tyre. The incident did not go unnoticed and the press reported that the new tyre, some 165 miles later, was 'as taut as when the race started'.

The road was unsealed and dusty for much of the way, and when the various bunches of riders reached Camperdown they were delighted with the refreshments Dunlop had arranged. Carpenter, determined to remain in the spotlight, astonished spectators by drinking four lipped tins of hot malted milk. Harry James, himself a scratch man in the first running of this long race, had the ingenuity to provide every rider with a calico satchel that could hang over their shoulders as they raced, and many of the cyclists consumed the titbits he provided as they rode towards Geelong where 'hot bread and milk' were awaiting them at the 125-mile mark. The calico shoulder-bag was to become common in long-distance races. In the 1930s, under the name of the bike bag, it was standard wear for hundreds of thousands of ordinary cyclists.

The cycling craze

Hubert (later Sir Hubert) Opperman leading the field in the 1924 Australasian Road Championship. He won, riding the 165 miles from Warrnambool to Melbourne in 7 hours, 15 minutes, 37 seconds. He made the Malvern Star a famous bicycle long before it became a Dunlop product.

At the 125-mile mark at Geelong, 'hot bread and milk' awaited the riders at another Dunlop feeding station. And then the race leaders pedalled across the plains towards Melbourne, pushing into a slight head wind. To their dismay they found the highway packed with clay-pans and scarred by the deep ruts from passing drays. One rider, a farmer named Vaughan from Learmonth, decided to take a short cut, and on the advice of a passer-by he rode across a paddock for a mile or so and then returned to the route. The paddock proved to be much faster than the highway and, unknown to the leading bunch, Vaughan now led the field. When the 'leading bunch' reached Flemington and finally sprinted across the finishing line at the haymarket, its riders were astounded to hear that they were not the leaders. Farmer Vaughan, when questioned, honestly admitted his mistake, and Jackson of Ararat was given the verdict by the margin of one wheel.

Harry James thought well of his company's tentative venture into the expensive game of sponsorship, the first of thousands of such it would enter. He had reason to be pleased. The four place-getters, though each riding a different brand of bicycle, had used Dunlop pneumatic tyres.

The desire to break cycling records became almost a mania. As the travelling distances and road surfaces and climate differed from one nation to another, real comparisons between a long-distance ride in Australia and other lands were difficult. On a racing track in an enclosed sports ground, however, a time trial over a set distance gave speeds that could be compared internationally. Australian cyclists had won dozens of these international records in the early 1890s, winning and then losing the records as faster times were recorded overseas. As a new world record led to increased sales of certain models of bicycles and brands of tyres, the cycling firms set out to assist the record-breakers. Dunlop began to used tandem cycles — pedalled by two classy riders — to set a fast pace for the lone cyclist attempting a record. The private ledger reported that in December 1896 a total of £9 4s was spent on coloured sweaters, knickers and caps for the Dunlop 'racing team'. On 23 January of the following year more than sixteen pounds was paid in weekly wages to these pace-makers. Summer was the height of the cycle-racing season and of the record-breaking attempts on country and bush roads. Presumably the racing team was virtually disbanded and the members went back to their normal jobs before Easter.

The tandem bicycle could set a fast pace. Perhaps a bicycle pedalled by three skilled men would go even faster. Before long the Dunlop racing team were dashing about on bicycles built for four or five — popularly called quads and quints. An even faster pace could be set by the internal combustion engine, in short by a motor bike. In 1898 Dunlop in Melbourne imported from England two ordinary tandem bicycles, each of which was equipped with a small engine and triangular petrol tank fixed to the frame between the two riders. The engine was made by De Dion, of two-and-a-half horsepower, lacking a carburettor, and driven by an imported brand of petrol of such

Dunlop pacing team and officials near the Exhibition Building, Melbourne, about 1897.

volatility that if the petrol filled a saucer almost to the brim, it would evaporate in a couple of minutes. When the two cyclists pedalled, and the engine too was running, the tandem could reach forty miles an hour, thus setting a brisk pace for the cyclist following behind.

Special cycling tracks were constructed on various sports grounds in the late 1890s. The best-known asphalt track in Australia stood in the grounds of the Exhibition Building in Melbourne where big crowds paid to see and bet on cyclists competing over set distances. The Australian Natives Association, the friendly society and nationalist lobby which boomed in Victoria at the turn of the century, became the biggest sponsor of cycle racing; and its cycle carnival at the Exhibition grounds on Australia Day — or ANA Day, as it was called in Victoria — was one of the main events on the sporting calendar of the whole nation. On Australia Day in 1900, Dunlop caused a stir by sponsoring a race with the handsome prize of fifteen gold sovereigns and providing their two tandem motorcycles as pace-setters. When the contest had first been announced, it was pointed out with indignation that the raised riding track around the arena was so steep that it was a danger to the tandem riders and the cyclist in pursuit and, of course, to the watching crowd. W. J. Proctor, as Dunlop's manager in Australasia, replied that his motorised tandems had already tried out the track and judged that it was safe. Even so there was high tension amongst the spectators as they watched the tandems pace each of eight invited riders, lap after lap, over a three-mile course. No rider fell, and G. Sutherland of New Zealand won in a time of five minutes and thirty seconds.

By 1910, semi-liberated women were taking up cycling in large numbers, as this advertisement proclaimed.

Cycling was becoming a way of life for people of middling income in the late 1890s. In the countryside young parsons cycled to outlying churches. Teachers at remote country schools bought a bike so that they could ride occasionally to the nearest town. Young men and women bought bikes and came together in hundreds of cycling clubs. A few shearers bought bikes to travel from one shearing shed to another. The plains were ideal for the bicycle, except when the wind was blowing in the wrong direction. But most bikes were in the cities, though they were not yet so cheap that the typical child of fourteen could afford one. A major attraction of the post of telegraph boy was that, from 1898, a bicycle was often provided with the job so that he could quickly carry telegrams from the post office to houses, shops and businesses.

The Victorian politician, Alfred Deakin, was taught how to ride a cycle in 1895. With his twelve-year-old daughter, he explored the suburbs on early morning rides. When the family went for holidays by the sea the bicycles went too. Deakin lived in South Yarra and cycled regularly to parliament house in the city. It was his distinction in 1906, when prime minister, to receive a summons for riding on a Melbourne footpath.

In city streets the speed of fast cyclists could arouse a sense of outrage. Regulations, devised by municipalities rather than by the central governments, tried to control these wild dashes. Justices of the peace began to express their indignation. Even in the early 1890s the City of Melbourne tried to compel cyclists to carry lights after sunset, to ride no more than two abreast, and to shun that practice of which Deakin would be guilty. It is widely believed that it was the noise of early motor cars which created terror amongst horses in the streets. In fact many horses were surprised more by the silence of the cyclists. The City of Melbourne was one of many bodies which enacted that when cyclists approached a horse which was alarmed, they should 'dismount as speedily as possible'.

Cyclists began to wear garments and knick-knacks designed for the cycling craze. They wore metal clips to prevent the bottom of their trousers from brushing against the greasy chain on the machine; they fixed on a bell to ring as they approached pedestrians crossing a street. Cycling shoes and sweaters and knickers appeared in shop windows. For half a guinea a keen rider could buy a cyclometer which recorded — to an aggregate of ten thousand miles — how far he cycled in a year. For a little more money a woman could steer her bike not with a metal handlebar but one specially made of hickory. 'No more numbness in the hands, wrists, and arms', was the promise made in 1898 by the big emporium of Foy and Gibson which sold these novelties. By a stroke of genius a manufacturer even devised a self-lighting cigarette which chain-smoking cyclists could carry in their pocket and light up while the wind was rushing past. The cigarette could simply be lit by striking its end on the special tin. How the tobacco tasted, after the end of the cigarette had been dipped in an inflammatory chemical, can only be imagined.

No district in Australia and New Zealand escaped the excitement about cycles. The hottest regions were more wary of cycling. In Queensland in 1899 it was said that 'all the riding was done in the winter'. On the goldfields of Western Australia, however, the vast plains and the absence of cheap alternative transport made the bicycle popular on even the hottest days. Sydney remained less enthusiastic than Adelaide and Melbourne, the hub of the cycle trade. New Zealand on the other hand was eager, with the South Island leading the way.

Sales of tyres and cycles boomed in 1895, 1896 and 1897. One trader estimated that sales of cycles in Victoria were multiplied by about twenty in little over a year. Many of the machines and tyres imported from Europe and England were unsuited to Australian roads, climates and preferences. Moreover, too many crates and boxes of cycles reached Australian ports. By the end of 1897 the market was temporarily glutted. One of the leading importers was the confectionery and chocolate maker, Mac Robertson of Fitzroy, and at the end of the summer of 1897–98 he was reducing the price of his American-made monarch cycles from twenty-five to sixteen pounds. 'We are quitting the cycle business', he announced. The flood of imports was now challenged by local factories producing for local needs and preferences, and by June 1899 perhaps half of the bicycles sold in the continent were made in Australia.

The Dunlop factory in Tattersall's Lane gained, being the main supplier of tyres and tubes for cycles built in Australia. But even in the period of heavy imports it was busy supplying replacement tubes and tyres. Its profits in most of these years must have been heartening. One of the few surviving figures for the 1890s covers the six months ending in January 1897 when Dunlop's profit in Australia — according to the private ledger — was 7607 pounds. That was a big profit for a relatively small business. On the other hand the tyre and tube formed a larger part of the total cost of making a cycle in the 1890s than in later years. For example Cooper Cycles of England, seeking an agent to sell its product in Australia, offered to provide at the London docks its own bicycles securely packed and boxed for the following prices:

Cycle, with cushion tyres	£5. 15
Cycle, with standard pneumatic tyres	£7. 15
Cycle, with Dunlop pneumatic tyres	£9. 00

In the light of such a difference between cushion tyres and Dunlop tyres — and that difference in price would increase once they reached Australia and were moved from wholesale to retail outlets — the boom in the cycle trade must have been a bonanza for Dunlop. The public, of course, had to be persuaded that the Dunlop tyre contained more rubber and also lasted longer. Increasingly they were persuaded.

Year after year the pneumatic tyre became less vulnerable. A series of major and minor improvements in the raw materials, the manufacturing process, and the cyclists' knowledge of how to look after the tyres made them more durable than the first such tyres imported to Australia. The frequent leaking of air at the point where the valve was inserted in the tube was largely remedied. The joints in the tyre and tube leaked less often, and Proctor, by 1898, was telling newsmen that the joints were 'hermetically sealed' as a result of a process that removed sulphur from the rubber. The tyre was so strengthened with a concealed lacing of thin wire that the tyre was less likely than in the past to slip off the rim. The punctures caused by sharp pieces of road metal,

Three stenographers at Tattersall's Lane—the 'Correspondence Department'.

Factory employees at Tattersall's Lane, 1897.

Horse-drawn wagons and carts rattled along the cobblestones to the Dunlop factory in 1897 to deliver materials from the wharves or to take away the finished tyres.

protruding stumps, horseshoe-nails and broken glass became less frequent with the arrival, about 1897, of the so called 'puncture proof tyre' with its thicker layer of fabric and thicker layer of outer rubber. Dunlop's own Thornproof Tyre was widely bought in the bush. A very wide tyre, it slowed down the bicycle on normal roads though in compensation it was ideal on sandy roads.

The three-storey factory in the Melbourne lane was bulging by 1897, such was the demand for pneumatic tyres. In just two years its weekly output had leaped from 100 pairs of tyres to 1500 pairs. The factory was modernised as it grew. When in February 1897 the proprietor of the *Australian Cyclist* inspected the factory he noted telephones linking the office and work-rooms, the novelty of electric light, and an Otto gas engine supplying compressed air so that every bicycle tube could be tested. He reported that tyres were being made especially for horse-drawn buggies, and he observed the big stocks of bicycle pumps and the Dunlop Midget outfits which cyclists bought for a shilling and placed in their vest pocket in readiness for the next puncture.

He peeped into the correspondence department and noted three stenographers and three typewriters presided over by Mr Green, whom he described as 'a competent man from the old country', while the accounts department was presided over by Mr Percy Iredale who kept the firm's cash in a safe which only 'a gang of forty thieves' would be able to shift. In the cobbled lane, a horse-drawn wagon could be seen bringing from the wharves the cumbersome rolls of cotton fabric — like massive carpets all rolled up — and the sheets of rubber. Onto another cart were loaded the packing cases containing new tyres and tubes or the steel rims on which they were now fitted: by now a wooden rim had been rejected as too fragile in the Australian heat. W. G. Rae, a sporting journalist, wrote such a glowing description that Proctor issued it in February 1897 as a special photographic booklet for Dunlop's customers.

The sales of tyres and tubes continued to soar. Even when sales of new bikes fell, sales of tyres remained strong. The work-rooms of the factory became crowded, more and more hands were hired. Proctor wanted more space but in the network of lanes fronted by smallish buildings the floor space was not easily found. Moreover the risk of fire was high, and visitors noticed the 'no smoking' signs, the fire hydrants and hoses, and the fire-buckets filled with water in readiness. The insurance officials were conscious of the inflammability of the rubber and also the adhesive or solution used to join together the parts of tubes and tyres: 'they charge us very heavy premiums in consequence', Proctor noted. The biggest hospital in Melbourne stood less than a hundred paces away, and its doctors might occasionally have wondered whether the tyre factory, now that it was so large, should be in such a spot. Proctor began to talk of a new factory. But before a new factory could be planned on a new site, a new owner arrived.

Behind the smoke at Montague

I N ENGLAND the Dunlop company rose like a rocket. In one of the most spectacular displays of corporate fireworks ever seen, the company also showed signs that it might fall almost as rapidly.

In short, the company fell into the hands of the most plausible of tricksters. Ernest Terah Hooley, the new promoter of Dunlop, came from a family of lacemakers in the Midlands. He found it easier to make money than lace, and by the time he was thirty he was a stockbroker in Nottingham, looking out for new ventures. In 1889 he began to exploit the craze for bicycles. He bought small cycle-making workshops — including Raleigh, Singer and Swift — and floated them into public companies, from which he was a large beneficiary. An utter optimist, he inhabited a mental world in which a puncture was a sheer impossibility. His optimism inspired people and his personal background calmed their doubts. He seemed to be a public-spirited man who shunned the normal vices. He did not smoke and he did not touch alcohol. His Baptist connections were first rate, and on Sundays — until his own timetable blew out — he played the organ in a chapel.

Hooley also gained from aristocratic connections. Buying a farm next to the royal estate at Sandringham, he found a way of being introduced to the Prince of Wales. He did not waste his widening network of titled acquaintances. Earls and lords were persuaded, for a fee much larger than company directors normally received, to appear on the prospectuses of the companies Hooley floated and to sit like silver cruets at the board tables. Becoming more ambitious, he took an option on large and profitable firms and, after showering them with publicity, floated them into larger companies. He floated Schweppes and Bovril, and turned them into two of the most popular brand names of the day. As a rule he tried to float only worthwhile companies, but too much of the cash received from the share-buyers went into his own pockets and those of the previous owners rather than into financing an expansion of the business. Most of his actions — the exceptions were notable and twice were to land him in prison — were within the law. He was simply a bird of prey circling overhead during a financial boom.

In 1896, at the height of a British speculative boom, Hooley thought that the tyre firm of Dunlop was yet another appropriate vehicle in which he could make money. For a man who had made a reputation as a promoter of cycling companies it was easy to take up the bicycle tyre. He decided to pay the huge sum of three million pounds for the business and then sell it to the public for five million. It was carried through with charm and speed. As the Chairman of Dunlop recalled, 'Two gentlemen arrived in my office and made an offer of 3 million pounds. I had not met them before'. The Chairman, Harvey du Cros, summoned together his directors in Dublin on the following Saturday and 'by the next Wednesday the deal was completed'.

To raise the purchase money, Hooley invited three noblemen to join the board of his new Dunlop Pneumatic Tyre Co. Limited, and issued a prospectus that forecast a glorious future for cycling and for the firm that already manufactured most of the tyres. He pointed out that his new company held in its hands virtually all the important tyre patents, having just paid the huge sum of 196 000 pounds for William Erskine Bartlett's patent which boldly supplanted the wiring, cementing or bolting of the tyre to the wheel rim with a version of the tension technique used to this day. Hooley, to his delight, saw English investors rush to apply for shares. So many clamoured for shares in May 1896 that he could have raised his five million pounds twice over.

Hooley then bowed out of Dunlop, another fortune in his hand. Unknown to the new shareholders, the structure of the company had been damaged, though to all appearances it seemed little changed. Dunlop retained its existing management with the du Cros family in control, and three peers — the Duke of Somerset, Earl De La Warr and the Earl of Albemarle — now ornamenting the boardroom under the chairmanship of Harvey du Cros. While the du Cros family and the other owners of the pre-1896 Dunlop company had made substantial sums from the deal, the company, as a commercial organisation, was the loser. Henceforth it had to earn much larger profits to pay the expected dividend on one million preference shares, one million ordinary shares, two million deferred shares, and one million debentures. If the bicycle business continued to boom, Dunlop had a hope of earning the required profits. But the London stock exchange had many newly-floated bicycle or tyre companies each competing for a market which did not grow quickly enough. In the English summer of 1897 the boom in bicycle sales came to an end. The export markets shrank, partly because American cycles were competing everywhere with British exports, not least in Australia which, despite its population of barely three million, was America's eighth largest export market.

The new Dunlop company made less profit than expected, and much of it went in litigation. To protect its vital patents it initiated 730 legal actions in the space of four years, and that cost a fortune. The slump in its shares, in all their variety, was chastening. The largest category of shares, the two million deferred shares, each with a face value of one pound, fell from 37s 6d to 6s 6d in just over two years. The result of the Hooley transaction was that Dunlop was gravely over-capitalised and could not earn enough profits to pay a worthwhile dividend to its small army of shareholders. By 1899 it had no hope of raising new capital, for all its shares were far below their par value. And yet Dunlop now needed capital to strengthen its fragile position.

Several patents which Dunlop believed were important would expire in the first years of the new century. The company was also vulnerable because it depended on outside manufacturers for its main raw materials, rubber and cloth. In London the board of Dunlop decided that the time had come to manufacture the rubber sheets and even perhaps the cloth and other fabrics used in making tubes and tyres. That venture, however, required more capital than Dunlop itself could provide. The solution was to sell its factories and agencies outside Europe. In 1898 the American business, with its factory in Chicago, was sold to an American syndicate. In turn the Canadian and Australian tyre businesses, patents and rights were offered to the local managers in what is now called 'a management buy-out'. On 19 December 1899, at the annual general meeting of shareholders held in the Hotel Cecil in London, the chairman apologised for the company's plight and for the absence of a dividend even for the ordinary shareholders and, according to the next day's *Economist* he 'explained at great length' why they had to sell the American and Australian businesses. It was all very embarrassing.

Richard Garland of Toronto was the main buyer of the profitable tyre factory being run in Melbourne. Born in Ireland, he was like nearly all of the first generation of Dunlop leaders — obsessed with outdoor sports. As a cyclist in Dublin he had met the du Cros brothers, and through that contact he was given the job of promoting Dunlop's tyres in Toronto and New York. Though limited in his business experience, Garland had personality and energy, a persuasive tongue, and enough mechanical knowledge to repair tyres. Slightly above middle height as measured in that era — he was about five feet eight inches tall — he had dark hair, thickish lips and rather a serious manner from which charm was not excluded.

While managing the Dunlop tyre business in Toronto, Garland gave his spare time to sport, becoming president of the local cycling and lacrosse clubs. He also enjoyed football until an accidental kick on the knee made him slightly lame, and by the time he reached his thirties one leg was so stiff that he could not ride a bicycle with ease. Mainly at his own expense Garland brought out a team of amateur Rugby players from Ireland — the Duke Collins team — and arranged fixtures in Canadian cities. A surviving notebook

Richard Garland, who came from Canada to float the company.

records that tour of 1899. Alongside Garland's handwritten figures of the money lost, his wife wrote playfully the words 'as usual'. In business affairs he was not usually a loser.

When the English board of Dunlop gave Garland the opportunity to buy the Canadian and United States' businesses he jumped at the offer. To raise the necessary funds — possibly a sum exceeding two hundred thousand pounds — he formed a syndicate consisting of three other Toronto business-men and an Ottawa man. Garland himself was in the syndicate but perhaps not one of the major investors. The new company was called the Dunlop Tire Company of Canada, and it was intended also to form a separate American company to run the business at Belleville in New Jersey.

The English board likewise offered to sell to the Australasian manager, W. J. Proctor, the business he had hitherto managed. Proctor, unlike Garland, was not sure what to do. A few months previously he had let slip to a news reporter that he thought the business was worth more than 200 000 pounds. Now, on being offered the same business reportedly for a mere 110 000 pounds, he had second thoughts. While he had commercial contacts who might well join him in raising the money, he decided to do nothing.

In Toronto, Garland decided to buy the Australian and New Zealand interests of the English Dunlop company. In the small Australian market the sale of Dunlop tyres was probably more lucrative than in the huge North American market. For his buy-out in Australia, Garland formed another syndicate in which the main member was John Jackson Palmer, owner of a Toronto foundry that supplied the metal type which was the basis of the printing industry. Garland and Palmer duly sailed in the mail steamer to Melbourne and met bicycle dealers and talked with sharebrokers, bankers and directors. The Toronto visitors observed that in the year ending January 1899 the business had sold a grand total of 55 600 Dunlop tyres. The net sales for that same period were 92 000 pounds and the profit was rising, and in the opinion of a Sydney and a Melbourne accountant the bad debts were normally low. Here was an enticing business, holding the monopoly of Dunlop patents throughout Australia and New Zealand. The Canadians decided to buy control of what already was called the Dunlop Pneumatic Tyre Company of Australasia. The price agreed was 136 861 pounds.

At that time it was rare for overseas investors, let alone Canadians, to buy out well-established Australian businesses, especially in manufacturing. The plan of Palmer and Garland, however, was not to seek full ownership but to invite Australian shareholders to supply part of the capital needed to buy the business from Dunlop. To enlist Australian shareholders was not as easy as they had thought. Australians were keen buyers of mining shares, enjoying the gamble, but were less excited by industrial shares. Most factories of any size in Australia were owned privately, and those manufacturing or industrial shares regularly traded on the Melbourne stock exchange could be counted on the fingers of two hands: five brewing companies, two brickworks, Swallow and Ariell which made biscuits, the Colonial Sugar Refining Company which refined sugar from its mills and plantations, and Kitchen and Apollo which made soap and candles. It was not at all clear that public support would enable Dunlop to join that list.

As the parent Dunlop company in England had been in the headlines following the exploits of the adventurer Hooley, the sale of its Australian business was probably looked on with suspicion by many investors. They wondered whether there was a hidden reason behind London's sudden resolve to sell the Australian business. Moreover every Victorian investor had been taught by the banking disasters only six years previously that there was no such thing as a completely safe public company. Admittedly, 1899 was proving to be Victoria's most prosperous year for an entire decade but that did not necessarily give the green light to cautious share buyers.

Garland and Palmer, staying at Menzies Hotel in Melbourne, now wondered whether the 80 000 pounds they hoped to raise from the Australian public was too high a sum. They realised that they must sacrifice part of their own potential profit in order to woo the sharebrokers; in short, the issue of shares must be underwritten. Whereas the practice of sharebrokers agreeing to underwrite or guarantee the success of a new issue of shares is now commonplace, it was a novelty in 1899. Surviving letters reveal that the leading Sydney firm of sharebrokers, Mullens and Co. of Pitt Street, agreed to underwrite ten per cent of the issue in return for a commission of twelve and a half per cent, to be paid to them more in cash than in shares. Mullens accepted the risk that if they could not sell the shares to clients in the space of a few days they would have to pay for them. In Melbourne two stockbrokers, J. B. Were and Son and William Noall and Son, almost certainly underwrote another parcel of shares. In all, eleven stockbroking firms in cities ranging from Launceston and Brisbane to Dunedin and Auckland appeared on the printed prospectus as agents, but it is doubtful if all were underwriters.

On Saturday 19 August 1899, Garland and Palmer formally appealed for Australians to invest by issuing a simple pamphlet setting out the prospectus of a company with a capital of 170 000 one-pound shares. In an unusual arrangement the shares were divided into three categories. The least attractive were the 70 000 ordinary shares, for they were not entitled even in a boom year to a dividend of more than nine per cent. Every one of these humbler shares was issued fully paid to Palmer and Garland. The second, and rather more attractive category, was the deferred non-cumulative preference share. Such shares, numbering 20 000, were also issued fully paid to Palmer and Garland. These two lots of shares, totalling 90 000, constituted the main payment to Palmer and Garland for selling part of their newly-acquired interest in the new tyre company to the Australian public.

The final category of shares, and far and away the most attractive, were the 80 000 '7 per cent Fixed Cumulative Preference Shares', now being offered to the investing public. Indeed they were entitled to an annual dividend of seven per cent, and if in any year the company was unable to pay that dividend, it had to promise to make up that deferred payment once the company again ran into profits. These shares were also entitled to the bulk of the profits in a bumper year: once the maximum allowable dividend of nine per cent had been paid on the ordinary shares, any surplus set aside for dividends went to the two categories of preference shares. In other words these 80 000 shares, so long as the company kept its head above water, were almost guaranteed a dividend in the lean years and entitled to high dividends in the good years. It could be argued from the viewpoint of the early 1990s that these shares now offered to the ordinary public would receive a minimum dividend of only seven per cent on their face value, but that was a pleasing dividend at a time when a fixed twelve-months deposit in a trading bank earned only three per cent. More-over, in the event of the company going into liquidation, the holders of these cumulative preference shares had first call on the remaining assets.

The package seemed enticing. As the promoters pointed out, even if the business were to earn less than half of its present annual profit of 14 000 pounds, it could still afford the seven per cent dividend. This dividend was virtually assured by the popularity of the Dunlop bicycle tyres. In fact the back cover of the printed prospectus was devoted entirely to chanting the praises given to Dunlop tyres in 1898 by fourteen cycling writers in newspapers in various colonies. Thus the *Queensland Sportsman* claimed that 'in the sprint home they leave their rivals as if anchored', and the *New South Wales Cyclist* insisted that Dunlop was the centre of cycling just as 'the sun is the centre of the solar system'. The writer of the prospectus said that it was 'no mere clap-trap to declare' that Dunlop tyres were the first in 1888 and were still the first.

When the subscription lists for the shares were opened, there was no rush. Big investors largely ignored the new shares, but a few score of humbler investors paid their deposit. The manager of a general store in sleepy Port Albert in Gippsland bought five shares, and a railway clerk in Christchurch bought his five, the minimum number that was allowable. A warder at the lunatic asylum at Ararat and a pastry-cook working in Swanston Street, Melbourne, each bought ten shares. The shire engineer at the Victorian town of Yea and the Presbyterian pastor at Kelso (in New Zealand) each bought fifty shares. John Marsh of the Sydney suburb of Leichhardt, who called himself an etcher, bought seventy-five. Small parcels of shares went to spinsters, graziers, doctors, solicitors, clergymen, an Adelaide cycle-manufacturer, two Wagga Wagga bank clerks, and a squatter's wife, Mrs Black of Noorat in western Victoria. The only celebrated name in the early shareholders was Sir Charles Todd of Adelaide, who more than anyone was responsible for the building of the overland telegraph which in 1872 joined Australia at Darwin to the world's system of telegraphs. Todd held 143 shares. The two Proctor brothers, presumably with not much money to spare, each held 250 shares. Of those investors who had no previous connection with the company, the biggest was probably Alfred Tooth, the Sydney sharebroker, who held 4 500 shares.

In one sense the floating of the Dunlop Pneumatic Tyre Company of Australasia Ltd was a flop. Though the surviving records are patchy, they show that many of the 80 000 one-pound shares were not bought by the public. Of the target of 80 000 pounds, a total of 45 000 was to have been paid to Palmer and Garland in cash, and 35 000 pounds was to serve as the new company's 'cash working capital'; but it is not clear that every pound of the 35 000 pounds was raised. The Canadian vendors much more than the local stockbrokers were the real underwriters.

For the Canadians, Palmer and Garland, the issue of shares was disappointing rather than disastrous. From the outset they had envisaged holding only 90 000 of the company's 170 000 shares — all shares in the riskier of the three categories. Instead they held closer to 117 000 shares, just one year after the company had been floated, and had to wait for the market in Dunlop Pneumatic shares to develop before they could slowly unload their surplus shares onto the public. Accordingly the initial company was essentially owned by overseas interests though its board consisted solely of Australians, meeting at the head office in Melbourne. A survey of the shares list in September 1900 reveals that no more than 30 000 of the 170 000 shares were held by those who ultimately would dominate the company — the Australians and New Zealanders. Ultimately the company would be overwhelmingly owned by Australians.

For the first couple of years Dunlop was mainly owned in Canada but effective control was in Australia. There an experienced board of directors was selected by Garland and Palmer to run the company. The only way of persuading the Australians to join the new board was to assure them that they would have power to make nearly all the main decisions. The directors formally met in Melbourne soon after the company had been floated. They were to shape Dunlop in Australia for a long period. Indeed three of the five directors still sat on the board a quarter of a century later, and one was to remain a director until the Second World War.

The four main directors lived in Melbourne but most had business interests throughout the continent. The chairman of the board was the Honourable Nicholas Fitzgerald, the head of one of Australia's few brewing empires. Celebrating his seventieth birthday a few days before the company was launched, he gave his main occupation as the chairman of the National Trustees, Executors, and Agency Co. of Australasia, an organisation which he helped to found and whose strong Catholic following he helped to attract. Educated in Dublin for the law, he had become a businessman in India and Ceylon before migrating to Victoria where he joined a brother in a brewery on the goldfields at Castlemaine. By the end of the century Fitzgerald was in control of breweries in South Melbourne, Adelaide, Newcastle and Brisbane — the genesis of the famous Queensland firm of Castlemaine Perkins — and owner of sheep runs in New South Wales and Queensland. A public as well as business man, Fitzgerald sat in the Legislative Council of Victoria for what was an astonishingly long time in that era of part-time politicians, from 1864 to 1906. In Sydney in 1891 he was one of the seven Victorian delegates who attended the National Australasian Convention to draw up what was the nucleus of the constitution for the proposed Commonwealth of Australia. A reading of his numerous short speeches leaves no doubt of his eloquence. Believing that the spirit of give and take was the 'essence of British parliamentary government', he followed that spirit when chairing a company meeting. Utterly independent, he would not have consented to chair the Dunlop Pneumatic Tyre Company of Australasia Ltd if his board had not been promised a high measure of independence.

Alongside Fitzgerald at the first meeting in 1899 sat Valentine Saddler. Australian-born, he began his commercial life as a clerk in a bank. Now in his early sixties, he was probably the best known builder of railways in Australia. Nobody knew more than Saddler about the cost of moving a cubic yard of earth with a horse and dray on the Queensland plains or the mountains of Tasmania. In some years he employed thousands of railway navvies, as well as the small army of labourers mining the huge open cut at Broken Hill under contract to BHP. Under the business name of Baxter and Saddler his firm built more miles of railway, both public and private, than probably any firm in Australia. The name is forgotten but in the cities and the bush it was once as well known as that of Dunlop. While Saddler was chairman of the most profitable private railway in Australia, the Silverton Tramway Company, his much younger colleague on the Dunlop board, John Grice, was to become chairman of what proved to be one of the least profitable of private railways, the Emu Bay railway in western Tasmania.

John Grice, one of Melbourne's pillars of financial prudence, was not normally associated with risky investments. He had engaged in shipping and trading in the south-east of South Australia for nine years before returning to Melbourne where, in the space of a couple of years, he won three of the city's prized positions. He was elected to the council of the University of Melbourne — he remained one of the few university graduates to be prominent in big business in Australia — and to the committee of the Melbourne Hospital which stood in Lonsdale Street, only a few dozen paces from the Dunlop factory in Tattersall's Lane. In 1887, when only in his mid thirties, he became a director of the National Bank, one of those numerous Melbourne institutions which eventually he was to preside over. Grice owned a large summer house at Mount Macedon, but so far as is known he did not ride a bicycle on the steep slopes. Why he decided to join the Dunlop board is a puzzle. He already had more than enough meetings to attend and meeting-papers to read.

Major Frederic G. Hughes, aged forty and the youngest of the directors, was the closest to the species of sporting lad which had come to be identified with the running of Dunlop in many lands. He had played football for Victoria, had rowed for Victoria some years after Grice had been in the champion Victorian four-oared boat, and had been a keen runner and volunteer rifleman. Beginning as a humble gunner he became commander of a semi-private military group, the Rupertswood Battery, which was financed by his brother-in-law, Sir William Clarke. In 1891 a team from this Battery, with Hughes as leader, won glory at military tournaments in the British Isles. Like his chairman Fitzgerald, Hughes lived in the seaside St Kilda, twice becoming its mayor. His wife Agnes was to become just as prominent in public life, being one of the six women who in 1904 founded the Australian Women's National League, perhaps the strongest women's group Australia had known.

Major Hughes, while not as experienced in business as other members of the board, was soon taking an intense interest, and as late as the 1940s he was taking more interest than his colleagues, on certain occasions, would have wished. On the other hand the fifth director, presumably selected so that Sydney would be part of the company, took no interest. Z. C. Rennie was the Australian head of the Mutual Life Insurance Company of New York, and he must have realised that he could not find the time to travel regularly by train to Melbourne for meetings of the board. He did not attend a meeting, and resigned in 1900.

The ultimate ability of the new Dunlop company to climb over the waiting obstacles owed much to the prestige and experience of these four Melbourne directors. They believed in Australia and in making it more self-sufficient. Strong individuals, they were capable of working as a team. Moreover they were willing to give time to the business, though their financial stake in it was small. Under the company's articles each director had to buy three hundred of the cumulative preference shares. In the early years they probably held in total no more than two per cent of the company's capital.

The directors still had 'Jack' Proctor as chief executive, a post he was to hold in one form or other for three decades. On 10 October 1899 he was formally appointed as general manager, though his power was to be diminished a little when Garland later migrated to Melbourne and took a seat on the board. The secretary of the new company was Proctor's younger brother Charles, who had spent exactly two years with Dunlop in Melbourne. Also a member of the Dublin cycling fraternity, Charles Proctor had joined Dunlop in Dublin in 1892, gaining more experience at the tyre factories and offices in Coventry and Birmingham. Promoted to Nottingham as sub-manager of the tyre depot, he remained in trim as a rider. When a racing cyclist attempted to break the road record between Edinburgh and London, Charles Proctor gladly acted as one of his pace-makers. He took over the pace-making at midnight, rode until daylight, and then went home for breakfast before proceeding to the Dunlop depot for the day's work. When he became the secretary of the new company in Melbourne he was wiry and athletic and — in the phrase of the *Australian Cyclist* — 'rather dark complexioned'. His ability — he was more talented than his highly-paid brother — was soon evident. In 1910 he was to return to London, at a time when there was little movement of senior staff between the separate Dunlop companies, and eventually became the chief executive of English Dunlop.

In the rented head office of the company at 108 Flinders Street — a two-

*The head office was decorated in 1920 for the visit of the Prince of Wales
(later King Edward VIII).*

storey building of old bluestone just five minutes' walk from Tattersall's Lane
— Nicholas Fitzgerald and his colleagues met nearly every Tuesday afternoon
at two-thirty. Soon they resolved that the time had come to build a new
factory capable of manufacturing 100 000 bicycle tyres a year, with space for
expansion. If their company was to become a real manufacturer of rubber
goods rather than an assembler and stitcher of imported parts, it must move
to an industrial suburb where the odours and smoke of the vulcanising and
other processes were tolerated. In 1901 such a site was found on low-lying land
just across the Yarra River, close to the Montague station on the Port
Melbourne to Flinders Street railway, the oldest line in Australia. The large
bluestone and iron buildings and the vacant surrounding land could be rented
for 325 pounds a year plus the municipal rates and the insurance against fire.
The option to buy the property for the sum of 11 000 pounds was to remain
open for three years. Here was the main home of the ever-expanding rubber
industry for the following eighty years.

The Australian company turned to North America rather than Dunlop in
England for skills and advice. Palmer in Toronto was sent a telegram
requesting that he hire a factory superintendent and a senior assistant. Early
in 1901 he chose John Kearns and his assistant Dan Cronin, who sailed for
Melbourne that winter. Kearns was experienced in every phase of making

John Kearns, Montague mill manager (centre) and his salaried staff. Two women stand behind him, outnumbered.

rubber products out of the raw imported rubber. Reared before the advent of delicate equipment for measuring and testing rubber, he knew almost intuitively whether the newly-made sheets of rubber were of the right quality, and when in doubt he applied a simple test. One of his Montague employees recalled how every morning John Kearns would bite off small chunks of the previous day's output of bicycle tyres: 'If his teeth left too great an impression on the rubber there was trouble for someone'. Normally he was genial and courteous, but if he pulled his cap down over one eye he was considered to be in a touchy mood. Kearns was to prove himself again and again as an excellent choice. He had not long settled in Melbourne when he was sent in the mail steamer to England with Major Hughes, one of the directors, to decide whether the Doughty process for vulcanising tyres should be adopted in the new factory.

At Montague, after piles had been sunk on the river flat to provide a firm foundation, and the boiler house and tall smoke stack had been built, the mechanical troubles began. In early tests the English steam engine, made by the well known firm of Tangye, consumed too much coal for the power it produced. In February 1902 two consulting engineers of distinction, Anderson and Monash, were called in to meet the directors in the boardroom, so urgently was their advice wanted. On 6 June 1902 Monash drafted a letter threatening legal action against Tangye. A fortnight later, seeking a remedy more practical than litigation, he advised the board to order a new flywheel for the engine. On 26 November, with the rubber factory now at work, he attended a special meeting of the board to talk over 'the serious position', for the steam plant was not pulling its weight. In the new year directors had no alternative but to order from the Melbourne foundry of Kelly and Lewis a new three-hundred horsepower engine. They also ordered a new Babcock and Wilcox boiler and indicated that they were short of ready cash by negotiating special terms of slow payment.

In the weekly newspapers the large advertisements for Dunlop tyres began to depict the new 'rubber mill', as it was now called. Consisting of four buildings, the main one being a long shed with a saw-tooth roof, the factory was described as 'ventilated to perfection, and lit with a prodigality of cheap sunshine from scores of skylights'. Such was the praise from the reporters who in August 1902 arrived for the grand opening inspection and banquet. Escorted in two groups led by Kearns and Charles Proctor, the journalists and leading customers saw the crushing of the lumps of raw rubber fresh from the South American jungle, saw them washed and rolled into long rough sheets, inspected the hot drying room where each sheet was dried for some four weeks, saw the mixing of the additives that gave rubber the desired qualities, and watched the great rollers of the calendering machine — 'under the absolute control of the operator, whose smallest desire is gratified' — press the rubber into sheets of varying thickness in readiness for the vulcanising process. Finally they saw the moulded rubber placed in a huge waffle-iron, with eight to ten tyres successively 'cooked' in each Doughty press in every hour, each emerging red hot. Walking along the narrow spaces between the machines and the benches the visitors saw bicycle tubes being tested, wheel rims made to precision, puncture-repair outfits being assembled, and garden hoses being extruded. Still smelling the coal-smoke and cooked rubber, the guests ate and drank at the late-afternoon banquet. Before the champagne was poured and the numerous toasts were drunk, chairman Fitzgerald assured journalists that an endless variety of rubber goods would go out the gates of what would become the world's 'perfect' rubber mill.

The cost of constructing the factory was a continuing worry. The old works at Tattersall's Lane in the city had earned enough profit to pay the required dividend of seven and seven and a half per cent on the two categories of preference shares held by the public and a smaller dividend on the ordinary shares. The new works, however, were greedy for money. There was no hope of a further issue of shares: the public would not have bought them. Accordingly, Dunlop had to borrow. By July 1902 the Bank of Australasia was owed about 15 000 pounds — a sum exceeding that paid by Dunlop in dividends in the normal year. A year later the borrowings from the bank exceeded 24 000 pounds. The bank extended its borrowing limit to 30 000 pounds and took the unusual precaution of securing its loan by debentures.

The time soon came for Dunlop to exercise its option to buy the land on which its new factory stood. The land had to be bought — it was packed with buildings and other improvements which could be lost when the lease expired in less than two years. After parleying with the owners, Dunlop was given a time-payment deal whereby the final payment of five thousand pounds was not due until May 1908. Even the prompt paying of the first instalment was a burden. Fortunately Mrs John Grice, wife of a director, had property in her own name, and she lent two thousand pounds to the company at the ruling rate of interest.

It was during the financial troubles that news came from the branch in Perth — a busy centre for selling tyres — that the accountant had been quietly embezzling. The Perth manager could not say how much money had vanished. At head office, where every halfpenny was now carefully counted, the news was heard with incredulity. How could a branch manager fail to detect embezzlement over many months? It was resolved that each Dunlop employee who was in a position of financial trust should take out one of those guarantee policies — so common after the widespread defalcations of the late 1880s — whereby the firm was partly insured in the event of fraud amongst its own staff.

The directors found themselves fighting minor frauds and illegal actions on various fronts. They spent much of their time at board meetings in the guarding of the firm's patent rights. The company's main asset, and bought dearly from England, was the exclusive right, held throughout Australia and New Zealand, of using the Dunlop name and trademarks and selling Dunlop tyres or any tyres made under the Doughty patents. To the surprise of the directors, many imported tyres were flouting the company's rights. Imported tyres labelled Dunlop filtered into bicycle shops in scores of towns. News would come from the wharf that a ship had just unloaded crates of bicycle tyres bearing a Dunlop trademark. Inside a bicycle shop one of Proctor's salesmen would observe, on open display, new bicycles equipped in England with Dunlop tyres carrying as insignia the bearded face of John Dunlop — a face now widely used in marketing. A dealer would report to the Proctor brothers that he had just received from American Dunlop a booklet inviting him to order his tyres from America. A confidential letter would arrive from New Zealand to disclose that English Dunlop tyres were being shipped there by Brown Brothers of London. From a customer at the Melbourne Sports Depot would come word that some of its tyres carried the trademark of 'Two Hands', proof that American Dunlop tyres were illegally creeping into Australia. Usually a letter from the firm's solicitors — Moule, Hamilton and Kiddle of Market Street — halted the illegal imports, but by then much of the damage had already been done. Sometimes legal action had to be initiated before the tyre dealer or importer promised not to infringe.

The printed reports sent to shareholders from the head office at 108 Flinders Street gave few details of the company's financial troubles. One curiosity in the meagre reports is that Dunlop's formal financial year ended on a different date each year — ending on 26 July in 1900 and then, in successive years, on 25, 31, 30, 28, 27 and 26 July. Eccentric and frugal, the reports could not conceal the truth that the assets of the Dunlop Pneumatic Tyre Co. of Australasia had been sold by London at too high a price. The preference shareholders at least received their promised dividend of seven or seven and a half per cent a year, but the ordinary shareholders were less fortunate. In the company's first year they received six per cent, in March 1901 they received an interim or half-yearly dividend at the rate of five per cent a year, and in September they received a final dividend at the rate of four per cent. By March 1902 it was down to a miserable two per cent. For the three following half years no dividend was paid to ordinary shareholders, and from time to time angry gentlemen must have been seen jumping from the cable tram in Flinders Street and entering the head office to speak their mind. They were assured that once the new plant was working smoothly and once the rural drought was over, a time of high prosperity would come again. At last in 1904 they received an interim dividend at the rate of seven per cent a year.

Dunlop's advertisements in the press sometimes showed a black and white sketch of the new factory, smoke pouring from the brick chimney in the background, and the sign DUNLOP RUBBER MILLS standing in huge letters high up the long corrugated-iron factory wall. Beneath the sketch was the promise that 'we are now prepared to supply rubber goods of every description'. While bicycle tyres remained the mainstay, the firm was alert for any rubber product for which Australia offered a sufficient market. A procession of inventors called at Flinders Street or the factory gates to show their ideas. During four months of 1906 a man came from Albury to submit his novel rubber heel for shoes, another inventor offered to sell his process for reclaiming the rubber in old tyres and other goods, while Kearns and Garland assigned to the company their own letters patent for a new kind of rubber-based golf ball. In each month a few overseas inventions were investigated. Thus in 1906 the firm offered a Mr Lindsay one hundred pounds and a regular royalty in return for the Australian rights to what he called his 'Beer Waste Preventor' — presumably a rubber hose or pluto with a device that cut off the supply of beer so tightly that none was wasted through spilling or dripping. Alas the firm was unable to buy another seductive invention — the rubber hair-curler, which was firmly in the hands of the grandly-named New Century Hair Curler Co. Limited.

Usually it was easy to make the mould which shaped a new product in readiness for vulcanisation. It was not so easy to make rubber of the specific quality demanded by different products. Nearly every type of rubber good was made to a different mixture of rubber and other ingredients. The manufacturing formula was secret. John Kearns had been hired from North America partly because he had acquired these secrets in his migrations to senior posts in various rubber firms. For some years he kept the recipe in his head or his

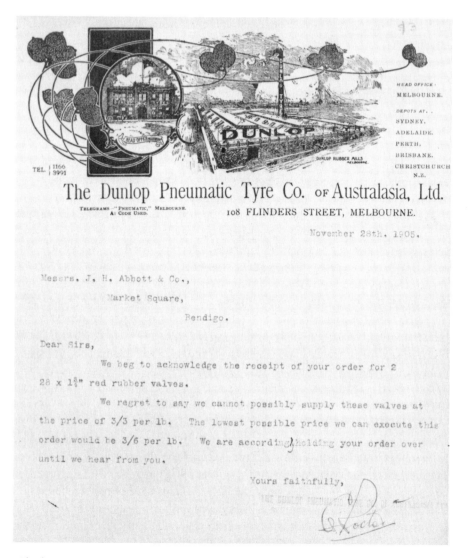

Charles Proctor, company secretary in 1905, knew how to write a lean letter to a customer.

secret notebook, but the time came when the board of Dunlop, willing to renew his contract for a period of a further five years, insisted that as a part of the contract he write down the various formulas on which the factory at Montague depended. The promise of an annual salary of 1500 pounds — more than any professor then received in Australia — induced him to part with his tightly-held knowledge. He divulged it, however, as if it were as important as a nation's defence secrets.

The firm treated with the same vigilance the document he handed over: an expensive exercise book of three hundred pages with marbled paper on the covers and the written title, 'Book from the Montague Mill'. Inside, the recipes for mixing the rubber needed for various rubber goods were written in a neat hand — probably the handwriting of a clerk rather than the more rugged hand of Kearns himself. The book, by order of the board, was placed in the safe deposit of a bank and was not to be removed even for the purpose of a peep or a check-up unless a specific resolution was passed by the board to authorise the consulting of the book. The director, Colonel Hughes, went to the bank and supervised the placing of the book of secret formulas in the deposit box.

Eighty years later, long after many of the rubber products were obsolete, and long after Kearns had gone to his grave, the book still carried all the wrappings of secrecy. It was hidden inside a very large sheet of blue-lined notepaper, tied up with a thin tape of green cloth, and the tape was sealed in three places with blobs of red sealing wax so that the directors could tell if someone had surreptitiously tried to untie the parcel. On the wrapping paper was the signature of one of the early directors, J. H. Riley, reminding one and all that the red sealing wax was not to be broken without a resolution from the board. As a double precaution the managing director, Richard Garland, had signed his name across the point where two ends of the wrapping paper met. If anyone broke the seals, unlawfully perused the book, and then tied it up and added blobs of sealing wax, they would have to be unusually meticulous to ensure that the wrapping-paper was so arranged that Garland's broken signature was again joined to form a whole.

Today, after the tape is untied and the wrapping paper removed, the volume inside has the appearance of a personal cookery book. And so it was. To make a batch of Doughty tyres, wrote Kearns, first take five pounds of fine Para rubber, ten pounds each of Rambong and Peruvian rubber, along with six pounds of old pure gum, four of litharge, four of lugo, three of best sulphur, two of zinc, one of Doughty trimmings, and three-quarters of a pound of nanthusi. The curing or cooking time, he added, was eight minutes. Scores of different ingredients, some of them exotic, were used in his recipes. Thus in mixing the rubber used as a red-coloured eraser to rub out pencil errors in school and office, Kearns used forty per cent of pumice stone. For tennis-balls — which he first made in 1909 — he used magnesia and talite and zinc as well as various kinds of crude rubber. The red soles he made for tennis shoes consumed a large quantity of Old Red, as well as such additives as red oxide, antimony, dry pontianiac, whiting, lime and sulphur. The composition of the rubber tobacco-pouches, coming into favour in an era when pipes rather than cigarettes were normal, included antimony as well as 'best vermilion'. Sponge rubber included such unexpected ingredients as cork dust, old tubes, and best baking powder. In the light of such a formula it is easy to understand why in earlier times the manufacture of sponge rubber had remained a virtual monopoly of the Russian–American Rubber Co. of St Petersburg which alone held the secret recipe.

Sometimes the grand chef of the rubber kitchen changed his recipe when he discovered that his product was not quite suitable for Australian conditions or when one of the ingredients became too dear. Thus, in 1907 Dunlop had trouble with its football bladders, of which so many were deemed defective that the board minutes noted the 'injury done to the trade'. After the Perth office complained about the football bladders, Kearns was summoned to the boardroom and told that all bladders should be made of his 'better quality' rubber. Certainly in 1909 he asked that the secret book of formulas be temporarily withdrawn from the bank so that he could write in the amended or new recipes. Several of the fresh recipes were for relatively new products such as massage brushes, tennis-balls, and green motor-goggles; but the recipe for bladders was also altered for the 1909 football season, with the substitution of five pounds of Best Ceylon rubber in place of fine Para rubber.

Kearns had a special formula for reclaiming rubber from the old tyres that were increasingly carted to the factory at Montague. The tyres were tossed into a vat and boiled for three or four hours in an acid solution so that the wires and beads used in the construction of tyres could be salvaged. Then the remaining mixture of rubber and cloth was ground down and boiled in a tank containing sulphuric acid solution until the cloth disappeared. The rubber residue was boiled in a solution of caustic soda. At one stage during these processes he added four per cent of that universal panacea — Australian eucalyptus oil. The reclaimed rubber had many uses including the manufacture of the cheap rubber mats on which the beer jugs stood in hotel bars.

By the standards of the time, rubber was one of the most secretive of industries. The kind of sales figures which in an annual report would now be deemed harmless were carefully excluded from Dunlop's annual report. As the chairman was to remind shareholders on 18 October 1912, in the course of delivering the vaguest of annual reports: 'In a manufacturing business of this kind — subject to the keenest competition — details of the progress of our trade cannot be placed before the shareholders, as they would thus be more or less public, and our rivals become acquainted with them'.

The easiest way for a spy to penetrate the rubber curtain was to become a manual employee at Montague. There he could quickly ascertain vital information that was never hinted at in the official reports. In a week, with the aid of a little mental arithmetic, he could calculate such crucial facts as the rough proportion of revenue that came from making bicycle tyres compared to all other rubber products — a calculation that shareholders themselves could not glean from the information inside the reports of the company they owned.

Side by side with tight-lipped secrecy was an eagerness to give publicity to the startling variety of rubber products available from Dunlop's branches in Australia and New Zealand. Farmers and their families could happily spend most of a Saturday night sitting beside the kerosene lamp with the latest Dunlop catalogue in front of them. The wife learned that for cold or wet

"This
is the way
to stop the
Colds"

The quality and construction of every DUNLOP Hot Water Bag
ensures long service without leaking. Being recently made
and free from perish, they are better than imported bags.
Ask your Chemist or Store for "Dunlop" brand - it's your
guarantee of Value and Service. Guaranteed against defects.
All States.   DUNLOP RUBBER CO.   And N.Z.

*In winter, hundreds of thousands of Australians went to bed with their
Dunlop rubber bottle at their feet.*

weather she could buy rings for an umbrella and a waterproof coat and rubber
boots, and of course a hot-water bottle. For summer they could buy a red-
coloured hose for the garden — so long as the creek contained water. Perhaps
they discussed buying rubber tubes for the new milking machine or rings to
seal the milk cans, rubber tyres for the horse-drawn buggy, rubber to cover the
hand wringer in the wash-house, pads to protect the feet of a lame horse, or
rubber heels for the husband's best Sunday boots. And when they drove into
town on market day they saw a host of other rubber products ranging from the
cushions on the hotel's billiard table to the rubber stamp which inked the
word 'paid' on the family's grocery bill.

Dunlop employees sitting by the new chimney at Montague, about 1912.

The Montague factory began in a decade when rubber was finding many new uses. More and more industries and inventors were utilising rubber's remarkable elasticity. It had the capacity to be stretched out to many times its original size and then return to it, and the same capacity in reverse — to be so compressed that in its resilience it bounced back. Every bank clerk, telephone operator, housekeeper, and railway shunter saw rubber goods, gadgets and fittings, all taking on new tasks and not always with complete success. Thus the rubber washers that sealed soft drink bottles were reported as defective in 1906. In the same year the heavy rubber belting made for the ore-treatment plant at the Junction North mine at Broken Hill proved to be inadequate, and the directors, who tended to handle the more serious complaints from customers, ordered a reprimand for their foreman at Montague and the purchasing of the 'requisite plant' for making a stronger kind of belting. In 1908, Kearns gave instructions that an employee should make the long journey by coastal steamship to Thursday Island in tropical Queensland in order to report on the adequacy of rubber hoses and other items used by pearlers in their diving equipment.

As new rubber products were launched, the factory at Montague was extended. It grew like Topsy, spreading into neighbouring streets where old warehouses and cottages were demolished, or intruding onto vacant lands when a lease could be arranged. New stores and warehouses and dumping grounds were needed as well as factory floors. The nearby paddock, where coal was stocked in readiness for the next coal strike or stoppage in coastal shipping, came to resemble the vicinity of a coal mine, so high was the pile. The rubber industry was hungry for steaming coal, and by the start of the First World War the rubber industry in Victoria, while not a large employer of labour, generated more horsepower than all but three industries; and most of that power was generated by Dunlop at Montague. A director of Dunlop, reading his agenda for board meetings, soon became familiar with economiser fans, superheaters, mechanical stokers, condensers, cooling towers, Babcock and Wilcox boilers, and any equipment likely to give mechanical trouble or sink, by its sheer weight, four or eight inches into the deep silt of the riverflats of South Melbourne.

Another frequent item on their agenda was 'the smoke nuisance'. Smoke rising from the Dunlop mill could be seen in distant streets. A banner of black smoke from the main chimney and puffs of steam and smoke from other equipment were normal. The smoke, soot and smell would have aroused few complaints in the 1890s because people desperately wanted work and knew that the smoke nuisance was another way of saying 'workers wanted'. By 1906, with prosperity back again, the smoke angered local citizens. The city of South Melbourne, in which the factory and Montague belonged, received strong protests in 1908. Mr E. Norton Grimwade, crossing Princes Bridge each day, noticed that the chimney of the paperworks on the South Melbourne bank of the river was pouring out dense smoke. As he had recently reduced the smoke nuisance at his own chemicals factory at West Melbourne he thought South Melbourne should do likewise. He wrote that the smoke was 'an absolute disgrace'. A chimney puffing out smoke so effortlessly, 'I assure you, would not be allowed in any city in Europe', wrote Grimwade. At a meeting of a committee of the South Melbourne council in August 1908 the letter aroused excited discussion. Those who were against capitalism called for prompt action, the mayor himself drawing attention to the odour usually emitted from Grimwade's own motor car, while others insisted that South Melbourne was not the smokiest suburb. The outcome was that Dunlop, which was possibly the most polluting factory in South Melbourne, was threatened with prosecution. The matter did not reach court, and Dunlop fitted to one chimney or furnace a device which possibly reduced the volume of smoke in the air.

Several councillors insisted that 'this wealthy firm' should fit further devices, while others warned that local factories and all the jobs they created might move out to Footscray if they were penalised too often. Dunlop must have taken further steps. In June 1909 an inventor, William Aston, erected a 'Smoke Consuming device' at Montague. The board minutes do not reveal the result of the experiment, but the threat of prosecution seems to have faded. It returned four years later when two councillors and the city engineer arrived at the works and promised legal action if the powerhouse at the mill continued to emit so much smoke. The erection of a taller smoke stack quietened them. Ironically, Dunlop still advertised its products by showing in the newspapers a black and white sketch of Montague, its chimneys belching smoke. Six smoking chimneys can be seen in the Dunlop advertisement in the Sydney *Bulletin* for Christmas Day of 1913.

While some local residents were perturbed by the factory's smoke, they did not realise that fire was the greater danger. Ted Wellington began at the new factory in 1902 and worked alongside Scotch Tom who took a deep pride in his long beard. Ted used to mix the inflammable chemical solution which fixed the outer tread to the bicycle tyres, but one day, in the mixing, a fire broke out. 'I looked round', said Ted, 'and there was Scotch Tom standing with his beard in his hand — swearing to some order. His beard had just been "singed off at its roots".'

Large piles of rubber goods and raw rubber were stored around the factory. In the event of an accident they would serve as fuel for a mighty blaze. In 1906 more water mains were laid to provide water for fire-fighting. A mill fire brigade was formed, and the workers willing to learn how to fight fires were paid an annual bonus of about half a week's wages. Next year they received an additional bonus when they successfully fought a fire until the professional fire brigade arrived from Eastern Hill. In 1909, at the massive expense of 2450 pounds, or more than a major extension to the factory had cost, Grinnell sprinklers were installed by Wormald throughout the works, thus lessening the danger of a runaway fire.

The only serious fire in Dunlop's first quarter of a century was in New Zealand. Christchurch was the main selling office, and imported most of its bicycle tyres and other goods from Montague, but also moulded various small rubber goods such as heels for shoes. The risk of fire was appreciated, and insurance was taken out on a liberal scale, including 1500 pounds on the office and 9700 pounds on the rubber goods in store. Without such insurance one fire could have inflicted enough damage to wipe out a full year's dividend for all the shareholders.

At about four o'clock on the morning of 19 April 1906, a 'newspaper runner' saw smoke gushing from the Dunlop building in Lichfield Street. He gave the alarm and fire carts fortunately stationed in the same street raced to the fire. By then the smoke was dense, and the melting rubber increased the hazard. Several firemen were badly burned, several were overcome by the smoke, and only after two hours of hosing was the fire controlled. When at last the firemen could inspect the damage they found that only a few frames and rims of bicycles survived the intense heat.

Christchurch supplied not only a warning of how quickly a fire could destroy a rubber warehouse but also a commercial warning of how easily a small competitor could poach Dunlop's business. George Skellerup, a young man of Danish descent, learned how to make bicycle tyres at the first Dunlop factory in Tattersall's Lane in Melbourne. He was energetic, and quick to seize opportunities. That he had left school at the age of twelve was more a spur to him than an impediment. Crossing the Tasman Sea he landed in Dunedin in 1902 and seeing the sign on a bicycle shop, 'Man Wanted', he went inside and announced that he was just the man. Eventually moving to Christchurch he worked for Dunlop again. His Melbourne skills, learned in a factory with the minimum of machinery, were ideal for Christchurch where carters and carriers wanted solid rubber tyres fitted to the iron wheels of their horse-drawn wagons and where the occasional bicycle with odd-sized wheels called for a tyre to be specially made. He later claimed that with his own hands he put together the first pneumatic tyre made in New Zealand.

George was in his late twenties when his wife received a bequest that emboldened him to leave Dunlop's and set up his own shop. His first windfall came when he bought a bargain lot of eight thousand bicycle tyres from the Continental Rubber Co., a German firm, and sold them to cyclists, one by one. In a bold gesture he even hired the giant marquee previously used by Dunlop to display wares at agricultural shows, and himself began to supply the rubber parts used in the primitive milking-machines that were becoming the vogue on large dairy farms. His business did not look back. In 1984 the sales of the firm he had founded, the Para Rubber Company, reached $184 million for the year.

Inside the Dunlop works it had soon been forgotten that George Skellerup was twice on its payroll, working for eight shillings a day. Again and again the firm was to suffer from the drive and bounce of young Australians who, beginning as humble employees, soon were on their own and outselling the firm that had trained them. In theory the self-made manufacturer had no chance against a big public company, but in practice the story was different, as Barnet Glass was proving only a few miles from Dunlop's own head office.

An indiarubber ball: the ups and downs of Barnet Glass

A T THE start of this century Barnet Glass used to travel each workday from what he called his 'handsome villa' in the riverside suburb of Alphington to his factory in North Melbourne. Travelling by train he was delighted to notice at the level crossings a steady increase in the waiting cyclists. His business was rubber — nobody in Melbourne had done more to pioneer the manufacture of rubber goods and with the soaring demand for tyres he believed the rubber industry was approaching a new heyday. His dilemma was whether to enter the tyre business.

The waterproof garment was the original speciality of Barnet Glass. The time, he sensed, was coming when he must turn his energy to the rubber tyre. His only worry was Dunlop. Could he compete with that expanding firm and its international name? By 1900 he was a jump ahead of the Dunlop Pneumatic Tyre Company of Australasia, but he knew that Dunlop's new factory rising at Montague would give him tough competition.

Barnet Glass was a two-time emigrant. Born in Russian Poland he had joined the stream of Polish Jews moving from Tsarist Russia to Manchester when it was the textile heart of the world. He married in Manchester in 1869 and the next year he was busy making waterproof garments for troops fighting in the Franco–Prussian War. His entry into the rubber industry was thus through its earliest popular product, the waterproof coat, which had been invented in the 1820s by the Scottish chemist, Charles Macintosh. The mackintosh or 'mac', in its origin, was really a product of a by-product from those gasworks that were beginning to dot the industrial landscape. Macintosh had dissolved indiarubber in the naphtha which he collected as a waste from the gasworks, and this mixture served as cement for the cloth fabric. After coating two pieces of cloth with the sticky solution he stuck them together like a sandwich, thus creating a strong waterproof cloth. The

Barnet Glass, whose surname became a household name in Australia.

waterproof garments made in Manchester delighted all those passengers who travelled in all weathers on the top of the stage coaches that were becoming the vogue. It was in Manchester nearly half a century later that Barnet Glass learned those skills which were his stock-in-trade when he emigrated with his family to Melbourne in 1876.

About two years later Glass began to ply his trade in Lincoln Square, Carlton. He must have been working on his own in a couple of rooms or in a backyard shed because the Melbourne household directory of 1881 does not mention him when listing half a dozen who manufactured or sold oilskins and other waterproof garments. His address in the 1881 directory is Devonshire Terrace, a row of four cottages hunched together on the west side of upper Bouverie Street. In 1882 he moved about a quarter mile to the south-west and opened a factory on a shallow block of land with a frontage of nineteen feet (less than six metres) in Queensberry Street, North Melbourne, just west of Elizabeth Street. He made full use of every square inch of land. On an upper story of his house as many as twenty-five employees were busy making what was then called indiarubber clothing. He made rubber capes for mounted troopers to wear in the rain. He made the heavy waterproof coats which miners came to prefer when working in the wet of the deep-alluvial gold mines. He also made 'the Baptist trousers' used by evangelical pastors who had to step into a river or a large stand-up bath in order to conduct the Christian ceremony of baptism by total immersion.

These rubber garments were not cheap compared to the clothes proofed with an oil substitute, but they lasted much longer. As they offered no ventilation, they were sweaty and unhygienic: indeed about the 1890s many people preferred to carry an umbrella and wear a porous waterproof coat that was less sweaty but more liable to become soaked in the heavy rain. Ultimately, about the 1950s, the rubber garments were to be seriously challenged by the plastic, PVC.

At first the Jewish manufacturer appears to have called himself Bernard Glass rather than the more exotic Barnet Glass; and when his sons Ezekiel and Jacob began to learn their father's trade they likewise anglicised their names to Ernest and Jack. The family pulled its weight in the business with its crowded workshop and long working hours. The Glasses did so well in the boom of the late 1880s that they added work-rooms to their new residential villa in the outer suburb of Alphington. Barnet Glass saw no ceiling to his expansion, and in 1890 went to England, hoping to buy machinery to build what would almost certainly have been the first rubber mill in Australia. After buying some of the machines to turn raw rubber into waterproof sheets and other goods he returned to Melbourne and quickly saw that the economic barometer was falling. He waited a time. Finally after heavy investment in land and machinery he opened his new rubber mill in 1899, on the lowlands near the Moonee Ponds Creek. The mill stood on three acres on the north side of Macaulay Road, between the Macaulay and Kensington railway stations. The present Barnett Street is presumably a later mis-spelling of his name and marks the western boundary of his land.

Barnet Glass must have borrowed heavily to build his rubber factory. The bonus was that now he could make all kind of goods which previously had to be imported from England and the United States. Under the new name of Barnet Glass and Sons he made rubber hoses, rubber valves and washers, rubber mats, the rubber rollers which wrung the water from the washing in the wash-houses of thousands of homes, and the tubing that carried the gas to the jets. The Victorian Railways, the Harbour Trust and other public agencies sent to the Kensington factory to order rubber parts. Barnet Glass also made rubber garments with the brand name of Hercules; and it was a proud day for the Glass family when the future George the Fifth of England, on his visit to open the first Commonwealth Parliament in 1901, accepted a pair of Barnet Glass wading boots designed for fishermen. To the delight of Barnet Glass, word came to him secondhand of royal surprise that such boots could be made in Australia. The factory also made tyres for children's prams, and for tricycles and bicycles. Judging by the emphasis in Glass's advertising — and he did not advertise on the scale of Dunlop — he succeeded in selling only a moderate number of bicycle tyres, a product for which Dunlop had the name and prestige. But he did well with the heavy double-wired solid rubber tyres now in demand on bakers' carts and brewery wagons. Many delivery carts drawn by horses were fitted with solid rubber in place of the iron tyres, and for the time being these horse-drawn vehicles provided a much larger market for rubber tyres than the new automobile. The automobile age did not come with a headlong rush: it crept in steadily.

Glass was keen to expand his small output of bicycle and car tyres. He was even happy, if the money offered him were large, to sign a contract to make tyres bearing the Dunlop brand rather than his own 'Pioneer' brand. In October 1900 he sent to Dunlop a specimen outer cover or tyre and a specimen tube made in his factory at Kensington. Would Dunlop's directors, he asked, be willing to place an order for large quantities? He could make tyres from raw rubber by the latest process whereas Dunlop's factory was still making them by hand from imported materials. Knowing that his firm and Dunlop were heading for a collision, he sought a truce whereby each firm could survive and make reasonable profits. In Victoria there was probably room for only one efficient manufacturer of tyres. Dunlop directors now had to decide whether they should sub-contract much of their work to Barnet Glass or build their own modern factory. Their decision was to build the factory at Montague, a decision which must have been received with dismay by Glass and his sons and financiers. The biggest maker of rubber goods in Australia, he was now confronted by Dunlop's competition in Victoria and, almost at the same time, by the creation of the Commonwealth of Australia and the simultaneous dismantling of the tariff wall which hitherto kept out New South Wales rubber goods.

Barnet Glass prepared for the tussle by bringing in fresh capital for his Pioneer India Rubber Works of Australia. With the aid of a leading importer of soft goods, he formed a new company called Barnet Glass and Sons Limited in October 1900, exactly one year after Dunlop had become a public company in Australasia. Of the initial shareholders in the new company the Glass family held at least 4500 shares, presumably received as payment for their stake in the business. The importer was Frank Stuart, and he paid for 1250 shares. A New South Wales lad who had eloped to Victoria with the daughter of his employer, Stuart was a live wire in Victorian business. At the age of forty-one he became the president of the Victorian Chamber of Manufacturers and at the age of forty-six a member without portfolio in the Victorian cabinet. A convivial fellow, a founder of the Beefsteak Club and a zealot for any sport, he claimed to have walked, for the sake of walking, over much of the terrain between southern Tasmania and his home town of Penrith. Later, like so many bush walkers, he took up cycling with enthusiasm.

As an importer and seller of garments Stuart was attracted to Barnet Glass because it was Australia's main manufacturer of waterproof clothes. Stuart's business — he called himself a 'warehouseman' — now included the manufacturing as well as the importing of clothes, and as far back as 1885 he had shown his zeal by accepting a contract to manufacture the uniforms for the New South Wales soldiers who at short notice were despatched to the Red Sea in order to fight in the Sudan. His contract called for the making of the uniforms within seventeen days. He succeeded: his name was made.

About 1900, Frank Stuart took over the chairmanship of the Barnet Glass company, leaving Glass himself to manage the business. But Stuart alone would not have given the business a new standing. Fortunately he joined the board along with W. L. Baillieu, one of the liveliest businessmen in Melbourne. Baillieu was in his early forties, a native of the fort-and-port town of Queenscliff, who began his career as a bank clerk, and quickly became one of the celebrated auctioneers of land during the boom of the late 1880s. Collapsing into the dust after the bank crashed he picked himself up and steadily built a new career. Mr Glass must have counted himself lucky that Baillieu took up almost twice as many shares as Stuart. There have been few businessmen in Victoria as creative as Baillieu. When he joined the board of Barnet Glass all kinds of customers must have taken notice that the firm was about to leap ahead. Baillieu's elevation to the board of this smallish rubber company was eventually to affect the international rubber industry, because the Baillieus, father and son, were to become two of the most influential names in world rubber.

A few other businessmen well known in Melbourne were persuaded to share in Mr Barnet Glass's promising future. David Syme, the proprietor of the Melbourne Age, was possibly the largest shareholder by 1904, and his representative sat on the board alongside Frank Stuart, W. L. Baillieu and the firm's two managing directors, namely Glass himself and his son-in-law Fred Ornstein. By now the company had a grander name, the Pioneer Rubber Works of Australia Ltd, but not so grand a future. It faced strong competition from Dunlop's new factory only a few miles away. Dunlop not only dominated the business in bicycle tyres but for the first time were manufacturing nearly all the products that Barnet Glass made. By 1903 the competition from the Dunlop factory at Montague was running Barnet Glass into the ground. Dunlop was a household name whereas Pioneer was little known. Dunlop was the master of the profitable bicycle tyre whereas Barnet Glass was second best in this product. Above all, the fierce drought in Victoria must have lowered the sales of Barnet Glass's main product, waterproof garments. Who would want to buy waterproof coats and trousers when everything was dry? Moreover, Victoria was depressed and rural storekeepers who normally paid on time now wanted time in which to pay. The outlook for Barnet Glass, so hopeful when the new factory opened in 1899, was now dour.

The likely option facing the Barnet Glass Company by 1905 was to close down. The more profitable option was to sell the business to Dunlop. Evidence suggests that Glass was in favour of a third and obstinate option — to fight to the end. But he no longer controlled the company. Sadly in January 1905 he saw Baillieu, at the request of the board, go away to propose a simple sell-out of the business to Dunlop.

Baillieu returned to the Glass boardroom with news that Dunlop was likely to buy Pioneer Rubber including all its liabilities and would pay by issuing new shares in Dunlop to the Pioneer shareholders. For Dunlop the deal was attractive because the cut-throat competition from Glass's firm had thwarted the high profits expected back in 1899 when Dunlop became a public company. For Glass and his sons, however, the deal was the end of a nightmare. They had been making heavy losses at their factory. Their bad and doubtful debts were high.

For the purposes of the sale Dunlop valued the Barnet Glass works at Kensington at the relatively low sum of 9316 pounds — far less than the cost of building them. Barnet Glass also carried large stocks of rubber, coal, cloth, chemicals and other raw materials, and orders completed or in production. The selling price of the company was further increased by the head office in Flinders Street and depots in various cities. In the end Dunlop was willing to issue 60 000 preference shares and 20 000 ordinary shares in its own company as the purchase price. Far more than the business would have earned at auction, the price was worth paying because it thereby removed the main competitor in an over-supplied market.

On 29 June 1905, W. L. Baillieu, accompanied by two Glass representatives — L. Stuart and E. H. Shackell — came to the boardroom of Dunlop to complete the formalities. On the following day the commercial editors of the *Age* and the *Argus* were informed that the deal was done. In the wake of the take-over, Dunlop found itself shaken up almost as much as Barnet Glass. Realising the worth of Baillieu, it invited him to join the board, where he was to become its dominant figure in nearly all financial matters. The 'new boy' had been a director for only two months when he moved that, in view of the failing health and frequent absences of Nicholas Fitzgerald, John Grice should take the chair whenever the chairman was absent. A few months later it was Baillieu who organised and actually underwrote a one for five issue of cumulative preference shares in order to raise another 28 000 pounds of capital. He too initiated the move to change Dunlop's bank from the Bank of Australasia, a London-owned bank, to the locally owned Commercial Bank of Australia.

He was so busy smartening up the company that in November 1905 he absent-mindedly lost his seat on the board by selling all the cumulative preference shares in his own name and thereby his right to sit on the board. For eighteen days this live wire ceased to be a director, finally arranging to buy from Richard Garland the necessary quota of five hundred shares.

With the purchase of the Barnet Glass business and its variety of rubber products, Dunlop moved far from its original function as a maker of tyres. Accordingly in September 1905 it resolved to take steps to change its name from the Dunlop Pneumatic Tyre Company of Australasia to the broader name of the Dunlop Rubber Company of Australasia. Its activities were reorganised, and each mill was given a special function. Montague concentrated on tyres and such lesser lines as moulded rubber goods, the rubber sealing rings widely used on the neck of bottles and jars, and sheet rubber. The former Barnet Glass mill at Kensington specialised in hose work, rubber packings and insertions, tubing, belting, mats, cushions, sporting goods, the rubber hot-water bottles taken to bed in winter, and waterproofed goods. Now the minor mill, Kensington no longer employed two hundred and fifty or three hundred at the peak of the manufacturing season.

The black-bearded pioneer of the local rubber industry, Barnet Glass, had behaved like a caged possum while the negotiations to sell his firm were clinched. Understandably feeling that his own soul and body were being sold against his will, he took no part in the detailed discussions with the Dunlop directors. His consolation, or so he hoped, was that he would remain managing director of the combined rubber firms. He soon realised that such a wish was very unlikely to be granted him. On the last day of his own Barnet Glass company he tried to prevent Dunlop officials from taking over his head office and warehouse in Flinders Street: he regarded them as a raiding party.

He now thought of litigation. He based his case on his original contract of 1900 when Stuart, Baillieu and others, on buying into his business, agreed that he could be joint managing director at the handsome salary of five hundred pounds a year until 1 August 1910. On the eve of the take-over, Dunlop offered to continue paying him the salary but insisted that he could not be managing director of the merged company and implied that it was hardly sensible to place the head of a failed company in charge of a successful company, especially when it was the failed company which had initially asked for help. Dunlop then offered him a specific post if he agreed to initiate no legal proceedings. Glass felt that his dignity would be lowered — and his contract violated — if he accepted this new post as manager of the waterproofing department at his old factory at Kensington. Like the Hercules of his trademark he summoned his strength and refused to give in. As a sign of his dislike for the new company he seems to have immediately sold the parcel of Dunlop ordinary shares allotted to him as payment for his Pioneer shares.

Glass engaged a fine solicitor and the best barristers to fight his case. He was represented in the Supreme Court of Victoria by Hayden Starke and James

Macfarlan: later they became celebrated as judges, Sir Hayden in the High Court and Sir James in the Supreme Court. Barnet Glass sued his old company, the Pioneer Rubber Works of Australia, for three thousand pounds in damages. He justified that large sum by explaining his working career, by pointing out that he no longer had the opportunity in Melbourne to practise his skills learned over a lifetime. He had had his fifty-sixth birthday at Easter 1906. He had little hope of starting a new business and if it did start he predicted that Dunlop 'would have knocked a little man out in no time'. Glass even sought work at another waterproofing firm in Melbourne but its part-owner informed the court that he could only employ him in a humble post. 'As an operative he would not be of much use', said Mr Zeltner. 'He is getting too old for my class of business.' The verdict was awarded to Glass but he received only one thousand of the three thousand pounds he had sought.

Other members of the Glass family joined Dunlop. The son-in-law, Frederic Ornstein, now received a higher salary than either he or Barnet Glass had received from their firm, and he remained in charge of the old factory at Kensington. But the new order did not please him. His machine shop and hose plant and various other departments were, to his regret, moved to Montague. After little more than a year he resigned with the bonus of six months' salary. Meanwhile the nephew of Barnet Glass, Philip J. Glass, was appointed as manager of Dunlop's busy branch in Perth, and showed his uncle's litigious streak by threatening to sue the firm which had removed his furniture and household possessions by sea to Perth and then overcharged him.

Not long after Barnet Glass was bought by Dunlop, the profits of the rubber business began to improve. The long drought was over, the world prices for Australia's exports were rising: the year 1907 was very prosperous in Australia. The public demand for tyres and other rubber goods was increasing, and the rising import duties against foreign manufacturers ensured that Australian-made products controlled most of the market. The profits of the renamed Dunlop Rubber Company of Australasia increased quickly. The elimination of competition from Barnet Glass helped those profits. Dunlop continued to pay the promised dividend on the preference shares and managed, for the year ending 31 July 1907, to lift the dividend on ordinary shares from five to five and a half per cent. A year later the dividend on shares was nine per cent and remained relatively high year after year. In a time of low inflation that dividend was handsome.

In the meantime the members of the Glass family, working for Dunlop in senior positions in Tasmania, Western Australia and Victoria, had increased their knowledge of Dunlop's business and its clients. They also saw Dunlop's increasing profits. They began to wonder whether they should again try to operate their own rubber business. On 4 March 1907 the directors of Dunlop held a special meeting to consider an agenda of only one item: should they yield to the request by P. J. Glass to be released from his Perth position at short notice? They agreed, maybe reluctantly. That was the beginning of the departure of the Barnet Glass brigade. The firm of Barnet Glass was born again, and the old founder returned to the smell of rubber. His cup was overflowing. He was happy to forget his court-room prediction that in no time Dunlop would knock out the little manufacturer.

In his new venture Glass was not knocked out. He and his family quickly showed how determination, drive and knowledge could tackle most obstacles. In their new rubber mill on the banks of the Maribyrnong River at Footscray they busied themselves at the old trades they knew so well. Some of their old employees returned. At 227 Swanston Street, Melbourne, they set up a new head office and display room. Thinking that a sure source of crude rubber could be handy, Philip Glass organised a group to buy a young rubber plantation in British Malaya. Floating it on the Melbourne Stock Exchange as the Port Swettenham Rubber Company, he persuaded a leading Melbourne physician and jack-of-all-professions, Dr James W. Barrett, to chair the company. In 1912 the company began to declare dividends, that year paying three in all. Dunlop had already contributed to the profits by buying a bargain consignment of Port Swettenham rubber at two pence a pound below the ruling rate. A senior member of the Dunlop board, James Riley, sat on the Port Swettenham board alongside two Barnet Glass directors, though Dunlop seems to have had no direct interest in the company.

The new Barnet Glass Rubber Company flourished. In 1910, only five years after the family's costly failure, the name of Barnet Glass stood again in large letters on roadside hoardings in Melbourne. In 1910 the payment of the handsome dividend of twelve and a half per cent on the company's ordinary shares surprised the share market. In the brief pre-war boom in Australia there was room for several strong rubber companies. There even seemed room for several manufacturers of car tyres, and Barnet Glass prepared to make a product that would make or break the firm.

Make way for the horseless carriage!

MOST OF the early motor cars, whether in Australia or the United States, were made by hand in backyards and stables. In Detroit, behind a two-storey house, Henry Ford busied himself each evening in building a car. As soon as he completed his daily work as an engineer at the Edison electric power-house, he resumed his task of assembling the parts of the car. It had four wheels on a light frame, a small gasoline engine, a chain drive like a bicycle, a tiller instead of a steering wheel, and a doorbell in place of a car horn. On 4 June 1896, at two o'clock in the morning, his car was ready, and a friend walked down the cobblestone lane ahead of the spluttering car to warn any drivers of horses and carts that a noisy mechanical animal was about to emerge. Ford's very first car was not a success.

While Ford was making his first car, other mechanics were busy in Australian sheds, putting together their automobiles. In 1896 in the Melbourne suburb of Fitzroy Mr Henry Austin began to design and assemble his Ridge-Austin motor car on behalf of the Australasian Horseless Carriage Syndicate, a group of twenty investors. Abandoning an engine of his own design he adapted a horizontal engine that used kerosene. Fitted at the rear of his car the small engine drove the rear wheel by means of a sprocket and chain device similar to the one used by Henry Ford. Austin first tested his car in Fitzroy's streets, and on 16 February 1897 he publicly displayed it, for all to marvel at, in a bicycle show in the nearby Exhibition Building. Like a four-wheeled mail cart, it had wooden wheels and iron tyres, and two seats for passengers, but no hood to protect them from rain. The Governor of Victoria, Lord Brassey, persuaded to climb aboard, was driven along a path in the surrounding gardens at a speed approaching ten miles an hour.

In the United States, most of the early cars were driven by steam or electricity. In South Australia a steam car was built about 1897 by John

Shearer, a manufacturer of ploughs, strippers and other agricultural implements at the river port of Mannum. A year or two later he drove his car along bumpy roads to Adelaide, where it was preceded along city streets by a man carrying a red flag as warning. City horses were apparently not as frightened as the Mannum horses by the sight and sound of this heavy monster. Not far behind Shearer as a pioneer car-builder came Herbert Thomson of Melbourne. The son of a wheelwright, he himself made steam engines and boilers in the suburb of Armadale where he tried his hand at making a lightweight steam car. Working mainly in his spare time, he was almost ready in 1899 to display his car in public by driving it around the Malvern cricket ground. The fittings of his car were ornate, as if it were designed to stand in a corner of the family drawing-room. Decorated with the fine-grained timbers and the elegant paintwork used on every classy horse-drawn vehicle, it was described as a 'six-seat Phaeton of fiddle-back ash and silky oak'. Its fuel was kerosene, which heated the water stored in a baby-sized rectangular boiler. The two cylinders in the engine worked in tandem.

The most celebrated but not the first of the early Australian cars was the Thomson. A hoodless Thomson car, reconditioned, now stands in the Museum of Victoria. Its original tyres and inner tubes, long ago worn out and thrown away, were apparently handmade by the Dunlop men at the original factory in Tattersall's Lane. The car carries the painted date of 1896 but is probably not as old as its inscription. A surviving photograph of the original Thomson steam car shows that its tyres were heavier versions of the bicycle tyres of the late 1890s. Like so many horse-drawn carriages of the era, the Thomson's front wheels were smaller than the rear wheels: the diameter of the front wheels was thirty-four inches (86 cm) while that of the back was forty-four (112 cm).

The Dunlop Pneumatic Tyre Company, deciding in November 1900 to promote motor cars, chose an imported car. Its directors signed an agreement to become the Victorian agents for the Paris company, De Dion Bouton, which was the leading maker in France. The demonstration model imported to Melbourne was soon a popular sight in a city where the motor cars probably numbered fewer than two dozen. Once or twice it presented a dashing sight on the rough country roads. On the eve of the Warrnambool to Melbourne cycling race of 1901 the Dunlop motor 'voiturette', as it was called in the press, conveyed the race's organiser, Harry James of Dunlop, and his boss, 'Jack' Proctor, along the route so that they could organise the final details. In all, four motorists decided to follow the cycle race. By agreement they did not leave Warrnambool until two minutes after the backmarkers set out, and their drivers remained at the very tail of the riding field.

Dunlop used its new French car simply to advertise the name of Dunlop and above all the Dunlop bicycle tyres. In the Melbourne *Herald* in May 1901 the readers saw a large advertisement showing a car labelled 'Dunlop' racing against a passenger train. Smoke streamed from the locomotive as it raced along a high embankment while, on the road below, the car's passenger and driver, both wearing French flat-top officer hats, bent their heads to escape some of the force of the rushing wind as the car, apparently, edged ahead of the locomotive. The dramatic black-and-white drawing was captioned 'RACING THE EXPRESS'. To our eyes it is unmistakably an early advertisement for Dunlop car tyres but, on reflection, it is not. At the foot of the advertisement, just below the speeding front wheel and its tyre devoid of tread, is a sentence inviting cyclists to write for a copy of Dunlop's 'Artistic and Beautifully Illustrated Booklet' containing forty pages of interest to all cyclists. Dunlop in 1901 was primarily advertising bicycle tyres, and the car was considered a glamorous way of advertising them.

The Dunlop company's De Dion Bouton was long remembered in Melbourne, where the average resident might set eyes on no more than one car a day. The car's fame, indeed its notoriety, increased after a mishap on 30 August 1901. W. J. Proctor was driving Harry James to the agricultural showground in Flemington where Dunlop tyres were in a special display. Chugging along Epsom Road at a brisk twenty miles an hour, the car came in sight of horses that were returning from a training run at the nearby racecourse. One of the racehorses, a two-year-old colt named Windsor, suddenly caught sight or sound of the car. The jockey, Sutherland, tried to quieten the horse. By now the car was close and decidedly noisy. Proctor, sensing danger, put on the brake to slow the car to seven or eight miles an hour. The racehorse in fright then tried to cross to the wrong side of the road, whereupon Proctor changed course. The horse reared, virtually charging the car, and damaged its right foreleg, whereupon it had to be destroyed.

When the owner of the horse, a St Kilda sharebroker named Samuel Bloomfield, heard of the accident he took the Dunlop company to court for damages. While Bloomfield had paid some fifty-three pounds for the colt, he thought it was worth close to five hundred pounds on the day of the accident. The Chief Justice, Sir John Madden, hearing the case in the Banco Court, knew so little about motor cars that at the close of the first day of the hearing he stood in William Street and watched the De Dion Bouton go through its paces so that he could be acquainted with what the horse must have seen. Madden observed the loud noise of the engine which witnesses had already sworn was boisterous enough to frighten any law-abiding horse.

The case was to be remembered outside the court for the wrong reason. It is said to have been a test case of the long-standing law that a traction engine or other mechanical vehicle must not exceed three miles an hour — the same law which decreed that such vehicles must be preceded by a man on foot and holding a red flag of warning. The reports of the case, however, do not mention that law. While the Chief Justice let it be known that twenty miles an hour was a very rapid pace, he did not dispute the motorist's right to travel

Make way for the horseless carriage!

RACING THE EXPRESS

'Racing the express', a Dunlop advertisement that appeared in many newspapers and journals in 1901.

without displaying a red flag of warning. His main concern was whether Proctor had been negligent in driving the car. Proctor for his part argued that the accident would have been avoided had he driven rapidly past the approaching horses, but the Chief Justice concluded that Proctor should have halted the car before reaching the horses. Proctor in effect was deemed negligent. To the dismay of the motoring fraternity, Bloomfield was awarded 250 pounds in damages. The Dunlop Pneumatic Tyre Company of Australasia paid the bill.

Owners of horses, drivers of cabs, carts and drays, grooms, stablemen and members of a variety of occupations had a vested interest in defending the horse. An opposing lobby that could speak for the motorists was urgently needed. Soon, automobile clubs were formed to press for favourable laws and smoother roads. In Melbourne in 1903, Harry James of Dunlop was the main promoter of what became the Royal Automobile Club of Victoria (RACV), and at the foundation meeting in the Port Phillip Club Hotel in Flinders Street on 9 December he moved and Proctor seconded the very first motion in the minute book. Sir John Madden, found to be a friend of motorists after all, was elected president and Harry James served briefly as first secretary. As in the English game of cricket in that era, the thorny question was whether the automobile club should be primarily run for amateurs or professionals. The wealthy amateurs, being the main owners of what the club called 'self-propelled vehicles', were not too sure whether the club committee should be tainted by the presence of the professionals from the new motor trade. After hot discussion the members of the trade — with the exception of Harry James, for someone had to soil his hands by organising — were formally excluded from the committee.

Dunlop, sensing that its distant future would lie more in the car than the bicycle tyre, continued to sponsor motoring. In 1906 the men who managed its branches in the large cities were each provided with a motor car. At head office in Melbourne in August 1906 the twelve-horsepower De Dion, traded in for 350 pounds, was replaced by a Beeston Humber described in the board minutes as of sixteen to twenty horsepower. The sale-room price of the new car was 695 pounds. The Montague factory specially made its tyres. For delivering goods in the cities the organisation mainly used horse and cart, but in Melbourne in 1908 a one-ton Argyll truck was bought.

South Australians, especially doctors and pastoralists, were early to see the benefits of motor cars. In 1906 their parliament, mainly copying the relevant English act, insisted on the registration of all motor vehicles using the public roads. In South Australia each car now had to carry a number and the name and address of its owner. Of the initial ten cars registered and assigned a number plate, four were Darracq cars and three were Talbots. The driver of the car also had to be licensed — a grave infringement of civil liberties, in the opinion of some drivers. New South Wales did not specifically regulate motor traffic until 1909 and Victoria waited until 1910.

Make way for the horseless carriage!

Photo courtesy of the RACV

An obstacle race for cars at the Aspendale racecourse, on the outskirts of Melbourne, 1904.

Sales of the bicycles were still soaring in these first years of the motor car. The market for bicycle tyres was huge, and the manufacture of these tyres remained the main activity at Montague. Its tyre builders occasionally made tyres for cars, but many of the Dunlop-brand tyres on Australian cars were English, having been imported from Coventry where the making of car tyres began in 1900. The Australian Dunlop probably did not begin to make car tyres with any regularity until 1903, and from time to time the tyres proved to be faulty. In 1906 the Montague factory must have been earning at least ten times as much revenue from bicycle tyres as from car tyres.

The early car tyres made by Dunlop's tyre-builders had no tread: the Thomson's tyres on display in the Museum of Victoria have a smooth surface. Even in Europe the car tyres had no tread until perhaps 1903 when a simple cross-groove design was adopted. As cars travelled slowly, the danger of skidding was not so high, and the tread was not deemed important. As the later cars travelled faster, a distinct tread pattern became necessary.

Car tyres were the target for the same complaints originally made against the bicycle tyres. In city streets the early car tyres were punctured by nails, broken glass and sharp stones. In the pot-holes of rural roads the car tyres were easily damaged. The motoring notes which appeared regularly in the daily newspapers were peppered with stories of tyre troubles. An Albury man, A. E. Fuller, riding his motor cycle home from Melbourne in December 1904, hit a sharp object just beyond Kilmore. When he alighted he found a long slit in the tyre and tube. He mended the puncture but when he reached Mangalore the tyre blew out. His roadside repairs enabled him to travel another twenty miles when again the tyre blew out. With further mending he advanced another twenty or so miles before more repairs were called for. Eventually he gave up, walked four miles to Wangaratta and completed the journey by train.

Start of the Reliability Trial, Melbourne to Sydney, 1905.

The owner of a car who completed a long journey without suffering from a puncture was inclined to tell newspapers about his good fortune. A long journey without one puncture was motoring news. When the Thomson steam car travelled the five hundred miles from Bathurst to Melbourne in 1900, its driver felt he was lucky to have almost completed the journey before he heard, for the first time, the loud hiss of a punctured tyre.

Before the quality of the car tyres was substantially improved, a few motorists turned to the solid rubber tyres. Unlike the pneumatic tyre, the solid tyre did not slip off the wheel and did not puncture. When comfort was considered of no importance for the passengers and driver the solid rubber tyre was preferred: it was much less likely to break down. But to those passengers who now were accustomed to the pneumatic tyre, the solid tyre was painful. Hour after hour the vibrations from the rough road were felt in the driving seat. In contrast pneumatic tyres not only cushioned the driver and passengers but enabled a car to reach a faster speed.

Dunlop decided in 1905 that the time had come to sponsor motoring contests in the same way that it had sponsored cycling races. In February it offered the Dunlop Cup, valued at the handsome sum of one hundred guineas, to the winner of the Dunlop Reliability Motor Contest. Twenty-three cars started from Sydney and after reaching Melbourne drove to Ballarat and back. Captain Tarrant, driving his home-made Tarrant, was the winner. In November, Dunlop conducted a second reliability test, beginning at Melbourne's

Make way for the horseless carriage!

Photo courtesy of Peter Darvell, Darvell & Associates, London

Two Dunlop directors, Valentine Saddler and James Riley, competing in the 1905 Reliability Trial.

Haymarket — the wide crossroads at the top of Elizabeth Street where now the huge Australian flag is flown. Of the twenty-eight cars that started, nineteen reached Sydney. Contrary to expectations, too many of the cars had proved to be reliable. To find a winner the race was continued on to Medlow Bath in the Blue Mountains and back, but those steep hills did not eliminate enough of the remaining competitors. The six surviving cars then set out on the return journey to Melbourne, which, if completed, would result in a total distance of 1276 miles.

Such was the national interest in this new form of the marathon race that reporters followed the cars along the present Hume Highway. At Victorian wayside towns the speed of the winning Mercedes, driven by G. Hobbs, thrilled the bystanders. According to the Sydney *Daily Telegraph* the Mercedes passed through the townships 'at a tremendous pace'. By our standards, however, the car was slow, averaging only twenty-seven miles an hour on the run from Albury to Melbourne. In fairness to this speedster, it should be added that his car would have averaged twenty-nine miles an hour but for the thirteen minutes wasted while waiting for railway gates to be opened. Sensibly the *Daily Telegraph* predicted that many of the outback's problems would be solved once motor cars were capable of averaging twenty miles an hour on bush tracks.

As advertising manager for Dunlop, Harry James spent weeks trying to set new records which would prove to doubters that the motor car was especially suited to a land where railways were far apart, the roads were rough and many creeks were unbridged. With a prominent car dealer, C. B. Kellow, as his co-driver, Harry James drove a four-cylinder Humber car shod with Australian-made Dunlop tyres. On several occasions, James and Kellow set out to break a world record by driving as far as possible in twenty-four hours. Choosing western Victoria where the flat roads were suitable for night driving as well as speed, they made their first concerted attempt on the record in May 1906. Leaving Melbourne at three in the afternoon they drove the ninety-two miles to Colac in just over three hours. After halting seventeen minutes to take on petrol and light their acetylene headlamps they drove on to Hamilton where they lost twenty-five minutes while replacing a punctured tube in a front wheel. Driving in the darkness from Hamilton to Camperdown they found they could not use their eye goggles because of the heavy dew; and their naked eyes — without the protection of a windscreen — were soon inflamed by the dust and grit that rushed past them. On the return journey through Geelong to Melbourne they were further delayed by a head wind, the poor state of the road closer to Melbourne, and a second puncture. Nonetheless in twenty-four hours they covered 556 miles, which they claimed was a world record. An *Argus* reporter, noticing the different driving styles of the record-breakers, reported that Kellow sat up straight while James crouched over the steering wheel and peered intently ahead. Their record was soon broken, but in November 1907 it was recaptured for Australia by Harry James and H. L. Stevens who drove a total of 777 miles in twenty-four hours.

The Melbourne–Sydney route was the favourite of the record-breakers. In January 1908, the experienced team of Kellow and James left Melbourne in the hope of completing the journey in only twenty-four hours, and would have succeeded but for the century heat, the hour-and-a-half they lost at night while they roused the gatekeeper at railway crossings, and the need to make a detour near Picton. Their final time was twenty-five hours and forty minutes. Newspapers and journals were willing to publicise the fact that the Talbot car again rode on Australian-made Dunlops. The fashionable journal *Table Talk* revealed that not one of the metal-studded tyres gave trouble, but the friction of the tyres on the road was such that the drivers from time to time appear to have stopped the car in order to throw a bucket of cold water against the driving wheels. The water, we learn, 'fairly hissed and rose in clouds of steam vapour'.

This faithful Talbot was photographed, probably at the end of the journey, with the drivers sitting high in their seats. Kellow is wearing a white collar and tie, and James is wearing a bow tie and both men wear white wide-brimmed hats: their dress and faces are clearly visible because the car had no windscreen and no hood. The drivers presumably decked themselves out neatly for the

C B Kellow & H.B.James
Melbourne to Sydney
576 Miles - 23 Hours 40 Minutes
16 H.P. Clement Talbot
WITH DUNLOP TYRES

Photo courtesy of the RACV

Harry James and C. B. Kellow at the completion of their Melbourne-Sydney trip in a 16 hp Clement Talbot. The face peering over the bonnet is that of C. O. Sherwood, Dunlop's NSW manager.

sake of the photograph but the car after its long journey could not so easily be made presentable. One mudguard is missing and the Dunlop tyres show signs of the long journey. Two spare tyres are tied to the driver's side of the car and at the rear sits an object that looks like a third spare tyre. The tyres on the front wheels are more like bicycle tyres than today's car tyres. Their tread is specially visible: it consisted of parallel indented bars that give the impression that the tyre is treaded with miniature railway sleepers. The one rear tyre visible in the photograph is distinctive. Its tread consists of small raised buttons of rubber that presumably held the metal studs. These rear tyres almost certainly were made by Dunlop of England.

In Melbourne, as late as 1906, Dunlop made thousands of bicycle tyres each month but few car tyres. The number of cars was still small, and most were imported complete with a set of new tyres and at least one spare tyre. Proctor had travelled to England and America in 1904 to learn what he could about the manufacture of car tyres, and about two years later the factory at Montague began the regular production of car tyres at a rate of about twenty a week. The venture required such a small amount of new equipment that it was not even discussed at the meeting of directors.

The early car tyres made in Australia cannot have been a startling success. Though protected against imports by a large duty, the local tyres could not defeat the imported tyres. Foreign tyres were obviously superior in quality and moreover they came ready-made with the imported vehicles which now dominated the new-car market. In addition there was a strong demand in Australia for replacement tyres for new and secondhand cars, and that market was even larger than that for tyres on new cars. Dunlop had to improve its quality to capture a good share of the replacement market. In May 1907 the 'wearing qualities' of Dunlop tyres were widely criticised by motorists. Two of the largest motor dealers in Melbourne, the Kellow Motor Co. and the Tarrant Motor Co., both complained that Dunlop tyres soon wore out. In reply, Dunlop's directors promised the motor dealers that the new tyres would be long-wearing. The hope was premature. In October 1907, Dunlop suspended the making of the larger sizes of car tyres, presumably importing them from England.

Many tyres of smaller sizes also were unsatisfactory. At the end of 1908 the directors appealed to English Dunlop for help in supervising the manufacture of tyres in Australia. The secretary, Charles Proctor, left in the weekly mail steamer for London where he joined a leading director, John Grice, for discussions with English Dunlop. On 23 April of the new year, Proctor was back in Melbourne to attend a meeting of the board. He handed out copies of the agreement whereby English Dunlop would help make the tyres in Australia, and every director agreed to take home a copy and read it closely. W. L. Baillieu, the company's supreme trouble shooter, then went to London to finalise the agreement.

Under the original consigning of territory in 1899, Australian Dunlop had a monopoly of Australia and New Zealand, and the right to exclude any Dunlop tyres and rubber products imported by other firms from English Dunlop. Australian Dunlop also held the right to inventions, patents and trademarks held by English Dunlop. Curiously it did not have the specified right to acquire what was often more important than inventions — a working knowledge of the techniques of making tyres. As Australian Dunlop had become independent in 1899, in the heyday of the pneumatic cycle tyre, it had already borrowed from its parent company the techniques of making cycle tyres. The more difficult techniques of making car tyres it did not fully possess. Admittedly, Montague had acquired some of the early techniques by hiring Kearns and his colleagues from North America, but it would have to keep on hiring new American or British tyre operatives if it wished to remain up-to-date. For these reasons the directors in Melbourne decided that it was wisest to make a permanent technical link with the big factory of English Dunlop in Birmingham.

On 14 September 1909, W. L. Baillieu, on behalf of Australian Dunlop, signed a reciprocity agreement with English Dunlop. In return for technical help, Australian Dunlop paid cash. For every tyre cover made at Montague in the next ten years Australian Dunlop was to pay a royalty which was not to exceed the sum of seven shillings and sixpence. The royalty, based on the cost of production, was to diminish from seven to four per cent for the second period of ten years. Likewise, when English Dunlop tyres were supplied on new English cars exported to Australia and New Zealand, the English company was to pay a similar royalty of seven per cent to the Australian company. The export of new cars to Australia and New Zealand from England proved small during the following decade, and so Montague's revenue from this source was tiny compared to the payments it made to English Dunlop. The signed agreement was very favourable to English Dunlop, but then the factory at Montague was in trouble and its bargaining position was weak. The factory either had to buy new skills or be content with only a fraction of the expanding market for car tyres in the south-west Pacific.

John Kearns, the mill superintendent at Montague, went to Birmingham where he examined all the techniques of the mother company, receiving free access to their detailed costs. He was also permitted to take down in writing — under a pledge of secrecy — the various recipes used for making the special kinds of tyre rubbers. His recipe or formula book was placed under lock and key when he returned to Melbourne. Kearns also was allowed to bring back to his factory a skilled foreman and his offsider from Birmingham, and use them as instructors in tyre-making for six months. He decided that two skilled men and six months were insufficient. The tyre specialists obviously had to be on call at every working shift if the tyre-making under the new methods was really to succeed. In May 1910 the board in Melbourne gave Kearns permission to hire six specialists and pay all expenses for the voyage to Australia. Meanwhile two directors, Riley and Grice, agreed to wait upon the Prime Minister, and gain consent to the hiring of the six men because, apparently, the importing of skilled labour formally required the approval of the Labour government. The English tyre-makers duly arrived and settled down at Montague. Meanwhile large quantities of tyres were imported from England to meet a demand which was as yet beyond the Montague factory.

To the dismay of the directors many of the tyres made at Montague, under English supervision, were 'highly unsatisfactory'. It was felt that Kearns could not cope. One of the best Melbourne tyre-makers, F. Wolff, after signing a new contract to work with Dunlop for five years at the high salary of four hundred pounds a year, was sent to England and Europe to work in the rubber mills and gain the latest knowledge. It was decided that the raw materials used at Montague were also at fault. As the fabric of the Montague tyres was not tough enough, Egyptian cloth was replaced by Sea Island cloth. Meanwhile English Dunlop, unable to meet the rising demand for car tyres in its home market, refused to supply all the tyres Dunlop needed in Australia. In desperation a consignment of German tyres, beginning at fifty tyres a week, was ordered for Melbourne.

Perhaps English Dunlop was not so competent after all. That suspicion gained ground in the Melbourne boardroom. The company turned to the

Americans again, buying an American tyre-making machine from Goodyear early in 1912. The company now appeared to be in the silly position — under the terms of the 1909 agreement — of paying royalties to English Dunlop for every tyre it made on a Goodyear machine.

At last Dunlop in Melbourne was making headway. Late in 1911 a big rambling building of wood and iron was built quickly to quadruple the output of tyres. A motor car was bought and driven for long hours each week solely to test the wearing qualities of a sample of freshly-made tyres. Kearns, who so far had clung to his job despite hints that his time was almost up, even made plans for the factory to enter the adventurous field of manufacturing steel-studded tyres. The quality of Australian-made tyres was improved. By February 1913 the complaint was not that too few tyres were being made at Montague but too many.

A year later the directors felt confident that their technical staff could begin to design special tyres for special regions. As the walls of the tyres used in outback Queensland and other rural districts were not strong enough, it was recommended that the walls be strengthened by the addition of more rubber. For New Zealand a lighter tyre should be specially made. Even the making of the solid rubber tyres favoured by motor lorries and heavy wagons now seemed possible, under the supervision of Roberts, the new rubber expert recruited from England. Soon Roberts was earning 1500 pounds a year, or more than ten times the annual income earned by many of his fastest employees. Under Roberts another large rubber mill was needed to meet the ever-increasing demand for car tyres.

The price of these technical advances was high. Much of Dunlop's profit went — for the first time — back to England in royalties. The drain of royalties vexed Sir John Grice and his colleagues in Melbourne, and they urged W. L. Baillieu, while visiting England to renegotiate the royalties agreement of 1909. In August 1914, in London, the two Dunlop companies resolved to replace the quarterly royalties with a once-and-for-all payment. The Dunlop Rubber Company of Australasia agreed to pay 35 000 pounds to English Dunlop in lieu of future royalties, and English Dunlop for its part agreed to pay 2000 pounds in lieu of future royalties. The final sum of 33 000 pounds, transferred in instalments from the Melbourne to the London company, now seems small, but it exceeded the total dividends paid by the Melbourne company in the year in which the royalty agreement was first signed.

The main cause of the sharp increase in the sales of car tyres in Australia — and of the soaring royalties paid by the Australian Dunlop — had been the Model T Ford. When it first ran in Australia it did not appear capable of transforming the motoring industry. Its axles, so important in rugged Australian conditions, seemed thin and weak. The car itself seemed too light: it weighed only about half as much as the strong English, French and American cars favoured by wealthier drivers. The Ford was fitted with only two forward

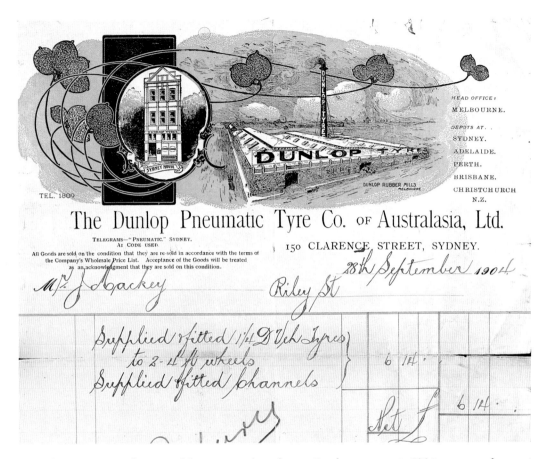

TEL. 1809

The Dunlop Pneumatic Tyre Co. of Australasia, Ltd.

HEAD OFFICE:
MELBOURNE.

DEPOTS AT . .
SYDNEY.
ADELAIDE.
PERTH.
BRISBANE.
CHRISTCHURCH
N.Z.

TELEGRAMS—"PNEUMATIC." SYDNEY.
AI CODE USED.

All Goods are sold on the condition that they are re-sold in accordance with the terms of the Company's Wholesale Price List. Acceptance of the Goods will be treated as an acknowledgment that they are sold on this condition.

150 CLARENCE STREET, SYDNEY.

28th September 1904

Mr J Mackey   Riley St

Supplied & fitted 1/4 D Veh Tyres to 2-4 ft wheels		6 14	
Supplied & fitted channels			
	Net £	6 14	

Sydney customers who received their account from the new Dunlop company in 1904 were treated to a coloured sketch of the rambling Melbourne factory and the narrow Sydney office.

One of the first share certificates issued following incorporation as a public company on 16 August 1920.

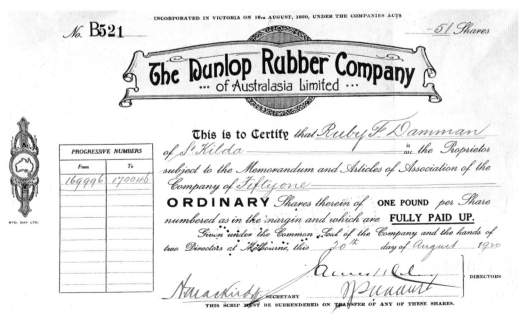

INCORPORATED IN VICTORIA ON 16th AUGUST, 1920, UNDER THE COMPANIES ACTS

No. B521   —51 Shares

The Dunlop Rubber Company
... of Australasia Limited ...

This is to Certify that *Ruby F. Damman* of *St Kilda* is the Proprietor subject to the Memorandum and Articles of Association of the Company of *Fiftyone* **ORDINARY** Shares therein of **ONE POUND** per Share numbered as in the margin and which are **FULLY PAID UP.**

Given under the Common Seal of the Company and the hands of two Directors at Melbourne, this 30th day of August 1920

PROGRESSIVE NUMBERS	
From	To
169996	170046

SYD. DAY LTD.

DIRECTORS

H Mackirdy SECRETARY

THIS SCRIP MUST BE SURRENDERED ON TRANSFER OF ANY OF THESE SHARES.

The elaborate Dunlop Cup, presented to the winner of the 1905 Reliability Trial between Sydney and Melbourne, is now displayed at the Royal Automobile Club of Victoria.

These glamorous cards, drawn by Jack Sommers, were printed in their thousands for Dunlop in 1907 and could be bought by sending a twopenny stamp to the Dunlop offices.

Around 1914 this was one of the best known advertising posters in Australia. It celebrated the race between Murray Aunger's Vauxhall car — on Dunlop tyres of course — and the Adelaide Express. Despite the poor roads the car won by three hours.

An eye-catching Dunlop price list issued around 1916.

Barnet Glass, a fierce competitor which later became a part of Dunlop, made its name amongst motorists with its Boomerang tyre. The tread of the tyre actually consisted of a procession of boomerangs. This big poster, fixed to the ceiling of an engineering shop for some 80 years, was restored in 1990.

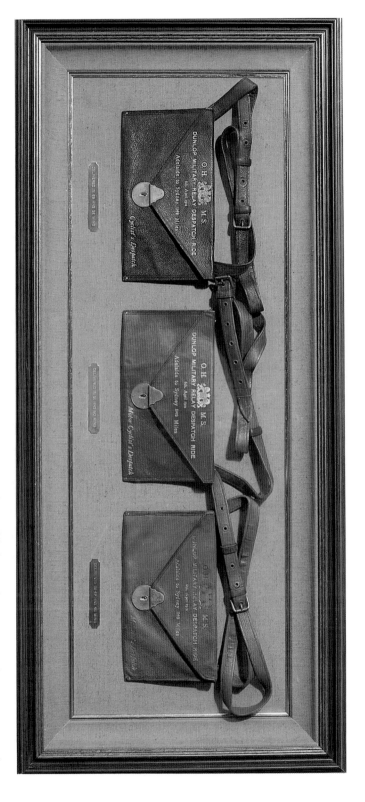

These pouches each held a military despatch and were carried in Dunlop's celebrated handicap race from Adelaide to Sydney in 1912. The contest was a relay race between bicycles, motor-bikes and cars — the bicycles won.

A Dunlop poster issued a few years before the First World War. It was found at Ballarat in 1993.

Make way for the horseless carriage!

*This clever Dunlop advertisement greeted the American warships, 'The Great White Fleet',
which visited Sydney and Melbourne in 1908.*

Jumping over the wheel

Dunlop's 'Railroad' tyre with its distinctive tread mark. Inch by inch the tyre was becoming wider.

gears instead of the three or four of the more expensive cars. Its virtue was its price — at 310 pounds it was only half the price of the normal car. It was an austerity car, a makeshift model for those who could afford nothing else. Indeed in Adelaide a leading car salesmen, S. A. Cheney, on seeing his first Model T Ford in August 1909, threatened to resign if his employer took on the agency for such an unglamorous car. The employer did take on the agency, and Cheney agreed to stay — so long as he could sell only the expensive cars and have nothing to do with the Ford which sold at less than half the price of the other cars. Before long he found himself, against his wishes, driving a Ford all the way to Loxton on the Murray. The strength and speed of the car astonished him.

The first car to appeal to American farmers, the Model T Ford attracted country residents in Australia for the same reason. Its cheapness and reliability also delighted city people. Those with a middling income could at last afford a car. The sale of cars in Australia soared, and the demand for tyres soared faster, for a tyre still had a short life compared to that of a car. More perhaps than any other Australian firm, Dunlop had promoted and popularised motoring. Now the box-shaped Ford car largely took over that task.

Dunlop's profits still lay mainly in bicycle tyres, for more and more people were riding bicycles. The Dunlop executives wondered how far they should glamorise the car at the expense of the bicycle, whose tyre was the mainstay of profits. One of their glamorous promotions highlighted their dilemma. In 1909, Harry James arranged for relays of Dunlop cyclists, travelling in pairs, to carry a sealed military despatch from Adelaide through Melbourne to Sydney. Their time was just under three days and nights, or sixty-three-and-a-half hours to be exact. The publicity accompanying the ride caught the public's imagination. Three years later Harry James found himself in a lunch-time discussion in which motoring enthusiasts argued that motor cars, now so improved, would cover the same distance in half the time: in short they vowed that the fast cyclist was no longer in the race. James sought permission from the Dunlop board to organise another military despatch ride from Adelaide to Sydney, with teams of cars, motor bikes and cyclists competing against one another. To make the race exciting, by ensuring that the competitors would not be too far apart when they crossed the finishing line in Sydney, he knew he had to impose a handicap on the motor vehicles. Public discussion on the relative speeds of cycles and motor vehicles, and the kind of handicaps that would be appropriate, convinced him that his race would arouse intense interest.

When Dunlop announced in the newspapers that the cyclists would leave Adelaide at five in the morning on Good Friday, and that the motor cyclists would leave at the same hour on Easter Saturday, and the motorists would leave another six hours later, the general opinion was that the cyclists had been shabbily treated. They could not possibly hold the lead for the 1148

£4
each.

Road Tests Demonstrate
the Value of a Tyre.

LOOK AT THIS SERVICE
— FROM —

DUNLOP TYRES

Extract from a Letter received from Koondrook (Vic.)

"The Car shown gets from 5,000 to 6,000 miles out of Dunlop "Ford" Covers, and at times makes trips of 120 miles over roads as shown in illustration. You can imagine what they are like on tyres when drying up."

All "Ford" Owners can have the same excellent service from these Special Covers which sell at **£4** each, or our Special "Ford" Rubber Non-Skid Cover at **£5 5s.** Why pay more when you can be sure of getting satisfaction and thousands of miles from these Reliable and Durable Covers.

OBTAINABLE FROM ALL GARAGES AND AGENTS.

THE DUNLOP RUBBER CO. OF AUST. LTD. ——— ALL STATES AND N.Z.

His Majesty's Mail
Bi-weekly Service Barham to Moulamein
Per Burdett's "Ford" Mudroplane
——— Using Dunlops ———

The Ford was becoming the favourite car in the bush, and Dunlop tried to capture the market for Ford 'covers' or tyres.

Make way for the horseless carriage!

ACROSS AUSTRALIA ON
ONE SET OF DUNLOPS

Francis Birtles was bogged during his 1912 Perth-Sydney trip, and the mishap was yet another opportunity to advertise Dunlop tyres.

miles. Several newspapers predicted that the cyclists would be overtaken before eight hundred miles — before they pedalled into Albury — or at best they would be overtaken before they reached Gundagai.

The directors of Dunlop were lobbied. The cyclists, it was explained, would be humiliated. Richard Garland came to James's office and as a director explained that the company's main profit still came from bicycle tyres, not car tyres. Was it therefore sensible for Dunlop to organise a contest in which the cyclists were downgraded? Why not give them another six hours' start? They debated the question for an hour but James would not give in. Cars and motor cycles were faster than bicycles, he argued, but were liable to break down. The cyclists had a fighting chance, he insisted.

On the first day of the race, the Good Friday of 1912, James must have doubted his confidence because the cyclists, riding in relays, pedalled into driving rain and a head wind. But the car and motor cycle used on the first leg made slow progress because they met their usual difficulties, not least the punctures. In fact the succession of cyclists surrendered their starting advantage much more slowly than expected. By the time the leading cyclist reached Goulburn on the evening of the third day, they were still far ahead of the motor cycle with its despatch, while the motor car had just reached Albury.

In the end the cyclists won easily, the last member of their 130-strong relay team riding into Sydney at three o'clock on Monday morning. Though the other vehicles carried a handicap, they were still — such was the state of the mechanical arts — not substantially faster than the bicycle. The cars averaged only twenty-four miles an hour, the motor bikes twenty-two miles an hour, and the cyclists sixteen-and-a-half.

The heyday of the fast reliable car awaited the coming of sealed roads, more reliable engines and stronger tyres. In a few series of statistics, however, the motor vehicle was coming to the fore. The car was now notorious for fatalities. In the annual list of accidental deaths the railways, with their millions of passengers, were being overtaken by motor vehicles with their few passengers. In 1916 in Victoria, forty-three people were killed by railway trains, thirty-eight by motor vehicles, and twenty-eight by horse-drawn vehicles. The age of motoring had almost arrived.

Turmoil

O N THE eve of the First World War the rubber industry was flourishing. Hardly a hut, hardly a house, did not use rubber goods. It would have been difficult to find one large factory and impossible to find one large mine not using rubber products made in Australia. Transport depended heavily on rubber. The roads, especially in the cities, had been transformed by cars and bicycles riding on pneumatic tyres, and the railways used rubber to cushion vibrations and shocks, while tens of thousands of horses pulled carts and wagons whose iron wheels were covered with a thin hoop of solid rubber.

More than twenty firms were making rubber goods, though many were hidden away in backyards. A tariff against imports had helped the rubber makers of Victoria even in the 1890s, and the import duty was increased by the new Commonwealth parliament. In 1902 the duty on imported rubber goods ranged from nothing on certain items to fifteen per cent on tyres for bicycles and cars and twenty-five per cent on such items as rubber boots and galoshes. Dunlop gained from these increasing penalties on foreign competitors, though curiously it did not bother to apply for a higher duty when lobbying was in the air and the government was eager to hear evidence from manufacturers wanting more protection. In 1908 all rubber factories were further protected by a duty of twenty per cent on rubber goods imported from the United Kingdom and twenty-five per cent on those from other lands. The whole spirit of the parliament, whether on the Labor or the anti-Labor benches, was now protectionist. The wish to subsidise and strengthen local industries was almost a national password for those seeking a seat in parliament. Nonetheless the imports of rubber goods still exceeded those made in Australia by a ratio of about sixty to forty. Germany was the main outside supplier, especially of rubber tyres and tubes, followed by Britain, the United

In 1910 tennis was growing in popularity, and the Dunlop ball was a best-seller.

*Miss Australia 1927, Phillis von Alwyn, farewells Francis Birtles outside Australia House,
London, as he prepares to drive to Melbourne in a Bean car.*

States, France, Canada and Italy. The Germans and the British between them earned two-thirds of the income Australia spent on outside rubber and rubber goods. The coming war, in cutting off German and impeding British supplies, was to give further protection to Australian rubber factories.

Within Australia the rubber industry was dominated by Dunlop. In 1914 the firm employed at least 1200 men and women. It was also the best known name in rubber, and one of the few trade names that was a household word. Indeed some people called bicycle tyres and car tyres by the simple name of 'Dunlops'. The firm drew attention to its products in daily newspapers as well as such popular periodicals as the *Bulletin* and the *Lone Hand* where its pictorial advertisements were of the highest class. Those who browsed through the weekly periodicals would come across a full or half page showing two women with basin-shaped hats driving a car with no hood and no windscreen and the white tyres clearly marked DUNLOP, or a smiling dark-haired girl, a black band around her white straw hat, holding a white tennis ball marked in flowing script with the word DUNLOP. To women who had little chance of sitting in a car, let alone owning one, Dunlop advertised hot-water bags or bottles said to be so well made that they would 'last several Winters', and the Dunlop rubber heels, each with their five bubble-like indentations. In many kitchens could be seen the handsome Dunlop calendar,

Jumping over the wheel

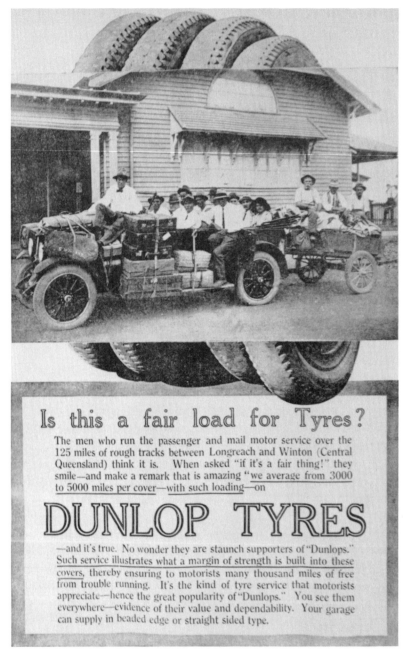

In 1923 Dunlop was spending a small fortune advertising in weekly papers such as
The Bulletin. Sales of tyres were aided by the fact that a successful tyre rarely lasted
more than 5000 miles.

and for the whole of 1910 the Australian actress Nellie Stewart in 'soft brown tones', looked down on families.

Dunlop at last had mastered most of the difficulties of making reliable tyres for cars. By 1912 the revenue from motor tyres almost equalled that from cycle tyres. By the last months of 1915 the tyres for cars and motor bikes provided forty-seven per cent of the company's revenue compared to a mere eighteen per cent from bicycle tyres. Dunlop, its profits largely riding on the car tyre, closely watched competing tyres. There was no official record of overall tyre sales in Australia, and so Dunlop periodically made its own count, sending men to the Melbourne Cup and other sports meetings where long rows of cars were parked. In nearly all counts the Dunlop tyres prevailed. Thus at an automobile rally at the bayside village of Aspendale late in 1914, the man hired to count every tyre on every car reported that Dunlop accounted for nearly half of all tyres — 236 Dunlops out of a total of 519 tyres. In those days the individual tyre had to be counted rather than the car as a whole because the one car could be shod with as many as three different brands of tyres. As the spare tyre or tyres were clearly visible — the car boot had not been invented — the spares were naturally included in the tally.

Dunlop's ascendancy in car tyres was about to be challenged. In 1914, Barnet Glass, the other Australian maker of tyres, was still cutting its teeth on this temperamental rubber product. At the Aspendale rally of cars, only fifty-two of its tyres were counted. For Dunlop the more dangerous competitor would be Perdriau of Sydney. Known for its Marathon, Sea Gull and Magpie brands of rubber shoes and now making for the first time those long rubber boots called gum boots, Perdriau had a potential to capture much of the tyre trade in New South Wales whenever it decided to make tyres: Sydney motorists were likely to prefer the local Perdriau tyre. When at last, early in the war, motorists in New South Wales were given the opportunity to buy the local Perdriau tyre they would buy it in large quantities.

More tension or unease in industrial relations as well as more competition slowly weakened Dunlop's commanding position. The rubber industry had its idle season, and Dunlop's factory tended to be slacker in June and July before picking up for the spring when bicycle tyres and other rubber goods were made in readiness for the main buying season. Dunlop's annual sales reached a peak in summer, partly because motoring, like cycling, was more a summer pursuit for many car-owners. Motoring was for pleasure, and many car-owners still went by train and tram to their daily work. These fluctuations meant that Dunlop did not provide a completely secure job for the average worker, which probably ruffled industrial relations. Turnover of labour was high, but new-comers learned the trade with relative ease. In 1909 Kearns of Dunlop told the Rubber Trade Board, which fixed the wages, that he himself could teach a newcomer any branch of the trade in the space of two months, though double that time was to be needed by the 1920s for the more complicated tasks.

Ernest Shackleton led expeditions to the Antarctic in 1908 and 1914, and he used not only dog-sleds but a car equipped with English Dunlop tyres filled with English air. His dogs and car were photographed outside the company's office in Christchurch.

In Kearns's opinion the rubber trade had the additional advantage that it was healthy. He claimed — maybe rashly — that Dunlop's factory had less absenteeism through sickness than any other factory. Some employees did not agree, arguing that a job in the compound room, where the mixing of chemicals and minerals took place, was not healthy. Unionists claimed during a wages hearing in 1909 that on one afternoon the odour of bisulphide of carbon caused several girls to faint, and that several operations led to nose-bleeding amongst men and even the cracking of their teeth. In the mixing mill, lead was part of the recipe for certain rubber products, and several men claimed to the trade union that they were suffering from lead poisoning. No doubt some processes in the factory could be unhealthy, especially if the foremen or the workers were careless but, rightly or wrongly, rubber working was not usually seen as a dangerous trade.

The company hoped for harmonious working relations and was prepared to make a few more steps than the average Melbourne factory to achieve such relations. The following gestures seem of little significance by today's criteria but were not yet normal amongst industrial employers. A large sum was given to the employees for their annual picnic. The widow of an employee killed in an accident or while on duty was likely to receive some consideration; and in 1906 the widow of J. Hall was given a sum of ten pounds and a weekly allowance of fifteen shillings — the allowance to be reviewed after a year. From the beginning the company set aside funds for hospitals and other charities, though it refused to help church charities in its early years. Naturally the Protectionist Association, which lobbied for higher tariffs against foreign goods, was a favoured charity, though it did not rank as high as the employees' picnic or the needs of a major hospital.

Dunlop paid its workers much the same weekly wage as other factory workers in Melbourne, with the unskilled men receiving forty-eight shillings a week and the unskilled women twenty-seven shillings at the outbreak of the First World War. On the other hand the very best rubber workers were highly paid by the standards of the time: a calendar hand received sixty-five shillings a week, a hose-maker and a tyre moulder fifty-five shillings a week. There was no shortage of labour. Each morning at the Montague factory, men and women were often waiting in a cluster or crowd at the main gate in the hope of being selected for a vacancy. In 1914, by overseas standards, the pay at Montague was high and the hours short. Dunlop employees, with their forty-eight-hour week, normally worked twelve hours fewer each week than a French or American rubber-worker. The protective tariff against imports meant that both employer and employee were more secure from foreign competition. The Australian customer, however, increasingly paid for this protection in the form of dearer tyres.

Sir John Grice and his colleagues on the Dunlop board could not be sure how their firm would be affected if European war broke out. Rubber did not seem to be an essential industry, in military eyes. In time of war, Australia was far more likely to be called upon for soldiers and horses than for rifles and a wide range of other manufactured goods. Accordingly, in the years before the war, Dunlop gave its attention — when it gave any attention to war — to promoting military training amongst its employees. In December 1909 the directors granted leave on full pay to all militiamen in its employ who wished to attend the 'Kitchener Camp' at Seymour. In 1911 they provided a trophy — worth about ten days' wages — to the Dunlop Rifle Club. In 1912 their bold publicity venture, the despatch ride between Adelaide and Sydney, was designed to publicise the dashing side of warfare as well as their own tyres.

When the European war began in August 1914, with Germany and Austria–Hungary on one side and Britain, France and Russia on the other side, the rubber mills were not affected at first. A trickle of Dunlop men enlisted in the Australian army but unemployed men soon filled the vacancies. A few of the mill foremen even returned immediately to England. G. S. Sheppard and W. I. Gibbard, who presumably were hired from England a year or two earlier, were still members of the British Army reserve; in their haste to enlist they left their families behind in Australia. The families, short

The hose room in Montague mill made long lengths of braided garden hose. Behind the ladder is a recruiting poster, which suggests the photo was taken around 1916.

of money, received thirty shillings a week as a patriotic gesture from the Dunlop directors.

It became the practice for Dunlop to pay an allowance to the wife and children or occasionally the mother of the permanent employees who enlisted. This allowance almost restored the weekly income the family had lost when its breadwinner joined the armed forces at a lower rate of pay. Married members of the salaried staff, as distinct from the wages staff, received an allowance which, after they enlisted, made up the exact difference between their peacetime and wartime income. The Dunlop scheme was not unique but was unusual. In the course of the war no more than a fraction of those Australian men who enlisted were to receive a bonus from their old employer.

Lieutenant-Colonel Hughes, sitting on the Dunlop board, helped to bring these war issues to the fore. As commander of the Third Light Horse Brigade he was ready to join the expeditionary force soon to sail for the Middle East; and at the board meeting on 13 November 1914 he was granted leave of absence for twelve months, presumably on the assumption that the war would last no longer than a year. Hughes at the age of fifty-seven landed at Gallipoli, and his men made the celebrated attack on the Turkish trenches at The Nek on 7 August 1915, suffering heavy casualties. Hughes himself returned to Australia, a victim of pneumonia and typhoid, and appeared again at the boardroom table. Lo and behold, in July 1918, Hughes — now General Hughes — gained from his colleagues on the board the leave to embark again on military service.

Dunlop was not a massive supplier of wartime goods to the government. Its contract in November 1914 to supply 17 200 ground sheets to the Defence Department is one of the few war contracts of which a record survives. The Montague factory's main work was to supply tyres, waterproof clothes and other civilian goods which eventually would have become unprocurable in Australia but for the existence of local suppliers. Even these goods were freely available in the first year or two of war because the United States, as a neutral nation, was only too willing to ship to Australia the tyres and other rubber goods which it had formerly sold to European markets now cut off by war. Tense competition from American tyres spurred Dunlop in November 1915 to advertise to Australian motorists the warning that 'every penny of yours that goes out of this Country — for foreign-made tyres' will tilt the financial scales against Australia and its allies.

The company, accepting an obligation to foster the war effort, devoted part of its profit to war loans and wartime charities. In the first month of the war 750 pounds was donated to the Motorists and Cyclists Patriotic Fund, and 250 to the Red Cross Society. Later donations became larger, with three thousand pounds to the Red Cross in Australia in 1915 for the benefit of sick and wounded soldiers, one thousand pounds to the French Red Cross in 1916, one thousand pounds to the British Red Cross in 1917 and an unspecified donation to the Italian Red Cross. The gift to some patriotic organisations was in the form of rubber — tyres for the car of the Salvation Army, a motor cycle ambulance for St John's Civil Ambulance, and the 14 500 rubber bands requested by the wife of General Hughes for her Australian Women's National League.

As the war went on and on, Dunlop's stocks of crude rubber dwindled. Every ounce of rubber used in the Montague mill came from distant lands, and the scarcity of shipping so disrupted the inflow that Dunlop's directors wondered whether they would have to close the mill. Nearly all the rubber used in Montague's early years had come from the tropical jungles of South America where the *Hevea* tree grew in the wild, usually close to the banks of a river. The trunk of this tall tree with the pale green flowers was regularly tapped to produce a flow of white sap which was collected in small cups fixed by a dab of clay to the trunk. Para in Brazil had for decades been the world's busiest rubber port, and the sap or raw rubber known as Fine Para was one of the most expensive of the main commodities in international commerce. Like wool, it was sold by the pound rather than by the ton, and normally it was much dearer than wool. Moreover its monthly price fluctuated even more than that of the base metals, and in the decade from 1900 to 1910, Fine Para fell below three shillings a pound and rose as high as twelve shillings. At the head office in Flinders Street the directors — whenever they sensed that rubber would rise in price — spent hours in debating whether they should instruct their Liverpool agent to stockpile more rubber.

The initial boom in automobiles had absorbed so much raw rubber that there were fears of a long-term scarcity of rubber. The rubber plantations, when in their infancy, were poor competitors to wild rubber. The plantations were the result of the courageous shipments of *Hevea* plants and seeds from Brazil to the Kew gardens near London where they were cultivated in hot houses and then distributed to British colonies in Singapore and Malaya, Borneo and Ceylon. By 1909 the new rubber plantations were producing about five per cent of the world's rubber; but by 1914, almost as if by a miracle, they were producing more than half of the world's rubber. In Australia, Dunlop probably used a little plantation rubber from 1911 — one can imagine Kearns biting into it before he mouthed his doubting verdict. By 1916 the factory at Montague was using more plantation rubber than Fine Para, Peruvian and all the wild rubbers combined.

The world's problem of how to produce enough rubber had temporarily been solved, but the problem of shipping it became acute. In the third year of the war the supply of rubber to Australia seemed likely to wither. German submarines sank so many Allied ships in the Atlantic that a scarcity of ships on nearly all long-distance routes delayed the arrival of cargoes. At the start of 1917 the mill at Montague held large stocks of plantation rubber but small stocks of Fine Para. Trusted recipes had to be changed, and a batch of one thousand car tyres was made with double the normal quantity of plantation rubber and only half of the normal quantity of the scarce Fine Para; and for months the directors waited anxiously for reports that the new-recipe tyres would prove to be as durable as the normal tyre. In the middle of 1917 the total stockpile of rubber at Montague so shrank that for seven weeks the mill worked at slow pace, and in the peak week of scarcity a total of 466 mill operatives were stood down.

Additives for the mixing room could no longer be imported with certainty. Pages of John Kearns's old recipe book had to be rewritten. Benzine was used in place of naphtha in fixing the tread to the canvas of the tyre, but some motorists found that the tread now tended to loosen itself from their new tyre. When zinc oxide was slow in arriving from the United States, alternative supplies were shipped from Sydney; but the Australian product tended to make the tread of the tyres too dark. When the supplies of fillers were endangered by the shortage of ships, 'Jack' Proctor was delighted to receive word that a South Australian had found a deposit of whiting and was only too happy to reveal, for a sum of money, the secret site of the deposit. Alas the company's agent, sent to find the discoverer in Adelaide, found no trace of him. At one time Proctor thought that, as a result of wartime shortages, the tread on his new tyres would have to be coloured red. He opposed the Fisk Rubber Company's application to register in Australia the trademark RED TREAD for fear that Dunlop might be prevented — in a time of scarcity of whiteners — from producing a tyre with a red tread.

The factory was busy in most months of the war — except for a drastic slump in sales late in 1916, and the temporary slumps during the rubber scarcity and the industrial strife of 1917. Record sales were made in many wartime months. To meet the demand, more buildings had to be erected and new storeys added on the crowded site at Montague. A smaller factory was opened on the banks of the Yarra at Abbotsford, near the Collingwood football ground, and there the plant for reclaiming rubber from old tyres began work in 1916. In the last wartime winter the two factories employed a peak of 1730 men and women, the night shift was almost as busy as the day shift, and sales revenue jumped by nearly a quarter over the previous year.

The company, generous in subsidising employees who enlisted, could not ensure that, if they returned, their jobs at Dunlop would be awaiting them. F. Dureau, one of the first employees to enlist, was wounded in the fighting and returned to civilian life in 1916. Applying for his former job as a traveller and salesman in rubber goods, he was deemed physically incapable of doing his old work for the time being. He was granted a living allowance and invited to return three months later. What eventually happened to him is not recorded. The promise to give returned soldiers their old jobs assumed that enough jobs would be available; but by September 1918 there was fear of a post-war economic slump. The directors then reached a compromise that if heavy retrenchments were necessary after the war, returned soldiers should generally be the last to receive notice of dismissal.

Hundreds of Dunlop employees must have enlisted. How many died is not recorded. Throughout Australia almost every church and many Sunday schools and day schools compiled an honour roll of those who had enlisted or died, but relatively few factories and mines erected honour rolls. No honour roll was erected at the Dunlop factory. The only official record of wartime deaths are two brief notes in the minute books. In January 1915 the board heard that F. O. Carr, an officer, had been killed in action. It was resolved that his widow be paid his salary for six months and that an instalment due on their house should be paid immediately by the company. The other death was formally noted in the minute book of 23 June 1916. The chairman, John Grice, and his wife had lost one son in the Boer War and now they lost another in France; the directors simply acknowledged without mentioning the sol-dier's Christian name — 'this sad loss in the Empire's Cause'.

The first post-war year was chaotic. The 'Spanish' influenza epidemic ran wild, especially striking young adults. In 1918 and 1919, 13 600 Australians died of influenza — a number equal to one fourth of the number of Australian soldiers who died during the First World War. At the height of the epidemic Dunlop immunised its employees, and the eight who refused were told to stay away from work until the 'epidemic was stamped out'. Two employees died, and the company paid allowances to the widows — Mrs Rees and her three children, and Mrs McLeod. So many workers used the Mill Sick Fund that the company had to pump money into a fund that normally depended on employees' contributions.

Near the peak of the epidemic, industrial relations began to show signs of strain. At numerous factories and mines the employees — even those who were reluctant to strike during the war — believed that it was now time for their wages to catch up with inflation. At the Montague factory the Federated Rubber Workers' Union was the main spokesman for the workers and became vocal for higher wages. It had not viewed kindly the creation, with the directors' blessing, of a rival body known as the Share Purchase Association. Essentially a co-operative designed to encourage workers to invest in Dunlop shares and thus to receive some of the profit in good years, the Association began to take on an industrial role. With 638 members at the start of 1918, it probably was as entitled as the union to speak for the work-force, but was seen by the union as a gate-crasher, a mealy-mouthed upstart.

In January 1919, after the union appealed to the Arbitration Court for more pay, the committee of the Share Purchase Association for the first time met two of the directors, Grice and Riley, as well as the three senior members of staff. Sir John Grice was full of courtesy: 'We shall be very pleased to hear what you have to say'. Mr A. Nordern responded with equal politeness, requesting an increase of ten per cent in the wages of mill employees. Pointing out that the present wages had been fixed some three years ago, he complained that the cost of living in that time had risen by at least a quarter. His second request was that the lunch break be extended from half an hour to three quarters of an hour. He argued that if a man, especially a big eater, 'is a smoker, he has to do without his smoke at lunch'. The employee would therefore try later 'to thieve a few minutes from his work' in order to have a quiet smoke out of sight. Nordern promised that the workers, if granted such a lunch-time concession, would find ways of making up for the time lost and would achieve the present daily output of work. In the end the company and the share association agreed to the new conditions. The agreement was to run for two years, during which time all employees agreed to seek no further concessions — unless their cost of living rose by more than five per cent, which it did.

In the second half of 1919 the two Dunlop factories, big Montague and small Abbotsford, were dislocated by the effects of outside strikes. Not since 1890 had strikes and disputes so disrupted the nation. The supply of coal was halted by a strike of marine stewards in interstate ships. In Melbourne there were strikes amongst gas workers and engine drivers working in factories. By June the coal scarcity had virtually closed Montague. So widespread was the distress amongst families who had no income from their work that at the end of June the company's general manager and secretary formed themselves into a relief committee to give money to families in need. Then the coal began to arrive from New South Wales, and 1200 operatives went back to work at Montague. The coal stocks dwindled again, and only five hundred people could be provided with work by the middle of July. At last more coal ships arrived but soon the coal stocks diminished again. Black coal from New South Wales was the industrial dynamo of the nation, and when the small coastal colliers were halted for a fortnight or more, factories like Dunlop's were in danger of closing down. The colliers resumed their sea route, but by February 1920 the marine engineers were on strike, and any observant stroller in Port Melbourne and South Melbourne could tell by the thinning cloud of steam and smoke above the Dunlop works that hundreds of employees had temporarily been sent home.

While people thought that winning the war would bring certainty, it brought uncertainty to daily life in the first years of peace. The swift rise of the car, especially in the United States, relied on cheap petrol, but soon after the war was over the long-term supply of petrol became uncertain. Few petroleum fields had been found anywhere in the world in recent years. What if petrol became dearer and dearer? One answer was obvious. The demand for new tyres would not rise quickly, and the heavy investment planned for the new tyre factory at Montague would prove to be a mistake. In October 1920 the directors of Dunlop, discussing the threatened shortage of petrol in the world, agreed that they, along with other rubber manufacturers, should finance research into a substitute for petrol. Their fears lasted less than a year. A dramatic series of new oil finds was made. Oil was even found near Los Angeles in 1921 and within two years California was the biggest producer of oil in the United States; by the end of the decade the finds in Oklahoma and Venezuela and other regions had led to a glut of oil.

The company, faced with frequent stoppages and technical hitches, was unable to cope adequately with them. Its managers were partly to blame. When Kearns returned to work in the United States in 1913 he was replaced as works superintendent by S. F. Roberts, who was recruited from the North British Rubber Company in Scotland by two Dunlop directors, Garland and Baillieu, then visiting the British Isles. Roberts lacked the all-round experience of Kearns. Arriving at a time when the making of tyres was beginning to change rapidly, he was soon a little out of his depth. The general manager, 'Jack' Proctor, went to North America and hired an expert in car tyres, a Frank Chamberlain of the Batavia Rubber Co., for the princely sum of 1400 pounds a year. The American was not long at Montague when he clashed with his superior, Roberts. He was more up-to-date than Roberts: perhaps he told Roberts so. Proctor felt obliged to tell the directors that the factory office was becoming a boxing ring. He parted the antagonists and pushed them back to their respective corners. Eventually Roberts, now in poor health, agreed to retire, and at the start of 1920 Chamberlain became the works manager on a five-year contract at an enhanced salary. Doubts about his capacity soon began to circulate. Clearly it was not easy to recruit top-class men because Australia's tyre industry — and therefore the salaries it could afford — was still a pygmy compared to those in North America. But the evidence suggests that Proctor the general manager was becoming the weak link in the organisation — a conclusion that the board was reluctant to make because of his long service and his powerful connections with English Dunlop.

While the imported technicians were fighting, the board lost its member with the most experience in the rubber industry. Richard Garland had virtually floated the original Dunlop Pneumatic Tyre Company of Australasia back in 1899. As one of the two largest shareholders in the firm's early years, his stake in the venture was high; and his knowledge of the North American tyre industry, of which he was a founder, was valuable because North America by 1910 had run past Britain as the pace-maker in tyres. As managing director since 1910, Garland was his company's number-one official, being strong in selling and shrewd in finance. His contacts were wide, especially in sport, and in Melbourne he was a sponsor of the Canadian game of lacrosse which was more popular then than today. In the eyes of many people he was Dunlop, and at one time a large part of his income must have come from Dunlop dividends.

Richard Garland lived in style — almost more style than he could afford — near the sea at Brighton. From his house, Bronte, in Dendy Street his full-time chauffeur drove him for his early-morning swim at the local sea baths. In the evening he was sometimes driven to the West Brighton Club, of which he was twice president. In his large house three servants attended to his wife and five children, but for long periods the house was almost empty. He travelled often — 'I hardly knew my father', recalled his youngest son Geoffrey in 1990 — and he travelled with almost as much clothing as a theatrical company on tour. When he prepared to leave with his wife on long trips on company business a furniture van called at the house to take all the cabin trunks, hat boxes and other luggage to the English mail steamship waiting at Port Melbourne. He, more than anybody in the company, was responsible for the policy of borrowing the latest technology, no matter where it could be found. To him the link with English Dunlop was worthwhile only if it produced the best, and often it did not.

Fanatical in his quest for fitness, Garland was disappointed when in 1910 an operation failed to improve his stiff leg. It became stiffer, and he could not even ride a bicycle, the machine on which his business career had been built. Several years later he felt poorly: the diagnosis was diabetes. He was only in his early forties but his business career was slipping slowly away. Towards the end of the war he could no longer attend the office regularly and had to seek leave of absence from board meetings for several months. He died in November 1919. Two of his sons, after distinguished war service in Europe, joined the Dunlop organisation in England and rose high; and a grandson, Patrick Garland, became a leading theatrical producer in England and New York.

The loss of Garland was more damaging than the company realised. Nobody replaced him, perhaps because he did less during his final years of sickness, and the vital gap was not noticed. The expanding factory at Montague was to become noteworthy for opportunities not seized. One of the most favourable periods in the history of the Australian rubber industry was coming to an end. Dunlop had earned high profits in two of every three years from 1908 to 1920 but that pleasing ratio of good years to medium years was not to be reached again until the late 1950s.

And yet when Garland died, Montague seemed to be in a safe position. The heart of the Australian rubber industry, it made a long list of products. For the motorist it supplied levers for removing tubes and an 'inflator' equipped with pressure gauge for pumping up a tyre. It made repair kits and patches for faulty tyres. It even supplied a dust coat for the car driver and tins of paint for smartening up his tyres. It made the handsome green or buff canvas bags to cover the spare tyres, spare tubes and spare wheel, thus protecting them from the weather in the era before a car had a luggage boot.

The variety of car tyres made by Dunlop was almost bewildering. In April 1920 it made fifty-eight different kinds of car tyres and supplied another forty-one different tyres for American cars. It did not have to worry about price-cutting and special deals, it simply advertised to the exact penny the price a motorist would pay for each tyre, whether some sixteen pounds for a Rolls Royce or Lancia tyre (the tube was always extra), fifteen pounds for a Crossley, or fourteen pounds for a Chandler and Daimler, Hotchkiss and Vauxhall tyre. Further down the list, a mere five guineas was charged for a special grooved tyre suitable for the Bean, Chevrolet, Ford, Maxwell, Overland and Palm cars. These sums sound small, but the cheapest tyre, even without a tube, absorbed about two weeks' pay from an unskilled worker. Frugal owners of secondhand cars allowed the tread of their tyres to wear down, month by month, until the last layer of rubber vanished and the canvas itself was visible. A bald tyre, however, was not yet considered to be dangerous because most cars travelled at less than thirty miles an hour.

A tyre was one of the most advertised products in the nation, and Dunlop, as the largest advertiser of tyres, went out of its way to stress that its tyre looked different. The tread of the tyre was then as important in advertising as the pretty woman's mouth was to become in selling toothpaste, and the tread was carefully depicted in newspaper advertising. Indeed the pattern of the tread usually gave its name to the tyre. Thus Barnet Glass tyres carried a tread shaped exactly like a pile of boomerangs, one on top of the other. Called Boomerang Tyres, they were sold with the nifty slogan 'There and Back'. On the other hand Perdriau of Sydney, boasting that its tyres were heavier and stronger than rivals, designed a tread consisting of three parallel rods running right around the tyres with deep grooves in between. Dunlop's prime tyres were called Railroads because the tread, viewed from the front, resembled a railway track running on sleepers placed close together. The Railroad seemed invincible in 1920, but was not.

Around the Dunlop board table in Melbourne in 1920 the debate about the future of oil was crucial, for Frank Chamberlain was busy supervising the design and foundations of a four-storeyed tyre mill at Montague. The big test of the new mill was how effectively it would make the cord tyre — the motor tyre coming into fashion. This tyre had originally been devised for the electric motor cars which were briefly favoured in North America. Its novelty lay in the cotton fabric rather than the rubber. Unlike the square-woven fabric that formed the carcass of the traditional tyre, the new cord tyre consisted of a fabric made of intersecting and parallel rows of cords — rather like fishing lines made from Arizona cotton or Sea Island cotton. As these cords were insulated from each other the tyre suffered less from internal friction and gained in resilience. A cord tyre was less likely to break down when the vehicle was overloaded or the tyre itself was under-inflated. As the fabric was now as strong as the rubber itself, the cord tyre would supplant the solid rubber tyres used on light trucks and eventually on heavy trucks. As every tyre expert in Australia knew, the cord tyre also promised a longer mileage. Here was a big gain in money as well as convenience.

Chamberlain set out to make the cord tyre, unwisely combining it with that other recent fashion, the non-skid tyre. The first of these new Montague tyres, fitted onto the wheels of cars with such enthusiasm, did not wear well. The public had been persuaded that here was the ultimate in tyres but the tyres contradicted the propaganda. Harry James, still in charge of advertising, drove along the inland plains for many days in March 1922, going as far north as Longreach before returning with the warning that if Dunlop was to give first priority to selling its cord tyres the new policy would be 'suicidal'. He emphasised that his firm's everyday fabric tyres called 'Railroads' were still favourites in the bush, indeed in all Australia. Garage men with a wave of their greasy hands assured him that the Railroad tyre would give three or four thousand miles of wear whereas the new Goodyear *cord* tyre gave only half that mileage. Michelin cords, he said, were rather better: Dunlop cords, he implied, were worse. His frank report was taken so seriously by the directors that it was actually embodied, word for word, in the minutes. No report from the general manager had ever been treated with such deep respect.

Perhaps a better tyre-making machine would produce a better cord tyre. Careful investigations were made into the best machines. The Thropp machine was the favourite of Proctor, who was visiting tyre factories overseas, while Chamberlain had complete confidence in the machine he had ordered.

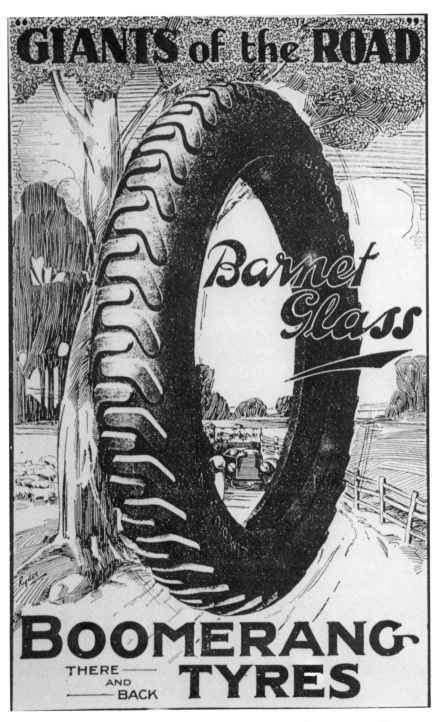

Barnet Glass, about1910, became well-known for its boomerang-brand.

In 1921 the motor-bike was still a strong competitor of the car and a major market for Dunlop tyres.

Finally two Thropp machines were hurriedly ordered from England in 1922 so that a trial of the rivals could be held at Montague.

F. O. Wolff of Montague went in the mail steamer to North America to learn how the Thropp machines worked. He returned to Melbourne in November 1922, convinced that the Thropp machine and Chamberlain's special machine were inadequate. Invited to speak to the directors — an honour rarely accorded to an employee of his status — he dropped the bombshell that the whole method of making cord tyres at Montague was unsuitable. Wolff was told to conduct experiments at Montague. An additional car, a heavyweight model, was bought by the factory so that tyres made under the various methods could be tested for durability.

The result of the tests can be guessed from the fact that six months later the general manager, 'Jack' Proctor, was sent from the quiet head office in the city to give his attention to straightening out problems at the factory. On the other hand, Chamberlain was invited to resign. As his contract still had several years to run, he was offered as compensation a lump sum of two thousand pounds and a free steamship ticket on condition that he went to America and remained there for three years: this would prevent him from signing up with any other tyre competitor in Australia.

Frank Chamberlain thought these terms were mean. The directors believed that they had been more than generous in view of the dislocation to their manufacturing plans and the loss of tyre sales, largely as a result of his errors. They gave him a few days in which to accept their terms or accept dismissal, without compensation. He promptly called at the office in Flinders Street and accepted the offer. As a gesture the directors loaned him money while he tried to sell his house in a sluggish real-estate market.

Changes in tyres became swifter. The cord tyre was no sooner made at Montague than tyre depots and roadside garages all the way from Auckland to Perth were asking for something else. They wanted the revolutionary balloon tyres which appeared on swish cars shown in the latest American silent movies. The balloon tyre ballooned out from the rim rather like a modern tyre whereas the earlier tyres were shaped more like enlarged versions of the bicycle tyres from which they had descended. The fat balloon tyre promised a smoother ride. In years when most suburban streets and main country roads in Australia were unsealed, such a tyre was bound to succeed. Perfected by the Firestone Tire and Rubber Co., it appeared on new cars in the USA in 1923, initially in a chaotic number of shapes and sizes. As Dunlop's main business was making replacement tyres, the lack of standardisation would be a nightmare.

In Sydney and Melbourne the strange-looking balloon tyres on the wheels of the latest batch of imported American cars were eagerly inspected by passers-by. In 1925 even the new Model T Fords landed at Australian ports carried balloon tyres. Those lucky enough to own a car shod with the balloon tyres marvelled at the ease with which a puncture could be mended and the tube pumped up — as the custom was — by the hand-held pump carried by every motorist. Whereas a typical Dunlop cord tyre fitted to a Buick, Dodge, Paige, Packard and Willys-Knight from America — and these cars were familiar to Australian motorists — required the very high air pressure of sixty to sixty-five pounds, the new balloon tyres on the same cars called for an air pressure of no more than thirty-five pounds. Better still, a balloon tyre on a Ford car needed an air pressure of only thirty pounds, or not much more than today's tyres. Pumping a flat tyre was suddenly made easy, for less air had to be pumped by hand into the tyre's tube. For much of 1925 the Montague factory could hardly meet the public demand for balloon tyres.

One slow change in the 1920s was not so popular. Many car tyres were now black. Hitherto the typical tyre was whitish, the white coming from the zinc oxide used in making tyres. Then the cord tyre came into vogue and for the first time the cord carcass lasted as long as — or longer than — the rubber tread itself. There was thus an incentive to strengthen the rubber which constituted the tread of the tyre, and a strengthener was already at hand — carbon black. At the big rubber works at Silvertown in London, S. C. Mote in 1904 had found out the qualities of carbon black, but it was little used for a decade, partly because it produced a tyre of an unwanted colour and partly because the rubber still lasted longer than the carcass of the tyre. The cord tyre changed that. By about 1925 many motorists were willing to accept the black cord tyre because the addition of carbon black increased the tyre's resistance to abrasion on the roads. The tyre-makers were happy because more carbon black meant less rubber: it was now the main filler in the recipe for tyre rubber. At the Montague factory this new ingredient soon gave the mixing department in No. 1 Mill a distinctive look, almost like that of a blacking factory. Carbon black had come to stay.

With more cars on the roads, the market for tyres soared. The pitfall was that additional firms were making car tyres in Australia. Furthermore, several of the popular American makes of cars arrived already equipped with tyres, thus reducing the market for tyres made in Australia. When Dunlop protested to the Tariff Board that this competition was unfair, the response was a shrug of the official shoulders. Some firms shipping new cars to Australian ports were willing to equip them with Australian tyres, but Barnet Glass and Perdriau often outbid Dunlop in supplying such tyres. It was a sign of Dunlop's struggle to compete in balloon tyres that the directors felt cheered when, in 1924, they won the contracts to supply balloon tyres to the imported Studebaker and Essex — not big-selling models.

Proctor just could not understand how these smaller Australian tyre-makers could outbid his firm. Perdriau and Barnet Glass succeeded because they were willing to sell new tyres to car-manufacturers almost at a loss, guessing that the owners of the new cars would choose the same tyres when they needed a replacement. In 1924 the Dunlop directors heard from their Sydney manager, obviously with surprise, that by 1924 Perdriau were making 2500 tyres a day and employing one thousand operatives. Such was the competition from all sides that Dunlop was now forced to guarantee its tyres against defects, and in one year it noted that three per cent of the total tyres it sold had sufficient faults to invoke the guarantee. In the tense competition from local and American tyres, several tyre-makers now appealed to the motorist to buy direct from them at a discount as high as fifty per cent off the list price. Secret and seductive discounts were offered to certain firms which, while stocking all brands of tyres, put their energy into selling one particular brand.

The selling of tyres was now highly competitive, but the Dunlop directors were reluctant to face the fact. Their minute book in February 1924 noted that the new ways of selling 'were diametrically opposed to the Company's policy'. For a time they obstinately stuck to their old policy while their customers went elsewhere. In July 1925 the selling of tyres was so cut-throat that all tyre-makers and importers of tyres came together and agreed simultaneously to increase the price of tyres by fifteen per cent. Such unanimity did not last. Soon there were whispers of deals done under the table — every firm believed that its opponents were the culprits.

As national statistics were not compiled on the annual sale of tyres, Dunlop continued to collect its own. The success of Dunlop's rivals was painfully obvious. When the Dunlop men went to racecourses and car rallies to count the tyres on the cars parked nearby, they reported the fading popularity of their own tyres. Thus at the Warrnambool races in western Victoria in 1917, seven of every ten tyres had been Dunlops; and of the new cars exhibited at the Royal Agricultural Show in Melbourne in 1918 about eight in every ten tyres were Dunlops; but such domination was not reported in any year of the 1920s. At the Melbourne Cup, said to attract the largest assembly of parked cars in the continent, almost fifty per cent of the tyres on the cars had been Dunlops in 1916 but by the mid 1920s the percentage had fallen to below thirty. Indeed in 1924 the men who counted the tyres returned from their day at the Melbourne Cup with the news that Dunlop with twenty-five per cent was not far in front of Goodyear's twenty per cent. Furthermore at least thirty other brands of car tyres could be seen in the rows of parked cars, including Michelin (thirteen per cent), Perdriau (nine per cent), the U.S.A. brand (eight per cent), Goodrich (six per cent) and Barnet Glass (six per cent).

In those years the Montague factory was saved from completely losing its ascendancy by the fact that it was largely shielded from English competition. Its sister factory, Fort Dunlop in Birmingham, was the giant of the British tyre industry and normally would have competed strongly in Australia, but it was debarred by the 1899 agreement from competing — without permission — in Australia and New Zealand.

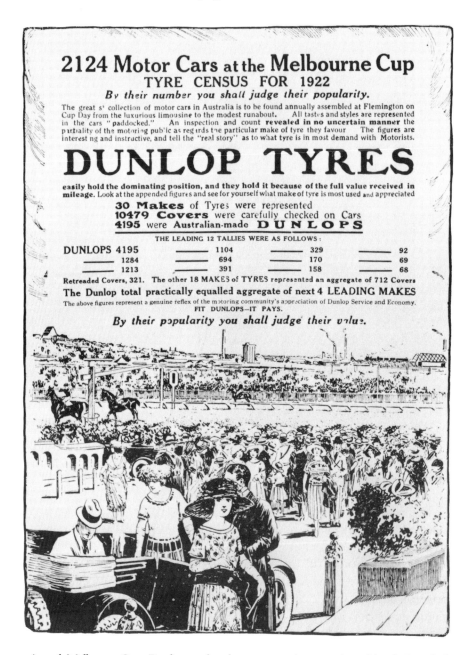

At each Melbourne Cup, Dunlop employed men to tour the car parks and list the brand of tyres on each car. Here is an advertisement announcing the scores for 1922.

Montague was saved partly by the boom in motor cars. It was losing its previously high share of the market but atoning for the loss because the market was increasing so quickly. New cars poured onto Australian roads in the 1920s in an unpredicted flood, and in some years there was almost enough business for every importer and manufacturer of tyres. Moreover the newest tyres, while more durable than the old, still did not last long, and so the replacement business was busy. Dunlop directors estimated at the start of 1927 that every car now on the road would need an average of two and a half replacement tyres in the next twelve months. In short, the typical car wore out a complete set of tyres in just over a year and a half. Most of the new cars, whether assembled in Australia or imported, were now equipped with Australian-made tyres, and so that helped the local tyre-manufacturers, including Dunlop. In the year 1926 at least one new car came onto the road for every three cars already on the road at the start of the year. In the Dunlop boardroom it was calculated that in Australia some 876 000 tyres had been manufactured in 1926 but that 1 401 000 would be needed in the following year. In such a market the leading manufacturer could only smack its lips in anticipation.

While motor tyres were the main source of profit, the factories at Montague and Abbotsford made hundreds of rubber products and were tempted to make even more. In 1924 they resolved to make sand-shoes. Sometimes called tennis shoes or just 'runners', they were becoming a popular leisure shoe. The sole was rubber but the upper was made of canvas. The rubber sole was light in colour — made possible by the use of an organic accelerator in the manufacturing process. The canvas top was usually coloured white and required frequent repainting by the owner. Whereas most of the rubber boots and shoes were traditionally designed for a wet climate, the sand-shoes were a summer shoe, ideal for Australian conditions.

The company became more ambitious, realising that sand-shoes must be made on a large scale with the latest machines if they were to be stylish in looks and fairly low in price. Through Clive Baillieu, the son of W. L. Baillieu, the maker of one of the world's best-known rubber shoes was persuaded to take an interest in the venture. Under the combined names of the Dunlop–North British Rubber Shoe Co. Pty Ltd, a new company was set up with Dunlop's money and North British's skills. A special issue of 293 000 ordinary shares to Dunlop's existing shareholders more than financed the venture.

An engineer named Ross came from Edinburgh to set up the shoe equipment in a new factory built next to Dunlop's Abbotsford factory, within sight of Dight's Falls on one side and the Collingwood grandstand on the other. N. T. Hay arrived from Edinburgh to manage the factory and Scottish rubber workers came out to teach Australian girls and women how to make a variety of rubber shoes. By October 1926 the factory was at work, and Sir John Grice in his courteous way was heard to inform young people about to play a set of tennis that he was sure they were all wearing the latest Dunlop–North British sand-shoes.

The head office in busy Flinders Street, while the nerve-centre of the company, did not look quite like the headquarters of one of the country's main firms. The directors attending a board meeting could hear hammerings in the yard at the back and sometimes the sound of packaging, because the building housed separate city dispatch and country dispatch depots where the new tyres were wrapped in hessian before being sent in the three three-ton T-model Fords to railway stations or city garages. At the rear of the head office was a brick building on stilts where hard Kelly tyres were fitted to the wheels of the buggies, jinkers and the other horse-drawn vehicles which were still common in city streets. Under the stilts were parked the cars of the high officials, the chairman's Marman roadster and the Buick belonging to the company secretary, H. MacKirdy, and the little Fiat used as a runaround by the warehouse manager. These cars found their way out of the yard, by way of a narrow lane, into the less narrow Flinders Lane.

The office was slowly mechanised. A fifteen-year-old, Ted Benbow, joined head office in 1928, graduating through a series of jobs which illustrated the new mechanisation. His first job as office boy was to place copies of dark carbon paper between the sheets of white typing paper so that the office typists could produce six copies of each invoice going out to customers. His fingertips must have been purple from the colouring long before the first hour was over. Eventually becoming a clerical assistant in the dispatch depot he combined his clerk's duties — when he turned eighteen — with numerous fast rides on a motor bike to city customers who urgently needed goods.

His big promotion was to become clerk in the office which made out invoices for the hard rubber or ebonite battery boxes, but his promotion was followed by a fall. Stock-taking on top of a precarious pile of stores he slipped when the edge of a board collapsed, and tumbled to the ground. When his injury had healed and he returned to work his job had gone, and he found himself in the basement of head office, wiping off the grease which had been rubbed on the metal rim of bicycle wheels in the English factory as a preservative. Even in this era of the motor car the familiar bicycle tyre was still an important line of business for Dunlop.

While Dunlop changed rapidly in the 1920s, it was prone to mishaps. For all its promise as the leader of a booming industry in a prosperous nation, it did not maintain the rate of profits earned in the previous decade. In the first five years of the 1920s it paid an average dividend of just under seven per cent on its ordinary shares. In the sixth year Dunlop's profits leaped, but some shareholders complained that the profit was not up to expectations, to which Sir John Grice quaintly replied that the shareholders had more valid cause for complaint in the five previous years than in this sixth year.

The chairman's confession that Dunlop should have done better had to be repeated in more apologetic words at the annual general meeting two years later — in September 1927. There he admitted to shareholders that his Australian competitors had had a bumper year but Dunlop had missed out again. What had gone astray? Dunlop had bought a large reserve of rubber in overseas markets at high prices in the belief that rubber would rise still higher. Instead it fell. As rubber was a crucial item in the wholesale price of many rubber goods, often contributing forty per cent of the cost, Dunlop's rubber was badly over-priced. Dunlop therefore had to sell many of its rubber goods at a loss. In some tyres the component of rubber cost more than the price for which the finished tyre was sold. 'Your directors admit they made a mistake in buying too far ahead', Grice told the shareholders in 1927. Next year Dunlop repeated the mistake. All the potential profits of the financial year of 1927–28 were gobbled up by these disasters.

For years the Dunlop Rubber Company of Australasia had been protected from world competition by high duties on imports. Now the problem was how to protect Dunlop from its own errors.

A Scottish 'steam-roller'

F ACED WITH troubles on all sides in the late 1920s, the Melbourne company did what European monarchies had so often done in earlier centuries. It arranged marriages, sometimes with handsome dowries changing hands. No major company in Australia had previously involved itself in such a quick succession of marriages and friendship pacts.

The first marriage was made in London. At the start of the decade the Dunlop Rubber Company of Australasia would not have dreamed of embracing its father, the Dunlop Rubber Company. Since 1899 the two companies had gone their different ways. At no time was a director of the one company a director of the other. No director from London had ever visited Melbourne, though a few of the Australian directors had called on the London board when visiting England. Neither company held shares in the other, though for a brief period in the early 1900s the English company did hold a small parcel of Australian shares mainly because it had not yet received from promoter Garland all the cash due for the sale of its Australian and New Zealand interests. The Australian company had the right to use the English company's trademarks and its latest inventions in tyres, but in practice it came to rely more on inventions and skills from the American rubber industry.

The Australians did not even seek its managers from the English Dunlop. Two of the three managers at the Montague factory — Kearns and Chamberlain — had been recruited from North America, and the third, Roberts, had come from one of Dunlop's competitors in England. Admittedly, several foremen who were experts in new processes had been loaned to Melbourne by Dunlop factories in England, and several Melbourne men, including Kearns, had gone to England to study the latest Dunlop processes; but Montague had just as many friendly links with American rubber factories.

Dunlop England still had the right to ship to Australia its own new tyres so long as they were fitted to new English cars, but until the 1920s not many Dunlop tyres came to Australia on English cars. Then the sales of England's new 'Baby' Austin Seven and its new Morris models soared in Australia, and Australian Dunlop noticed the effects. English tyres were generally lighter in construction than the comparable Australian-made tyres and sometimes fell apart on rough Australian roads, thus harming the wider name of Dunlop.

In most years the tightest bond between London and Melbourne was a blood relationship. The du Cros brothers, who dominated English Dunlop, were first cousins of the Proctor brothers, who were prominent in Australian Dunlop. Charles Proctor had been secretary of the company in Melbourne and was now with English Dunlop where eventually he would become the managing director; Harvey Proctor in Liverpool was the buying agent for Australian Dunlop and indeed purchased all the crude rubber coming to Melbourne; and, above all, W. Jack Proctor was general manager in Melbourne. This family bond was weakened in 1919 when the colourful Sir Arthur du Cros, for long the managing director and now the chairman of English Dunlop, was edged out of the chair. The thirty years of the du Cros family's control of Dunlop came to an end and Sir Arthur, a multimillionaire, set out on a world cruise in his nine-hundred ton yacht. He still had the title of president of the company and he was still the member for Clapham in the House of Commons, but his era of influence was over. Before long his name carried little prestige in the inner rooms of English Dunlop because the details were slowly unravelled of how he had manipulated company shares and made certain decisions in his, rather than the company's, interest. The report of his conduct was not made public. English Dunlop was in enough trouble without advertising episodes that would further lower its name.

Contact between the directors in Melbourne and the directors in London was rare. Accordingly, Sir John Grice was surprised when, a year after the end of the First World War, he received an urgent cable from the managing director of English Dunlop, Mr Bergin, who in a typical year probably did not even write one letter to the Australian board. The cable was so important that Grice called a special meeting of the board for Friday 10 October 1919. Even Richard Garland, who was close to death, attended to hear the cable read aloud:

> Wish to discuss with your company most important proposition affecting vital future interests of all Dunlop Companies stop. Can you or one or more of your colleagues visit England at early date with full powers to negotiate stop. Proposition would involve outright purchase or acquisition of controlling interest in Australian Dunlop. Whatever your present view most important in your own interests you should share our knowledge regarding future World Competition and confer with us here stop. Please cable.

What the directors thought of it can be predicted. They were Australians — all except one were probably born in Australia — and were proud of their country's industrial progress and independence. The telegram seemed to threaten that independence. Moreover Mr Bergin was peremptory in suggesting that Grice should suddenly cast aside all other business for three months in order to travel to England and back. Bergin offered no reason why, as an alternative, he or another London director or high executive could not visit Melbourne for negotiations. As for his ultimatum that total English control of Australian Dunlop was the only way of ensuring co-operation, this must have been the last straw. The directors in Melbourne had no hesitation in resolving that 'the offer be not accepted'. Four days later Grice cabled his reply, moderately expressed. He doubted whether Australian shareholders would agree to sell. He thought it would be appropriate if London first divulged the details of that world competition they so feared. Meanwhile London should send out a man to Melbourne if urgent negotiations were important. More than three weeks elapsed before a cable came from Bergin. His reply, conceding nothing and adding nothing, achieved nothing. Grice, always courteous, replied that since the secret information in the possession of English Dunlop was so important, he felt 'sure you can find some means of communication from your end'.

The 'world' competition feared in England was American competition. English Dunlop hoped to cope with the volume of cheap American tyres partly by building a factory in Buffalo, in New York State, as well as by regulating as many markets as possible outside America. English Dunlop also believed that the motor industry would boom, and that the demands on supplies of crude rubber would be heavy. So the company bought up rubber, huge quantities of it. The directors were mistaken in the belief that the world's price of rubber would soar in the early 1920s. Consequently they ended up possessing large stocks of rubber from their own plantations in Malaya and Ceylon and massive purchases from the output of other plantations, including a promise to buy future output as far ahead as 1924. Their rubber now was over-priced, which meant that the tyres they made usually were dearer than those of their competitors. Even the quality of their latest tyres was not up to the mark. They launched their non-skid tyre called the Magnu, which proved faulty. Dunlop could not even hold on to their own English market in the face of superior tyres from the United States.

Sir Arthur du Cros, who had succeeded his father as chairman, was out of his depth. His honesty was also questioned: the du Cros family tended to treat the company as their own possession. The head office in London could do nothing that was right. It was deluged with bad news. Dunlop had bought all the rubber in the hope of a boom but a post-war recession preceded the boom. In August 1921 it reckoned up the extent of the financial loss in the year just concluded. The total loss for the year was the huge sum of 8 320 006 pounds

— one of the largest losses ever recorded by a European company. Further losses could be expected because English Dunlop was committed to buying rubber at prices that were likely to be far above those paid by their competitors.

Amidst this flow of disappointing news, old John Boyd Dunlop, the inventor of the pneumatic tyre, died in Dublin. Though he had long ago severed his ties with the company, his personal signature and portrait — round-faced and bearded — was the actual trademark of Dunlop tyres. At the time of his death it seemed possible that the Dunlop company in England might not outlive its founder by many years. And if the English Dunlop company were to die or its name were henceforth to signify merely an inferior or lesser brand of tyre, then the Dunlop Rubber Company of Australasia would suffer too. It still traded on the international reputation of Dunlop products. The average Australian cyclist and motorist probably thought that the two Dunlop companies on opposite sides of the globe were one and the same. Though the Australian Dunlop company, in ownership and management, was completely independent of the English company, it depended equally on the reputation of 'Dunlop'. In the early 1920s that reputation was faltering.

In this crisis the English Dunlop company might have collapsed but for the organising skill of an Indian-born Scot named Sir Eric Geddes. In his forties, Geddes had a reputation as a trouble-shooter. His early career had yielded no sign of this talent, for he was asked to leave a variety of expensive and reputable schools, one after the other, finally travelling at the age of seventeen to the United States where for four years he did a variety of manual jobs in railways and steelworks. Settling down in India he became manager of a forestry estate and the light railway that carried its timber from the forests. Geddes developed a flair for organising in what was then one of the most highly organised of civilian industries, the railway. Returning to England he became a lesser and then a greater official on one of the hundreds of private railway companies, the North-Eastern Railway Company. When war broke out in 1914 his skill in organising was immediately used, at first for mobilising troops and then in munitions where his drive and leadership were detected with delight in 1915 by the new munitions minister, Lloyd George. Geddes reminded the minister of a heavy locomotive — the way 'he rolled into my room'. Geddes's talents were such that his services were competed for. The British army invited him to take command of its transport and the arduous task of supplying its forces at the battle front in France. The navy then used him to revitalise the building of ships, now being sunk in their hundreds by new German submarines. In 1917 he was invited by his patron, Lloyd George, now the prime minister, to fill a vacant seat in the House of Commons so that he could take up the key post of First Lord of the Admiralty. Curiously his younger brother, Sir Auckland Geddes, had followed the same meteoric path from civilian life to cabinet, succeeding Neville Chamberlain in 1917 as minister for national service.

When the war was over, Sir Eric Geddes, as minister for transport, rationalised the 123 private railways of the United Kingdom, arranging them in four main groups. He did not believe in free competition: he believed in regulating competition — a belief that was eventually to attract him to the idea of making Australian Dunlop a real ally rather than a competitor. After his railways bill of 1921, Geddes was deputed by Lloyd George to axe wasteful public spending, an unpopular mission. He handled the axe as easily as if it were a child's toy. After a remarkable political career of five years Geddes left parliament in 1922. Acclaimed as a wizard for his work in reorganising the public sector, he turned to the private sector, becoming chairman of Imperial Airways, his nation's major air carrier, and extending its operations step by step to Delhi in 1929 and Australia in 1934. Likewise taking on the harder task of rescuing the Dunlop Rubber Company from the chaos created by its over-optimism, Geddes as chairman steadily made headway. His early reaction to Dunlop was dismay. The losses reported in February 1922 at eight million pounds were found, two years later, to exceed eleven million. Geddes helped to make English Dunlop strong again; Dunlop returned to the paying of dividends in 1925 and three years later was one of the pillars of the British economy, employing 55 000 people.

Geddes set out to restore his firm as a global manufacturer. In 1922 it owned factories only in the British Isles, Germany, France and Japan (opened at Kobe in 1909). America was an alarming gap in the Dunlop empire, but a tyre factory was opened at Buffalo, NY in 1923: it was to earn a profit in only one year in the following thirteen. Canada was another gap, and an interest in a Canadian tyre firm was bought in 1927. An ardent believer in the British Empire, Geddes thought it was absurd that the independent Dunlop company in Australia did not work in harmony with his own Dunlop company in the northern hemisphere. He began to court the heads of Australian Dunlop when they visited London. Towards the secretary, H. MacKirdy, he was full of goodwill and advice in 1925. Control of Australian Dunlop was obviously one of Geddes's plans.

The Australians who met Geddes were impressed and at times overawed. Geddes could be as bossy as the vanished Bergin, his grey eyes cold and his jaw jutting out like a rocky headland; but he could also radiate charm and goodwill. In build he was big, and at first sight did not seem such a dynamo but he did everything at a half trot or faster, and when he drove his heavy Daimler 'Double Six' from the office in London to his country house at Hassocks on the Sussex Downs his butler at the house could occasionally hear the engine of the car roaring on the hills far away to the north. Those Australians who met him already knew of his ruthless streak and probably applauded it — so long as they did not suffer from it. It was Geddes who made the famous speech at the Drill Hall, Cambridge, in December 1918 calling for Germany, the defeated enemy, to be punished with massive fines or reparations. The

W. L. Baillieu joined the Dunlop board in 1905 and served as a director until 1933. He was the great arranger of company marriages and mergers.

victorious allies must take from Germany everything 'you can squeeze out of a lemon and a bit more', he thundered. 'I will squeeze her until I hear the pips squeak.' The quotation, to be found in most dictionaries of quotations, is one of the most celebrated in modern English history.

A few Australians from Dunlop must have had the passing thought that if they came to a closer business arrangement with Geddes he might — if they were careless — squeeze them until the pips squeaked. They were aware that Geddes had an instinct for identifying the starting point and finishing point, and for positively striding from one to the other. He expected his senior employees to follow the same course, even if they were almost exhausted. His former railway colleague, Sir George Beharrell, now the managing director of the English Dunlop, conceded that the acute individualism of Geddes did not always make for harmony but that in compensation Geddes displayed a special quality. In the words of Beharrell, Geddes 'asked for a great deal, but never more than he gave'.

A tight link between Australian Dunlop and English Dunlop became feasible when Geddes had an opportunity to engage in friendly discussions with W. L. Baillieu. When Baillieu's wife, Bertha, died in 1925, he spent much of the following year in England and had chances to meet Geddes to discuss the two Dunlop organisations. Though Baillieu was older by sixteen years they had much in common in their political and business careers and even in their big physiques. 'Big Bill' Baillieu had spent twenty-one years in politics in Victoria without approaching the level of dizzying fame Geddes acquired on his first day in the House of Commons. A part-time politician, Baillieu was for long the leader of the government in the Legislative Council in Victoria and for three years was minister for public health and commissioner of public works, but most of his time was given to business. No other Australian held such a variety of interests in important companies. Indeed some companies rose in importance because he joined their board. The Melbourne *Herald*, the Carlton and United Brewery, Mount Morgan Gold Mining Co., North Broken Hill, Electrolytic Zinc Co., Yarra Falls Spinning Mills, the London Bank of Australia, and Dunlop Rubber were amongst his directorships. The Dunlop board did not absorb a large amount of his time except when big financial events were in the air, and then he tended to take over those events. He thought big and he was prepared to bide his time, coaxing and hinting, until others began to fall in with his big idea. Between 1926 and 1929 he was to reshape Dunlop with the largest consolidation plan so far seen in Australia's manufacturing history.

In London in 1926, Baillieu's conversations with Geddes were cordial. Accordingly in August he wrote to Sir John Grice, the chairman, suggesting that the co-operation forged with English Dunlop in the last year should go further. For this scheme Grice easily secured the approval of the other directors in Melbourne. They saw, like Baillieu, the advantages in gaining access to English Dunlop's technology, especially to the revolutionary anode process which promised — a promise eventually broken — to revolutionise the manufacturing of rubber by using electrolysis to deposit raw rubber on moulds. The Australians could also see benefits in securing London's help in the hazardous task of predicting the price of crude rubber, a task in which neither company excelled. They were also worried that for the first time a big foreign rubber firm, the giant Goodyear, was about to set up a factory in Australia. Would their own company, they asked, necessarily survive in competition with an international giant which had shrewdly decided to join them in sheltering behind Australia's own tariff wall?

These arguments in favour of Anglo-Australian co-operation did not have to be sold to Sir Eric Geddes. He was as enthusiastic as Baillieu for a tight relationship between the Melbourne and London companies. He also knew that he was likely to control it. In any case he foresaw gains for his company in tapping the booming market in Australia where the population was small by European standards but the people were so motorised that they bought more tyres annually than all the people of Italy and Japan combined. Such was the Australians' enthusiasm for motoring, and their capacity to afford cars, that in 1926 they bought more tyres annually than all but the United States and Canada and three big nations in Europe (England, France, and Germany). In other words the general rubber and tyre industries in Australia were, by world standards, infinitely more significant than steel or glass. Car tyres formed perhaps the only major field of manufacturing where Australia was amongst the six world's leaders. In the eyes of Geddes that made Australia doubly important. As Geddes's company already controlled rubber factories in the nations which were the world's five biggest users of motor tyres, the incentive to move into Australia was strong. But under the terms of the agreement of 1899 English Dunlop had no right to manufacture rubber goods in Australia or New Zealand. Its only way of entering that manufacturing market was to buy into or buy out Australian Dunlop.

The aim of Sir Eric Geddes was almost certainly to control the Melbourne company. On the other hand that company wished to maintain a high measure of independence while enjoying all the support — including new inventions — that London could give. Negotiations proceeded slowly, with Baillieu and Geddes eventually working out a compromise. From the London head office in 56 Pall Mall in December 1926, Beharrell wrote to Baillieu, who was back in Melbourne, explaining the terms under which English Dunlop would share the rights it had acquired in the revolutionary anode process for manufacturing rubber. These rights would be expensive if the two companies remained separate but cheap 'in the event of the two Companies coming together'. Meanwhile the works manager from Fort Dunlop, D. G. Snodgrass, was travelling in a steamship via the Suez Canal to Melbourne, where on Australia Day, 1927, he was welcomed in the boardroom by Grice 'with a few well chosen words'. It was probably the first time that a high-ranking Dunlop executive from England had visited Australia. His task was to decide how much the Australian Dunlop was worth.

His initial private impression was that the big Australian factory was not worth much. From Snodgrass's nods and headshakes it was patent that Montague had slipped far behind in efficiency and costs. While it paid much higher wages than Fort Dunlop's huge plant near Birmingham, each member of the work-force produced less than their counterparts in England, the USA and France. Even at the end of the year, Montague's labour costs, though improving, were four times as high as those of Fort Dunlop in the production of an identical tyre. Wages at Montague were dearer, the machinery was less efficient (an 'enormous saving' could be made if motor tubes were made with a Circular Mandrel), and moreover there were perhaps one hundred too many operatives in the factory. Nearly every factory manager, on tour, likes to think that he can teach everyone a lesson in efficiency; but the evidence suggests that the Montague factory was not impressive.

Within a few weeks Snodgrass was acting as if he were general manager. At all board meetings his advice was sought. Jack Proctor, after thirty-two years as the firm's chief full-time executive, was being quietly elbowed towards the door. Proctor had come from England as a teenager, exulting in the task of making and selling bicycle tyres, and graduating at about the age of twenty-five to the post of general manager of the small company, but he probably coped less easily as the business embraced more machinery and stronger trade unions. His gifts were more in selling than in manufacturing, and the factory was now the weak side of the business. In 1902 he had been the driver of the 'speeding' De Dion Bouton car which collided with a racehorse at Flemington, thus occasioning an early lawsuit on the responsibilities of car drivers, but a quarter of a century later he may well have been almost as outdated as a fast horse in the glistening era of Austins and Morris Cowleys. Despite his long experience as chief executive of the company he was only in his early fifties. The manner of his going was mysterious. In the board minutes of 1928 no tribute was paid to him for his long and loyal service. So far as is known no presentation was made to him by the directors, but the mill workers gave him a silver coffee pot and the staff at the head office gave him a set of crystal glasses and decanters. The generous gifts pleased him: he himself was generous. Proctor had no further connection with the company but continued to live in Victoria, driving often in his Buick from his block of flats in Fitzroy Street, St Kilda, to his house by the sea at Sorrento.

Snodgrass — the messenger from English Dunlop — was running the company. He apparently informed Geddes and Beharrell in London of all he saw and heard, and he saw advantages to both sides if they worked together. On this question the Australian directors had no doubt. They permitted the Sydney accountancy firm of Smith, Johnson and Co. to report in full on their firm's assets and prospects, after which the report went to London for inspection. The report, steering clear of the performance of Montague, argued that the company was not as strong as the public believed. During the four disappointing years of the early 1920s the company had failed to provide adequately for depreciation of plant and machinery. Ordinary shares, priced at thirty-one shillings and sixpence on the stock exchange, were probably worth only twenty-six shillings. Nonetheless the company had advantages which English Dunlop could hardly ignore: it stood tall in public estimation, its directors were high in reputation, its products bore a 'splendid name'.

Sir John Grice sailed for London to talk with Geddes: everything so far had been handled by Baillieu, almost as if he were the chairman. In England the gracious seventy-six-year-old was received with courtesy. He discussed the fine details of a coming together, details which Baillieu had long ago set in place. The last odds and ends of the negotiations between the two boards were settled by cable. In August 1927 the shareholders in Melbourne were brought together to vote on the propositions that English Dunlop would buy five hundred thousand new shares, thus giving it some nineteen per cent of the total capital of the Dunlop Rubber Company of Australasia. Two meetings, one of the ordinary and the other of the preference shareholders, approved of the terms without dissent. Interestingly, in that era when women were a rarity at a company meeting, the two shareholders' meetings were attended by Dr Georgina Sweet, lecturer in zoology at Melbourne University and the daughter of a wealthy Brunswick brickmaker.

In effect, English Dunlop were given the right to appoint three of the eight directors on the enlarged board, including Sir Eric Geddes as the vice-chairman. As two of the directors — Geddes and Beharrell — were unlikely to visit Australia more than once in every four or five years, they were entitled to appoint alternate directors who lived in Australia; and promptly the mining engineer Colin Fraser and the Sydney accountant F. J. Smith were appointed as alternatives. The third representative of English Dunlop on the board in Melbourne was D. G. Snodgrass who for the next two years was to remain in Melbourne as managing director. So that the board of the Australian company would know what went on in the head office in St James's Street, London, W. L. Baillieu would sit on the board of English Dunlop as well as of Australian Dunlop — an unusual but sensible arrangement since he had largely negotiated the pact. Australian Dunlop would remain an Australian company, but English Dunlop had the option to buy another five hundred thousand ordinary shares at thirty shillings each, thus increasing its holding to one million shares or about one-third of the capital.

The Australians believed they would gain what they once possessed but in a fast-changing industry had somewhere lost: the latest skills of all kinds. They would plug into the information circuit of one of the world's biggest producers and consumers of crude rubber, using a special London committee consisting of Geddes, Beharrell and the powerful Anglo-Australian businessman, W. S. Robinson, to advise on the purchase of all rubber, cotton and other raw materials. The Australians would be able to tap the manufacturing skills and inventions of an English company which, with its American, French and German offshoots, claimed to be spending almost as much on research as

Australian Dunlop paid in dividends. The Australian company also gained an injection of capital at a time when its plant urgently needed modernising.

In retrospect the tight new link was not necessarily the wisest decision. Admittedly, without such a link, the Dunlop Rubber Company of Australasia could have been taken over by one of its Australian competitors or even by an American rival eager to expand in new territory. The Australian company, however, lost much of its independence. At times it was to be dominated by the minority of English directors. Moreover the new rubber technology, which was one of the prospective gains of the pact, proved of little value. Even the access to English Dunlop technology was not all-important because other Australian rubber companies were able to flourish without the aid of a big brother in England or the United States. In other words, Australian Dunlop could have survived by reshaping itself and recharging its flat batteries — without any help from England. The catch was that it was unlikely to reform itself unless its very existence was challenged.

More brides and grooms

THE AUSTRALIAN competitor which was selling tyres by the ten thousands was the Perdriau Rubber Company. A Sydney firm, it had been launched by a family celebrated on the north shore as the owners of steam ferries running from Balmain to Sydney. The founder of the family in Australia, Henry Perdriau, ran the Balmain Steam Ferry Co. and three times was mayor of Balmain. His eldest son, Henry junior, worked in the ferry business until he was in his thirties, and learned how to use rubber as a packing in the steam engines and pumps and wherever rubber could ease the friction and vibrations. Spare rubber, however, was not always easy to buy in Sydney, and so he ordered it by telegram from Europe. Most telegrams were sent in business code or cipher to save money and preserve privacy, and there must have been an error in decoding the cable. As Henry recalled the episode: 'At last I decided to order a specially large supply, and to my astonishment more than five times the quantity of goods we required was sent.' Making the most of the mistake he employed a salesman and set up as a rubber importer at the corner of Erskine and Clarence Streets in Sydney. There was enough profit in rubber for him to leave the harbour ferries. Much later he gave the foundation date of his business as 1881, but if that was the date it was a very tentative foundation.

Possibly the first manufacturer in Australia to make a variety of rubber goods, Perdriau began to mould rubber goods in about the year 1885: 'I remember, among the many moulded goods I made were the rubber grips for the sculls that helped William Beach to retain his title as the world's sculling champion'. Professional rowing was a popular spectator sport in Sydney, and Beach was one of Australia's heroes: and it can be deduced that the Perdriau rubber grips made for the end of his oars must have been moulded in Sydney about November 1887, when a vast crowd watched Beach defend his title on the Parramatta River.

Jumping over the wheel

A meeting at the Perdriau offices at Drummoyne. Sir Alexander Stewart is believed to be in the chair.

Perdriau liked to cater for sportsmen, and in the Christmas issue of the Sydney *Bulletin* he took up the entire front page to advertise his own Sydney-made tennis shoes as well as Slazenger rackets and tennis-balls imported from Europe. His traditional business of supplying rubber to the railways and the steamships, as a cushion against jolts and vibrations, prospered. One brand of his products was Dugong — the name of the tropical Australian sea-cow — and his Dugong and Titan jointings used in high-pressure steam engines were much in demand on the Sydney waterfront where steam was quickly surpassing sail.

As the business of Messrs Perdriau and Co. expanded, Henry Perdriau opened a factory on the waterfront at Drummoyne. It was then called Birkenhead Point, and the rubber products could be carted a short distance by horse and dray to the small coastal ships. While his brother George managed the factory on the waterfront another two brothers, Walter and Ernest, conducted their own rubber firm, called Perdriau Bros, at 305 George Street in the centre of Sydney, just a little down the street from Henry's head office and showrooms. For customers it was very confusing.

The new factory at Drummoyne was really just a workshop, and in 1899 it employed only ten people. One of its newest employees, Bob Mockett, was to remain there for fifty years, and when presented with a wrist-watch on his retirement day he amused his listeners by explaining how folksy was the early factory. Once a horse standing at the factory's loading dock took fright and

Aerial view of Perdriau's Drummoyne mill, Birkenhead Point, in the 1920s.

bolted, falling into Sydney harbour, and virtually everyone in the factory ran
to the rescue, with George Perdriau the manager calling out loudly 'Quick,
quick, with a line!' In the confusion one of the factory hands, thinking that
for some reason the boss wanted not a rope line but a bag of lime, ran to the
corner of the factory where a bag of builder's *lime* was standing and ran with
it to the wharf.

In 1904 Henry Perdriau floated his firm into a limited liability company,
the Perdriau Rubber Company. He was the first chairman, describing his
occupation as 'Indiarubber manufacturer and merchant', and his brother
George and his son Edgar joined him on the board, with Edgar taking the main
responsibility for managing the business.

At first the small firm of Perdriau gave few signs that it would eventually
challenge Dunlop and give it shock after shock. Its business was small time,
and in 1907 its total sales amounted to 61 000 pounds or a mere one-fifth of
those of Dunlop. Nonetheless its business was probably managed more
effectively than Dunlop's. Edgar M. Perdriau busied himself in pursuing
efficiency and finding out the invisible details of the business — why the
Queensland manager was selling so little, why his Melbourne manager did not
save money by dismissing his errand boy and telling his office boy to run the
errands. He was tenacious, and when he heard a report in 1909 that the

Montague factory was manufacturing waterproof riding and driving coats on which Perdriau had the patent he visited Melbourne and with his assistant manager, Harold Daniell, he personally bearded Dunlop in its den and, according to his own account of the visit, won from Charles Proctor, the company secretary, the admission that Dunlop had unwittingly made a small number of such coats and presumably would make no more. Edgar Perdriau had a precision and a tidiness in dealing with personal matters, and when he decided in 1912 that one of his factory managers was being fractious he carried out a painstaking correspondence with him on the matter:

> The point of the fact is that you have an altogether inflated conception of your position or that you are so thick-skinned that you're always on the lookout for pinpricks and nursing imaginary grievances.
>   I wish you to reply to this letter and in reply to state fully anything to which you take exception. After receipt of your letter, I will grant you an interview, but during that interview nothing will be discussed except what is contained in your reply.

Before long, Edgar Perdriau told his employee not to 'resume at the factory until you hear from me'. The employee replied by telling Perdriau to meet him in court, where he apparently sought damages of one hundred pounds. When about to submit himself to cross-examination in the court the employee had second thoughts and fled the court-house.

Unlike Dunlop in Melbourne the Perdriau Rubber Co. did not bother about the bicycle tyre and the car tyre though it did manufacture a few car accessories like the rubber bulb which, when pressed, sounded the car horn, or rubber shock-absorbers, and springs and radiator hoses for cars. As late as 1910 the mail-order catalogues depicting their wonderful variety of rubber wares gave almost as much attention to rubber goods designed for the drivers of horse-drawn vehicles as for motorists. They made dust wraps for people to wear as they sat in a sulky or buggy and the special Perdriau waterproof rugs were favoured by farmers and their wives as they sat in their sulky or cart, exposed to the rain.

The Perdriau Rubber Company imported as well as manufactured rubber goods but realised that with the increases in Australian tariffs the future lay in manufacturing. About 1912 it began to expand dramatically, importing machinery and skilled labour from England and Europe, erecting new factory buildings, and moving progressively into the production of footwear and car and bicycle tyres. By 1914 the Perdriau Rubber Company was manufacturing car tyres, and competing with Dunlop and entering into all the publicity gimmicks of the tyre trade. There was jubilation when a telegram arrived in Sydney reporting that a Melbourne racing motorist, J. W. Day, would try the new Perdriau brand of tyres. After the tyres had been fitted with care, Mr Day drove towards St Kilda Junction. He had covered just on three miles when a tyre blew out.

Perdriau tyres were slow to challenge Dunlop's supremacy but in the 1920s they succeeded, adding a new layer of icing to a cake that was already rich. In a normal year Perdriau now paid a dividend of twelve and a half per cent and also put away large sums for a rainy day. New share issues were rushed. By 1928 its paid-up capital was thirty times as large as in 1904. Financially it was outshining Dunlop year after year. At Drummoyne the factory, always expanding, was one of Sydney's biggest private employers with 2300 employees on the payroll.

The company was run with flair. No grand surnames adorned the board. No works managers were recruited at high salaries from Akron, Ohio, or Birmingham. The top executives — Edgar Perdriau, Harold Daniell, Albert Fenton and Charles Cross — had joined the firm when very young. Their teacher had been old Henry himself, and he must have had an eye for raw talent, an ability to retain it, and a capacity to care personally for his factory hands — until they were too numerous to be treated as members of a family.

Henry Perdriau remained chairman, even into his eighties, but most of his time was now spent at the bowling green, the Freemasons, or the Presbyterian church. The surname Perdriau, like the name du Cros of English Dunlop, denoted Huguenot origins, but the family was Australian to the brim of the hat, and proud that their firm — with the generous help of the protective tariff — could stave off foreign competition in almost every product.

Perdriau was possibly the kind of firm which, expanding so rapidly in prosperous years, risked severe concussion when the first blows fell in lean times. In 1928 there were no convincing signs of the bad times which we now know were lying ahead. Nonetheless Perdriau was not over-confident. And when W. L. Baillieu, the Merger Man, quietly suggested that advantages might come from a merger or pact between the biggest Melbourne and biggest Sydney rubber companies, Perdriau asked for further details. The advantage of a merger was obvious. It would quieten the cut-throat competition in the industry. It would also enable Australians to compete more effectively with American tyre firms which were becoming far more active and effective in Australian garages and tyre depots.

Sir Eric Geddes of the English Dunlop knew about the early talks with Perdriau, but had no strong views. Clearly he was interested in thwarting the Americans' drive for world dominance in tyres, and a merger would thwart his powerful rival, Goodyear, in Australia. At the same time a merger with Perdriau would instantly enlarge the capital and the size of the board of Australian Dunlop, thus diluting the influence which Geddes and his London colleagues had just acquired.

Baillieu did not push the negotiations too hard but he did lead and guide them. Whereas F. J. Smith, the Sydney accountant prominent a year earlier in the merger of the two Dunlops, thought an exchange of shares between Perdriau and Australian Dunlop would be the neatest knot, Baillieu favoured a proper amalgamation with a new company taking over all assets. An amalgamation was soon the favourite idea. But how should each company be valued? Baillieu was eager that the turnover of each company be treated as more important than the profits, for Dunlop's profits were now disappointing, at least for a year or two, because of the over-buying of crude rubber. As usual, Baillieu had his way.

The press was informed in April 1928 that discussions were taking place. Thereafter the to and fro of bargaining around the tables in the two cities was slow. Neither company was willing to merge if it was to be outvoted in the new partnership. Nor would they merge if they believed that the new company could be impaired by basic disagreements about policy. Dunlop admired Perdriau's success but thought it had been achieved with helter skelter methods and an inspired anarchy which they did not wish to see persisting in a combined operation. Perdriau were sometimes disruptive after all manufacturers and the main sellers had painfully reached agreement on a uniform price for tyres. Such incidents lined the memory of Dunlop salesmen. There was the recent time when Perdriau, its warehouses full of unsold tyres, erased the Perdriau name and serial number from ten thousand perfectly sound new tyres and — without breathing a word to competitors who normally were told in advance of such events — sold them as 'seconds' or blemished tyres at a discount of thirty per cent, thus upsetting the tyre market to such an extent that even a Goodyear executive in far off Akron was provoked to marvel at Perdriau's whims. No doubt the Perdriau men also had their legitimate complaints against Dunlop. They did not, however, feel their grievances so intensely because they were gaining the better of Dunlop and steadily lessening their leeway in sales, year by year. How could you be continually indignant towards a competitor when it was playing into your hands by following a lethargic selling policy?

Snodgrass, the Fort Dunlop man serving as managing director of Australian Dunlop, soon noticed the selling zeal of old Henry Perdriau and his team. As he wrote to a London colleague in a private letter on 23 April 1928: 'His business has been created from nothing, and for a good many years I am afraid his competition was not treated seriously'. That Dunlop had been too complacent was a frequent but tactfully-worded criticism from Snodgrass's pen. He privately praised the Perdriaus' enthusiasm for selling. Their brigade of travellers had no hesitation in bypassing garages and tyre shops in order to sell direct to the people. The closest attention to business plus sheer hard work, wrote Snodgrass, had made the Perdriau Rubber Company a power.

While Dunlop was vulnerable in tyres — and car tyres were the basis of the Australian rubber industry — it remained very competitive in many other manufactures. In lesser products such as rubber belting, Dunlop was supreme. Its salesmen did not so much count the orders they received in belting but counted the orders they failed to win. Broken Hill's mines and treatment plants were voracious buyers of conveyor belts, and there Dunlop won about

three-quarters of all business in 1927. Dunlop's Perth branch, which specialised in selling conveyors to the gold mines of Kalgoorlie, reported that in a
period of seven months all but one of its tenders for the supply of belting were
successful. Dunlop's weak spots were Sydney and the New South Wales
collieries and steelworks, where Perdriau and Goodyear and even foreign firms
were winning much of the trade in rubber belting. Indeed Perdriau was
installing at Port Kembla what its salesmen claimed was the world's largest
conveyor belt for the loading of coal.

Even while Perdriau was busily joining in negotiations for the merger its
hustle for new business did not diminish. Dunlop men felt like tearing out
their hair when, coming close to an agreement to prevent further cuts in the
prices of tyres and tubes, they heard on the grape-vine that Perdriau had
started a new price-cutting scheme. By the middle of 1928 the money owed
to Dunlop by tyre retailers was causing 'considerable anxiety'. The economy
was less buoyant, and moreover the dealers were victims of their own price-
cutting which cut profit to the marrow. Dunlop's directors, despite the
advantages from the new English ties, were experiencing probably their worst
year since the early 1900s. They were still paying the penalty for their
excessive buying of rubber, and were also bruised by their competitors. For the
half year ending December 1927 they declared no dividend on the ordinary
shares, and in the following half year they recorded such a loss that the whole
financial year ended in loss. In contrast their Australian-owned competitors,
Perdriau and Barnet Glass, ended their respective years with impressive
profits on the basis of a lower turnover than Dunlop's. The prospects of the
following year, running from 1 July 1928, were also sober for Dunlop. The
figures they collected for the registration of new cars in Australia in the
previous six months were down by twenty-nine per cent on the same period
of the previous year, and fewer new cars meant fewer new tyres. Owners of
secondhand cars were shunning new tyres to an unprecedented degree,
preferring to pay to retread or recondition their old tyres. The retreading of
tyres, hitherto a minor backyard activity, was said to form fifteen per cent of
the trade in replacement as distinct from new-car tyres at the end of 1928.

Dunlop was in deep trouble, and the Perdriaus also were looking for a way
out. In August the three big Australian tyre companies agreed that, rather
than cut prices and thereby cut their own throats, they would share the
Australian market for new tyres being fitted to brand new cars being roughly
four-tenths of the annual tyres sales. It was a sign of how far Dunlop had
slipped from dominance since 1920 that Barnet Glass accepted a quota of
twenty-five per cent and Perdriau accepted thirty-one and a half per cent,
leaving Dunlop with forty-one and a half per cent. Outsiders, it was anticipated, would nibble but not bite into those quotas. Within a few months
Goodyear, now running its own factory in Sydney, was actually biting. On 1
November, Snodgrass wrote privately to London that New South Wales had

a 'craze' for Goodyear tyres. In the leaner economy Montague was making 1100 tyres a day and Goodyear, with the latest machines and a team of American foremen, was making the astonishing total of 1250 a day, 'which gives you some idea of the speed at which Goodyear came into this market'.

At Montague the tyre factory, as distinct from other workshops, reduced its work-force even further from 1004 — including 124 women — to fewer than eight hundred in the space of two months. This chapter of woe seemed to have no end. The next problem was in the tube department. For some reason large numbers of tubes were faulty, and complaints came from 'all over Australia'. Tubes had even failed after a new car had travelled a few miles. Previously large customers such as Morris (New South Wales), Studebaker Corporation and General Motors (Victoria) simply refused to accept Dunlop tyres and tubes in certain sizes. By now the agreement on quotas for supplying new-car or so-called equipment tyres was being torn up. The Dunlop sales manager, Anivitti, reported that Perdriau had gone prospecting and 'found loopholes' in the agreement and was flagrantly discounting tyres. Nothing could go right for Dunlop. Signs of nerves and confusion were visible at head office. The December sales report must have been read with some surprise by the directors because it carried the date of 13.13.1928.

Sir Eric Geddes, about to make his first visit to Australian Dunlop, decided that some sanity must be allowed to enter the marketing of tyres in Australia. In Akron, Ohio, the Goodyear company agreed with him. It was even sending an emissary to board the steamship in which Geddes was travelling to Australia so that Geddes should be impressed with the need to tame the Perdriau company. Goodyear actually hoped that in Australia, Dunlop and Perdriau would amalgamate. In its view the competition of a combined Australian firm was preferable to the unpredictable price-slaughtering of the exuberant Perdriau company. On 3 December 1928, Geddes cabled a confidential message to Melbourne, using Bentley's code book so that the message would not be leaked. He reported that in North America, Goodyear was 'considered mad dog of industry'. He predicted that if Goodyear were to apply its aggressive American policies to Australia, where so far it had acted reasonably, the ferocity of its attack would stun even the Perdriau company.

In the end it was the vitality of the Perdriau staff which Australian Dunlop was really purchasing. Every member of the Dunlop board agreed with the conclusions expressed in clipped language in the confidential cable drafted by Baillieu for despatch to Geddes before he sailed from England:

> The ability of personnel Perdriau Company in the past to handle business has outstripped the Dunlop stop ... Snodgrass has revealed to us the great weakness in our organisation and executives and the prospects of improvement from within are not encouraging stop ... We have to recognise that the previously successful executives and organisation of the Perdriau Company will dominate the amalga-

mated Company subject to the control of the Board... We have given the situation careful consideration and have come to the conclusion that if we do not amalgamate Perdriau will be the mad dog of Australia.

In short it was wiser to have the mad dog as friend than as enemy.

Edgar Perdriau for his part was now willing to join forces with Dunlop. The competition of Goodyear was forbidding. Moreover it was becoming more difficult to sell tyres in a sagging economy. Perdriau, however, would not give in easily. He stipulated that he should be chairman of the combined company, a demand he later abandoned. He gained consent for his three leading executives to join him on the new Dunlop Perdriau board, and above all he knew that he and his lieutenant, Fenton, would control the new executive because Snodgrass would be the only other member.

Perdriau was even prepared, in deciding the shares to be allotted in the combined company, to sacrifice the larger share which his company's aggregate profits in the last three years virtually entitled him to expect:

	Perdriau Rubber	Australian Dunlop
1926	137 451	252 582
1927	183 181	132 462
1928	213 393	36 452 (loss)
Total profits	533 025	348 592

Instead of basing the apportioning of power in the amalgamated company largely on past profits, or largely on share-market values, Perdriau accepted a formula based largely on turnover. There Dunlop became the winner with 2.6 million to Perdriau's 2.1 million. Perdriau in this decision was sensible as well as generous. He must have suspected that if his company decided to fight alone, in months when the selling of tyres became harder and harder, his company might eventually sink, simply because it lacked the fighting funds which, in a crisis, Dunlop could summon from London and Goodyear could direct from Akron, Ohio.

Even before this merger was finally cemented, another was quickly being arranged in Melbourne by the resourceful Baillieu. His scheme for an efficient rubber industry in Australia would be enhanced if the other Australian-owned group joined the amalgamated company. The outsider was Barnet Glass. This old firm had flourished in its second life. Born again in 1908, three years after all its assets had been bought by Dunlop, the firm of Barnet Glass showed its old skill in enlisting well known Australians as shareholders and directors. Just as David Syme, proprietor of the nation's most successful newspaper, the Melbourne *Age*, was a big backer of the first firm, the second firm also had prominent backers. On the board of Barnet Glass were E. C. Dyason, a skilled financier and sharebroker who was heir to a Bendigo gold-mining fortune, and John Tait, a theatrical promoter who organised entertainments ranging from Nellie Melba's triumphal tour of Australia in 1902 to the forming of the early radio station, 3LO. As one of the five subscribers to the articles of association of the Barnet Glass Rubber Company in 1914, Tait listed his address as The Auditorium in Collins Street — the new concert hall in which the Taits were to stage many of Melbourne's major recitals. Although Barnet Glass himself died during the First World War, and the business was in the doldrums soon after the war, the family entered a highly profitable period in the 1920s. A wise step was to enlist one of Australia's ablest politicians of the 1911–20 decade, Willy Watt, who served as chairman of Barnet Glass even while he was Speaker of the Federal Parliament. In any negotiations with Dunlop and Perdriau he would be wearing full armour on behalf of his shareholders.

The Barnet Glass factory stood at Footscray, on low-lying land by the Maribyrnong River. From some of the higher factory windows a stone could be lobbed into the river. In most months the factory was crowded with men. Like a medieval town, the factory site had narrow alleys and crooked streets and cramped courtyards, all approached beneath a covered gateway with hefty wooden gateposts on each side. One of Footscray's largest employers in the late 1920s the works made close to nine thousand tyres in their busiest weeks, and a variety of other rubber goods. Six days a week the coal smoke drifted or gushed from the high chimney with its ornamental rim at the top — a landmark for a procession of lorries with solid rubber tyres and slow horse-drays coming along Moreland or Parker Streets. Today the factory is forlorn, with downpipes rusty, blades of grass growing in niches in the brick walls, the chimney cold, and the overhead walkways linking the adjacent buildings now silent. It is hard to believe that in a mere three years of the late 1920s this cramped factory earned net profits almost as large as Dunlop earned in the same years from its big factories and large capital base.

Barnet Glass as a company had flair. Even its name became an indirect advertisement because people on first encountering the name assumed it was a glass firm and not a rubber firm while many others wondered about a car tyre that was labelled 'Glass'. The firm won a big following amongst Victorian cyclists and motorists. Its advertisements, seen along the main roads and in hardware shops and petrol stations, were more catching than Dunlop's, partly because they were less sophisticated. An Aboriginal holding a boomerang was often depicted in Barnet Glass coloured hoardings, and the slogan of the Barnet Glass tyre was simply 'There And Back'. The tread on its motor tyre, for many years, had boomerangs as the pattern. In hardware shops a tall coloured poster advertising Barnet Glass's black garden hose showed a rustic gardener standing by his wheelbarrow, lighting his clay pipe, while two children with a black and white dog played around his feet, the brass nozzle of the hose clearly visible.

The Ormistons and the Glasses, who managed the firm, were managers of the old school who knew the business inside out and gave it all their waking hours. They thrived on attention to detail. They chased the highest standards. They made everything from tyres to bath caps, lawn bowls and tennis-balls. Generally their methods were empirical, and for years they tested tennis-balls partly by employing a man to hit them against a brick wall at the factory. While most of their employees were the typical Australian workhands, a substantial group of employees was Jewish. At least they were believed to be Jewish by those who employed them. Thus Bill Jacobs feels sure that he gained his job at the factory office in 1926 because his name sounded Jewish; and for months he was at a loss to know how to behave — should he try to attend the synagogue, what he should eat at lunch-time — so that he would continue to appear to be Jewish in the eyes of his employers.

W. L. Baillieu, in trying to unite Dunlop and Perdriau, knew that any Australian merger which excluded Barnet Glass was inviting trouble. It was hard enough discussing details with Perdriau alone, and yet perhaps the presence of Barnet Glass at the bargaining table at an early stage was essential. While the merger talks between Dunlop and Perdriau were continuing in the winter of 1928, W. L. Baillieu arranged a few private discussions with W. A. Watt, the chairman of Barnet Glass. The two had been ministers together in the Victorian Parliament, and indeed Baillieu had once stood in Watt's present shoes because as the leading director of the original Barnet Glass Company he had negotiated its first merger with Dunlop a quarter of a century earlier. Watt spoke from a position of relative strength. His company was flourishing. Run more tightly than its big competitors, it could survive unless by chance it had to face all-out war with its competitors.

Watt could see merit in a merger, especially if Barnet Glass joined in while it was strong. As he said later, the rubber manufacturers of Australia had long 'indulged in heavy competitive waste'. There were too many factories and machines, warehouses and selling depots, for the work involved. Now was the time to combine, before profits fell.

From the head office of Barnet Glass at 289–299 Swanston Street, Watt joined in the joint negotiations with Perdriau and Dunlop. He made it very clear what he wanted. He was so articulate and such a master of making the running in any discussion that he was invited to withdraw from the negotiations for the time being! E. M. Perdriau explained that it was easier for two firms than for three firms to negotiate a merger. Later, maybe, Watt could return to the discussions. Six months later, when the two had almost come to terms, Watt came back. His terms, one suspects, were now a little tougher. Indeed he ran the argument that his firm wanted a merger along with the retention of a high degree of independence. This impossible demand was met.

On 4 January 1929 the board of Dunlop approved a deal with Barnet Glass. Dunlop was to make a bid for the 550 000 ordinary one-pound shares in Barnet Glass, offering a premium of sixty per cent on each share. The ordinary shareholders in Barnet Glass, if they so wished, could then buy Dunlop shares at a favourable price. That left Barnet Glass with only a block of two hundred thousand cumulative preference shares each of one pound. The Barnet Glass Company would continue to exist, its profits would go to the preference shareholders, and those preference shares could be bought and sold on the stock exchanges. Dunlop even promised that for the next ten years it would guarantee a minimum dividend of eight per cent on such preference shares. In short if Barnet Glass did not earn enough for that dividend, Dunlop or the new firm of Dunlop Perdriau would subsidise the dividend.

Through this curious arrangement Barnet Glass retained its name and identity, its factory, its branded products, its advertising budget, its own board with Philip Glass as chairman, and its own guaranteed dividends. Australian Dunlop, as owner of all ordinary shares in Barnet Glass, in effect controlled its policies and trading methods, but some observers argued — and they were right — that Dunlop would not control Barnet Glass as much as it hoped. Dunlop even promised to maintain the existence of Barnet Glass 'indefinitely', but there were within Barnet Glass itself many senior employees who had no intention of being ruled by Dunlop. It was only half a merger and would provide an ants' nest of problems.

Watt resigned from the board of Barnet Glass early in the new year and joined the board of Dunlop, not as one of many directors but as chairman. His colleague, Frederic S. Ormiston — his name changed from Ornstein as a necessary act of wartime camouflage — was equally promoted to high office because he was to become managing director of Dunlop when later in the year Snodgrass returned to England. When in February 1929 Sir Eric Geddes attended special board meetings in Melbourne to discuss the implications of all this activity, the pact with Barnet Glass was in place, even ahead of the merger with Perdriau.

Friday 1 March 1929 was the long-awaited day in the merger of the three rubber companies; and at the directors' meeting Watt and his new deputy chairman, E. M. Perdriau, were present though they were not yet formally in office; and Sir John Grice — present as chairman for the last time — welcomed all and thanked all. On 8 March W. A. Watt formally took the chair. A gathering of all the clans was set down for Monday 22 April when the directors of the Dunlop Rubber Company of Australasia and the two new directors brought over from Barnet Glass met with five representatives of the Perdriau Rubber Company, including the venerable founder of the firm, Henry Perdriau, now in his eighty-fourth year. On 11 June the name of the amalgamated company was formally adopted, the Dunlop Perdriau Rubber Company Limited. The task of welding together rival and very different organisations was only beginning.

Melbourne remained the head office of the new company. The old Dunlop company remained the structure around which the new organisation was built. Much, however, went on as before. The head office and three other

In the mid 1930s, Dunlop Perdriau used Harley-Davidson motor-bikes and big side-cars to deliver goods in Sydney.

states continued to bank with the Commercial Bank of Australia, while Sydney and Brisbane kept the old Perdriau account at the Commercial Banking Company of Sydney. Under the same banner, Drummoyne and Montague remained rival factories, and at first little rationalising of their activities was attempted. The competing sales organisations in every state were tackled more speedily, and in each big city either the Dunlop or the Perdriau branch office was sold or leased out, and a new hierarchy of command was established in the one building. Ormiston and Fenton accepted six-year terms as managing directors, with Snodgrass continuing until Ormiston returned from his tour of overseas plants later in the year. And at head office a board of massive size, perhaps the largest board any major public company had been encumbered with, met regularly, waiting until death or voluntary resignation reduced its membership to a mere dozen. An early reward for all the amputation and plastic surgery was that in the difficult year ending in June 1929, the reshaped organisation earned close to fifty per cent more profit than would otherwise have been possible.

Meanwhile the last of the medical operations was performed. The New Zealand business had long given worry. For several decades it was a sound business selling cycle and motor tyres and a variety of other Australian goods. At the end of the First World War the two depots at Wellington and Christchurch together sold as much as Adelaide and Perth combined, or about one seventh of Dunlop's entire business. In the early 1920s, however, the New Zealand tariff turned against Australian tyres, charging them an import duty of twenty-five per cent compared to a duty of only ten per cent on English tyres. It was the bright idea of MacKirdy, the Dunlop secretary, to arrange tentatively with English Dunlop to provide most of the rubber goods for New Zealand, with England taking most of the risks and Australia taking most of the profits. In 1928, a total of seventy-seven per cent of the sales at Dunlop's New Zealand depots were of English goods. The sensible solution was for English Dunlop to buy back what it had sold in 1899, the sole right to the Dunlop business, name and products within New Zealand. Australian Dunlop agreed to the sale in March 1929, just when its Australian mergers were finalised. The sale was slight compensation to English Dunlop which in 1927 had bought a substantial interest in Australian Dunlop, only to find in the following two years that its proportion of shares on the Melbourne register and its proportion of seats on the Melbourne board were both diluted by an unforeseen wave of Australian mergers.

Meanwhile, Australian Dunlop, seemingly well, was suffering from a form of Alzheimer's Disease. It had lost much of its identity in the space of two years. By October 1929 its chairman and vice-chairman were newcomers, recruited from firms that were stubborn rivals only a year ago. Likewise Australian Dunlop's new managing directors, coming from rival firms, must have blinked when they found themselves signing cheques in the name of Dunlop. The three-sided alliance of Dunlop, Perdriau and Barnet Glass did not work smoothly. And yet as the world's economy began to shake, and customers decided not to buy new cars and even new tyres, the company's new leaders knew that they had come together just in time.

Surely the clouds will lift

I N 1929, as Christmas approached, the order books of the new Dunlop Perdriau company were disappointing. In the country towns many farmers, worried by the falling prices of wheat and wool, decided to cling to their horse and cart rather than buy their first car. Those who already owned a car and were thinking of replacing it with a later model postponed the decision. In the cities the tyre depots offered discounts on new Dunlop, Barnet Glass and Perdriau tyres — the distinctive brands were not yet affected by the merger — but did not attract the expected customers. Most people, nervous of the future, saved rather than spent. City shops reported a quieter Christmas while the tyre dealers reported a depressingly dull month.

Tyres and tubes were the first rubber goods to experience the slump in demand during the first year of the world depression. In a nervous economy the imports of new car chassis — most came from the United States — fell dramatically, and so the supplying of new tyres to car-assembly plants fell away. Those driving older cars put off the buying of a new tyre. When their tyres became bald they saved money by driving their car to tyre dealers for a cheap retread; and such was the demand for retreads that Dunlop wondered whether to enter a section of the industry which it previously despised.

In the main street of every town and suburb all those dealers who traded in new and secondhand cars, sold tyres and batteries and spare parts, served oil and petrol, repaired radiators, and recharged batteries and mended punctures — felt the pinch. The horse-transport in its heyday had not been so sensitive to the ups and downs of the economy (a thousand new horses were manufactured, without even a midwife or stall keeper in attendance, but the birth of a thousand new cars called for a small army of workmen). That the motor industry was a delicate barometer of the economy was a painful realisation. Everyone in Dunlop felt the shock. Thinking that the motor car on which so much of its profit depended was a necessity, they were dismayed to find that in bad times it was more likely to be deemed a luxury. Most of the other goods made by Dunlop, whether rubber galoshes or garden hoses or bicycle tyres, were somewhat vulnerable to a depression but they were still bought in substantial quantities: not so the car tyre. Australians almost ceased to buy new cars. Imports of motor vehicles fell startlingly from 98 000 in the year ending June 1929 to a mere nine thousand just two years later. Cars were still on the roads, but people who owned them drove fewer miles. That again reduced the demand for new tyres.

Thousands of motorists ceased to drive, placing their car permanently in the garage or sitting it on blocks, preferring to ride a bicycle or walk. As Dunlop made cycle tyres and rubber shoes it might at least gain from these activities but they were minor sources of profit compared to the automobile industry. Moreover people made their shoes last longer than in good times and most people still wore leather shoes — not a Dunlop product — and if they did use rubber it was only on the heels. Even the sale of first-rate bicycle tyres declined, though those of poorer quality remained popular.

The employees, and not least the teenage boys and girls who worked at the Dunlop factories in Sydney and Melbourne, wondered how long their jobs would last. Those making tyres were given a four-day week and then a three-day week. Sometimes production halted for a month, and when work was resumed no jobs were available for many of the former employees. Every morning a crowd waited at the factory gate, hoping that a vacancy might occur. In the offices and sales departments the few people who retired or left voluntarily were not replaced. As orders fell away, salesmen were told to come to work only on each second week. The evidence is overwhelming that Dunlop clung to more employees, especially salesmen, than its volume of work justified. An efficiency drive a few years later proved the extent of the over-staffing. Meanwhile employees, as distinct from shareholders, were delighted that Dunlop tolerated inefficiency in such lean times.

The manager of each factory was ordered to keep smaller stocks of raw materials, especially after the directors learned, a month before Christmas of 1929, that the company's stock of unsold raw materials and manufactured goods was valued at the huge sum of 1 648 446 pounds. Just as Dunlop bought less from its suppliers, so its customers bought less from Dunlop. In that way the depression spread from firm to firm, backwards and forwards again and again. As Dunlop decided to keep a smaller stock of ready-made tyres, garden hoses, hot-water bottles and a hundred other goods, those decisions meant that many departments required no further output, no work except mainte-nance, for months on end — until such time as the sale of goods to the public reduced the stockpile of each product.

Almost everything that could be cut was cut: directors' fees, executives' salaries, the dividends, the advertising budget. Wages too were cut, in line with the national policy. The first cut in wages was ten per cent in 1930 and, as the depression became severe, a further cut of ten per cent. Fortunately for the wage-earners the real fall of incomes was small because the prices of rent and food and clothes were falling rapidly, sometimes more rapidly than the wages. For the rubber workers, salesmen and clerks who lost their jobs the outlook was grim. 'Social security' was not even a phrase. The dole was precarious and pitiful.

Meanwhile the company's offices and foremen were swamped with calls for help or leniency. Customers wanted time to pay their bills. Redundant employees wanted relief money, and a sum was given to the Federated Rubber Workers' Union for distribution; ten shillings here, four shillings there. A second sum was given to each branch office with the instruction that the money be apportioned to former employees with 'the aid of the most efficient local charity organisation'.

The senior executives knew that a big sum might be saved by closing down certain sections in certain factories and concentrating all the production in one factory. The Dunlop factory at Montague, the Barnet Glass factory a few miles across the river flats, and the Drummoyne factory by the waterfront at Sydney were each duplicating the others; and one of the promised advantages of the merger was that costly duplication might be cut out. With the falling demand for many products, virtually all the production needed could come from one factory, thus permitting a large saving in labour and overheads. The delicate question, however, was which factory should be the loser? Should it be a Sydney or a Melbourne factory — a matter with fierce political implications.

The chairman of directors, Willy Watt, had a crucial say in this matter — as in every important decision during his eighteen years in the chair — and so his attitudes call for comment. Perhaps more than any other top politician in Australia in the twentieth century, Watt has slipped from public memory. He was once the wonder-boy of politics, a farmer's son with little formal education but the gift of oratory. Rising from little debating societies and the ranks of the Australia Natives Association around North Melbourne and Carlton, he became in 1899, the postmaster-general of Victoria and reputedly the youngest cabinet minister in the British Empire: he was then twenty-eight years old. In 1914, as Premier of Victoria, he resigned to enter federal politics, and for sixteen continuous months in 1918 and 1919 he was acting prime minister while W. M. Hughes was overseas putting Australia's case in the last phase of the First World War and in the peace negotiations that followed. Falling out with Hughes, Watt remained in the federal parliament until March 1929, though his era of influence was over. Indeed he was still the federal member for Balaclava when he was chairman of Barnet Glass and then chairman of the new Dunlop Perdriau.

Watt began his new full-time career as a business leader just before the

Willy Watt.

onset of the world depression. While he was to sit on many boards, his major board was Dunlop to which he gave such large slices of time that his colleagues were to vote him an annual remuneration such as few non-executive directors had hitherto received. To the boardroom Watt brought unusual qualities and experience, as well as a certain nervous tension of which his up-and-down health was a sign. As treasurer both of Victoria and Australia he had learned much about the role of government. As a compelling speaker he could express the company's view to shareholders or the press — not that he now concerned himself much about the press — with authority or charm or wit, and occasionally with an earthy phrase or metaphor that was just right. He was willing to listen to other points of view, and when presiding at a meeting he was alert for compromises. A left-wing liberal in the early part of his political career he did not see the division between capital and labour as a high wall. His sympathies were almost as much with a conscientious employee as with an employer, and that made him extremely reluctant, as the depression deepened, to pursue efficiency too breathlessly, for he probably believed that rising efficiency, in a slump of this magnitude, could be carried too far. After a certain stage, it was wiping out jobs and thus transferring income from workmen who needed it to shareholders who mostly needed it less.

Willy Watt, reluctant to go all-out in his company's drive for efficiency, was also the leader of one of the three factions within the boardroom. He led the Barnet Glass faction, having initially been invited to join the Barnet Glass board because of his friendship with the Glasses and other Jewish families. In the hunt for economies Watt was loath to inflict undue hardship on the Barnet Glass firm which still existed and whose preference shares were quoted on the stock exchange. Indeed Barnet Glass had been only half-merged in the Dunlop Perdriau alliance of 1929, was conscious of its independence, and knew that it had a strong defender in Watt. In short Dunlop did not have a neutral chairman. It was not even a company in the normal sense but a loose federation nervously engaged in sorting itself out. Many employees who retained their jobs in the rubber industry in the dismal years of the 1930s really owed their income to Watt and the way he saw his role. Whether his role was in Australia's national interests is a moot point. Dunlop did not become efficient enough at a time when the nation needed the cheapest possible tyres and other rubber products.

As a former politician Watt also hoped political action would ease the depression. On the eve of the federal election of October 1929 — the first time he had not been contesting a seat for nearly one-third of a century — the Dunlop Perdriau directors voted a 'special donation' of seven hundred pounds to an unspecified fund in each mainland state, clearly the conservative election fund. But Labor under John Scullin won the election after twelve years in opposition.

Watt, and probably every other Dunlop director, was an opponent of Labor, but he had no reason to complain of Labor's policy towards manufacturing. J. H. Scullin increased the duty against imported manufactures. Britain was still the main source of competition, and traditionally British goods were admitted to Australia at a lower duty than goods from other nations; but even the duty on British manufactures jumped between 1929 and the first months of 1932. The duty on the main kind of cotton-based waterproof cloth imported from Britain jumped from fifteen to thirty-five per cent. For German, Japanese and American waterproof cloth the general duty applied, and it was increased from twenty-five to fifty per cent. On clothes wringers — the manual device with which housewives squeezed water from the washing — the general duty went up from twenty-five to fifty per cent while on British-made wringers the duty leaped from twelve and a half per cent to forty per cent. On some rubber goods the duty was not increased. On car tyres and tubes the British-preferential tariff remained unchanged at twenty-five per cent, compared to forty per cent on American tyres and tubes; and on many other rubber imports the percentage duty was increased little if at all. But then the effective duty on these imports was really increased by the simple fact that most Australian goods were protected primarily by a duty expressed in money values. In the early 1930s the price of nearly all imports, whether tyres or golf balls, actually fell. As the import duty remained the same number of pounds and shillings, the real protective duty in effect increased without the tariff authorities having to take action.

Dunlop did not always receive the protection it wanted but the tariff was enough to keep out most imports so long as Watt's price was lean. His biggest complaint was that crude rubber, admitted to Australia without paying duty in the 1920s, now had to pay an import duty of four pence a pound. This new duty was simply a device to give Canberra sorely-needed revenue but it meant that in these years, when crude rubber was incredibly cheap the import duty was often as much as the cost of buying the rubber in Malaya and shipping it to Australia.

Dunlop Perdriau secured further protection from imports when early in 1931 the Australian pound, hitherto equal to the pound sterling, was devalued, at first by thirty per cent though later the devaluation stabilised at twenty-five per cent. Australian importers therefore had to pay twenty-five per cent more for rubber goods from overseas. This proved to be a barrier against Europe but not against Japan, for in 1932 the Japanese devalued the yen even more drastically than the Australian pound. Devalued by fifty per cent in the space of eight months, it enabled the Japanese merchants to penetrate Australia with ease. To buy in Japan was to buy in the world's bargain basement for factory goods. From Japan crates of rubber footwear poured into England, temporarily forcing the famous North British Rubber Company to close its factory. Apparel elastic from Japan reached Australian shops. Paying no import duty it outsold Dunlop's elastic, endangering the jobs of the forty people who made it in Melbourne.

In 1932 Dunlop's rubber gumboots and wading boots were suddenly undercut by low-priced Japanese gumboots. As Dunlop's main footwear consisted of gumboots and sand-shoes, and as footwear still employed 780 people, the blow was acute. Dunlop's machines were the latest, the employees received piece-work incentives, and the factory was believed to be efficient in manufacturing the black knee-height gumboot with its black binding and foxing. In winter nearly every dairy farmer in Australia wore Dunlop gumboots in the muddy milking yard, and hundreds of thousands of rural children wore gumboots to school on wet days in winter, but now they were turning to Japanese boots. These imported boots, though of good material and appearance, were likely to disintegrate after a short life, but they were too cheap to be overlooked by buyers eager to save money.

A pair of Japanese gumboots could bear high charges but still be cheap in

Australian shops. After paying the shipping costs from Yokohama to Australia, an import duty of forty per cent at the Australian port, a surcharge on that duty which in effect increased the duty to sixty per cent, a tax called primage which virtually increased the duty to seventy per cent, as well as the Australian wharf and handling charges, a pair of Japanese gumboots reached a Sydney warehouse for fifty-one pence. But an Australian pair reached the same warehouse for a minimum of 101 pence. On 15 September 1932 Dunlop Perdriau appealed to the government for 'adequate protection' at once, arguing that without it the factory would cease to sell gumboots. The sand-shoes, of which Dunlop Perdriau made more than two million pairs a year, were also endangered now that the Lyons government, elected early in 1932 (with the help of a 'special donation' from the directors) reduced the effective import duty to forty per cent.

Finally the Australian government, fearful of the loss of jobs in an economy which was slowly reviving, decided to protect nearly all Australian factories against the new competition from Japan. The policy of protecting jobs and capital in Australian factories remained so for at least forty years. It protected jobs more than efficiency. In Tokyo, for most of the next forty years, the comparable policy protected jobs but also spurred efficiency. Thus the day would come when the unbelievable would happen and a Japanese firm would buy the tyre business from English Dunlop.

In tyres the competition from overseas was not strong. The tariff against imports was high, the freight on tyres was costlier than on gumboots, and Japan was not yet a big exporter of tyres. Indeed the importance of Dunlop in the world tyre industry, whether in England or Japan, and the fact that in Australia the firm of Dunlop Perdriau was exempt from overseas competition stemming from other Dunlop factories, placed tyres in a special position. Imports of American tyres remained a possibility, but the American firm most interested in Australia was Goodyear of Akron and it had already decided to set up its factory behind the tariff wall in Australia. Goodyear had the misfortune to open its factory at the Sydney suburb of Granville on the eve of depression and was thumped by the collapse of the new-car industry. Whereas Dunlop Perdriau had dozens of varieties of other rubber products to fall back on, Goodyear had little. Its annual profits were slashed between 1929 and 1931: they fell from 249 000 pounds to 36 000. In contrast Dunlop paid a dividend on ordinary shares in most half-yearly periods of the depression.

Dunlop's other competitor was a new Tasmanian company, the Rapson Tyre and Rubber Company (Australia) Limited. Its financiers included the Thonemann family, prominent in Melbourne stockbroking and partners in the Elsey cattle station in the Northern Territory. Rapson's plans were followed with intense interest by Dunlop. In November 1928, Dunlop's sales manager, L. Anivitti, had inspected the new Rapson factory on the banks of the Tamar River in Launceston, with its own wharf almost in place and the boiler house for the two big Johnson 'colonial' boilers, powerhouse, and a cluster of other buildings including a main workshop as long as the Sydney cricket ground. Indeed the new factory settlement was grand enough to be called Rapsonia. Anivitti reported privately that its skilled operatives hired from England were soon to begin large-scale production with the unorthodox Rapson process and its vertical heaters which cured the tyres and tubes. The choice of Tasmania now seems strange but ships along the coast of Australia were not yet so unpredictable in port nor so snail-like at sea. The Rapson company won cheap hydroelectricity from the Launceston City Council and a remarkable promise that the Tasmanian government would guarantee, for the next seven years, an annual dividend of eight per cent on the cumulative preference shares which formed almost three-quarters of the paid-up capital.

A tyre factory, as the depression gathered way, was as risky as a cattle run in the bush. Within one year of the arrival of Rapson tyres, the company was negotiating to sell its factory to Dunlop. The discussions dragged on, the wedding knots were almost tied and then untied. Dunlop would not positively agree to use the Rapson formula for making tyres but seemed willing to keep alive the factory in Launceston and so collect the government guarantee of profits which was now Rapson's main asset. By the middle of 1930, however, the tyre market in Australia had so shrunk that Rapson lost its earlier bargaining position and Dunlop lost its enthusiasm.

Dunlop feared that the Rapson factory would fall into the hands of a strong company, perhaps an overseas company keen to capture part of the tyre trade. If the factory were bought by a company aggressive in its selling, it would promptly undo all the potential gains that Dunlop made by merging its former competitors into the new Dunlop Perdriau company and by the effective sales truce with Goodyear. Meanwhile Rapson survived. The coastal steamships unloaded the Rapson tyres at Melbourne wharves and the tyres, heavily discounted, ate into the meagre national markets. As Rapson made only a dozen or so different tyres, for each of which the Australian demand was high, it was not burdened with the losses inevitable in manufacturing in small batches of special tyres for which demand was small. Rapson fought strenuously in 1930 and 1931. At many meetings of the Dunlop board in Melbourne, details were revealed of each new selling campaign mounted by the Tasmanian company. In April 1931 Dunlop made a decision which seemed revolutionary at the time. It resolved, after careful research, to save a big sum by ceasing to wrap new tyres sold in the Dunlop, Barnet Glass and Perdriau brands. Hitherto most tyres were elaborately wrapped in strong paper in the belief that a tyre, like a box of chocolates, deserved to be packaged as if it were a gift. A fortnight later the directors decided to produce new 'second-grade tyres' to recapture trade lost to Rapsons on the one hand and the tyre retreaders on the other.

The Rapson tyre had its admirers, especially in Tasmania and Victoria.

In the 1920s, Barnet Glass competed with Dunlop in garden hose and a host of other rubber products.

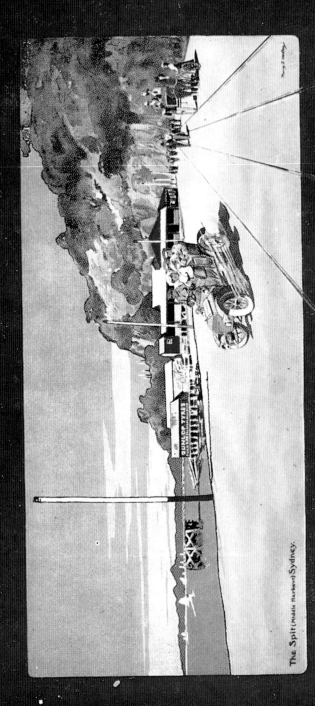

An early Dunlop poster, depicting Sydney's Middle Harbour, when a car was still a novelty.

In 1949, to mark its fiftieth anniversary as a public company, Dunlop invited the well-known artist Rhys Williams to depict its two main factories, the Montague mill in Melbourne (above), and the Drummoyne mill in Sydney (below). This was the prelude to the Dunlop Art Contest of the 1950s in which many of Australia's greatest post-war artists competed.

*Sir John Grice sat on the first board of the company and was chairman from 1911 to 1929. This portrait, by
Sir John Longstaff, hangs in the offices of National Australia Bank, of which Grice was also chairman.*

Dunlop's advertising was quick to make the most of world events. Britain and Australia entered the First World War in August 1914, after Germany had violated a treaty ('just a scrap of paper') and invaded Belgium. Dunlop's billboards around Australia appealed at once to patriotism and the British Bulldog.

TYRES -
that make light of heavy work

DUNLOP PERDRIAU
RUBBER CO.,LTD.

A 5L

SPORT & SAND SHOES

RANGER
Double texture bleached duck, tan leather toe-cap and eyelet facings, crepe sole, wedge heel. Men's only.

CONQUEST.
Oxford, double texture bleached duck, eyelets ventilation in vamp. Rubber toe cap. Crepe sole, flat heel. Men's only.

PASTIME—WHITE
Heavy unbleached duck, unlined, white rubber toe-cap, white sole, flat heel. Men's, Women's, Youths', Boys', Children's.

PASTIME—CREPE FINISH
Oxford, heavy unbleached duck, unlined. Crepe finish sole, flat heel. Men's, Women's, Youths', Boys' and Girls'. and Children's.

PASTIME—TWO TONE
Heavy unbleached duck, unlined, brown rubber toe-cap and foxing, drab crepe sole, flat heel. Men's only.

PASTIME—
Heavy unbleached duck, unlined, white rubber toe-cap, crepe sole, flat heel. Men's, Women's, Youths', Boys', Children's. Also with drab crepe sole for Men and Youths.

Dunlop

Above: An advertisement from the early 1930s following the merger of Dunlop and Perdriau.

Left: By 1934, the era of the sandshoe, Dunlop was a force in footwear.

The company's leather-bound ledger (1893–96) and first minute book (1899).

'Let Berlei discover the Enchantress in you!': a wartime slogan of 1941, just before clothes were rationed by the Australian government.

Only a united attack — and a continuation of the economic slump — would drive Rapson to the wall. In February 1932 the representatives of Dunlop Perdriau and Goodyear agreed to make an all-out assault on Rapson by cutting the price of all tubes by thirty per cent, subject to the consent of Goodyear's head office in Ohio, and by slicing fifteen per cent from the price of second-grade tyres, which were Rapson's speciality. Rapson hung on, hoping that sales of tyres in Australia would at last begin to rise.

In autumn 1932 Rapson's directors could wait no longer. Their firm went into liquidation and their factory and stock were bought by Dunlop. Many of the Rapson machines, especially the twenty-seven watchcase heaters used for vulcanising the rubber in the tyres, were shipped from Launceston and installed at Dunlop's three tyre factories at Montague, Footscray and Drummoyne. A Victorian dealer bought the remaining Rapson tyres at the bargain counter, at fifty-nine per cent off the list price. He agreed to dispose of them within four months, after which the tyre market would cease to be the scene of continuous price-cutting. Or so it was hoped. Meanwhile the Rapson factory on the riverbank in Tasmania remained a white elephant and attempts to sell it did not succeed until 1938.

If Rapson had lasted for another four months it might have gained new life from the revival of sales of tyres. Signs of recovery from the depression were visible in June 1932. Compared to the previous June, the total sales of Dunlop Perdriau were almost five per cent higher in money terms and much higher in quantities. But the increase in sales was weak in Queensland and invisible in New South Wales, now the most important state for the company's business. In Sydney the radical policies of the Labor Premier, J. T. Lang, and the closure of the huge Government Savings Bank of New South Wales had punctured economic confidence. The Dunlop directors, like most business leaders, remained suspicious of Sydney. In January 1931 they had taken out an expensive insurance policy against the possibility of damage being caused to their factories and overall trade by riot and public commotion; a year later it was not renewed for five Australian states but was specifically renewed for New South Wales. The sad story of commerce in New South Wales was reflected in the sales returns: in June 1932 the Sydney branch's sales of all Dunlop products were half of one per cent lower than in the comparable month of 1931, but in the Melbourne branch the sales had risen in the same period by twenty-four per cent and in Adelaide and Perth by just over thirty per cent. The Dunlop directors had been eager to save money by closing the big footwear factory at Abbotsford (Victoria) and concentrating all footwear activities at Drummoyne (New South Wales), but the risky political and economic outlook in Sydney made them defer the decision year after year, until 1935.

'Surely the clouds will lift,' said Watt, the chairman. The clouds were blown away more by his firm's sales of the general rubber products than of tyres. Dunlop made many different items, and some were essential for households and were bought both in poor and prosperous years. People might sell their car but they rode their bike — perhaps more than before — and it needed a new tyre once in every few years. Walking more often than in the past, people needed new shoes. Hospitals and other public buildings were still busy and their rubber flooring became worn, and Dunlop had to replace it. Moreover during the dismal years of 1931 and 1932 the firm entered new fields. It made the strong boxes in which the car battery was fitted; under the guidance of a Swiss specialist it made webbing. The Barnet Glass factory, with the help of a visiting English expert, T. O. Heappey, was soon making five hundred dozen golf balls each week. In the rising enthusiasm for plastics, Dunlop moulded a variety of bakelite and synthetic resin products though it unwisely sold its plastics interests — the genesis of the profitable firm of Moulded Products — just when plastics were about to boom. During the depressed years a corner of the factory at Montague also began to make small batches of foam rubber for cushions and seats, though the foam-rubber seat did not catch the public's imagination until a few years later when the mania for erecting suburban cinemas gave many Australians their first experience of the most comfortable of all seats.

In the second half of 1932 the recovery of sales was heartening, but revenue was recovering from a miserable base. In a typical month Dunlop Perdriau's sales were about twenty per cent above those for the same month in 1931. In November 1932 there was silent cheering when monthly sales returned to the figure — still a lean figure — for January 1931. The sales of tyres were now recovering: more cars were on the roads, and new cars were bought in numbers unimaginable one year ago, though far behind the sales of six years ago. After the closing of the Rapson tyre factory in Tasmania, Dunlop had a clearer field with Goodyear its only competitor. There was only one catch. Dunlop had developed the habit of buying out competitors rather than smoking them out by sheer competition. Competitively Dunlop was not strong. Its only competitor, Goodyear, was full of drive. Though Goodyear was hit hard by its dependence on tyres — the most miserable part of the whole rubber industry — it was highly skilled in this speciality and could call on technical advice and designs from its own parent in the United States, still the world's leader in tyres. Moreover Goodyear could not be bought out by Dunlop. It was not for sale, and Dunlop traditionally had difficulty in coping with competitors that were not for sale.

Goodyear snatched business from Dunlop in the early 1930s. For three years in succession it supplied about half of the tyres on the new cars registered in Australia. It made the most of its American connections. The Ford and Chevrolet (General Motors) and most of the major makes of American cars sold in Australia were usually fitted with Goodyear tyres made in Sydney. The notable exceptions were the Essex and Hudson cars which ran on Barnet Glass tyres. On the other hand the makers or assemblers of English cars sold in

Australia preferred Dunlop and Perdriau tyres, but the English car was not so popular as the American in the showrooms of Australian dealers. In the market for replacement tyres — the tyres bought in ones and twos for the older cars — the Dunlop brands were more successful. Nonetheless competition between Dunlop and Goodyear became so intense, and profits so precarious, that in February 1933 the two firms agreed to sell their tyres at the same price to dealers. Adventures in retail price maintenance were embarked on every few years in the tyre industry. This pact survived for about eight months. It was ended by those tyre dealers for whom a fixed price would mean slow strangulation.

A successful seller of tyres traditionally relied on the quality of the particular make of tyre he sold and its relative price. Quality, however, was not all-important. The latest model in car tyres might be sold with ease for a year or more before a deficiency in its wearing quality became apparent. Even then many customers were happy to cling to the brand name they usually bought or the brand name favoured by the tyre dealer or garage they patronised. In addition to quality, brand name and price, the tyre trade was influenced by the skills of individual salesmen. The selling of new tyres was a profitable circus for gifted salesmen. Even in the depression Dunlop alone employed, on its own payroll, about two hundred outdoors salesmen who, driving a company car, went to the suburban and country dealers and used all their persuasion to make them buy more Dunlop tyres. Concessions went to the tyre dealers who sold big numbers of tyres. Part of the concession, sometimes all, was passed onto the customers. As a result the price of tyres normally differed from one tyre dealer to another. If the official price did not differ, the secret price did. Price cutting was almost a disease in the tyre business, and in some seasons it was an epidemic.

The tyre companies now knew roughly how many tyres were sold each year in each state but in the various districts they still relied on the old practice of sending a man to a football final or the agricultural showgrounds where he walked between the parked cars and counted the total tyres of each brand. Such counts privately made in Victoria about September 1934 show the remarkable variations from district to district. Thus Barnet Glass had only thirteen per cent of the tyres in cars parked outside the Geelong showground but twenty-four of the tyres at Benalla. In turn Goodyear could claim only twenty-one per cent of the tyres at the Benalla show but double that percentage at Corowa, on the Sydney side of the Murray River just across the river from Victoria. At Corowa the Dunlop Perdriau tyres were only one-third of all the tyres present on cars but at Benalla they constituted half of all tyres on the parked cars. Neither the quality nor price of tyres could explain such remarkable contrasts in the popularity of the same tyre in different districts. The main explanation was the zest and flair of the company salesmen servicing a district and the skill of the local tyre dealers.

In the head office of Dunlop there was a reluctance to face the conclusion that the company was not succeeding as it should have succeeded. Some of its executives knew that their car tyres were in no way superior to those of their main competitor. They knew that their truck tyres were inferior, though they were not sure whether the 'tread cracking' in many truck tyres arose from the Lancashire cotton fabric purchased through Dunlop England or from the zinc oxide used in the rubber compound. In July 1933 Dunlop employed Robert Blackwood, previously a lecturer in engineering at the University of Melbourne, to take charge of the systematic testing of tyres. His appointment, not of high status at the time, was the first public hint that the company was determined to improve its engineering standards. Fourteen years later, Blackwood was to become chief executive of the company, which by then was far more proficient technically than the one he had entered.

The officials at 108 Flinders Street were increasingly confident. They had survived the depression. Sales of nearly all their rubber goods were rising. Their company had a prestige which was enhanced by its part in the celebrations held in 1934 to mark the centenary of the colonisation of Victoria. The richest road cycle race in the history of the British Empire was sponsored as a major celebration, and S. R. Lough and Harry James of Dunlop were the co-organisers of the race.

While cycle tyres were now a lesser source of income than car tyres, Dunlop's factories still made a greater number of cycle tyres than car tyres. The typical household in Australia owned several bikes but no car; a cycle race was still glamorous. Therefore the public interest was high on the morning of 20 October 1934 when the cavalcade of racing cyclists, including two French champions, Nino Borsari of Italy and Victoria's own Hubert Opperman ('Oppy always rides on Dunlop tyres') assembled at the gates of government house in St Kilda Road for the start of the first leg to Warrnambool. Seven days later a big crowd assembled around the asphalt cycling track at the natural amphitheatre at Como Park in South Yarra to wait for the cyclists to complete the final leg from Mirboo North. Mel Morris of 3LO was there to broadcast the spectacle in his deep slow-speaking voice, old Sir John Grice, then in his last months on the board, was probably at home, 'tuning in' to his radio to hear the exciting finish, while His Majesty's Grenadier Guards Band was ready to march onto the arena as soon as the race was over. But no matter how exciting the finish, no event of that year could match, for W. A. Watt, the news that the Duke of Gloucester, on his official visit to Australia, was being driven to all his royal engagements on the latest brand of Dunlop tyre.

Dunlop's supremacy was not entirely secure. A Melbourne businessman was about to test the popularity of its tyres. He believed that he could manufacture a superior tyre and outsell Dunlop. At the end of 1933 Frank Beaurepaire, a humble retreader of tyres who knew how to sell new tyres, began to build his Olympic tyre factory at West Footscray. Here was an undeniable sign that Dunlop's merger of 1929 had not really succeeded. One of the biggest mergers in Australia's industrial history, it had seemed certain to sew up a large part of the tyre market in the continent, but less than five years later it was being challenged by a complete newcomer who often purchased wholesale from Dunlop but was not even able to pay all his tyre bills on time.

When the first rumours of Beaurepaire's tyre venture reached the head office of Dunlop, they were not treated seriously. How could he, a simple retreader working at the humdrum end of the tyre trade, finance a tyre factory and actually compete with the biggest tyre firm in Australia? In theory Beaurepaire should have had no hope of competing. Dunlop, however, was complacent and inefficient. Even six years after the great merger, Dunlop, Perdriau and Barnet Glass virtually continued as three separate firms, each firm with its factory and sales organisation and distinctive brands of tyres and each with its own spirit and set of loyalties. It was a phantom merger, and the time was coming when a leader would have to convert it into a real merger.

That man Holbrook

H OLBROOK MANAGED the rubber factory at Drummoyne as if he were an old captain of a sailing-ship running into a storm. His orders were delivered in few words. His tone of voice and manner were blunt. He expected employees to work hard and he roared like a lion when incompetence was reported to him. If a visitor came to the open door of his office and he did not wish to see the visitor he slammed the door. He was utterly independent. He symbolised the way in which, after the merger, most activities went on as if the merger had never happened.

When the head office in Melbourne sent instructions that displeased him or challenged his authority he gritted his teeth. He knew that with patience a way could be found to circumvent the Melbourne orders. He was proud of his subordinates who helped him to frustrate head office but he did not easily express thanks to them. His emotions he expressed more easily with gestures and shouts and occasionally an impetuous action. His brother Reg managed a part of the factory which occasionally produced more than its quota of faulty truck tyres. Shown a faulty tyre, Holbrook lifted it and threw it with all his strength at his brother, knocking him over.

It was a sure sign of the reserve with which he was viewed on the factory floor that he was mostly spoken of simply as 'Holbrook'. To his face, however, he was Mr Holbrook or Sir. Originating in the Isleworth Rubber Company in England, he was one of those self-made managers who was promoted from job to job because he could control men and do his work with maximum results. It is fair to say that the exact opposite of the Holbrooks, the English shop stewards of the next generation, were partly a reaction to his kind of manager. Holbrook's bark was louder than his bite; he begrudgingly respected those who were forthright towards him. He even had a dash of humour, though he could completely batten it down for days on end.

A crowd of Drummoyne employees, gathered to farewell Holbrook in 1935.

His sense of fun was more often quiet than boisterous. It was the custom for foremen or other bosses on the factory floor to send a lad to collect a billy of hot tea; but a decision to dispatch the boy for tea just before the shift was about to end — in short to dawdle and to drink the tea in the last minutes of the shift — was seen by Holbrook as malingering. One day, about twenty minutes before the whistle blew, he saw a factory lad carrying a billy of tea.

'Who's tea is that?' shouted Holbrook.

'Bushell's, sir!' called back the lad, displaying a sense of fun. Holbrook was so amused, so taken with the lad's presence of mind, that he asked somebody else for the name of the boy and awarded him a small rise in pay. At the back of his mind was probably the thought that the factory should reward those who were bright and alert. At Drummoyne a surprising amount of experience and talent worked under Holbrook. In an old time way the factory was efficient, and by any definition it was innovative.

When a large factory was taken over by an outside firm, a frequent dilemma was how to handle the Holbrooks. That species of factory manager was common, though declining. When companies like Dunlop, Perdriau and Barnet Glass all merged, the main advantages of the merger could be lost if the factories continued as if they were independent empires. Holbrook, in managing the big Perdriau factory at Drummoyne, gave the impression that for him the merger hardly existed. Barnet Glass's factory at Footscray was also continued with a high level of independence. The fact that W. A. Watt from Barnet Glass was chairman of the merged company and that most of the senior executives did not come from Montague meant that people like Holbrook received a heartening measure of protection.

In Barnet Glass the equivalent of Holbrook was F. S. Ormiston. He was more courteous than Holbrook but almost as pigheaded. He was in a stronger position to guard his old firm of Barnet Glass and his own independence because he was joint managing director of the merged company. Under his wings, Barnet Glass went its own way. Three episodes in 1933 reveal the power of his protection. In January at a time when the account books of the merged company were spotted with bad and doubtful debts, and every effort was made to collect them, the Barnet Glass office privately decided that its favoured customers should be given an extension of time in which to pay. Accordingly Dunlop, making successful efforts to collect bad debts, learned later that some customers were able to pay because Barnet Glass had simultaneously been persuaded to grant them more credit. In April it was revealed that Barnet Glass, exceeding the budget for advertising which had been precisely set by head office, had privately been given permission to make its own rules with the blessing of Ormiston, the very man who was in charge of enforcing the budget in that cheese-paring year. Ormiston himself went on an overseas tour early in the year but feared that in his absence Barnet Glass might lose some independence — in short that the interests of the merged company might be given precedence over one of its parts. So he urged Watt, the chairman, to protect Barnet Glass, arguing that its profits were essential to the well-being of Dunlop Perdriau. Watt could well have replied that co-ordination between the three former firms might have ensured even higher profits.

Despite the merger the three old factories continued in most ways as before, selling the same products, under the same brand names. The only difference was that in competing with one another they were not allowed to cut each other's throat. In 1931, at a directors' meeting of Dunlop Perdriau, Major-General Hughes pointed out that the merged company was more than two years' old but that little reorganising of its activities had taken place. E. M. Perdriau made the same complaint when he was acting as chairman of the company. The severity of the depression was a powerful argument for rationalising the activities of the three big factories but the argument was not accepted by the chairman and a majority of directors. The employees certainly gained from the existing duplication because there were more jobs than would otherwise have existed. The shareholders, however, lost because profits were lower. The Australian motorists lost also because their tyres were more expensive, coming from three plants, rather than one more efficient plant.

In these years of indecision, Holbrook flourished. He announced, privately but loudly, that he did not want his staff at Drummoyne to be 'tainted with the

Melbourne brush'. From time to time the head office in Melbourne made efforts to develop a uniform method of recording the costs and analysing the efficiency of the various factories, but Holbrook was hostile. He did not care for paperwork — some of it he did not fully understand — and he was suspicious of Melbourne interfering in his domain.

At the Drummoyne factory, a young accountant, Bert Wittig, was chosen by Dunlop's accountants in Melbourne to learn the system of factory accounting used by Barnet Glass and carry it back to his own factory. Wittig did not realise how perilous was this mission to Melbourne. While Holbrook sanctioned the month-long visit he was reluctant to allow Wittig to introduce changes to the time-honoured method of accounting used at his own factory. Wittig on returning by train to Sydney with the new ideas made various attempts to speak to Holbrook. He called on Holbrook's secretary, and that man put the request to Holbrook who replied that he was much too busy. Three more times the same request was refused: Holbrook was always too busy if he detected a danger of being infected by ideas from Melbourne factories. Wittig, knowing the instructions he had received from Melbourne, made a fifth attempt to inform his boss early one morning with no result.

That afternoon he waited in the street for Holbrook to return from lunch. At last he would corner him. Holbrook came into sight, saw the young accountant and told him 'to get to hell away from me'. For good measure he announced that he would see nobody tarred with the Melbourne brush. Holbrook then walked into the factory and, to his surprise, he was followed everywhere by Wittig. After an hour Holbrook turned on the Melbourne-tarred accountant and repeated that he did not wish to speak with him, and raced over to his office which he entered by a side door, slamming and locking it. Wittig — his determination deserved a medal — calmly walked around to the front door of the office and walked in, pulled a chair alongside him and sat down in front of the enraged Holbrook. Only when Wittig threatened to catch that evening's train to Melbourne and report his dilemma did Holbrook calm down a little, light his pipe which he kept in his desk, and say in almost a fatherly way: 'Well, laddie, what's your trouble?' The trouble was outlined and discussed for more than an hour, after which Holbrook gave permission for the introducing of a new method of costing the factory's work. The method apparently eliminated the work previously done by some twenty clerks. Even Holbrook eventually appreciated the daily and weekly figures he was given in the form of simple graphs. For all his rages and eccentric ways he was highly efficient in managing most activities in the factory but he was reluctant to accept change in those activities he did not understand, especially if the orders for change should come from Melbourne.

The chief accountant at the Montague factory once invited Wittig, then visiting head office in Melbourne, to come out to his home for dinner. Inside the house Wittig, on meeting the host's son, asked him what he hoped to do when he grew up. Instantly the father interjected with sharp wit: 'I am going to keep him away from school and make him a factory manager'. In categorising factory managers as uneducated, he had Holbrook in mind.

Holbrook, while not strong in tact, formal education and other qualities, was a man and a half. He was probably the best manager Dunlop possessed. This was recognised at head office, where as early as 1931 a move was initiated to bring him to Melbourne and place him in charge of Montague, the firm's largest but least efficient factory. At Montague the rumours that Holbrook might be arriving were heard with squawks of dismay. To invite Holbrook to Melbourne was like inviting the fox to live in the henhouse. Ormiston, who was the managing director with a portfolio covering the factories (his partner Fenton controlled the sales and administration), could not bear to think of Holbrook coming one step closer to Melbourne. So when the executive committee of the board met on 15 May 1931 and actually proposed the transfer of Holbrook to Melbourne, Ormiston said 'no'. Perdriau, opportunely chairing the meeting in the absence of Watt who was attending to company business in Queensland, had no doubt that Holbrook would perform wonders at Montague. He also was quietly pleased with the idea of an old Perdriau man taking over the Dunlop factory, which he still instinctively saw as a rival. In the end all the members of the executive committee except Ormiston voted that Holbrook be transferred to Montague.

When Watt returned to Melbourne and heard of the decision he was angry. Why he was angry is no longer clear. Perhaps he thought such an important decision should not have been taken in his absence; possibly the topic had been discussed at an earlier meeting and Watt, not approving of Holbrook, had managed to derail the idea; or perhaps, because he was the Barnet Glass chairman before the merger, he sided with his old colleague Ormiston. When the executives of the board met again one week later Watt spoke his mind. The minutes of the meeting are the essence of tact, for they simply state that Watt deplored 'the impropriety of the procedure adopted in his absence'. He was so angry that he disbanded the committee and set up a new executive body called the 'sub-committee of directors' of which Ormiston was a member but Fenton was not. The astonishing decision to include one but exclude the other was a sign that Watt's emotional temperature was close to boiling. The outcome was that Holbrook did not come to Melbourne, the inefficiencies at Montague lay untackled, and the merger really lay unconsummated, though Fenton was eventually forgiven and invited to join the powerful sub-committee.

Why Watt was so touchy and so reluctant to consolidate factories which were not co-operating with each other remains unclear. Nearly three years later a consolidating plan was discussed again, at a time when the profits of the Dunlop factories were disappointing; but Watt would not allow much change. He said he was supported by 'several reasons, economical, legal and political'.

Admittedly Barnet Glass was still legally a separate company with its own preference shares but that was not an insuperable reason, for when in 1941 the time for urgent action finally came, Dunlop made a public offer for the two hundred thousand preference shares in Barnet Glass and so ended the old firm's life as a public company.

Holbrook, whose mere presence at Montague would have galvanised operations, remained in Sydney. To refuse to make full use of Holbrook's rough drive and dynamism was perhaps wise. It was not wise, however, to delay tackling the inefficiency which ran right though the big company.

As business recovered from the depression and the sale of rubber goods increased, Dunlop Perdriau did not gain its full share of the increased prosperity. It was not one company: in practice it was at least three companies, sometimes working together and sometimes working against each other. In a real sense the merger of the 1920s had proved to be a myth. It was, in retrospect, a merger stitched together to defend existing rubber companies rather than to hunt for new business. Therefore it was still vulnerable to competition from rivals.

The new rival, the Olympic Rubber Company, beginning to make truck and car tyres at Footscray in 1934, gave Dunlop Perdriau a fright. Expected to struggle for business, it snatched business, much of it from Dunlop. As most of the new executives employed by Frank Beaurepaire of Olympic had worked with Dunlop, they knew the weak points of their old employer. Dunlop, bruised and humiliated, still refused to make unpalatable decisions. Rather than bring down the raging lion from Drummoyne, or rather than close down the Barnet Glass factory and transfer its activities to one Melbourne and one Sydney factory, it looked for another solution. Ormiston as managing director had the idea of moving the head office from the city of Melbourne to the Montague factory, so that contact between directors and senior staff would be enhanced. In November 1934 the plan was 'abandoned temporarily' — in other words, permanently.

Major-General Hughes, a Dunlop director since 1899, was not regarded by his younger colleagues as the most wide-awake of those who sat at the crowded board table. Accordingly he must have surprised them with his blunt hint that the company was acting like a fool. His letter of 31 January 1935, deploring the fact that the company owned so many competing factories, asked why all the machinery could not be concentrated on one site? Though his scheme was rejected he gave momentum to the move for change.

At last, during the first half of 1935, the directors acted. The old Barnet Glass family of Ormiston, now deemed unsuited for the posts it held, was dethroned. F. S. Ormiston, who was one of the two managing directors of Dunlop, was removed from his post. No vote of thanks was expressed to him, such was the tension. In another provocative but necessary move, Gerald Ormiston was removed from his position of head of the factory at Montague.

In retaliation the Barnet Glass board, still possessing much independence, invited him back to the Barnet Glass factory at Footscray and appointed him a director as well as head of the factory. The Dunlop Perdriau board intervened. In May 1936, after a brief struggle, the independence of the Barnet Glass board came to an end with the appointment of three directors from Dunlop Perdriau.

The fireworks were only beginning. Meanwhile Fred Holbrook was brought down from the old Perdriau factory at Drummoyne in Sydney to become 'acting controller — Montague factory'. After a show of strength, he was made superintendent of all the factories. At Montague he said constantly that he was astonished at what he found. His indignation, some observers said, was mixed with concealed pleasure that the heartland of his old enemy was so incompetent. In March 1935 his report to the board on the No. 1 unit at the Montague mill was damning. The equipment was poor, the 'Festoon' method of building tyres was poor, the specifications to which tyres were made were slipshod, as were many of the employees. The board read with alarm — but satisfaction that they had found the right man for the job — that forty-seven per cent of tyres produced in the unit were defective. The wastage rate, under Holbrook's fierce gaze, suddenly fell to twenty-seven per cent. Soon, he promised the directors, only five per cent of the tyres might be wasted. A team of trouble-shooters arrived from Drummoyne to show Montague what could be done with improved machinery, techniques and supervision.

The directors approved of swift reforms. C. W. McKay, a friend of Holbrook, was hired as the motor-tube expert from the Firestone Rubber Co. in Akron, Ohio, his two-year appointment a sign that Dunlop's products were open to challenge by fierce competition from Olympic. The Drummoyne factory was expanded with the installing of the shoe machinery from Abbotsford (Victoria), and the truck-tyre section from Montague. Barnet Glass factory at Footscray was warned that it might progressively be closed, and its leather-shoe department was sent to Drummoyne. The engineering department at Montague was reduced to a simple core, with most of the work let out by tender. Obsolete machines — and scrap heaps piled high with unwanted parts and machines — were sold at each of the major factories. A junkyard is often a sign of indecision: for some six years Dunlop had been undecided.

Amidst all the pruning, grafting or relocating of activities, one weakness persisted. It was the inefficiency of the whole operation, whether factory men and women, foremen and managers, or the machines themselves. The quality of certain sizes of tyres was suspect. Many tyres were too dear. In consequence Dunlop did not gain its share of the nation's increased volume of tyre sales fostered by the recovery of confidence. In March 1935, Chester Cross, the sales director, decreed that the company employed far more commercial travellers and salesmen than the size of its business could justify. He recommended that they be reduced from 224 to 178.

The early effect of a smaller selling force was a loss of sales. Many of the sacked salesmen had excellent relations with garage owners and tyre dealers in their own network of towns or suburbs, and with their departure some of the business passed to Olympic and Goodyear. At the end of July 1935 the Dunlop board learned that in the last twelve months the registration of new cars in Australia had risen by sixty per cent but Dunlop's share of the tyre market had risen by only forty-five per cent. Some of the loss was beyond control. In the new-car market, the Dunlop and Perdriau tyres were mainly fitted to new English cars but in the last year the English makes had been outsold by American and other foreign cars. Of American cars, Ford was the main user of Dunlop's tyres, but for the time being Ford was being outsold by General Motors who favoured Goodyear. It was a blow to Dunlop in what was intended to be its year of resurgence.

At the board meeting at 108 Flinders Street, Melbourne, on 16 August 1935, two visitors from 'The English Co.' were introduced, F. R. M. de Paula and Reay Geddes. Perhaps only once in a decade did senior staff from Fort Dunlop make the long journey to Australia, but these were urgent times. A specialist in organising the shop floor by 'time and motion study', de Paula told the directors that the stop watch, the measuring tape, a little common sense and, above all, the patient observing of every movement in every job on the work floor of every factory would make Dunlop competitive again. The directors agreed. What Holbrook thought of the work-study teams invading *his* factory floor is not on record. In the new year D. V. Merrick landed in Sydney, fresh from the Dunlop factory in Buffalo, NY, and began to apply the latest techniques to the factory in Drummoyne. R. W. Ashley, a cost accountant sent up from Melbourne, was the understudy. Sometimes this new method called *time and motion* was dubbed 'time and commotion'; and yet some uproar was necessary if Dunlop was to continue to give work to thousands.

There was urgency. The company's profits were slipping at a time when other manufacturing companies in Australia were recovering. In the opening months of 1935 the price of Dunlop's ordinary shares fell by one-fifth. No explanation came from the directors. The most recent statement by the chairman, W. A. Watt, was as far back as September 1934 when he told the annual meeting of shareholders that they could expect to share in the nation's and the company's returning prosperity. The company still was divided into preference shares, on which a dividend of ten per cent was the first priority, and ordinary shares which received a low dividend in poor years and as much as 10 per cent in the prosperous year of 1928–29. The ten per cent preference dividend required a profit of 93 000 pounds. In contrast, to pay a mere two and a half per cent dividend on the big number of ordinary shares required almost a similar sum in profits. In the year ending June 1934 Dunlop Perdriau had paid a five per cent dividend on ordinary shares, and still had a small sum left over for a rainy day. In the following year, however, everything seemed to fall to pieces. The net profit was almost halved. Watt's sole comment in his printed statement to shareholders was that the 'net trading result is much below specifications'. He did not specify how much: presumably the figure was acutely embarrassing. The pitifully shrunken profit actually earned would have permitted the payment of a dividend of one per cent on ordinary shares but the directors wisely decided not to pay such a derisory dividend. After the end of the financial year 1934–35, for the first time in shareholders' memory, no dividend was paid on the ordinary shares. In a year of hope amongst the big manufacturing companies, Dunlop was an exception.

Even after the vigorous wielding of the accountants' axe, Dunlop's costs remained too high. Latest reports from Dunlop's team of travelling salesmen were disturbing. For September 1935 the total sales of all products actually fell by six per cent compared to sales in the previous September. For October they fell by eight per cent, for November one per cent, with a token recovery of one per cent in December. Footwear was one weakness. The Dunlop sand-shoes (the common name for runners or trainers or sneakers or tennis shoes) were not capturing their share of the market, and sales actually fell in the space of five months by the enormous total of 471 000 pairs. Compared to the corresponding months of the previous year the sale of new tyres in place of old tyres on existing cars, motor bikes and trucks all fell away in the five months from June to October. The sale of solid tyres for the big lorries fell; so too did sales of the best-selling Kromhyd heels and soles which in the 1930s were fastened in their millions to the leather soles of new or worn shoes. As consolation the rubber hot-water bottles boomed. In a diverse business involving hundreds of rubber products there were always winners as well as losers, but now the disappointments were everywhere.

There was one remedy. A powerful general manager had to be found. It was agreed that he must arrive without preconceptions, and without allies or enemies. He must sum up the company's defects and strengths and recommend to the board what should be done in the interests of the company. In April 1935 the search for superman was begun. Sir Colin Fraser, who since 1927 had acted as an alternate director for one of the absent heads of English Dunlop, took on the task which W. L. Baillieu had previously fulfilled. On a visit to England he looked for experienced managers who might be suitable for Australian conditions. By July 1935 he believed he had found his superman. Charles Proctor, the former Melbourne secretary who was still with Dunlop in England and still rising up the executive ladder, agreed with Fraser that the chosen man would fit in with Australian conditions and practices. In Melbourne, W. A. Watt, the chairman, was persuaded by all the papers and references sent to him that the right man had been found.

Watt called a special meeting of the board to consider the applicants, for Australians as well as Englishmen were amongst the contenders for the post.

Watt shrewdly decided that a unanimous decision was called for. Otherwise the old Perdriau or Barnet Glass sympathisers sitting on the board might decide eventually to sabotage the sweeping reforms which a new general manager would make, reforms that inevitably would destroy the concept of three separate rubber organisations working side by side. That concept of the threesome was expensive. It was doomed. Watt called the directors together on 11 July 1935 in order to appoint a strong general manager. As two directors — the 'indisposed' Alexander Stewart and the Sydney accountant F. J. Smith — could not come to Melbourne, Watt made the rare concession of permitting the board meeting to be held in Sydney to ensure the fullest possible attendance. At the meeting in the Hotel Australia in Sydney, Watt read aloud the letters and cables, each of which recommended the appointment of the same English contender. The directors agreed that here was the superman they had sought.

His name was plain Bartlett — the board minutes gave him no initials. His salary was to be a high five thousand pounds. His task was to bring cohesion and order to the three separate manufacturing organisations, and to cut out duplication. In short his mission was to make the merger created half a dozen years ago a fact rather than merely an intention. He was placed on the payroll eleven days after his appointment. After touring various Dunlop plants in England and North America he went to California, boarded the Pacific steamship *Monterey* and sailed for Australia, landing on 6 December 1935. The company would not be the same again.

Wallace Andrew Bartlett, the new general manager, was aged forty-one. Born in Midhurst, Sussex, he had emigrated at about the age of fifteen to Canada where he was trained as an electrical engineer. One of his early jobs was with the Westinghouse Company in its Hell's Gate power-station in New York State. Not quite twenty-one when the First World War broke out, he joined the Canadian army and went to war. Transferring to the Royal Flying Corps he is said to have become a captain. Back in North America he moved into the new radio division of Westinghouse. The wireless was in its infancy, and he grew with the infant. Returning to England on behalf of a Canadian firm he opened a radio factory in Slough, near London, and made headphones for crystal sets. At the age of thirty-five he was managing a radio factory in Sidcup, Kent, and supervising several thousand employees when he was appointed general manager of a new public company, Kolster-Brandes Limited. When he was chosen for the Australian post his experience in rubber was probably negligible. Quick tours of Dunlop plants on both sides of the Atlantic gave him some familiarity with rubber manufacturing before he set out for Australia. People tend to prescribe their own experience for others, and when he tried to recruit outsiders for very senior positions in Dunlop in Australia he did not regard experience with rubber as vital. It was just another manufacturing process. He saw himself as essentially a manager.

Wallace Andrew Bartlett.

After he had been in Melbourne less than three weeks he was invited to the annual dinner of the Dunlop Staff Club at the Montague factory. He shook dozens of hands: he felt all eyes were watching him. The chairman, W. A. Watt, a wonderful chairman of a dinner, welcomed him with magic phrases. Bartlett stood up, to applause, and made a sincere speech people long remembered. In essence he said: 'I thank you for your generous welcome, but I think it would have been better for you to withhold your applause until you have had time to judge me on the results of the job I do. Mine is no easy task, as some part of it will be unpleasant for both you and me'. A slight shuffle must have been heard from the floor as the feet of his hearers moved uneasily.

At every office and factory of Dunlop the rumours and news of Bartlett's activities and decisions were heard with a mixture of fear and hope: fear of employees that they might lose their jobs, hope that the oppressive atmosphere at some of the factories would be lifted. The early impressions of him — by those who had nought to fear — were favourable. He was good-looking in a quiet way, his hair was brilliantined and neatly combed back with a studied-casual sweep, his clean shaven face was pleasant, and sometimes he smiled with utter spontaneity and warmth. There was a style about the way he walked and the way he climbed out of his expensive English car. He was energetic around the factories; he was easily approached by those who carried worries; he talked easily with the grimy rubber-workers but kept a certain distance and remoteness that seemed to safeguard his authority. After a time the chief engineer at Montague, E. N. White, came to the conclusion that Bartlett was one in a hundred: 'We all knew that our worries and troubles were his, and our triumphs and successes were his pride'.

His standards were high, and in his first year he saw much that fell short of his standards. In December 1936 a reporter from *Rydge's Business Journal* asked him his formula for personal success. His first requisite, he said, was thoroughness. Already he was showing what he meant by 'thoroughness'. Every department and every operation — he inspected them all. At Montague those loyal, long-suffering sub-managers and foremen who had already been inspected by Holbrook were scrutinised again. Bartlett was willing to delegate, to assign full responsibility and interfere as little as possible. An experienced sales manager, he saw that the manufacturing and selling sections of the organisation largely went their own way. In the storerooms he found a mountain of tyres — about two hundred thousand embracing all sizes. Knowing that this was a larger number of tyres than the firm could expect to sell in the next six months he called for a sharp fall in the output of new tyres. An overloaded warehouse, he insisted, was a waste of money.

At 108 Flinders Street, which was both the head office and the headquarters of the Victorian sales branch, he wondered what so many staff were doing. They were busy writing letters and producing statistics but he decided that many of the letters and statistics were of little use. He set up a small general manager's department — a mere five people of ability — and reduced the staff of head office by thirty-four. The Victorian branch was next pruned, eleven employees departing. As big retrenchments in clerical and sales staff had been made at 108 Flinders Street in the previous year the extent of over-staffing under the old order can easily be imagined. On the other hand it could be argued that the firm, in the worst years of the depression, had shown unusual loyalty to its old staff and tried to retain as many as possible on the payroll, though at the shareholders' expense.

Bartlett turned to the major issues of policy. He wondered why Dunlop and Perdriau were each producing their own best tyre. Why not produce one tyre even if it was branded differently? He looked a second time at the company's selling methods and found them chaotic. Many of the sales staff he found lethargic or dispirited. Were they the victims of earlier management which squashed suggestions and crushed individuality? He did not know the cause but he could see the effects. While the new firm of Olympic Tyres was sweeping all before it, its factory working around the clock, Dunlop sometimes had idle machines even during the day shift.

Bartlett looked at the purchasing of rubber and other raw materials and shuddered at the waste. Driven out to the riverbank factory of Barnet Glass at Footscray he admired its relative efficiency but wondered at its financial operations. And how, he thought, could he justify two duplicate factories each operating no more than three miles apart, and producing so many of the same products. P. J. Glass, still the chairman of the public company Barnet Glass, was persuaded that the duplication should cease. In October 1936 his board agreed to plan for the evacuation of its Footscray factory. Henceforth the Barnet Glass brand of tyres and other goods would be made either at Montague or Drummoyne and sold under the 'BG' label. Significantly, Barnet Glass retained a big following of customers, especially in Victoria, and the fear was that these people would desert Barnet Glass for Goodyear or Olympic once they learned that Barnet Glass tyres were now made by Dunlop Perdriau. As Bartlett argued, the economies of the situation outweighed the risk. For another three years Barnet Glass retained its own offices in Sydney and Melbourne and its own sales organisations. Finally, in November 1939, the Barnet Glass factory, which still stands in derelict state at Footscray, was bought by Bradford Cotton Mills of Sydney.

Bartlett's savings at the end of his first year were astonishing. Without counting the economies that would eventually accrue by transferring the Barnet Glass tyre-making plant to Montague he estimated the savings at 130 152 pounds. Those were not once-up savings but likely to be repeated every year. With his sharp knives he had saved a sum almost equal to the net profit of Dunlop in the last full year before he arrived. Of course he did not always carry the knife. He relied heavily on subordinates. 'I do not keep dogs and bark myself', he often said, meaning that he employed officials to do his barking.

Most of Bartlett's rivals were shown the door. Charles Cross, the sales director, resigned after Bartlett arrived. It was also easy to predict that Holbrook, in effect the head of all manufacturing, would fall out with Bartlett. The directors were told that at Montague, as a result of Holbrook's 'bullying tactics', the able men were leaving. A spirit of sullen resentment hung over the buildings, reported Bartlett. And so Holbrook resigned after less than two years at Montague. He was to be long remembered, and even today old employees talk of him with blunt indignation. Stan Orton, a tyre-builder who started in 1925 and wrote a short reminiscence of his years at Montague, tells how one day 'an animal called Holbrook' arrived with his team of executives: 'These people found fault with everything we did'. In fairness to Holbrook he found inefficiency everywhere and he pounced on it, but some of his reforms were as harmful for the employees as they were beneficial for the tyres.

Holbrook was replaced by William M. Holbeach who arrived from England in November 1936. The names of Holbeach and Holbrook were confusing, and when news of Holbeach's appointment was passed by word of mouth around the grimy mills at Montague, some workmen on mishearing the new name said with dismay: 'Not old Holbrook again! We thought they'd got rid of the animal.' The directors must have wondered when the confidential procession of disturbing reports would end. Holbeach the newcomer, while benign in manner, began to write about Montague as if Holbrook and Bartlett each had done nothing to improve efficiency.

Fortunately the company now depended less on tyres, the problem product. Between 1914 and 1934 the contribution of car and bicycle tyres to revenue had fallen from eighty to fifty per cent. 'We are now almost universal providers of rubber goods', said the chairman in September 1934.

Bartlett had no intention of reversing the trend. He proposed to the directors that at the Footscray works, they should make the wheels to go with the tyres. The directors announced the proposal and in 1938 Bartlett went to North America to cost it, eventually deferring it because Australia did not yet produce the special steels from which wheels were made. In the same year, he explored the possibility of erecting a factory in Australia to make from cotton the high-grade cords used in manufacturing tyres, and discussed the project with Davies Coop, the textile firm, and with English Dunlop and even Goodyear, his competitor in Sydney. One of the first long-distance telephone calls in the history of the company was made to speed the negotiations on cords. On Friday 11 February 1938 the board instructed Mr Bartlett to telephone London for advice, and at the weekend he spoke through the static to Charles Proctor who, now a director in London, had originally worked for Dunlop in Melbourne before wireless telegraphy was even invented.

While nothing came from the proposal to make wheels and the cotton cords used in tyres, another venture was astonishingly successful. Foam rubber was one of the few innovations which came to Australia straight from the research laboratories of the English Dunlop. Made from latex, the milky fluid of the rubber tree, and patented in 1929, it combined a sponge-like quality as well as a strength not achievable in a foam rubber manufactured from the normal dry rubber. This latex foam first appeared on the market as the comfortable Dunlopillo seat for the pillion or rear rider on a motor cycle. At first the riders of motor bikes found it hard to believe that a seat could be so compact and yet so soft. The product immediately spread to the drama and picture theatres where the normal chair was a padded seat without springs, and two plain wooden armrests. In 1932 in the Shakespeare Memorial Theatre at Stratford-upon-Avon the latex foam was used in the upholstery of seats — a permanent landmark in comfort, the foam rubber was about to work a miracle in the western world.

In Melbourne the company began to import latex in steel drums. Experimenting with the new process at Montague, R. M. Fitzpatrick reported privately in May 1932 that he could produce foam rubber by the new Dunlop patent. He called it 'latex sponge rubber'. Too busy at first with the making of trial batches of party balloons and surgical and household gloves — they too were made from the liquid latex rather than from the dry rubber — he soon was making the foam rubber. In June 1933 the 'Dipping Department' at Montague was making sponge cushions for the seats in Sydney trams and a total of 324 sponge seats for the Athenaeum Theatre in Collins Street, Melbourne. Then came a period when the sales of foam-rubber products were doubling every ten or twelve months. By mid-1935 the revenue from Dunlopillo was well over two per cent of the company's total revenue, and soon it was five per cent. Here was a product in which the Australians were at least as efficient as their colleagues in England and North America.

In the space of a few years the upholstery trade was turning to foam rubber. The seats of the latest motor cars and railway carriages made in Australia now consisted of Dunlop cushions encased in leather or leather-cloth. The new picture theatres in every major town and suburb of Australia were another market, and when Hoyts Theatres in 1936 decided to buy tens of thousands of Dunlopillo seats, they were given hire-purchase terms and allowed credit for three years (soon increased to five years) at an interest of five per cent a year. When people sitting in the theatres experienced for the first time the luxury of the new seats they asked for it in their armchairs and lounge suites. The new product was booming, and it was largely Dunlop's own. From 1936 A. N. Thomson Co. of Sydney, specialists in providing seats for picture theatres, was controlled by Dunlop.

At the start of 1939 the grand total of 126 000 cinema-goers could sit on Dunlopillo seats at the one time. The Dunlopillo mattress was not quite so fast in seducing people. At first there was suspicion of a bed of foam rubber, and the typical mattress with its filling of hair, kapok and flock remained normal: not until 1959 did Dunlop make a serious assault on the market by producing an inner-spring product. Meanwhile the foam rubber, being less dusty than

Men at the Woolston factory, near Christchurch (N.Z.), remove the lid from a Dunlopillo mattress-mould after curing.

the traditional mattress, was a boon for those suffering from hay fever. It was also the ideal cushion for those suffering from fractured limbs.

Amidst Bartlett's new ventures, one wide-open opportunity was lost. He failed to persevere with the new plastics industry in which his company was an early leader. In May 1934 the firm briefly increased its stake in plastics by taking over a small firm called Moulded Products and concentrating all machinery from Montague in the Moulded Products factory, a disused cable-tram depot in Scotchmer Street, North Fitzroy. For a time F. S. Ormiston became chairman and C. S. Butt the secretary of Moulded Products but the losses of the venture continued. Bartlett could not foresee the enormous increase in the uses for plastics nor the mass market for many plastic products. In essence the plastics section was making losses, and in 1936 the Dunlop board decided to sell the venture for a relatively small sum, on time-payment, to F. J. W. (John) Derham and his partners. Plastics boomed, Moulded Products was floated in 1939 into a public company which was innovative and quick-growing, and under its eventual name of Nylex Corporation was one of the top 150 companies in Australia. One sign of its success was its sale in 1981 to Dunlop of half of the shares in the cable-making firm of Olex. The price of that single transaction with its old-time owner was 56.2 million dollars.

Adrian Quist, one of Australia's greatest tennis players, worked for Dunlop when he was in the winning Davis Cup team of 1939.

In the fascinating history written about this small plastics company which Dunlop jettisoned, wonder was understandably expressed that such a prize should be eschewed by Dunlop. Tim Hewat, in *The plastics revolution: the story of Nylex*, presumably was expressing the speculations of Nylex officials of a later generation when he explained why Bartlett in 1936 walked away from the plastics industry. He said that English Dunlop in effect gave the order to Bartlett; that moreover Australian Dunlop was in a phase of concentrating on rubber and cutting out other activities. In fact, so far as can be ascertained, English Dunlop took no interest in the sale of Moulded Products. Similarly, Australian Dunlop generally was trying to expand beyond a dependence on rubber rather than trim down its operations. On the evidence at present available, Bartlett came to the conclusion, then shared by many, that plastics was not the great product of the future and that the losses already made by his company in plastics should not be increased, especially at a time of cost-cutting. In retrospect it was a mistake of magnitude.

Preferring sports goods to plastics as an avenue for expansion, Dunlop bought the Empire Racket Co. in 1937. To bring together all its sporting goods, it formed Dunlop Sports Co. Pty Ltd under A. A. McPherson. Adrian Quist became one of its directors, used Dunlop rackets when he played tennis for Australia, and was a wonderful asset for the company as well as a skilled promoter of its interests. Sporting goods became one of the glamorous sections of Dunlop, and were often advertised in the programmes which Dunlop, in a new adventure, sponsored on commercial radio at the prime time evening slots of a quarter part seven and eight o'clock. When Donald Budge came to Australia he used Dunlop equipment. When Australia defeated the United States in the final of the Davis Cup in September 1939, the heroes Bromwich and Quist brought more glory to Dunlop. Every Dunlop employee interested in sport was proud that Quist, who played in both singles and doubles, carried Australia towards victory by defeating the reigning Wimbledon champion, Bobby Riggs.

Under Bartlett the company's muscles grew, its vitality increased. The staff — those who remained — liked his way of doing business. The morale everywhere seemed to be higher. He personally took charge of selling, and the sales increased — aided by the return of prosperity. Profits were certainly higher. As a reward Bartlett's salary at the end of his first full year was increased from five thousand to six thousand pounds and just over a year later he was receiving the big salary of eight thousand pounds. In July 1937 he was made the alternate director to the chairman, and when W. A. Watt made the long sea voyage for discussions with English Dunlop, Bartlett occupied his seat. Now, in many ways, Bartlett was Dunlop.

The success of Bartlett came partly from the streamlined board. The company had begun the 1930s with an unwieldy board of thirteen — the outcome of the merging of the three rubber companies. So many voices around the table were unmanageable. Moreover many spoke primarily in the interests of their old factories and colleagues. In addition eight of the thirteen directors were chief executives, past or present, but the complexity of the company's situation and the fact that the merger was only half digested really called for a majority of independent directors who could see the tensions and impediments with fresh or neutral eyes. By the time Bartlett reached Melbourne the core of old executives had departed, the board had pared itself down to nine members, and before long it retained only one man, Harold Daniell, who could be seen as representing one of the three companies which had merged in 1928.

The smaller board had a different outlook on England. It was sympathetic to English Dunlop, and much more willing to co-operate with it and to share information and plans than had been the large and unpredictable board of thirteen members. In 1938, with the resignation of Clive Baillieu (son of W. L. Baillieu) from the board of Dunlop Perdriau, English Dunlop agreed henceforth to nominate two directors instead of its former quota of three directors to the board in Melbourne. This was not a defeat for English Dunlop. They needed only two representatives because they were already so influential. Why they should have become so powerful at that time is not clear. Presumably Dunlop Perdriau, having fallen on its face in the mid 1930s, was far more willing than before to seek and accept advice from London.

The staff began to share in the new prosperity. A superannuation fund, much wider than those of the past, was planned with the aim of embracing 'all staff and permanent employees down to second foremen'. The long-standing scheme encouraging employees to buy shares was pepped up, and by 1945 about three of every ten employees were members — a record matched by few, if any, big public companies with primarily a blue-collar work-force. For the average employee, especially the hundreds of younger women and men of limited skills, the dramatic change was the new social life fostered after work at the main factories. Thus at Montague in 1936 a social club was formed with sports, musical and social sections. On a winter Saturday night in 1936 a 'free get-together dance' was held at the mill. Bartlett himself was invited, and as he watched the 1100 people on or near the dance floor he quietly exulted that 'a different spirit is apparent'.

The spirit of fun was not everywhere. Trade unions in the rubber industry, though subdued after the hammering they had received from the depression itself, became more assertive. In March 1938 there was friction at Drummoyne, partly because Dunlop was that rarity — a company which did not pay overtime for Saturday work. Bartlett admitted privately that the engineers and maintenance workers who were on strike for two days at the Drummoyne machine shop had a good case but he disliked their militancy. He told the board he planned to close the shop completely, perhaps in two months' time, when it had completed the manufacture of all the moulds needed in the rubber mills. 'By taking such a step', he added, 'we will rid ourselves of the militant section of the employees who joined the Company recently'.

Bartlett could close a militant stronghold of unionism: he could not close down the rival factories which chipped away at his business. Even in the year ending June 1938, Dunlop, despite its new products, did not quite equal the sales revenue it had earned in 1929. Its competitors, however, were thriving. Olympic was rumoured to be about to move into new products, including hosing and conveyor belting. In equipping new cars Olympic had gained another scoop by snatching fifty per cent of the Humber-Hillman orders from Dunlop. Goodyear was also flourishing, partly aided by a price-fixing agreement with Dunlop. In Sydney there was even a hustling rival called the Progress Rubber Co. which ate into Dunlop's shoe market and was threatening to make a range of six tyres in popular sizes, using only the six-ply casing which, once the tyre became well worn could be used for retreading. Was this another Beaurepaire? The man behind Progress Rubber was the fiery, obstinate F. O. Holbrook.

A topsy-turvy world

'IN THE present topsy-turvy condition of world affairs', said Willy Watt, 'you will not expect from your Board any predictions as to the prospects of the immediate future'. He was speaking to shareholders on 23 September 1938, just a year before the Second World War began. 'No one alive knows what a month — or even a week — may bring forth', he added. He did not add that in the previous week Dunlop had been forced to pay an increased new rate of 'war-risk insurance' on its cargoes in ships on the Australia–Europe route, the increase on the Suez route being eightfold and on the North Atlantic route twentyfold.

From his long political life Watt had learned to appreciate the force of the unpredictable in human affairs. He thought a war was probable. Where it would be fought and by whom he could not be certain. That the war would virtually cut off the western world's sources of rubber and thereby trigger a revolution in its future supply was beyond any forecaster's power to foresee. As long ago as 1936, Watt had been worried about the prospect of war and its effect on supplies of imported rubber and cotton, and sometimes his company built up stocks but then, as fears of war were eased, let the stocks run down a little. To carry high stocks, especially of rubber, was very expensive and a drain on profits. In February 1939 the directors sent a telegram to Bartlett who was visiting South Africa and enquired urgently about the adequacy of the company's stockpile of rubber, cotton, chemicals and the special wire used in tyres. The stockpile would apparently last for four months. Bartlett when he returned to Melbourne reassured the board by pointing out that Australia, in the event of a war, would soon ration petrol, all of which was imported. As the ration of petrol might be only one-third that of peacetime, the demand for tyres — the main outlet for rubber — would quickly dwindle, and even the stock of tyres in dealers' warehouses and garages would only be sold at a slow rate. On 23 February 1940, when the war was in its sixth month, the directors looked at their rubber stocks and decided, rather optimistically, that for the duration of the war they should carry a minimum stockpile of three months' supply of rubber. Bartlett, not Watt, was the optimist. In Bartlett's defence it should be said that early in 1940 Europe was engaged in a cold rather than a hot war. The fighting was intermittent and indecisive. In the eyes of most military observers it was inconceivable that during the coming summer Hitler would swiftly conquer France and thereby expose the isolated French colony in Indo-China to an effortless Japanese take-over — the beginning of Japan's stride-by-stride advance to the world's greatest source of crude rubber.

In the first months of the war the factories were far busier than in the previous year. In September 1939 sales were up twenty-three per cent on those of the previous year. In October they were thirty per cent higher, and in April 1940 they were eighty-five per cent higher than in the corresponding month of the previous year. Peacetime and wartime needs were competing with each other in a booming economy. Soon after the outbreak of war, the Commonwealth government began to set up tall fences and guarded gates around essential parts of the economy. Bit by bit new regulations diverted effort to essential tasks. The company had an early experience of the new order in November 1939 when, faced with mounting costs in its factories, it tried to raise the prices of tyres and tubes. Permission had to be sought from the Prices Commissioner, Professor D. B. Copland, who after examining all costs, consented to an increase of seven and a half per cent. As the war became more serious, as Hitler over-ran most of Europe in 1940, and as central London was blitzed (in September 1940 the board sent a large donation of 2500 pounds to 'British Bombing Victims'), the Australian government controlled more and more economic activities: profits, prices, manpower and raw materials. Petrol was rationed later that year, thus dramatically curbing the sales of tyres and tubes, and allowing large parts of the factories to turn to war production.

The sense of urgency emerged slowly in Australia compared to Europe. 'Montague will be there', announced the headline in the Dunlop *Gazette* in October 1939: the headline was an echo of the First World War song 'Australia will be there', but people enlisted at a slower pace than in 1914. In the first war months of 1939, men enlisted from a variety of sections and departments at Montague and Drummoyne — from Sporting Goods, Budgets Office, Mixing, Moulding, Tread Extruding, Dipping, Surgical, No. 10 Store, Rim Shop and other work-places, but in the first year and a half the total enlistments reached only three hundred. The company gave its employees every incentive to enlist, usually making up the difference, for the duration of the war, between the pay received from the armed forces and the higher rate of civilian pay. But the government increasingly prevented the enlistment of those working in industry.

Many of the Dunlop employees thumbed their nose at the government's attempt to prohibit them from enlisting. Claude McFarlane, a tyre builder, was so persistent in trying to enlist as an airman that in the end Robert Blackwood, the technical manager, trained somebody to fill his place. Stan Orton, working in the tyre department at Montague and aged thirty, decided in June 1940 that he should enlist. Going before the Dunlop industrial officer to seek permission he was told that he was in a protected industry and could not be released. Stan shrewdly went to the army's recruiting office and claimed that he was a bricklayer working around the suburbs. With the housing industry in decline, bricklayers were plentiful and were permitted to enlist. At the end of the year Orton sailed for the Middle East as a motor mechanic in the First Australian Corps Vehicle Park. His military career is worth tracing. After taking part in the war in Libya and Lebanon he returned to Australia early in 1942, missing by the narrowest of margins the expedition which sailed to the Dutch East Indies where it was captured quickly by the Japanese. Instead he found himself working at the No. 1 Tank Workshops in Neils Motors in Sturt Street, South Melbourne. As he was close to his old Montague factory he hopped in a General Grant tank one lunch-time in 1943 and drove it down the tramlines to show 'the people at work'. Suddenly he was hit by a tram. In the history of the Melbourne trams published later Orton was delighted to read, so he recalls, that 'I was the only man in Australia who had been hit by a tram while driving a 20 tonne tank'.

Even in 1940, when Orton enlisted, more and more of the Montague output was directed to the armed forces. After the fall of Dunkirk, Britain was gravely short of munitions; and Australia was urged to supply bullets. As Montague held one of only three lead presses in Australia — the press was normally used for extruding hose — the company was ordered to use it for manufacturing lead bullets rather than rubber hoses. From slugs of lead Dunlop produced the nucleus of .303 bullets and sent them to the munitions factories for further processing.

The air force and army demanded big quantities of military tyres. In England, Dunlop had long manufactured tyres for aircraft — tyres that resembled bicycle tyres and carried no great strain because the planes were light and moreover they landed at slow speeds. As aircraft became heavier and landed at faster speeds they required special tyres, usually squat so that they could be stowed away in a cramped space, and usually inflated to a very high pressure so that they could carry the weight of the heavy aircraft and also cushion the impact of the wheels hitting the ground at high speed. Aircraft tyres became a special interest of English Dunlop. In the first decades, the aircraft normally landed with a wire or chain trailing along the landing strip, acting as an earth, and thus preventing electrical energy from setting the aircraft on fire; but eventually the English Dunlop perfected a kind of rubber that reduced the risk of an aircraft, on landing, catching fire. Australian Dunlop, borrowing English technology, manufactured aircraft tyres as early as

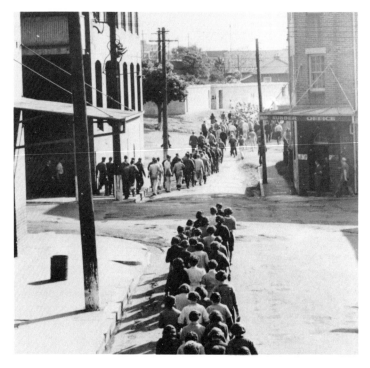

Drummoyne mill workers filing into shelters during an air-raid drill.

1926. By 1940 it was manufacturing tyres for Australian-built aircraft and soon was to make even larger tyres for American-built aircraft.

The war had its minor advantages. In the interests of efficiency, Watt at last cemented the merger and dismantled what remained of Barnet Glass. The Dunlop Perdriau Rubber Company made an offer of thirty shillings for each of the two hundred thousand preference shares in the Barnet Glass Rubber Company Limited, and in May 1941 the offer was overwhelmingly accepted. The way was also clear to remove Perdriau from the name of the company, and in September 1941 the company became known simply as Dunlop Rubber Australia Limited. The company's fourth name, it would last until 1967.

Early in 1941, the chairman of Dunlop Rubber Australia wondered whether the company held sufficient reserves of rubber to last throughout a long or disruptive war. On 14 February Watt and his fellow directors resolved on 'grounds of urgency' to obtain another one thousand tons of rubber from overseas. By the end of the month they had bought but not taken delivery of it. In July, one month after Hitler invaded Russia and carried the war into a hazardous phase for the Allies, the directors decided to increase rubber stocks by another fifty per cent. The arguments behind the decision were not reported. Almost certainly they feared that Japan would enter the war and

THE WAR EFFORT 1939-1945

In a million ways the qualities of rubber contributed to the final victory. Among the interesting wartime developments at Dunlop were the important reclamation of old rubber for new uses; the production of virtually a bullet-proof tyre; and the manufacture of a range of war material, comprising hundreds of various items in rubber, not to mention the aircraft parts, lathes, jigs, wheels and so on, made by Dunlop engineers as well. On the coming of V.P. Day, Dunlop looked back on six years of unceasing and tireless endeavour in the interest of the nation.

Most Australian built aircraft which served in the South-West Pacific Area were fitted with Dunlop wheels, tyres and brakes.

Life savers for Allied Airmen — Dunlop Rubber life rafts, and life preservers, commonly known as "Mae Wests".

The Dunlop Company also manufactured Jungle Green clothing for Australian troops in New Guinea and the islands north of Australia.

Respirator face-pieces and hose, also helmet linings were another big item of Dunlop wartime production.

Dunlop Sand Tyres equipped the vehicles and guns used by our troops in the Middle East.

Dunlop Australia at war.

thus endanger the supply of rubber from Malaya, where Dunlop of England ran its plantations. It is reasonable to surmise that Japan was in the company's mind, for a month later — on 22 August — the board discussed arrangements for blacking-out the rubber mills so that they would not be a target for a surprise air attack should Japan enter the war. A rubber mill was not only a strategic target but easily turned into an inferno. Admittedly, Japan was not yet at war with any western power but her forces had just moved into the southern part of French Indo-China, thus hinting of expansionist ambitions to the south. Watt usually gave a pithy, shrewd comment on the state of the world at the end of his annual address to shareholders, and on 5 September 1941 he said, 'What man amongst us is daring enough to predict the length, or outcome, of this WAR?'. He spelled the word war with capital letters, as well he might.

On 7 December 1941 the Japanese bombed the American naval base at Pearl Harbor and invaded Malaya. As the Japanese advanced quickly down the Malay peninsula and moved into the Dutch-defended islands along the Indonesian archipelago, the future supply of rubber was anxiously discussed. In Australia the government arranged to buy a big stockpile of rubber from Malaya and Indonesia, partly to prevent it falling to Japan and partly to replenish Australia's own inadequate reserves of raw rubber. Some 25 000 tons of rubber, it would cost the big three tyre companies the enormous sum of 4 200 000 pounds, much of which they would have to borrow from banks. On 24 January 1942, Dunlop was informed that shipments of the rubber had begun. The question of how to finance the purchase of this rubber — it would absorb a sum equal to many years' dividends — and the long-term storing of such a huge stockpile, did not long absorb the Dunlop directors. The Japanese penetrated the British and Dutch colonies with such speed that they began to capture the warehouses full of rubber destined for Australia.

Bartlett was negotiating in Britain and the USA in the first weeks of the Japanese war. Early in 1942 he discussed with Mr Pratt of the Lend Lease Department in Washington the possibility of supplying Australian tyres to China. At that phase of the war — a phase lasting only a few weeks — it was too risky to ship tyres all the way from England to Burma and so across the Burma Road to China, and it was too difficult and roundabout to ship tyres from the USA because of Japanese naval forces in the Pacific. On 22 January in Washington, Bartlett was summoned to a conference in Pratt's office. How many tyres, he was asked, could Australia produce for the urgent needs of India, China, the Malay States and other lands? It was then assumed that the rubber of South-east Asia was still in the Allies' hands and would be freely available, thus enabling Australian tyre factories to enter a remarkable era of expansion. Within three weeks of the private conference in Washington, however, virtually all that rubber was endangered.

Singapore fell to the Japanese forces on 15 February 1942, and Australia lost hope of replenishing its rubber stocks, Dunlop held only eight months' supply of rubber at the current rate of consumption. Fortunately there were rubber plantations in the Australian territories in New Guinea. In many peacetime years Dunlop had bought the entire peacetime output of New Guinea. Suddenly these plantations — the hope of Australia — fell to the Japanese or ceased, because of shipping hazards, to be a practical source of supply.

The speed of the Japanese thrust astonished observers. Malaya had not been expected to fall, let alone the islands to the north and north-west of Australia. Now the fear was that Australia might be invaded.

Before the Japanese began to bomb the outback town of Darwin, the company had taken steps to protect its workers in the event of air raids. At a meeting of directors held five days after Japan entered the war, it was resolved to place sandbags around the big factory at Drummoyne and to paint the roofs 'in a protective colour'. Drummoyne, being on the shores of Sydney Harbour, was the most vulnerable of the Dunlop plants. In addition it now employed as many women as men, whereas Montague employed twice as many men as women. At the same meeting of directors the head of all factories, Mr Holbeach, told Watt, Sir Alexander Stewart and Sir Colin Fraser — the only other directors present on that Friday morning — that the fire brigades at the main mills were in readiness to fight any fires lit by enemy bombing. E. A. Kellam, the secretary, who was soon to leave for war work, similarly assured the directors that the company's main records were protected against damage from air raids. By March 1942 the board was making special precautions against air raids in Melbourne. The digging of a trench shelter for five hundred employees was authorised close to the Montague mill, and at head office at 108 Flinders Street the bricking up of the windows was authorised to prevent glass flying during an air raid. At Drummoyne the air raid shelters were already being dug.

Almost as soon as the Japanese invaded British Malaya, the Commonwealth government resolved to ration rubber. After talks with rubber companies, it announced on Christmas Eve that it would ban at once the making of car and motor-bike tyres and restrict the sales of those already in stock. The common or half-inch garden hoses and the floor coverings of rubber were no longer to be made except for Defence orders. Golf balls and tennis-balls, presumably because they consumed little rubber, were treated leniently, and their production was to be cut only by half.

In effect the big three tyre companies and the dealers had to take charge of the rationing of car tyres, a hit-or-miss method which made them very unpopular with customers. Soon the Commonwealth began to ration tyres on the same basis as the rationing of petrol, and by May 1942 the Commonwealth had printed the application forms without which a car-owner could not replace a worn-out tyre. The onus was on the owners to retread their tyres. Only when a tyre could no longer be recapped or retreaded was the motorist eligible to buy a new tyre. Moreover before he took delivery of the new tyre he had to hand in the worn-out tyre. The penalty for those who gained a new tyre on the basis of misleading statements was a fine of one pound or imprisonment for six months.

The rationing of petrol and tyres, and the complete absence of new cars for the civilian market, thinned out the traffic. Spare parts, especially for imported cars, became rare. Before long, thousands of motorists did not even bother to register their car or light truck and simply placed it on blocks in their garage — this was the era when nearly all vehicles were still kept under shelter at night. Within Dunlop it was estimated that at the end of the war Australia had a total of nine hundred thousand cars and commercial trucks, of which one hundred thousand were not on the roads. As a result of the shortage of motoring necessities the demand for new tyres would have fallen sharply even if there had been no rationing of tyres.

Rubber could be saved in countless other ways. At Abbotsford the company's plant for reclaiming rubber now worked around the clock. At Drummoyne another plant was built to reclaim rubber. The government ran an advertising campaign for waste and scrap rubber to be handed in, just as aluminium saucepans had been a little earlier. In April 1942, after the directors had been assured by Robert Blackwood that rubber could be further diluted without much loss of quality, they agreed with the other major rubber companies to reduce the amount of rubber in all products, the rubber in a tractor tyre declining from seventy-eight to fifty-five per cent and in industrial hosing from forty-two to thirty per cent. The new ceiling on the rubber component of a bicycle tyre meant that the popular red-coloured Dunlop tyres, which consisted of seventy-six per cent rubber compared to fifty-three per cent in black-coloured tyres, were manufactured no more.

As the war went on, reclaimed or recycled rubber became vital. Interstate ships and long-distance trains carried tens of thousands of old tyres and tubes to Melbourne and Sydney for dispatch to the reclaim plants. Great consignments of used tyres were brought as back-loading from army vehicle depots as far away as North Queensland and even the Middle East. Towards the end of the war about one-third of the rubber in most new rubber goods in Australia consisted of Dunlop's reclaimed rubber.

Once rubber products were either rationed or not available to the public, the normal competitive methods of selling were pointless. By mid-winter of 1942 Dunlop employed no salesmen in the country areas and only a few in the cities where they served more as trouble-shooters and procurers than as sellers. Late in 1942 the big three tyre companies agreed to apportion Australia into distribution zones, and Olympic withdrew completely from selling tyres and tubes in Queensland and New South Wales while Goodyear agreed to serve only those two states. Dunlop was the oldest and most widespread distributor of rubber goods, and as it was represented at the negotiation table by Roy Simkin — as always he refused to budge an inch — it won the right to continue to sell in all six States though on a strict quota. Before the zones and quotas were finally allocated, the big three had to make a frank exchange of information about their current sales of tyres, and the information shocked Bartlett. He realised the full success of Olympic's selling campaign in the last eight years. In Victoria it was now the leading seller of tyres and tubes, and in Australia as a whole its annual sales of car and motor-bike tyres were not far behind those of Goodyear and Dunlop, each of which sold about 132 000 tyres compared to Olympic's 102 000.

With an increasing fear of raids by Japanese aircraft, Australia's precious stocks of rubber had to be carted to safer sites. As most of the crude rubber was held in warehouses and bond stores near the docks, and as a couple of bombs could have destroyed most of Australia's reserves of rubber, Dunlop moved its rubber to safer sites. In Victoria, Dunlop's stock of crude rubber — a stock that could not be augmented in the near future — was dispersed to fourteen different sites by September 1942, the largest store being in the residential suburb of Elsternwick. There was even a highly inflammable stack of 450 tons in a store or warehouse in Collins Street in the city. In Perth, where scarcity of interstate ships led to the holding of large stocks of tyres and other rubber goods in Dunlop's city warehouses, the danger of a bomb was suddenly realised, and a large store, possibly a wheat store, was rented at the inland town of Merredin for the holding of rubber goods. The fear of air raids declined after the Battle of the Coral Sea and the fighting on the Kokoda Trail halted the advance of the Japanese. On 24 September — four months after the Battle of the Coral Sea — the company decided that it no longer had to take out air-raid insurance policies for all its employees in the southern states. For the few employees in Queensland, however, the insurance policies were renewed.

The year 1942 was almost certainly the most arduous in the company's history. Much had to be done quickly in the face of obstacles. New products were urgently called for. Shortages of raw materials and labour were almost an epidemic, and the two crucial materials — cotton and rubber — were amongst the most vulnerable because neither was produced in Australian territory in any quantity. The sea routes to the outside world were precarious: cargoes from England had to pass through the North Atlantic where submarines were waiting; and cargoes from the United States had to come in convoy. Even then the cargo — whether machinery or cotton — was liable to be comman-deered suddenly by American authorities. The mail crossing the world was jeopardised by the dangers of transport and by wartime censorship, and for the sake of preserving confidentiality the directors in Melbourne for several months refused to send even the minutes of board meetings for perusal by the two absent English directors.

Within Australia the transport was strained. In July 1942 the Montague factory, depending on coal shipped from New South Wales, was down to a stock of two weeks. Motor vehicles were so scarce that Robert Blackwood, the factory's technical manager, had to stop the regular testing of new tyres. The supply of labour was also erratic, and heavily controlled by manpower regulations; the closing of one section of a factory produced a surplus of employees while in another interstate factory labour remained in short supply until all hands were working the fifty-six-hour-week which the government insisted upon before it would allow the recruiting of more labour.

Even with the best will in the world, work disputes arose. At Drummoyne, more volatile than Montague in its industrial relations, disputes disrupted vital production. Thus in a phase of very hot weather the workers who made the battery boxes were given the privilege of taking a cold shower in working time. For some reason — perhaps because it was seen as a privilege likely to spread to all parts of the factory — the right to shower was withdrawn, and the workers went on strike for several days. In the shoe factory where male labour was scarce, twenty women who were doing men's jobs struck for the right to receive men's pay. As this issue had national implications the Arbitration Court intervened. The women went back to work only after Dunlop promised to back pay them, giving them the difference between men's and women's rates if it should become the nation's policy to grant equal pay to men and women. Then in the winter the tyre-moulders working on a defence contract went on strike, arguing that the piece-work incentives for two sizes of tyres did not give the fastest workers the chance of earning fifty per cent above the base rate. Bartlett twice went to Sydney in the overnight train to try to solve the dispute. Judge Drake-Brockman held a compulsory conference and ordered the tyre men back to work. They refused: they ignored the order from the executive of the Rubber Workers Union that they should return on the old basis. Week after week the stop-work went on, more and more government authorities entering the fray, while urgently-needed tyres were not produced. Finally on 8 September, the celebrated unionist, Jock Garden, acting on instructions from the federal minister for Labour, Mr E. J. Ward, addressed the militant group of tyre moulders at Drummoyne and told them to obey their own union and return to work, threatening those men of enlistable age that if they refused they 'would be drafted into the Army'.

More of the factories' space was given over to war production. Forming fifty per cent of all production by early 1942, it rose to ninety per cent. The Australian aircraft factories which now supplied Wirraways and Beaufighters and Beauforts to the air force depended heavily on Australian rubber. The first Wirraways, made at Fishermen's Bend within ten minutes' bike-ride of the Montague factory, used Dunlop tyres and brake equipment. In other war planes Dunlop rubber was used in crash-proof and bullet-proof petrol tanks, fuel pipelines, engine mountings, window strips, flooring, Dunlopillo cushioning, radio panels, shock absorbers for the radio valves, buffers for the retractable landing gear, parachute cord, electro-pneumatic gun-firing equipment, and a dozen other items. On the airfields in the Pacific Islands many bomb carriers used Dunlop tyres from Australia. In making the airstrips the earth-moving equipment often ran on heavy Dunlop tyres. The company's machine shops made much of the machinery vital for new manufacturing projects, and until the machinery was ready the second-best had to suffice. Early in 1942 the shortage of aircraft tyres was so acute that the company had to make truck-type tyres for aircraft at front-line airfields.

At sea, sunken ships were raised with the aid of salvage bells of which rubber was a component. The navy also used Dunlop rubber in torpedoes, kneeboots and seaboots, in fuelling hose, in reconnaissance boats, mooring buoys, and flare floats and fuelling hose. In the army the Dunlop brand was on tyres and tubes of military vehicles of all kinds, including the sand tyres fitted to trucks used in desert war. The company's rubber also appeared in machine-guns, machine-gun belts, searchlights, water purifiers, the bogey wheels for tanks, petrol hoses, jungle-green trousers, rubber boots and ground sheets — millions of them.

When supplies of rubber medical equipment were cut off by war, Dunlop set out to make surgical equipment. When a huge rubberised air bag, a device nicknamed a camel, was contrived to raise sunken ships and aircraft from the sea bed, Dunlop made many camels. Once inflated under the water, they raised vessels to the surface. Submarines also benefited from inventions. When the enemy's depth charges sent shock waves that damaged the batteries and therefore the mobility of submarines, Dunlop's engineers devised an ebonite battery cell which more readily stood up to the shock waves.

The company was involved in unusual projects. One arose from the unexpected fact that many wartime pilots, flying at high speeds and suddenly changing the direction of their aircraft, suffered a momentary 'black-out'. Professor F. S. Cotton, a research physiologist of Sydney University, thinking that insufficient blood might be reaching the pilot's brain after the aircraft suddenly turned, became absorbed in the question. He decided that if pilots donned an aerodynamic suit, the suit would help maintain the circulation of blood throughout the body and so prevent black-outs. He arranged for Dunlop staff at Drummoyne to make the rubber parts for his complicated pilot's suit. Tests showed that the regulated pressure of the rubber against the pilot's skin did help to keep the blood circulating. Indeed, in the opinion of the war historian, Professor D. P. Mellor, the Cotton suit increased a pilot's tolerance by about thirty per cent when an aircraft was making a fast turn.

Bartlett was proud of the way his staff adapted old equipment and factories to new needs. In dinner conversations he liked to explain — if military security permitted — that in the factory where golf balls were once made, the gas masks were made; where tennis-balls were made, the rubber lining for steel helmets was now made.

Natural rubber had been scarce ever since the Japanese overran Malaysia. Month after month Dunlop's factory managers wondered whether they held enough rubber to continue defence tasks at the planned rate. As compensation they were promised stocks of the synthetic rubber, but that revolutionary form of rubber at first was even rarer than natural rubber. It had been invented by Germany in the First World War. Later the Germans developed a more satisfactory synthetic called Buna rubber, the *Bu* standing for butadiene. In 1942 the Americans began to gear up for the mass production of a similar synthetic which they called GR-S, meaning Government Rubber-Styrene. American factories could not produce it quickly enough. Even after the fall of Singapore the huge American automobile industry was still devouring the fast-falling stockpile of natural rubber at an enormous rate, and the United States government actually began to ration petrol across the nation late in 1942 in order to reduce the consumption of rubber, which was dangerously scarce, more than the consumption of petrol, which was merely in short supply.

Australia was promised a supply of synthetic rubber long before America was able to ship it. In preparation for treating the new rubber with its very different qualities, Australian technical men went to the United States to study the maze of production changes which would be required in Australian rubber mills. Robert Blackwood, on behalf of Dunlop, and Charlie Grainger, on behalf of Olympic, were absent for about five months. For a time the Australian government itself planned to sponsor the manufacture of synthetic rubber, and as Australia lacked the oil refineries which could produce vital ingredients it had no alternative but to consider manufacturing Buna synthetic rubber from grains. The Council for Scientific and Industrial Research (CSIR) examined the possibility of extracting alcohol from wheat and sugar — a costly way of making Buna rubber. Some seventeen million gallons of alcohol annually would be enough to feed a synthetic rubber factory, and in fact four factories with an annual output of twelve million gallons of alcohol were constructed in the wheat lands in the last phase of the war, though in the end their 'power alcohol' was destined simply as an additive to petrol. If the government had boldly decided to go ahead and make synthetic rubber in Australia the plan would have collapsed on the eve of its completion. Drought destroyed the surplus wheat needed to produce the alcohol.

From January 1944 synthetic rubber was imported in small lots but throughout that year the Australian rubber factories still depended primarily on natural rubber or scrap rubber scavenged far and wide. On New Year's Day 1945, Australia held a stockpile of natural rubber which, even if augmented by ships expected to arrive that month from Africa and elsewhere, would last only five weeks. Dunlop believed it could make its own stock of crude rubber last until 31 March if it used an increased component of synthetic rubber, but even the use of that tricky type of rubber might be impeded by other scarcities. Unless synthetic rubber or GR-S was processed with the aid of carbon black, the resultant tyres lacked tensile strength or were prone to become excessively hot. In January, the technical manager, Blackwood, reported an 'alarming' nation-wide shortage of carbon black: he blamed the myopia of the federal government's Import Procurement Division in refusing to order, well in advance, sufficient quantities from the United States where it was a product mainly of the oil refineries. The scarcity of carbon black meant less synthetic rubber could be processed, and so the scarcity of crude rubber became perilous.

As Montague was now far and away Australia's biggest maker of vital truck tyres for civilian or military purposes, any delays at Montague would disrupt the supply of war equipment to Australians and Americans in the war zone. Montague, however, was hit by delays. Forced to use more synthetic and less natural rubber, Montague's mill could not, initially, cope with the new mixture. The synthetic rubber at first was mixed and dried at a slower rate: it usually needed more manpower. As a result, Montague's output fell temporarily from twelve hundred to nine hundred tyres a day. Moreover Bartlett computed that, with the increased costs of using synthetic rubber, the company — unless the prices commissioner altered his view — would actually trade for the whole calendar year at a loss.

There was no alternative but to use more synthetic rubber — so long as the carbon black could be obtained. Early in 1945 Dunlop was producing goods partly made of synthetic rubber even before the goods made by the new formula had been adequately tested. The tennis-balls consisting of one hundred per cent synthetic rubber (except for the seams of cement) were bouncing truly but the tests of truck tyres were much slower. On Victorian roads the new synthetic tyres on a timber-carting lorry and on a passenger bus were still being tested when the need to set a production run at the rubber mill was imperative. On 18 January all truck tubes and tyres at Montague were being made with ninety per cent of crude or reclaimed rubber and ten per cent of synthetic rubber, but now the synthetic percentage had to be raised quickly in order to save the scarce stocks of crude rubber. In these difficulties Robert Blackwood showed his skill and patience. By September 1945 half of the input of rubber at the Dunlop mills was synthetic rubber. By the end of the year, if the war had still been raging, two-thirds of all rubber used by Dunlop would have been synthetic. The new material would eventually transform the rubber world, but it still had to fight natural rubber which was ready to return in cheap abundance from the tropical plantations recaptured from the defeated Japanese.

In June 1945, soon after the defeat of Hitler, the pressure on the company as a supplier to the defence forces quickly eased. Canberra's restriction on the sale of garden hose to civilians came to an end. The restrictions on selling kneeboots to the public was removed, and the 65 000 pairs in Dunlop's warehouses were rushed and sold out in an instant. In August the Drummoyne factory was so free of defence contracts that it began to make shoes again. Bartlett, now looking for fields in which to expand, was thinking of buying control of a firm that made golf-clubs and another that made gut. The big military orders — American and Australian — for heavy tyres for trucks and aircraft came to an end within weeks of the Japanese surrender in August 1945, and Dunlop's only remaining defence contracts were the making of tyres and tubes for the Douglas aircraft carrying prisoners-of-war from the Japanese camps and the tyres for Mustangs on aerial patrol around Japan. All over Australia, at general stores and clothing shops, people were beginning to enquire — usually in vain — for the galoshes and bathing caps and hot-water bags which were almost unprocurable in the war years. Above all, they were hoping for tyres, which were rationed until 1946.

Dunlop's improved relations with its employees were proving an advantage at a time when in many factories the relations were often tense. Even in 1940, when the company employed just over five thousand people — a record — it took steps to try to make all employees, as far as possible, satisfied with their work. Of the big industrial employers, Dunlop was now close to the most paternal. While it could not be called paternal by the standards of the 1980s, it clearly was paternal by the pre-war standards. One minor mirror of the new attitude was the attempt at Dunlop factories, when employees were about to leave, to find why they were dissatisfied. At Montague, the son of a rabbi, Saul Ziven, who was formerly a Barnet Glass employee, accepted the task of pastoral care on the production line; and in old age he recalled in his droll way how he did this work:

> I went to one particular girl who was leaving and asked her if she was unhappy, would she like a change? She said no. I asked if she would like a seat so she could sit down? She said no. I asked would she like to go on bonus?

Nothing could be done to make this young factory operative stay on. And why then was she leaving, he asked. Her answer came strong and clear.

> She told me that in the Department there were thirty people and she had been there ten days and not one of the 'bloody cows' [strong language in those days] had asked her to go to the pictures.

Saul Ziven did not offer to take her to the picture theatre. He confessed that his effort to promote the contentment of employees could only go so far.

Those who enlisted or those who took leave of absence to train in the militia were treated by the company with generosity. As a rule they received topping-up allowances from the company so that they did not lose income, and this scheme was continued throughout the war. Early in the war the salaried members of staff — mainly the white-collar employees — were given a new superannuation scheme that was well ahead of its time. In the year 1940–41 the company also launched, without demanding a financial levy from employees, two unusual schemes. The Group Insurance scheme promised to pay to all employees, whether in factories or offices, a sum of one hundred pounds if they died 'whilst in the service of the Company'. One hundred pounds was still a sizeable sum, and for the family of many employees it equalled five months' income. Another wartime innovation provided sick-leave on full pay if the employee had given long service and sick-leave on a lower allowance for a newer employee. As social security in Australia was still elementary, these schemes must have cheered up many of the older hands at Montague and Drummoyne, people whose life savings, because of the depression or other mishaps, were small.

For those returning from the war Bartlett devised his post-war training scheme. An experimental course in 'tyres' was run over three months early in 1945 and the ten 'students' did a written exam at the end. In May a mechanical course was begun: already servicemen were being released so that they could return to rubber and other essential industries. In August, the month in which the Pacific War ended, a course was begun in salesmanship for 'returning servicemen and others in the organisation who express a desire to improve their position'. Nearly all Dunlop employees in the armed forces received advance notices of these courses and an invitation to apply to take part when they were demobilised. In the typical course, lectures and 'cinematographic films' occupied the morning and practical work the afternoon.

By the last months of 1945 scores of former employees were reporting back for work and some were enrolling in the training scheme. The return to Dunlop was not always smooth. Ted Benbow, who had sold rubber flooring for Dunlop before enlisting in the army in 1941, returned after a distinguished war career to his old company. There was 'one jarring note', he recalled later. A senior officer at head office told him that his holiday was over and that he would have to settle down to solid work. 'Having lost good men over there', recalled Ted, 'I nearly punched the person in the nose'. Becoming a sales representative again he was given a well-worn Nash car to do his rounds in Melbourne suburbs. Later, Benbow was one of the first representatives to receive a new Holden which he found to be a complete 'lemon' because its engine, gearbox and differential had to be replaced after 14 000 miles. For millions of other Australians a brand-new Holden was not a lemon but a golden apple. The era of massive sales of new tyres was arriving.

The servicemen who returned to head office in Flinders Street after an absence of four or six years instantly noticed, on the days when the directors assembled in the boardroom upstairs, that old faces were missing. Even in 1939 it was an oldish board. Major-General F. G. Hughes, a director since the inception of the company, was in his eighties and others were close to seventy. In the space of a few years, death reshaped the board. Sir Colin Fraser — 'whose invariable dignity and wisdom added strength to our deliberations' — died in 1944: he had been on the board for seventeen years and did more than anyone to recruit Bartlett in England. Hughes, who gave mainly dignity and goodwill to the deliberations of the board, died in the same year at the age of eighty-seven. F. J. Smith, a Sydney accountant in his seventies, died in 1946, only months after the death of the Right Honourable W. A. Watt, the chairman.

Watt was frail in his last years, having suffered a stroke in 1937. Such was the concern for his health that when he returned a little later from a visit to

England the company postponed its annual meeting so that he would not be forced, in order to reach Melbourne in time, to travel by ship through the Red Sea at the hottest time of the year. His strength recovered, he remained an active chairman; and when Bartlett went to England and North America for a short official visit that was prolonged to six months by difficulties in finding civilian seats on wartime air routes, Watt seems to have taken up some of the managerial duties. As Bartlett was in the northern hemisphere when Malaya was invaded and when Singapore fell, Watt accepted the main responsibility, because the acting general manager, Simkin, was inexperienced in some issues of policy. Slowly Watt slipped back to the normal role of chairman, after a long period when he was almost an executive chairman. By 1946 he felt poorly on many board days and could no longer attend with ease. His resignation as chairman was accepted with regret on 2 August 1946 but curiously it was backdated to 30 June.

Besides his political knowledge and public standing, Willy Watt had brought unusual talents to the board. After an uncertain period as head of the hurriedly stitched merger between the three rubber companies, he became a source of strength. We can glimpse his power in the portrait, painted in 1914 by Phillips Fox for the Yorick Club, and now hung on a wall of the Melbourne Savage Club. His face is lean, shrewd, cynical but dignified. His skin is red and almost weather-beaten, and its black shadows give the appearance of someone who, having shaved only two hours ago, has to think of shaving again. A striking figure, he looks like a statesman and a gypsy. Probably he was the best-known man ever to occupy the chair of a major public company.

Nobody could really replace Watt as chairman. At first sight, nobody on the board could hold a candle to him, which made his death all the more perturbing to those whose future lay with the company. In the end Wallace Bartlett, the chief executive and already a director, was chosen as chairman. It was the first time the chief executive of the company had simultaneously held the post of chairman — a combination of posts which was then most unusual in Australia. But there was little fear that Bartlett would become too powerful. He was frank with the directors and listened closely to them. There was no fear that he would become too pushy, for he was rather a private than a public person, and his entry in Who's Who was the ultimate in privacy, listing neither his own age nor his wife's name. His appointment to the dual posts was also sanctioned because he would provide continuity in policy, for he saw eye to eye with Watt. Though they had not met until Bartlett stepped ashore in Australia for the first time, they became firm friends and eventually close friends, even living in the same street — Orrong Road, Toorak.

Most employees felt deep satisfaction that Bartlett was chairman — even those who did not know what the chairman specifically did. As he was in his early fifties he was expected to enjoy a long reign. There was just one hitch — he held more power than any previous officer of the company but he had no clear-cut successor as chief executive or chairman. What would happen if he was poached or fell dangerously ill?

Watt perhaps more than Bartlett had been conscious that the question of finding an outstanding deputy to the general manager was vital. We know that not because of any surviving document in the Dunlop archives but because of a typed sheaf of reminiscences written maybe three decades later by a New Zealander who was offered the post of understudy to Bartlett. Philip Proctor, the general manager of Dunlop in New Zealand, was the favoured man. The son of Australian Dunlop's first secretary and the nephew of its first general manager, Proctor was passing through Melbourne in March 1945 while on his way from London to Wellington, an arduous wartime flight. Spending a few days in Melbourne, staying at the Athenaeum Club in Collins Street — only a few minutes' walk from the head office — and busily inspecting the Dunlop factories, he had no idea that he was being observed closely as Bartlett's possible successor. He had no official connection with the Melbourne company, for his own company based in Wellington was owned by English Dunlop from which he had been recruited. But there was something about him — his personality and drive and his interest in social questions — that made him appealing. Both Watt and Bartlett believed that a new broom, a gentle broom, was needed in industrial relations in the western world. Proctor was of like mind. In fact, when he returned to England in 1932, at the trough of the world depression, after working three years for Dunlop in Czechoslovakia, he was appalled by the poverty. He then joined the Labour Party and the Fabian Society, becoming a speaker at street corners while still a middle-ranking employee of Dunlop. The position he was later offered in New Zealand by Sir George Beharrell, a blunt-speaking Yorkshireman, was on the strict condition that he abandon party politics. He did but his social sympathies remained. It was therefore likely that Bartlett's policy of welfare-ism then pursued at Montague would be supported fully by Proctor. To Proctor's surprise, just before he left Melbourne, Watt in an eloquent speech made his offer. It was 'a veritable bombshell', said Proctor. He sought — and was given — some months to consider it. The decision, however, was made for him. English Dunlop resented the attempt to poach him, and Australian Dunlop withdrew the offer.

Bartlett still had no sure and satisfactory successor as general manager, even thirty months later. Now he was both chairman and chief executive, while his second in charge, Roy Simkin, was a fine but pugnacious salesman with no great factory experience and in Bartlett's view no flair. Then in the autumn of 1947, after only nine months in the dual post, Bartlett fell seriously ill.

His condition became so serious that on 4 July 1947 an emergency committee of four executives was set up to manage in his absence. It consisted of Roy Simkin, William Holbeach who ran the factories, Eric Dunshea in charge of administration, and A. T. Collins in charge of purchasing — the buying of materials had been a key responsibility ever since the unwise purchases of crude rubber had wounded the company two decades previously. The caretaker committee was not long in place when, on 20 July 1947, Bartlett died.

The sense of loss was acute. He was not only the best leader the company had known, but the best liked. A contingent of employees from Montague went to his funeral at St John's church in Toorak. Some still talk vividly of the occasion, of the emotion felt even amongst humble employees. The funeral procession to the Box Hill cemetery was memorably long, by the standards of those days when petrol rationing restricted the use of cars, and when the hearse had turned from Glenferrie Road into Cotham Road in Kew the procession of cars stretched back as far as the eye could see, way into the Hawthorn shopping centre. After his death a black and white photograph of Bartlett was published in the *Gazette*, which periodically went to all employees. It was a sign of Bartlett's quiet magnetism and his civilising achievement that all around Montague, on grimy walls, on pillars, on doorways, in dingy workplaces, employees spontaneously pasted or pinned up his photograph which they had cut or torn from the magazine.

In the space of three years the company had lost five members of the board, including two chairmen. Suddenly it needed a new chairman and a new general manager, for no man was likely to fit into both of Bartlett's shoes. Sir Alexander Stewart, the senior director, was elected chairman. A Scot who had worked as chief engineer in ships of the Aberdeen White Star Line and who immigrated in 1904 after meeting a Melbourne girl aboard ship, he became a consulting engineer in the city and, initially through his father-in-law, James Cuming senior, a director of fertiliser companies. A good board-man, he accumulated directorships until they far outnumbered the fingers of his two hands. He sat on some of the nation's major boards including ICIANZ, Broken Hill South, Electrolytic Zinc and MLC. He had joined the Dunlop board back in 1924, one of the group of men who shared directorships of the important mining and industrial companies centred on Collins House at 360 Collins Street, and by the time he became chairman the Dunlop board was dominated by men from Collins House. Sir Alex Stewart was an alert seventy-three and an energetic golfer. He did not quite view himself as a caretaker whose task was to keep warm the chairman's seat warm for just a year or two — until a younger man was ready to take over.

Bartlett the general manager was far more difficult to replace than Bartlett the chairman. He had no successor on the managerial staff. The directors were reluctant to accept too long a delay in searching overseas for a new general manager. Soon they turned to, of all places, Melbourne University. There the new professor of mechanical engineering, Robert Rutherford Blackwood, was a former Dunlop employee. As a lad he had gone from Melbourne Grammar to the university where he took out degrees in civil and electrical engineering before becoming the lecturer in agricultural engineering. It was as a tester of the performance of machines that Dunlop enticed him away to Montague where he began research and testing in 1933, eventually serving ten years as technical manager of Dunlop. He left Dunlop on the last day of 1946, presumably thinking his long-term future in the company was dubious: he was not in the top five employees. Above all, he was not on the same wavelength as Bartlett.

With Bartlett's death, Blackwood was suddenly courted. On 3 October 1947 he was appointed general manager, with the university agreeing to release him at the end of the year. He was only forty-one. It was rare and possibly unique for a big company in Australia to appoint a research and development man to its highest post, and Blackwood was soon to show his concern for building up a team of talent by persuading the directors to send four young officers overseas each year for experience. Blackwood himself had benefited from an earlier short-lived such scheme, and in England in 1935 he had been the first Dunlop Perdriau employee to meet Bartlett, then about to leave for Australia.

'Bob' Blackwood was very different from Bartlett. Whereas the previous head was a production and sales man, Blackwood knew nothing about sales and had not managed a rubber mill. Indeed at no time had he directly controlled a large number of employees. Robert Blackwood had little time for commercial huzzah. He liked nothing better than to be discussing how to make a new product or improve an old product; he was practical in his approach to production. He liked to make things himself — his hobbies were joinery and gardening as well as music — but he was happy to delegate tasks, though he kept his eye on the progress. In speech he was rather quiet but forthright. He said exactly what he wanted to say and said it with courtesy — unless he thought the subject of his remarks was a fool or scoundrel.

Blackwood's manner was slow and deliberate rather than dashing; he did not jump into decisions before the jump was absolutely called for. Receptive to new ideas he took his time in chewing them over and testing them before introducing them. He saw no merit in the new, unless it worked. He had the same belief as Bartlett in quality and good service; he simply sought them in a more measured way, detouring to dawdle and fill his pipe with tobacco where others would have lit a quick cigarette and pressed on.

Presumably the directors selected Blackwood partly because he was more likely than Simkin, who was second in seniority to Bartlett, to carry on the emphasis on cordial relations between bosses and workers. For a manufacturing company Blackwood was an asset because he already had an impressive record of improving the quality of the company's products. On the other hand he sometimes looked like a leisurely seeker of truth who had lost his way in a rubber factory. Never before had the chief executive of a top Australian company been plucked from a university. Some observers wondered whether Robert Blackwood would be able to keep Dunlop abreast of its hustling competitors.

Blackwood had the advantage of inheriting a robust company. Moreover Australia was prosperous, and in his first year he could point to a net profit of 536 000 pounds — or about 26 000 pounds above the previous record earned in 1928–29, on the eve of the world depression. He, of course, knew that the company's real profit had not yet returned to the heights of the late 1920s because in the intervening years the general price level had risen by some thirty per cent. He knew that much must be done to keep Dunlop in the top list of manufacturers, and in his quiet way he began to do it.

◆   T W E L V E   ◆

Blackwood and the
buzzing years

A T THE END of the 1940s Australia was in a buzz of economic activity such as had not been experienced for at least forty years. Every adult who wanted a job could find a job and overtime as well. Migrants from the British Isles, the Baltic states, and many parts of northern Europe were now landing in their thousands at Port Melbourne, and for most newcomers the first sight of a big Australian factory was Dunlop, which their train passed on the way from the pier to the city. The new all-Australian car, the Holden, was on the roads and admired by those families whose increasing prosperity made them believe that one day they too would own a car. The public demand for tyres and cars was about to soar because the end of nine years of petrol rationing was announced on 8 February 1950 by the new Menzies government.

Robert Blackwood knew that Dunlop, though in a hectic period of expansion, was not capable of fully meeting the demand for rubber products. Labour was scarce, and every week dozens of employees left with virtually no warning. Intending buyers of timber, steel, bricks and other building materials, which were scarce, placed their names on a waiting list. The waiting time for some imported machines was as long as three years. At times even electricity was rationed, especially in a cold winter or when the coal miners of New South Wales went on strike. Government permits were sometimes needed to engage in new activities, and the price of most rubber products was still regulated by government officials.

The existing factories stood in crowded inner suburbs and had no room for planned expansion. Montague was the main worry. It had long outgrown a site which, even when chosen, was not ideal. Certainly in 1900 the factory had advantages which had since faded. It was within walking distance of the cottages of a large work-force, both women and men, and near train and cable-

Robert Blackwood, in his first month as general manager.

tram stops. It was close to vacant blocks of land and small workshops and warehouses, so that the tyre factory for a few years could expand onto new ground. Above all it was wedged between the ocean piers at Port Melbourne and the main interstate wharves on the Yarra River at a time when sea transport was vital. In those years coastal shipping was relatively efficient for carrying bicycle and car tubes and tyres and conveyor belting and rubber mats to Sydney, Brisbane, Hobart and Adelaide, and indeed as late as 1914 the coastal ship was the only way in which Dunlop tyres could reach Perth, Townsville and Darwin, for road and rail services did not yet reach the remoter ports. By 1950, however, closeness to the wharves was no longer vital.

The factory at Montague, once it could acquire no surrounding lands, became like an ingrown toenail. The pain of making more and more products on the same ground affected each factory manager. New storeys were added, old buildings were extended right to the street frontage, roadways inside the property became narrower, and new mills and workshops were erected on

Presentation of the 'Dunlop Brotherhood Cup' to Dunlop Australia in recognition of Australia's gifts of food parcels to Dunlop employees in Britain. To the left of the cup is Sir George Beharrel and to the right is Sir Alex Stewart.

waste land where once coal or spare machinery had been stored. One of Melbourne's busier streets and several side streets cut through the straggling factory, and a covered bridge had to be built over Normanby Road to link No. 1 Mill and No. 2 Mill. Each mill, being divided by the busy street, had its own boiler house. A high conveyor belt carried new tyres across Munro Street to the warehouse. Tunnels carried steam in pipes under the public road, from one mill to the other.

The buildings at Montague had so expanded that main delivery routes ran through the mills while delivery doorways opened onto the street. Pilfering was rife; some employees were alleged, while on night shift, to have dropped tyres and tubes from a factory window to the public footpath where they were picked up by waiting friends. Naturally the exact development of the rubber industry could not be predicted, and so factories for new products occupied space which, with hindsight, should have been reserved for the expansion of the plant next door. At one time as many as 2500 people worked on this crowded site. At lunch-time on sunny days dozens of employees could be seen sitting in the street eating, and when Bartlett decided to build a grand canteen seating a thousand inside, the congestion became more acute.

As the buildings became taller and as the machinery inside became heavier, the foundations began to creak. Montague factory had originally been built on a swamp, and although the water had vanished from the surface the deep layers of mud remained below. Each major building and many sagging old buildings had to be propped up. The thump, thump of the pile-driver was heard again and again. Telegraph poles sixty feet long were driven into the soft ground, row after row of them, shoulder to shoulder, before the concrete foundations of new buildings were poured. When a pole disappeared completely, a thirty-foot pole was driven down on top of it. When a heavy machine, perhaps the latest Banbury mixer, was installed on foundations that proved to be soft, the machine was jacked up while the ground below was reinforced. The land was like a drunken sailor who, no matter how often he was set upright, eventually sagged again.

The working conditions in the crammed site were just tolerable. I asked a group of old employees how they would describe the factory to someone not even born in the 1930s. Back came the reply, almost as a chorus: 'The Black Hole of Calcutta'. The walls, ceilings and floor of some buildings were dark and grimy. Particles of carbon black, an ingredient of tyre making, seemed to coat everything in the mixing department of the No. 1 Mill, but in the No. 2 Mill the white talc or soapstone gave a lighter colouring. There was a scarcity of natural light, for the site was so jammed with buildings that even the windows did not admit much light — unless they faced a street. The ceilings were low and the few windows and numerous internal walls retarded any flow of outside air in the summer. On hot days the buildings were very uncomfortable but in winter they were warmer than most factories of that era because of the heat created by the rubber-making processes. The tempo of work — most people were paid a piece-work bonus — and the cramped conditions gave much of the factory a hyperactive air. In its bustle it looked more like a crowded jerry-built department store than a modern factory. The whistle from the steam-engine ruled everyone. At set times it gave a loud blast: at 7.25 and 7.30 in the morning, then at 12.15, 12.50, 12.55, and at 4.05 and so on through the changing of the shifts. In very busy periods, parts of the factory worked three shifts, and in dull periods in the inter-war years much of the factory was closed for weeks on end, especially in the first half of the year.

While Montague on a dark day seemed like a scene from the industrial revolution, it had its own attraction: the camaraderie of people who played jokes and bantered, who had known each other for a long time, who lived in nearby Port and South Melbourne and shared the same leisure activities. A sense of belonging, a kind of factory loyalty, was present in a proportion of the work-force, and the loyalty was focused on certain events: the annual picnic in the bay steamer to Sorrento, the factory dances and celebrations, and the Dunlop football team which won premierships in the Saturday morning league, then a major competition. In pre-war years such famous footballers as Tommy Lahiff and the winner of the Brownlow Medal, Herb Matthews, had played with Dunlop in the morning and then hurried to a league or association ground to play senior football in the afternoon.

The people working in the factory showed many social and sartorial divisions and distinctions to those with powers to observe them. Thus in the 1930s the senior executives walking to visit a part of the factory always wore their felt hat. The clerks and higher technical staff always wore a suit but rarely a hat. The foremen mostly wore grey or white dust-coats. The employees wore anything that caught their fancy or was serviceable: a waistcoat from an old Sunday suit, big farm boots, maybe a former best shirt from which the clip-on collar had been discarded. D. H. Kemp, beginning in 1934 a career which would take him to the boardroom, began work at the factory by reading the numerous power meters for several weeks. 'The dynamic movement of the whole bustling factory fascinated me', he wrote years later.

Bartlett did not think well of this Black Hole of Calcutta. He had his own phrase for it, 'the Bottomless Pit', by which he denoted both the sinking soil and the big sums of money required for the constant renovations to the factory. Setting his heart on a brand new factory on a new site, he first favoured Fishermens Bend, not far away. In 1939 he turned some twelve miles along the bayside, to Beaumaris and its market gardens, and persuaded the directors to buy land quietly on a large scale. By June, when they could no longer keep their plans secret and expected Sir Keith Murdoch's *Herald* to scoop them on any afternoon, they had bought 248 acres. They agreed that they could easily finance a new factory if they reduced the annual dividend from seven and a half to five per cent for the following five years. Admittedly the factory site was far from Melbourne's industrial suburbs, indeed was one of the most remote of the factory sites chosen by an industrial company in the 1930s, but Bartlett believed that the finished products could be sent away either by railway or from the Black Rock pier where lighters and tugs could carry them to the piers and wharves where the interstate ships were berthed. This was not only to be a big factory but it was to be surrounded by its own garden city for employees. At once two executives were deputed to go overseas to learn all they could from overseas factories and employee cities.

Ten weeks after the announcement, the war broke out, halting the scheme. By April 1940 when the war was merely simmering in Europe, Bartlett resumed the planning. The board authorised the surveying of the site and the levelling of the ground. Then the war exploded with Hitler's invasion of France. The plans were put away. In November 1942 Bartlett took them again to the boardroom and said the time was ripe for the building of the aircraft annexe at Beaumaris. The time was not ripe; it was easier to add new buildings to cramped Montague. But many employees decided it was only a matter of time before the new factory was built at Beaumaris, and some even went so far, after the war, as to build or buy houses close to the roads that bordered the actual factory site — Balcombe, Haydens and Reserve Roads and Pacific Boulevard.

For Bartlett the new factory and garden city became a burning ambition. On 28 April 1944, even before the Allied invasion of Europe, he thought the end of war was sufficiently in sight — maybe two years away — to justify the drawing up of building plans for Beaumaris and tentative orders for machinery so that he could begin bit by bit once the war was over. At the board meeting on Friday 28 April 1944, Bartlett spoke at length, seeking immediate permission to acquire or order or recondition machinery in readiness for Beaumaris. The board gave its 'unanimous affirmative vote'.

In Sydney, Bartlett sounded out a high government official about his prospects for securing the building materials for factory and houses. In Canberra he spent an hour with J. B. Chifley, the federal treasurer who was soon to become prime minister. Chifley, after examining the exhibits and factory plans that Bartlett placed on the table, said that the timber for building would probably have to be imported but imports might not be easy after the war because the rebuilding of war-torn Europe would have an early priority. He agreed with Bartlett that there was no large saving in building prefabricated houses in the garden city, and he revealed that the Labor government was thinking of regulating the housing rent payable by the lowest-paid worker at one sixth of his income. In short Dunlop would have to accept a low rent in its housing estate. Would Mr Chifley give a priority to the bold Dunlop scheme? Yes, he was willing to grant the same priority for labour and materials as he would grant to similar government and semi-government undertakings. Bartlett said privately that he thought Chifley was 'favourably impressed with what I had to show him'. In fact Chifley 'gave instructions to his secretary that he should be reminded to call' at Dunlop's head office when he next visited Melbourne.

When the war ended — almost a year earlier than Bartlett expected — labour and materials remained too scarce to allow an early start on Beaumaris. After his unexpected death in 1947 his plan retained a high priority, and there was talk of giving the name Bartlett to the garden suburb at the planned factory. Three years later Dunlop finalised a huge debenture loan of one and a quarter million pounds from the Australian Mutual Provident Society. Borrowed for twenty years at an interest rate of a mere four and a quarter per cent, it gave some shareholders the idea that at last Bartlett's dream factory would arise, overlooking the sea. Times had changed, however, and the swift expansion of suburban Melbourne made the acreage at Beaumaris too valuable for factories. Moreover the cost of building a huge factory — even without the garden suburb — had jumped to about four and a half million pounds. The money could yield higher dividends elsewhere. The Royal Melbourne Golf Club had every reason to cheer when its long-announced neighbour, Dunlop, decided in the winter of 1950 not to settle alongside some of the world's finest greens and fairways.

If Bartlett had lived, he probably would have found a way to build an economical version of the factory and suburb so important to him. His successor, Blackwood, preferred less dramatic and quieter solutions. Almost without announcing it he was establishing low-price versions of Beaumaris around the countryside and in outer suburbs. In the space of about five years, at a fraction of the cost, he provided additional factory space with a total output at least as high as that of pre-war Montague.

As labour was scarce in the cities Blackwood set up small factories in those country towns where female labour especially was plentiful. To these factories was moved equipment from Montague and Drummoyne, where space was thus released for the expansion of tyre making. The weatherproof clothing factory had already been started at Wagga Wagga during the war. In the late 1940s, in Victoria, Bendigo began to make industrial V-belts, fan belts and rubber heels while Bairnsdale made rubber threads. At Frankston, then an isolated bayside town rather than an outer suburb, a small factory began to make golf balls. Of course the supply of labour in these towns, while more reliable than in the cities, never quite reached expectations. At Bendigo the manager was dismayed to see his employees, when the tomato-picking season arrived, leave the factory to take on the better-paid seasonal work, while at Bairnsdale many of the employees did not arrive if the day was very cold. Compared to the city factories these small places were at least manageable.

At Drummoyne and Montague the turnover of labour each year was the despair of the foremen. Employees, trained by the company for a new task, left before their training was complete. Montague was bad enough with an annual turnover rate of more than sixty per cent in 1949 and 1950. Drummoyne's turnover of labour reached 163 per cent in 1950. The manager there even tried the revolutionary step of making a short movie about his factory and showing it at the crowded suburban cinemas. Hundreds, maybe thousands, who saw the movie were not in the least influenced by its message that they too should work at the Drummoyne factory. They had worked there and then moved elsewhere.

The difficulty of running the big Drummoyne factory was partly eased by opening factories in other suburbs of Sydney. The best-selling Maxply tennis racket was made at Beverly Hills and shoes were made at St Mary's. On a large site at Blacktown a variety of products was made beneath the sawtooth roofs of separate factories: quality trousers and sports coats made of fine worsted cloths, the new plastic gardening hose which was challenging the heavy rubber hose, and Geon plastics. By 1954 the Dunlop factory at Bankstown was making more shoes than any factory in Australia. Amongst its numerous products were leather fur-topped ladies' boots for the ski season, small rubber boots which were laced to the feet of sheep suffering from foot-rot in the Monaro winters, kneeboots tailored for handicapped people, and those sandals known as thongs. At first the thongs were assumed to be a fast-passing fashion, but production soared to meet the demand and that section of the Bankstown factory was busy for fourteen years until the market was seized by cheap imports.

At its peak, over a thousand people worked at the footwear factory at Bankstown and a lot of the folklore of the suburb still centres around events on the factory floor. At reunions and get-togethers the old hands will ask each other: don't you remember the time when the man on night shift was found fast asleep in a warm autoclave? Just before the doors were shut and the steam turned on? And they recall the day when a factory hand unlocked the door of the vulcaniser too early: the door swung open, the sudden rush of air blew him out, and he was thrown through the thin fibro wall of the building, landing on the grass, more bruised than battered. 'Later on we had a good laugh', William Pask says, recalling the incident. 'The fibro wall showed a perfect figure of a man with arms and legs spread wide just like in a cartoon!'.

In Western Australia a factory much humbler than Bankstown was planned. The state was isolated and when certain machines broke down, replacement parts were too slow in arriving, thus curbing production and even causing unemployment. Accordingly at the back of the Dunlop offices at 424 Murray Street, Perth, a small workshop was opened to turn rubber into simple shapes. With power from a steam boiler, an autoclave cured rubber articles such as washers, hoses, and wringers made to the specification the customer required. It was like a small baker's shop, except that rubber rather than dough was the raw material. Two men, Bob Dickson and Harry Walker, did all the tasks, and with a little more equipment they could tackle a variety of orders from factories, mines and other users of machinery.

The government railways of Western Australia were potentially the main customers for simple rubber products. Their rolling-stock was run-down, and the braking mechanisms were vulnerable. The steam train's brakes worked on the vacuum system, and each of the flexible hoses linking locomotive and carriage or carriage and carriage required nine rubber components. When the government began to re-equip its railways and replace the brakes, it saw advantages in the rubber parts being made locally. Blackwood was easily persuaded in 1948 that a small factory should be established, and Gerry Young went from Montague to Welshpool to manage it. A Lancashire boiler, burning firewood, supplied the heat for working the rubber. The fire was lit each morning at half past five so that the boiler held a sufficient head of steam by the time the men began work at eight o'clock. Two secondhand torpedo tubes, no longer needed by submarines, were converted into autoclaves, thus enabling the manufacture of hose up to ten feet in length. Primarily depending on orders for railway brakes, the makeshift factory soon employed eight men. More and more orders arrived, and in 1952 the machinery was moved to a larger factory built at East Fremantle.

Blackwood believed that small was often best and that factories with a small work-force usually had smooth industrial relations. He hoped that no Dunlop factory would have more than 1500 employees and that most working-places would be small. Of the Victorian factories opened in the first decade after the war, the largest was at Bayswater. It was chosen when a site at Jordanville, much nearer the city, had to be jettisoned in 1950 after the Mulgrave Shire Council refused permission for a factory to be built. The forty acres of farmland at Bayswater was bought for eight thousand pounds. The land was close to the Dandenong Ranges, and some of the first employees, arriving by electric train from the smoky, grimy and flat mills of Montague, said the new site was too pretty for a factory. The first intention was to use Bayswater primarily for making the aircraft wheels and brakes, the pneumatic and hydraulic equipment, and the oil and fuel hoses which were in demand by the air force, by the Commonwealth Aircraft Corporation factory at Port Melbourne, and by the Department of Civil Aviation. In 1950 the commonwealth government gave this project a high priority for defence purposes and offered to supply the machine tools if Dunlop built and staffed the factory.

The Bayswater factory was built in stages. It was an alternative to Montague, taking on products that were squeezed out when more space was needed at the old factory for the manufacture of tyres. The machinery too was sent out from Montague where there was reportedly a popular saying about very old machinery: 'Don't scrap it — send it to Bayswater'.

Bayswater made a wide variety of products, and it might have made even more but for the fact that it proved to be a poor recruiting ground for manual labour. The work there, though hard, was relatively well paid, but the system of two twelve-hour shifts working around the clock was not very popular. Every Friday afternoon thirty or forty men collected their final pay and vanished. Every Monday morning another thirty or forty appeared at the office, were signed, and then were led in a procession along the various factory floors, with men dropping out of the procession here and there to start their new job of making hoses, or rubber parts for aircraft or milking machines, or the rubber lining for the inside of huge metal tanks.

For a time Dunlop even awarded the substantial bonus of twenty-five pounds to each employee who could recruit one outside labourer and persuade him to work at the Bayswater factory for three continuous months. Many of the employees drove from the Dandenong Ranges where they worked their own farmlet at the weekend or on long summer evenings. In the early days of Bayswater it was possible to buy from fellow workers a dozen eggs or a bag of potatoes or a live hen at bargain prices. A few days before Christmas, small pigs were for sale inside the factory.

In addition to the post-war factories scattered between Fremantle and Brisbane a network of new workshops retrod tyres. This form of manufacturing was done near the main street of many towns and suburbs rather than at one central location in each state. The retreading of worn tyres was vital in wartime, because new tyres were strictly rationed. Dunlop apparently decided that it should have a hand in the business when the opportunity arose to buy the small firm operated by Barney Hamill, who in 1943 was on the verge of retiring. His firm, B. A. Hamill Pty Ltd, in its factory in Spencer Street, Melbourne, made the moulds and much of the equipment used in retreading and recapping tyres. With this business as a base, Dunlop began to buy out a few tyre dealers who sold tyres and sometimes petrol at the front entrance and retrod tyres at the back. In the mid-1940s, private tyre businesses were not bought systematically but simply when they came on the market. At the end of the war Dunlop owned fifteen, including eight in Victoria and four in New South Wales. In the following decade (1945–55) another seventy-two tyre dealers and retreaders were bought out, making the dealerships an important asset in their own right.

There were distinct advantages in owning a factory-shop-depots chain for retreading old tyres and selling new. The main Melbourne rival, Olympic, had begun with its Beaurepaire retreading outlets, and many rubber firms in America owned nation-wide outlets. Blackwood's deputy, Roy Simkin, bought more outlets, though for a long time he was reluctant to make it known which dealerships were actually owned by Dunlop. Thus Bill Gurton sold his three tyre depots to Dunlop and continued to play golf regularly with the managing director of Goodyear without breathing a word that he had sold out to Dunlop. A typical tyre subsidiary sold every brand of tyre but it definitely favoured the Dunlop brands, and by the mid-1950s about four of every five sales were Dunlop tyres. Thirty years previously Dunlop had no time for the retreading firms because they inevitably restricted the demand for new tyres. Now they found that it was better to join the enemy than to defeat them. This proved to be a sound decision during the Korean War when the world price of rubber soared and new tyres were judged too dear by most Australian motorists. In the seven months ending January 1953 Dunlop's chain of tyre firms made 1.1 million pounds from the sale of new tyres, 1 million from the retreading of old tyres and 0.35 million from selling petrol, oil and accessories.

Dunlop's policy was to buy a successful tyre and retreading business in a busy street, retaining the former owner as manager. In its buying policy it was to make one major mistake. Kenworth Rubber Limited made general rubber goods and also sold retreads. From its factory in Lennox Street, Richmond, it unwisely expanded to Bendigo in 1951 and lost money there before planning to build a big factory at Tottenham in Melbourne's western suburbs. Lacking the money to complete the factory it eventually fell so heavily into debt that three nominees of the Commonwealth Bank were placed on its board. In 1955 Dunlop was approached to buy Kenworth Rubber. The price was low, and long lists of arguments seemed to justify the purchase, but Kenworth was not successful under Dunlop's ownership.

The 1950s was almost a magical decade for the motor industry in Australia. Sales of cars leaped year after year, the buying of a car was an endless topic of conversation, and new service stations sprang up at nearly every big crossroad — Melbourne and Sydney probably had more petrol outlets then than today. The tyre business also prospered and Dunlop won a share of the market it had probably not regularly achieved since the First World War. In the year ending June 1952, sixty-six per cent of the new cars and sixty per cent of the new trucks sold in Australia were equipped with Dunlop tyres, and one-seventh of the company's entire income came from the sale of new tyres to four big customers: General Motors–Holden, Ford, International Harvester and Austin.

Changes in the qualities of tyres added to the excitement and ultimately the profits. In the previous twenty years the tyre had been in a state of flux, with synthetic rubber challenging natural rubber, and rayon and then nylon supplanting cotton as the fabric in the tyre casing. The tyre was changing shape, with the wheel rim wider and the tyre fatter — the ratio of height to width was falling. The pressure of air in the tube that lay inside the typical tyre was almost halved in the years 1924 to 1958, and the lower air pressure combined with the wider tyre meant that a higher proportion of the total tread of the tyre actually hit the surface of the road at any given instant. Such tyres, and their grip on the road, enabled a car to corner safely at a higher speed. To cap these changes came the tubeless tyre. Perfected by the Goodrich Co. in the USA, it became the vogue in the early 1950s. Its special qualities were explained by D. H. Kemp of Dunlop who often spoke on science on ABC radio. He explained that the new tubeless tyre combined 'the air-holding attribute of the inner tube with the load-carrying characteristic of the outer casing.' No amount of explanation could convince a big number of Australian motorists that the tubeless tyre was safe and less likely to be punctured. When Dunlop released the new tyre in February 1955, and it became common on new cars, some motorists went to high expense in removing the tubeless tyre and fitting the orthodox tyres with their dual fitting of an outer casing and inner tube.

The company was earning about seventy per cent of its revenue from tyres in the mid-1950s, and most of the tyres were made at Montague. But the company operated another twenty-one factories, making a wide variety of rubber goods. In 1956 the real output of the company was two and a half times what it had been in 1947. Under Robert Blackwood the company had grown like Topsy and yet it was generally efficient, with each new factory occupying a site that had a special advantage in either attracting scarce labour or in serving local needs. True, the scattered workshops and factories were not so easily co-ordinated from head office, but Blackwood, usually practical, was content with any management structure that worked.

The 1950s were dream years for big Australian manufacturers. There were pressures but new opportunities appeared almost monthly. The tariff kept out most imports and for many years Canberra's method of licensing imports was an added protection. In 1958, for example, the government issued licences to importers for only two hundred thousand tyres for the year, and yet if licences were abolished some six hundred thousand tyres would have flooded in. A local manufacturer could naturally flourish under such protection.

Towards the end of the decade Japan was looming as a serious competitor, and at first the Japanese were often enlisted against European brands intruding into Australian shoe shops. Thus in March 1959, R. N. Dowling of Dunlop made a short visit to Japan and arranged to import three hundred thousand pairs of thongs, stamped with the Dunlop brand and priced to outsell any other imports. In another trial shipment he arranged to import 16 000 pairs of

The Dunlop advertisements were becoming a common sight in Papua New Guinea.

Japanese shoes, with imitation leather uppers made of PVC. It was the Dunlop business in Australian New Guinea which first faced stern competition from Japan. By July 1961, Japanese goods were allowed to enter on equal terms, and Dunlop's agents there tried to compete by advertising that Dunlop bought the entire output of Papuan rubber and that therefore its rubber goods should be preferred by customers in New Guinea.

In almost every month of the late 1950s, Dunlop was tempted to manufacture new goods. It gave in to the temptations. It now proclaimed that its formal policy was to depend less on tyres, and instead to diversify. It bought three-quarters of the shares in Trilby, makers of ladies' footwear. It bought Buesst and Bills, manufacturers of bedding. It bought out the Sydney and Brisbane factories making the Sleepmaker brand of inner-spring mattresses. At Nowra in New South Wales a factory making hoses and other rubber products was taken over from the John Bull Rubber Company. In 1960, Dunlop joined with its rival, Olympic, and the company Ralph McKay Limited to form Wheels and Rims Australia which produced disc wheels for trucks. Already at Regents Park, Dunlop was the nation's largest maker of polythene piping and at Sandringham it was the largest maker of automotive batteries, including the new 'dry charged' batteries. The biggest of the plans discussed in these years

Peter Thomson, five times winner of the British Open, used Dunlop clubs and golf balls.

*Two of Australia's finest tennis players, Evonne Cawley and Margaret Court, used Dunlop
and Slazenger racquets and Dunlop shoes.*

— a partnership with oil companies for the manufacture of synthetic rubber
— did not eventuate.

It became Dunlop's practice to claim that nearly every Australian adult and
child used at least one of its products nearly every day. Dunlop products were
seen on every tennis-court and golf-course. In October 1958 the company
chairman proudly told shareholders that for the fourth time the Australian
golfer Peter Thomson had won the British Open using, of course, the Dunlop
65 golf ball and the Dunlop clubs carrying his own brand name. In the
following year the purchase of the Australian business owned by Slazenger
increased the investment in sporting goods.

The sixtieth birthday of Dunlop Rubber Australia Limited came during
these exuberant years. In August 1959 the company made the most of its

Debut of teenagers Lew Hoad and Ken Rosewall in Australia's 3-2 victory against USA in the Davis Cup, 1953. Hoad worked for Dunlop and Rosewall was linked to Slazenger.

birthday, though it was mistaken about its own origins, confusing the floating of the Australian company in 1899 with the earlier founding of the little factory which put together the bicycle tyres in a Melbourne lane. In celebration, 671 Dunlop displays were mounted in shop windows and tyre depots in Sydney alone, while in country towns in New South Wales some 350 automotive sales points, 195 footwear shops and 110 sports-goods shops arranged special Dunlop displays. In Sydney those who turned their new television sets onto Channel Seven saw that ancient retired Dunlop director, H. Daniell, reminiscing in the programme 'Person To Person' about his seventy years in the rubber industry. In Geelong many listeners heard on 3GL the government's whip in the federal parliament, Hubert Opperman, plead for a national network of sealed roads and recall in passing that his early wins as a champion cyclist were in races sponsored by Dunlop. Even the *Rubber Workers' Journal* promised to write an editorial about Dunlop, the largest employer of its members. For the long-standing employees a memorable night of the diamond jubilee was the first dinner of the 25 Year Club, with speeches, fellowship and the presenting of inscribed watches to those who had been with the firm for twenty-five years or more. A quarter of a century later, these annual dinners were to be a victim of the new federal Fringe Benefits Tax, and in part, of the task of coping with the crowds of people entitled to attend them, especially in Sydney and Melbourne.

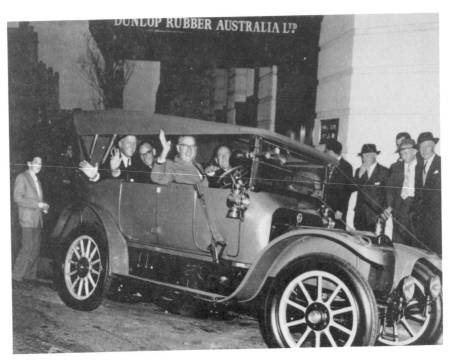

Some employees came in vintage cars to the inaugural Dunlop 25 Year Club dinner in Sydney in 1959.

Dunlop had never experienced such a prosperous decade as the 1950s. Dividends of ten per cent were easily paid on preference and ordinary shares, leaving large unpaid surpluses to help finance the expansion of factories and tyre depots. After the big debenture issue of 1950 and the share issues of 1950 and 1952, the company in the remaining years had raised no further capital. Indeed in 1959 it issued bonus shares to its members. And yet these were years when new factories were ravenous for capital, for the work-force of less than five thousand in the late 1940s exceeded ten thousand a decade later. The sheer size of the work-force was making some of the old social occasions almost unmanageable, and when in Victoria on 10 December 1960 the Dunlop Social Club ran its annual picnic by the bay at Mornington, its secretary calculated that 3206 people were present amongst the hundreds of parked cars and vans.

In the following year, out of the blue, came the first short break in the long post-war prosperity. The balance of payments gave acute trouble, the government imposed a 'credit squeeze' to quieten the economy, and people feeling the intended squeeze decided to buy fewer new manufactured goods. The car

A Christmas picnic of Montague employees at Mornington in 1950.

industry was especially squeezed. In June 1961 the new vehicles registered in Australia were twenty-eight per cent lower than in the same month of the previous year. The sale of fewer cars meant the sale of fewer tyres. A month later, in most states, the sales of Dunlop goods were lower, but in Victoria they were down twenty-one per cent compared to sales in the corresponding month of the previous year. Dunlop's profits on tyres fell more rapidly than the sales, because the relatively new tyre firms, Goodrich and Hardie, were advertising their own brand of tyres at slashed prices. This economic slump in 1961 shocked most Australians. In the federal election at the end of the year, they almost voted out the Menzies government, because in those balmy years an unemployment rate exceeding two per cent was deemed a sign of an economy in peril.

Remarkably the Dunlop sales in Western Australia did not fall during this short slump that so harmed the eastern states. Western Australia was beginning to jump ahead. Frank Merry, who left the navy and joined Dunlop in Perth in 1958, made his first visit to the far north-west before the start of the iron-ore boom. In isolated Wyndham the sale of tyres was so slow that at the general store and Dunlop agency he came across a pile of 'new' Dunlop truck tyres. They had been sitting there for some time, and the white ants had bored holes through the carcass of the tyres. Before long he was in Port Hedland and Dampier, the early iron-ore ports, opening tyre depots which eventually blossomed into big Dunlop agencies that sold everything from huge tyres for road graders to long conveyor belts of a strength and toughness previously unknown in Australia.

In the motoring boom the sales of tyres soared, and about seventy per cent of the company revenue again came from tyres. The Montague factory, after shedding so many activities to other factories, was free to concentrate mainly on tyres. Usually it produced at least half as many tyres again as Drummoyne; but it was hardly efficient. Montague was congested, the operations could not be physically placed in the correct sequence, and there was double-handling of raw materials and the half-finished products. The cramped sites of Montague and Drummoyne had originally been selected in the era of the bicycle tyre and the indiarubber doll, and it was natural that their deficiencies should be discussed again and again. In July 1956 the managerial members of the Dunlop board proposed a brand-new tyre factory to supplant Montague. Where exactly in Victoria that factory should be sited they had no firm view. But they believed that high-grade tyres could never be manufactured cheaply until they erected a new factory, all on one level to promote the efficient flow of production. Using as a rough guide the tyre factory operated by English Dunlop at Whitby, they calculated the price of building an Australian factory that would make four thousand tyres a day. Bartlett's dream was again on the drawing-board, only to be pushed aside by other ventures, other calls for funds.

His dream was revived in 1960. Out amongst the orchards and paddocks on the Springvale Road, just to the north of Wellington Road, was a large block of eighty-one acres which seemed ideal to Blackwood and his right-hand man, Eric Dunshea. Before a factory could be erected the land had to be rezoned, and Dunshea put a powerful argument to the authorities. Permission was granted, but again Dunlop had second thoughts. The recession of 1961 arrived and unemployment jumped over two per cent, causing a fall in the demand for tyres and a postponing of plans for a new factory. Moreover Blackwood looked again at his big tyre factory at Montague, and saw its numerous advantages, including its contented, skilled and stable work-force. When he compared inner-city Montague with the big Dunlop factories in the outer suburbs, the contrast in the work-force was astonishing. Thus in the month of April 1962, Montague had a labour turnover of only one per cent compared to seven per cent at Bankstown and ten per cent at Bayswater. Absenteeism at the grimy old tyre factory at Montague was only half as frequent as at the other big Dunlop factories where the average employee was absent — and not sick — for about a fortnight a year. In time lost through accidents Montague was again the winner. The message was clear.

For a time the demand for a big modern tyre factory in Melbourne was forgotten. Instead several states applied political pressure and made enticing offers in the hope of winning a small tyre factory for their own capital city. In Perth, Charles Court, the dynamic minister for industrial development and the north-west, offered all the government's tyre business to the company that would build a tyre factory. Dunlop knew that if it did not act, another tyre-maker — perhaps an overseas firm — would step in and capture the valuable South Australian and Western Australian markets. In 1963 Dunlop and Olympic did what was once thought impossible. They agreed to combine in financing and running two new factories, with Olympic managing a tyre factory in the Adelaide suburb of Elizabeth and Dunlop managing the Western Australian factory. There, in the suburb of O'Connor in December 1964, Dunlop manufactured its first Western Australian tyre, a tubeless four-ply.

The original hope was that the increased cost of producing the more popular sizes of passenger tyres in these small interstate factories would be offset by eliminating the freight from Melbourne, but the factories proved to be too small to be economical. In Perth the new manager, Claude McFarlane, was dismayed to find a chronic shortage of unskilled labour, for the new outback mines were paying high wages. Moreover his factory had to face competition from the Hardie Tyre and Rubber Co. which began to build a local tyre factory after gaining — through quick negotiations — the government contract for which Dunlop had hoped. In three years the additional cost of the tyres made in the new Adelaide and Perth factories was well over half a million pounds. A technical hitch increased the loss. The tread on the rayon tyres made in Western Australia tended to separate itself from the tyre, mainly because the rayon ply transported from Montague collected moisture before it reached the factory.

The clear gain of the Perth tyre factory was in industrial relations. When it closed in February 1967, after making 157 000 passenger tyres and some 11 000 truck and tractor tyres, it had experienced not one strike or demarcation dispute. The factory which Olympic managed in Adelaide was closed at the same time. The efficient manufacture of tyres, more than ever before, called for large-scale production and the latest equipment; and the dominance of Sydney and Melbourne in tyre production was not challenged again.

In the boardroom at 108 Flinders Street there was a touch of disillusionment with tyres. Sir Dan McVey, who had succeeded Sir Alexander Stewart as chairman of Dunlop in 1956, was something of an expert on government policy. A Scottish-born engineer, he had fought in the First World War, had risen rapidly in the Australian public service to become head of departments, and had then moved into manufacturing where he was managing director of the big Port Kembla firm, Metal Manufactures. He did not think highly of Canberra's zigzag policy towards tyres. Since the war the federal government had firstly encouraged the manufacture of tyres in Australia by regulating imports both by duties and licensing restrictions, and then in the late 1950s it had backed down, creating too much competition in a limited tyre market by encouraging foreign tyre-makers to set up factories in Australia. Six companies — Firestone was the latest foreign arrival — made tyres in a nation where there was barely room for two efficient factories. Moreover several of the older manufacturers, including Dunlop and Olympic, had further splintered the market by spreading their machinery and output over several scattered factories.

Imported tyres increased the competition. By the mid-1960s large consign-

Sir Daniel McVey, with a group of Dunlop ladies, at the 25 Year Club dinner, in 1960.

ments of cheap Italian, Japanese and other foreign tyres were often arriving. In the year ending June 1967 one in every six replacement tyres fitted to a motor vehicle was an imported tyre. Here were early signs of the foreign competition that would become stronger and stronger, challenging the existence of local manufacturers in scores of industries.

While Dunlop had nothing like the diversity of today, it was selling so many different products that its warehouse and sales staff in the remote parts of Australia felt they were becoming general-storekeepers. Neville McAvoy, Dunlop's full-time 'representative' in the Mackay and Bowen districts of North Queensland in 1965, would visit a local sugar mill or the Collinsville coal-mine to discuss their needs in conveyor belts, spend the next day trying to persuade tennis officials to use the latest Dunlop ball in their tournaments, and devote the following day to visiting shoe shops to sell footwear — including the distinctive Canecutters Leather Boots made in Dunlop's Bankstown factory. Occasionally he would hire a room in a motel — the motel was the very latest in accommodation — and display for the benefit of customers the newest styles in Ladies' Winter Fashion Coats and Bikinis under the brand name of 'Bobbi by Dunlop'. He even had to sell surfboards: 'I will never forget my struggling around the streets of Mackay with my sample of a ten-foot fibreglass surfboard under my arm'.

With the steady move away from an overwhelming reliance on rubber goods, Robert Blackwood was in complete agreement, but his agreement was no longer as essential as in the past. Inch by inch he was edging out of the detailed running of the business. Blackwood in his spare hours was absorbed in the task of creating the new Monash University, of which he had become the first chairman of council in 1958, and three years later — the year of his knighthood — its first chancellor. In Dunlop's head office by the early 1960s

In 1992 Dunlop Slazenger introduced the Bradman collection. At the request of Sir Donald Bradman
all licence fees and royalties from sales of the Bradman range go to the Bradman Trust to develop cricket.

Photo courtesy of Kelvin Aldred

A Dunlop poster of 1950, when far more Australians owned a cycle than a car.

Above: Robert de Castella, winning the Boston marathon in 1984 in his Adidas shoes, was a member of the Adidas sales team for 16 years.

Left: Footscray champion, Ted Whitten, alias Mr Football, is one of many well-known sportsmen working for Dunlop. For several decades he has been promotions manager for Adidas.

Golf Shoes by NIBLICK

In 1976, Greg Norman began wearing Niblick golf shoes.

Above: *Surgical gloves made at Ansell's factory in Malaysia.*

Below: *The rubber glove was becoming popular for household tasks in 1953, and readers of the* Australian Women's Weekly *saw the leading model, Bambi Shmith, wearing the Ansell gloves in the house and garden.*

A model life-style.

BAMBI SHMITH, famous model and busy housewife, says...

"STOP WORRYING about 'housework hands'
START WEARING ANSELL RUBBER GLOVES"
—for ever-beautiful hands.

"The wonderful thing about these Ansell Rubber Gloves", add that they're so easy to slip on and off. They fit they feel so light and the

In the weekend Bambi likes to potter in the garden. "I just couldn't enjoy this pleasure without the protection of Ansell Sure-Grip Rubber Gloves", says Bambi. No dirt to scrub out afterwards . . . no scratches, either . . . when you garden with the help of Ansell.

Sleep**maker**

Comfort with support

MARSHALL BATTERIES

The company's first logo had been a serious portrait of bearded John Dunlop, the inventor, but by 1990 the typical logo was more skittish.

Above left: 'Sleepmaker' of Dunlop Bedding.

Below left: 'Holler for a Marshall'.

Above right: Holeproof's celebrated 'Computer Socks' commercial.

Below right: Holeproof's award-winning 'No Knickers' commercial.

Sir Frank Beaurepaire, painted by Sir William Dargie.

the executive who set the pace was Eric Dunshea. In 1960, on the retirement of Roy Simkin, Dunshea had become in effect the assistant general manager, a position which was made more powerful by the fact that he already had a seat on the board. Dunshea and McVey soon became allies. Senior staff felt certain that Dunshea would soon become general manager, in place of Blackwood, not only because he was Blackwood's right-hand man but also because he was McVey's right-hand man.

In April 1966, at the age of sixty, Blackwood stepped down, while remaining a director. Without any flamboyance, any grand theorising, any ideology of management, Blackwood had proved his all-round competence in his seventeen years as chief executive. He handed over to Dunshea the control of one of the five biggest manufacturing companies in Australia, and no observer had reason to doubt that Dunlop was in sound condition.

If a company can be likened to a horse, then Dunlop was a steady and even impressive work-horse at the time when Blackwood handed over the reins. Dunshea, in eagerly accepting the reins, had other preferences. He thought he would turn the draughthorse into a charger. With McVey urging it on, it began to gallop off in a new direction.

The ascent of Dunshea

Y EAR AFTER year Eric Dunshea must have longed for the day when he
would produce the play, be the leading actor and arrange the stage
scenery. He had been secretary since 1944 and a director since 1951;
now in his late fifties, he had a strong wish to make his impact. Definite in
many of his views, inclined to steamroller through opposition if he thought
he could get away with it, utterly absorbed in the firm, he also had a fatherly
attitude towards employees and an ability to inspire them to give their best.
Bald with a little white hair on the sides and neck, wearing old-fashioned
spectacles with brown rims, and talking with a sense of conviction and a
slightly gravelly voice, he soon gave the impression that he had held the top
post for years.

Eric Ernest Dunshea was a chartered accountant, not an engineer. For the
last four decades the permanent head of Dunlop had normally been a
technical man familiar with a rubber factory, but Dunshea's skill was in the
office. A Sydney-sider, born in a relatively humble house in the Old Canter-
bury Road in Summer Hill, he was brought up a Baptist with the Bible at his
side as a boy and still not too far away when he was sixty. In April 1971 a
journalist from the *Australian Financial Review*, visiting Dunshea in his wood-
panelled and green-rugged office, was surprised to receive several freshly-
typed copies of the biblical texts which had most influenced Dunshea.
Dunshea informed him that 'as a matter of fact my life is based on this
particular verse of scripture'. It was Joshua 1:9, ending with the assurance that
'the Lord thy God is with thee whithersoever thou goest'. Dunshea added
that the sayings remembered from his childhood had moulded his life. One
saying, passed on to him by an old Sydney manufacturer, remained a favourite:
'You should never be satisfied with second-best'.

He was not satisfied to be second-best. Though his early schooling was

*Eric Dunshea and the premier of Queensland, Frank Nicklin, presenting the
Dunlop Rural Awards in 1968.*

limited, he rose steadily in the office of Perdriau in Sydney, and soon after the
merger with Dunlop he was sent, at the age of twenty-three, to head office in
Melbourne to install what was a primitive precursor to the computer: this was
the latest punch-card equipment which enabled the collecting and sorting of
information for analysing Dunlop's sales and supervising its annual budget.
Dunlop never had a more dedicated, more eager employee. He was systematic,
obliging, quick to learn, and even at an early age he was imitating his superiors
in Melbourne and quietly preparing himself for higher office. Dunlop and the
local Baptist church absorbed him; in the 1960s, as the dynamic chairman of
the council of the Carey Baptist Grammar School, he was to transform that
school's buildings and equipment. He had imagination and big ideas as well
as the accountant's concern for correct detail. Though the detail of the
company's business quickly became less appealing to him as his power in the
company increased, he felt it was a sign of power to produce the kind of detail
that took a listener by surprise. Thus a year before his death he could tell a

journalist the exact number of public speeches he had given so far in his life: a total of 542 including thirty-seven at church services. Possibly the number was plucked from the air; more likely it was true, and the notes for every one of those speeches were in safe keeping at home or in the office.

For long Dunshea, as general secretary, had ranked third to the general manager, but in the early 1960s, as Blackwood approached retirement, Dunshea began to act as pace-maker. Aided by his own seat on the board and by a growing friendship with Sir Daniel McVey, Dunshea quietly planned a reorganising of the power structure of the company. His plan began to emerge soon after he went overseas in March 1962 on a three-month tour of investigation. Making his very first inspection of a rubber plantation — in Malaysia — and examining the tyre factories of Japanese Dunlop before visiting London, Fort Dunlop, Germany, France, Ireland and North America, he returned with two strong impressions. Firstly, he said, 'what a wonderful family is the Dunlop family!', and secondly he announced that the time had come for the Australian branch of the family to smarten itself.

Dunshea saw grave disadvantages, and Sir Daniel agreed, in Australian Dunlop's traditional method of management whereby those who controlled the factories had inadequate contact with those who controlled the selling of the products. The branches in each state sold the tyres and other rubber goods but even in Victoria, where the factory and the sales headquarters were less than two miles apart, the contact was minimal. Some of the goods they manufactured, either in design or in quantities produced, were not quite suitable for the markets they were serving. Dunshea's solution was to reorganise the company, and set up five separate divisions, each with its own general manager who would control the factories as well as the relevant sales and service organisation. In other words Dunlop would consist of five organisations or divisions, each with a large degree of autonomy. With the aid of McVey, Dunshea's scheme was accepted by the directors.

On the first day of January 1963 the reorganised Dunlop set to work. The big automotive division centred on tyres was led by H. E. Pill, the industrial division by H. W. Watt, the footwear and weatherproof division by R. N. Dowling, the flooring division by I. C. Stevens, and the sporting goods division by the former tennis star, Adrian Quist. The new organisation worked well. Several years before Blackwood stepped down as general manager the company was reflecting several of Dunshea's major views. When finally he became general manager he was quick to savour the job and increase its power.

Eric Dunshea had waited years for the day when he could dominate a board meeting. His day came on 1 April 1966. The first agenda he arranged for the board was humdrum, and the meeting went quietly. The chairman, Sir Daniel McVey, congratulated him on becoming chief executive and assured him of the 'utmost help'. Within a few months it was clear that Dunshea wanted little help.

Dunshea decided that the title of general manager was inadequate. At the second board meeting it was agreed that he be called the Chief General Manager. Such a commanding title needed a house to match. For the first time Dunlop bought a home for its chief executive, an expensive house at 6 St Georges Road, Toorak, where Sir Edgar Coles of the celebrated retailing family had lived. It was quickly agreed that Dunshea would pay three per cent of his salary in rent and that the company would pay all rates and taxes and the wages of two domestic servants and a part-time gardener. He intended to entertain in the name of the company: it was right that the company should help. With Sir Dan's consent the house was bought even before the directors heard of such a proposal. At the next meeting the board agreed that at head office a private dining-room be provided for Dunshea to entertain important clients.

'The company must cut a dashing image', said Dunshea. He quietly discarded the familiar insignia of Dunlop seen on hoardings and advertisements: the word DUNLOP printed in black on a yellow background. Instead he borrowed the phrase THE FORWARD LOOK, from English Dunlop. His desire for change was as much conservative as radical. He liked to imitate English Dunlop and he also wished to entertain in the manner of other heads of big companies.

That he made many of these changes with haste was the first sign that he intended to lead Dunlop along a new road. Quickly he centralised power. The board agreed with the proposal that the Executive Directors' Committee be abolished and that all its duties be passed on to Dunshea. A new management chart was shown to the assembled directors who expressed satisfaction that Ern Kellam, the deputy general manager, would retain oversight of sales. In his quest for efficiency Dunshea was given all support: the making of tyres in South and Western Australia was abandoned, the making of conveyor belts at Bayswater was agreed upon, and research was fostered.

Directors were heartened to hear Dunshea talk of plans as far as twelve years ahead. Only with long-range plans, he announced, could the big American competitors be held at bay. On 7 April 1967 he privately revealed the most detailed, co-ordinated plan for capital works ever conceived by a public company in Australia. He said he would spend eighty-seven million dollars in the following dozen or so years, financing it all from the soaring profits: he would not sacrifice the dividend and he would even wipe out existing debts. Lord Baillieu, absent from the meeting, sent along a letter which reportedly acclaimed the plan as 'the best thing of its kind he had ever seen'. As Dunshea was now lending a hand in the wording of the board's minutes, Lord Baillieu's exact words could be less a reflection of his enthusiasm than of Dunshea's. The minutes give the impression that Dunshea's long-term plans were hailed with evangelical fervour: 'Each director in turn complimented Mr Dunshea on the thoroughness and excellence of the proposals he had presented to the Board and expressed complete agreement with the scheme'.

Enthusiasm from the staff was, for Dunshea, as intoxicating as the enthusiasm of the directors. Soon after becoming the chief he called together the senior executives for occasional conferences. His warm personality, rapport with all around him, and faith in Dunlop persuaded them that there was a new drive for perfection. With an almost childlike eagerness he told the directors about the staff's urge to excel. He conveyed the impression that he was an evangelist producing born-again managers. To each conference he gave rousing names such as 'The Forward Look' or 'The Turning of the Tide'. The idea of a turning tide implied that Sir Robert Blackwood had handed over to Dunshea an ebbing business. Blackwood was too gentlemanly to protest.

The minutes of the monthly meetings of directors, usually a desert of dry facts, now became a torrent of praise and thanksgiving. When a record profit of $5.3 million was announced in July 1967 the chairman was reported in the minutes as saying, 'the achievement was most remarkable'. Dunshea's key words were *challenge* and *forward*: everything was a challenge which led to another step forward. After two years he was granted a large increase in salary for his 'outstanding service'. In these bumper times the old employees also shared, and the news of a Dunlop retirement fund was 'received enthusiastically' even by shop stewards at the factories.

Exciting times; they were to become frenetic. The twelve-year programme of capital works was advancing with such speed that new projects were needed. A foretaste was given at the board meeting of 1 March 1968: 'Business', said Dunshea, 'should be sought in new fields with a significant potential for growth'. He began to buy out other companies, and his shopping list grew long; he began to go Christmas shopping throughout the year. The capital works programme was almost forgotten.

The day of days in Dunshea's shopping spree was 6 December 1968. That morning the board of Dunlop discussed concrete proposals to buy all shares or a controlling interest in Ernest Hiller Holdings, Taft Australia, Julius Marlow Holdings, SA Rubber Holdings, Hollandia Shoes, and Frankwil Engineering Industries. The appetite to consume other companies was temporarily satisfied but then it quickened in the following year. On the first Friday in May 1969 the directors tackled a banquet consisting of Pelaco, Yarra Falls, Universal Textiles, Warrnambool Woollen Mills, and Qualitaire Holdings. At the next meeting Factors Limited was on the menu, and at the next Ansell and Davies Coop. Some of the meals were not entirely eaten. Two deals that fell through in the winter of that year involved the large textile firms of Pelaco and Davies Coop.

Dunshea's policy of buying out companies was now the talk of all Australians interested in the share market. His buying, so incessant, seemed so effortless. There were exciting periods when at least one major company a week would be the subject of new take-over bids from Dunshea. Sir Leslie Froggatt, coming to Australia as chief executive of Shell, was invited to a luncheon in Dunlop's new dining-room where he found the optimism was contagious. Dunshea knew that his constant buying was the talk of Melbourne, and with a mixture of fun and seriousness — the latter predominating — he quietly broached the topic. As Froggatt recalled: 'We were having a drink at the bar just before sitting down for lunch, and Eric turned round to Kellam and said, "Well, tell me Ern, what will we take over this week?"'

The question was asked with a sense of theatre. Of course Dunshea knew what was on the shopping list but he half-pretended that the list was so long that it could not easily be carried in his head. Years later, Froggatt was to join the board of Dunlop and eventually become the chairman. The effects of Dunshea's buying spree lasted for years. 'It taught the company a lot of lessons', recalled Froggatt. One of the lessons was that a company entering a new field in a big way needed to plan its approach with the utmost care.

Nearly always a Dunshea take-over was friendly. He saw no point in taking over a firm whose senior staff were hostile to a new owner. His Dunlop family, he said, did not want malcontents. On at least five occasions his first approach to a company was greeted with 'no', and he accepted as final an answer which other raiders would have ignored. He seemed to buy some firms with only the flimsiest investigation, but other firms were bought because he had watched them for years or because his staff reported favourably on their prospects. He rarely made tentative offers, and rarely did he stipulate that the final deal was subject to the verification of assets and profits of the targeted firm. As he made more and more bids, other firms approached him about the possibility of selling to Dunlop. He was easy to approach; the negotiations were invariably pleasant and prompt. In his desire to be fair, and his desire to acquire, he leaned more to the seller than to Dunlop. On several occasions the sum he offered was beyond the owners' sweetest dreams. One owner, reminiscing years later, recalled that he was so nonplussed by the sum mentioned that he was temporarily silent, during which silence Dunshea raised the offer.

Several directors, when asked to approve one take-over, cried 'wait'. They thought the price offered was too high or the stated reasons were inadequate for entering an industry new to Dunlop. One of the first objections came from Sir Robert Knox in October 1966 when Dunshea wished to buy 50.2 per cent of the shares in Frank O'Neill Industries for the relatively small sum of $351 000. In effect Sir Robert Knox must have wondered why Dunlop was about to go in for the construction of swimming-pools and the supplying of the necessary equipment. In response Dunshea went out of his way to find further information, even meeting the head of O'Neill for a discussion. He reported that he found 'him to be a man of excellent quality'. It was one of Dunshea's axioms that if he was dealing with a man of sound character and high principles the deal was safe. The board approved. Dunshea estimated that his company would win an annual return of fifteen per cent on the investment. After each such protest, Dunshea was more careful; but before long he was again making offers without the board's prior approval. Six years later the company, finding itself in deeper and deeper water in this minor activity, decided that the entry into the swimming-pool industry had been 'something of a disaster'.

At times a minor rebellion seemed likely to be staged by a few directors who thought that they were being deprived of the opportunity to have their say in the shaping of the company. Dunshea's briskness in taking over other companies was sometimes discourteous to the board. Thus a director who read his board papers carefully before coming to the meeting and then, on arrival, found that the main item of business — the buying of yet another company — was not even listed on the preliminary agenda was likely to feel a surge of resentment. If he then learned that Dunlop had already moved some way towards buying the company, and could not easily withdraw, he was entitled to feel that the board under Dunshea was being treated as an advisory body rather than as the ultimate source of power. Prestige Limited, a huge purchase, was hustled through in this manner, being introduced by Dunshea as a special item of business. It was the most important transaction since the marriages with Perdriau and Barnet Glass four decades previously, and deserved careful consideration. Prestige Limited and its various brand names, including Holeproof, Brandella and Heathermoor, was one of the best-known firms in the clothing industry, with a name for quality as well as quantity. It made hosiery, lingerie, socks, shirts, knitwear, fabrics and schoolwear, and was the first company in Australia to enter the fine weaving industry. From its head office in East Brunswick it controlled factories in eight Melbourne suburbs and in the country towns of Ararat and Horsham. Outside Victoria it had a factory in Parramatta and in four towns in New Zealand. In all, Prestige employed close to five thousand people.

The firm of Prestige was respected in Melbourne's northern suburbs. Its chairman, George Gotardo Foletta, belonged to families that had emigrated from the border of Switzerland and Italy to the Victorian gold-fields around Daylesford in the 1850s. His father Henry was a wholesaler in a tiny way in North Carlton and North Fitzroy in the 1890s, visiting his clients in a horse and trap. Venturing into manufacturing he began to make the sticky fly-paper which was used to catch house flies in kitchens. His son George, entering the business, was alert for new kinds of manufacturing that could prosper behind a protective tariff, and soon after the First World War he became the first general manager of the little hosiery syndicate that became known as Prestige. When Dunlop sounded him out in the winter of 1968 he was in his mid-seventies and tempted by the offer from such a big firm. His group was valued on the share market at more than ten million dollars: Dunlop offered him much more.

The ten directors who attended the meeting of the Dunlop board on 5 July 1968 were presented with a report of thirteen pages on Prestige and its activities and profits. All the information appeared to come from Prestige's own published reports. There was no independent evaluation of the company, not one comment on difficulties it might face in the future, and no argument justifying the price to be offered for each Prestige share. Possibly such information and advice was given verbally by Dunshea though the minutes give no hint of it. After discussion the board agreed that Dunlop should make a formal offer for all the issued ordinary capital in Prestige.

After the meeting Sir Daniel McVey, as the chairman, must have received some pointed complaints from a few directors who knew they had been railroaded. At the next meeting he raised the matter formally, conceding that they had grounds for disquiet at the speed of the Prestige transaction. There was now no possibility of reopening that matter; the printed offer had already gone out to Prestige shareholders, and acceptances of the offer were pouring in. In fact at head office the preparing of the formalities and fine details of the offer and the printing and posting of it had been accomplished by senior and junior staff with such celerity that Dunshea, soon after the opening of the next meeting of the Dunlop directors, expressed his praise for the staff involved before Sir Dan could even raise delicately the question of whether Dunshea had been quite fair in hustling the decision through the board.

McVey was now seventy-five. Living in Sydney and making visits to Melbourne mainly to preside over the monthly meetings of the board, he was no longer so close to the details of the business and was inclined to allow Dunshea to make the running. At this stage he trusted the ability of his chief executive. He knew Dunshea's quick-fire method of doing business, and realised that his tendency to treat the directors as his faithful assistants rather than his colleagues could cause a rift with the board. An important principle was at stake, the right of directors to make the decisions for which they were held responsible, and he aired the principle. In the end the board resolved that when a take-over proposal was in its infancy the top management should consult two senior directors — McVey and Marshall L. Baillieu, a director since 1952 — and keep them informed so that discussion on the board's behalf should be well advanced before any proposal came officially to the full meeting of the board. Sir Dan is reported in the official minutes as saying: 'While the need for speed was often of paramount importance there were at times other aspects present in take-over proposals which precluded earlier disclosure than desirable to a full meeting of the board'. As Dunshea had taken firm control of the wording of the minutes, there must be some slight uncertainty whether this quotation caught the exact spirit of Sir Dan's remarks. Their wording implies that not all directors could be trusted even with the simple disclosure that tentative discussions had begun with a certain company. At least the important matter had been aired, a gnome-like concession had been wrung from Dunshea, and for a time all went well. In effect, however, the directors had surrendered. Soon the take-over committee ceased to meet.

Three months later, on 1 November 1968, Sir Daniel McVey, in his thirteenth year as chairman, stepped down to become deputy chairman. Dunshea now took the chair. As he held the dual posts of chairman and chief executive, his control of the business was even tighter. That his appointment as chairman was accepted by all directors was a sign that no matter how much they might raise their eyebrows at his hustle and haste, they respected his ability and the vision he set down for the company. Perhaps they also privately decided that peace was preferable to waging war against this resolute guerrilla fighter.

Now and then Eric Dunshea exasperated one or two directors with his breathless pursuit of other companies. In November 1969 he resolved to buy the Wendouree Woollen Mills, an old Ballarat enterprise owned by the Myer Emporium. He believed that Wendouree could be run in harness with the newly acquired Warrnambool Woollen Mills (resulting in 'definite econo-mies, the extent of which has not yet been determined') and that through the purchase Dunlop could cater for the increasing Australian demand for knitted fabrics. Another bonus was that the great Myer stores, which hitherto had not sold Warrnambool blankets and furnishing materials, would now stock them throughout Australia. Dunshea called a special meeting of the Dunlop board to approve this purchase. Why a special meeting was needed when the normal monthly meeting was only a fortnight away he did not reveal. As Wendouree was not listed on the stock exchange there was little chance of another buyer elbowing out Dunlop and offering a higher price.

Dunshea seems to have given the board very short notice of the meeting. Thus he wrote to Sydney directors on Tuesday 18 November to call them down to Melbourne for a meeting three days later! In the event only five directors turned up to the meeting — three outside directors and the two internal directors, Dunshea and Kellam. Dunshea informed the meeting that he had discussed the proposed purchase, presumably on the phone, with four other directors each of whom gave 'full agreement'. The odd man out was Brian Massy-Greene. He did not give his full agreement. Instead he had sent a telex on the eve of the board meeting, complaining with pithy courtesy:

> am disturbed it apparently necessary to call another board meeting at short notice especially as submission under review does not give me feeeling of urgency stop respectfully suggest matter be deferred for consideration at regular board meeting stop if in your judgement deferment impossible please submit my apology

To purchase all these other companies, a huge sum of cash was required. Dunlop paid for most of its purchases with a lump sum of money and a large parcel of Dunlop shares. As Dunlop's shares were priced high on the stock exchanges, and as the company was travelling like a bullet, Dunlop shares were viewed as attractive. Those selling their business to Dunlop were usually happy to receive part of their payment in Dunlop shares. It was therefore important for Dunshea that the Dunlop shares, being the currency he used so often in his take-overs, should remain high. That Dunshea set higher and higher goals for annual profits, and reached those goals, helped to raise the price of the shares, and his flair for publicity helped to keep them high.

There were two main reasons for all this buying. He was ambitious for Dunlop and for himself. He was also logical and far-seeing, and so he concluded that Dunlop did not have an assured future in its traditional rubber products — the tyres, hoses and typical industrial goods. His intuition was correct. Tyres, his main product, were subject to periods of what Dunshea called 'turbulent price cutting'. Profits from tyres could become perilously low. If Dunlop were to become dominant again in tyres, and make higher profits from them, it would have to streamline its present factories. Those two grimy juggernauts, Montague in Melbourne and Drummoyne in Sydney, were hemmed in by other factories and by residential suburbs. To design and build a factory in an outer suburb required a huge sum. Dunshea hesitated, arguing correctly that the profit on the outlay would be dubious.

In the long period from 1950 to 1965 Dunlop had made seventy-two per cent of its after-tax profit from serving the automotive industry, mainly with tyres. Another eighteen per cent of its profit came from Dunlopillo, leaving all its other activities to provide the remaining ten per cent of profit. So long as Goodyear and Olympic were the only Australian makers of tyres, the competition was manageable — except in the mad bursts of price-cutting that broke out periodically. But by 1965 three other tyre makers, Goodrich, Uniroyal and Firestone, had entered the market, shaking it and reshuffling it. Dunshea did not think tyres would henceforth be a reliable source of profit. Moreover the tyre industry was changing more quickly than in the past, and the need to spend heavily on new plant was accelerated by a torrent of innovations — the change from square-woven to cord fabrics, from cotton to rayon to nylon fabrics, from tube to tubeless, and from natural rubber to a procession of synthetics. The tyre was altered by the rise of radial ply and steel-cord tyres, and was tinkered with almost annually by minor technical variations which the advertisers and marketing firms persuaded the public to see as essential to smooth motoring. For all these reasons Dunlop would be unwise to rely so much on tyres.

Dunshea's aim was to make Dunlop less dependent on tyres, but the major innovations in tyres he could not ignore. Thus he set out to manufacture steel-cord truck tyres, modelling them exactly on English Dunlop's tyre. The meeting of directors in October 1969 was long remembered because the first lumbering steel-cord tyre, straight from Montague, was bowled into the boardroom in Flinders Street. By then a gigantic novelty in truck tyres seemed puny compared to the targeted companies that Dunshea wheeled into the boardroom for approval and ultimate purchase.

He chose to expand into new areas where the profits outstripped those of tyres. At first he bought factories producing many types of consumer goods. In December 1968 he informed the board that Dunlop would eventually enter 'the foremost ranks of Australian industry' largely through a policy that he described as 'unrelated diversification' or 'selective diversification'. He would make Dunlop 'a conglomerate'. It was perhaps the first example of such a policy, pursued on a grand scale, in the annals of Australian business.

His goal was apparently the kind of conglomerate found in big 'zaibatsu' industrial companies in Japan or in such American companies as Litton, General Electric and General Tire. In a paper he prepared for the board in October 1968 he argued that the conglomerate has these inherent advantages:

- It is relatively insensitive to fluctuations within a particular industry.
- It is well positioned to channel capital investment into the most productive areas.
- Its ability to obtain financial resources is a function of the characteristics of the firm as a whole rather than of the individual parts.
- It can produce competent top management in greater depth than any other form of organisation.
- It has the ability to ride out the traditional phases of industrial develop-ment, the tendency to be unprofitable when very new, profitable but under-capitalised when the growth rate is highest, and then a generator of cash when mature and successful.

This was more a speech borrowed from a management manual than a sermon based on experience. It justified almost any purchase. Dunshea first concen-trated on textiles, clothes and other fashion items partly because he liked the kind of person in the industry and partly because they were very profitable in those easy-money, high-protection years. 'Colourful, artistic people appealed to him', said Ian Clark, whom Dunshea had appointed as the new company secretary.

Dunshea also saw room for more efficiency in clothing, textiles, footwear and several other fields. Once he had the lion's share of the manufacturing capacity, he could cut out wasteful duplication and make the main products more profitably. There was one catch. The firms he bought were in highly protected industries. If he made them more efficient and lowered the price of their shirts and shoes and suits, the federal government would probably reduce the import duties, and so cut Dunshea's anticipated profits. Dunshea could at least feel confident to assume, in 1968, that relatively high protection of Australian manufactures was assured. Furthermore he was rightly proud of his persuasiveness. He frequently went to Canberra, delighting in his contacts with those in power. Several times he dined with the prime minister, William McMahon. Eager to impress he spent part of the afternoon before his first dinner discussing with a senior employee what tie to wear.

Without doubt his visits to Canberra were successful. He reported that Dunlop's image in Canberra was beginning to shine like a neon light. In 1969, Leslie Bury, whose star was rising as minister for labour and national service, set up the Productivity Promotion Council of Australia, a ginger group charged with making the nation more efficient. He selected Dunshea as chairman, and a lively chairman he was. 'Productivity' became one of those bee-like words, heard almost everywhere for a year or two. 'Productivity' was soon acclaimed by Dunshea as increasingly the hallmark of the work-force in nearly all of his own factories and offices.

While he swept more and more firms into Dunlop's keeping he was not completely sure how to manage them. In 1963 he had achieved his radical plan of breaking the company's various activities into self-contained divisions, almost in readiness for a buying spree. Having bought them he was hesitant in placing each new acquisition in the appropriate division. He was reluctant to place the self-made men who had created their own businesses under the control of traditional Dunlop men, divisional heads who might not understand the new lines of business taken over. Above all, Dunshea — in the opinion of some who knew him — 'wanted to be loved'. He gave the new leaders, individualists all, a free hand partly for fear that if he regimented and controlled them he might lose the special respect they seemed to show him. He did not mind tramping on old Dunlop men, whose attitudes he knew, but not on new Dunlop men about whose attitudes he was nervous.

Most of the leaders of the bigger firms acquired by Dunlop retained their independence. They were pleased to report personally to Dunshea. This certainly made for contentment. Life under the Dunlop umbrella was almost a continuation of their old existence — without the financial worry. For his part Dunshea relished the contact with the newcomers, especially those who had succeeded in the exciting corridors of fashion.

At the back of Dunshea's mind was also a respect for the companies he had bought out and the loyalty they inspired in their work-force. He did not wish to shatter or weaken that loyalty. People gave their best, he argued, when they were loyal and when they received loyalty. In a business, loyalty is 'a priceless quality, immeasurable in money value'. In a pep-talk he prepared for the directors he praised the loyalty of Dunlop men and women and the loyalty of those in the subsidiary companies: 'Having determined that qualities such as loyalty are of inestimable value, they must be treasured and safeguarded and not allowed to deteriorate by any loose appreciation of their worth'.

As the take-overs were multiplied, Dunshea summoned nearly all the new leaders to a conference in Melbourne. He spent much of the day making short and long speeches: loyalty was one of his themes. Cordial and welcoming, he seemed slightly disorganised. At subsequent meetings he would outline a problem facing the company and call for inspired team-work in solving it. Late in 1969 he announced that Dunlop needed liquidity and that subsidiary companies should sell surplus stocks and collect overdue money, but he did not set down firm rules. Many of the managing directors went away and, eager to co-operate, increased the liquidity of their business by borrowing money from banks. The company's total borrowings soared.

Dunshea understandably hesitated to control too firmly what he called 'the Dunlop family', for he knew that the newcomers would only remain profitable if they were permitted to be themselves. Much of their efficiency and individuality would fade if they were submerged in massive new divisions and departments. Instead many of these subsidiary companies were loosely gathered into the Dunlop Textile Group, with wide autonomy for each company member.

Dunshea gave colleagues the impression that he was living on the top of a mountain while the company was expanding. The personal contacts involved in the take-overs, and the political negotiations sometimes called for, elated him. One colleague described him as 'a consummate actor'. Here was a new theatre in which he played all leading roles. A deep sense of purpose prevented showmanship from taking over for very long. He remained a Baptist, and sometimes he revealed his assumption that in revitalising Dunlop and in injecting 'productivity' into a thousand Australian workshops and factories, he was one of God's instruments for delivering abundance to Australian families.

His control of the board increased year by year. When Sir Dan McVey stepped down from the chair, Dunshea as chairman controlled the discussion as well as the flow of information. As the board met only on the first Friday of each month, it could not keep as closely in touch as did the directors of earlier years when usually they met each fortnight. His manner of introducing a new item of business tended to discourage questions. A probing question at a board meeting became a rarity. An observer could not help noticing that Dunshea positively discouraged questions even on issues where his answer, if a question were asked, would have been perfect in the eyes of the questioner. He was now so identified with Dunlop that to criticise him seemed to be an act of disloyalty to Dunlop. The most loyal, least questioning directors were singled out for special praise in the minutes of meetings. On hearing of the death of Sir Giles Chippindall, for eleven years a director, Dunshea lent a hand in shaping the gracious sentence in the board minutes which reported that Sir Giles's 'loyalty to Dunlop and unswerving faith in its future endeared him to his colleagues on the board'. It was not quite the reason for the affection in which Sir Giles was held. In death Sir Giles served as fuel for the throbbing propaganda machine.

At the height of Dunshea's power only one challenge was made to his authority inside the boardroom. Brian Massy-Greene, a substitute for one of the English Dunlop directors who rarely visited Australia, expressed his unease at the way Dunshea was railroading the board on certain matters. Dunshea, feeling his authority was in danger, came out fighting. Jumping to his feet he denounced the very suggestion. His face was red and he thumped the table and roared like a lion. While Dunshea seemed to have lost his temper he was in control of it. His display of force was successful. Massy-Greene, whose complaint was legitimate and in the company's interest, apparently received scant support from other members sitting at the long table.

English Dunlop was one potential source of criticism but Dunshea visited London regularly and paid court. Moreover, could London criticise Dunshea when in general performance and concrete results he was superior? Dunshea's deputy, Ern Kellam, knew that the Dunshea's garden was not quite as blossoming as the public imagined it to be. As Kellam held a seat on the board he could have quietly warned several other directors that some facets of the business were decidedly unfavourable. Kellam said nothing, knowing that he might be retired if he opened his mouth.

That the directors should have had such confidence in Dunshea was not a surprise. Normally he was competent, far-seeing, and utterly dedicated. By nearly every measure Dunlop flourished; and its success was a topic for incessant talk in Melbourne. In the space of one year net profits leaped from seven million dollars to the magical mark of ten million. The Dunlop take-overs seemed to be proving their worth. In March 1970, Dunshea reported proudly that the new acquisitions in all were earning 9.5 per cent on their gross assets whereas old Dunlop, with its tyres and conveyor belts and Dunlopillo and Slazenger products, earned only 4.7 per cent. English Dunlop acknowledged this unusual success. Through careful diversification, it announced, Dunshea and his directors had inaugurated a new era. In 1970 they were awarded, on behalf of their company, the Baillieu Trophy for 'outstanding contributions to the competitiveness of Dunlop' throughout the world. Sir Reay Geddes, chairman of English Dunlop, took time off from organising the new corporate alliance between Dunlop of England and Pirelli of Italy to come to Melbourne and personally present the trophy to Dunshea at a meeting of the board.

The award marked the peak of Dunshea's career as chief. Already the economic climate was cloudier. By the winter of 1970 the federal government was restricting credit, and the wholesale and retail firms supplied with textiles by Dunlop were keeping smaller stocks and buying less. Dunshea's empire relied on ever-rising sales to pay the costs of the take-overs, but sales now grew slowly. The fear of lower tariffs on imports of clothing and footwear was also increasing. The likelihood of such a policy perhaps explained in part why so many successful firms were eager to sell out to Dunlop, though hardly a word about the potential effect of lower tariffs on the Dunlop businesses appeared in the board papers. At the same time unexpected changes in fashions in clothes forced Dunlop to write down heavily the value of stocks in its warehouses. The profit for the year ending 30 June 1970, though higher than in the previous year, was far below the target which had seemed within reach for much of the year. Dunshea, to his surprise, was refused permission by his board to buy the remaining shares in Hollandia Shoes.

The take-over feast was not quite finished. While its heyday was in 1968 and 1969, the company snapped up tasty morsels even when it realised that it could not fully digest what it had begun to eat several years ago. Thus in September 1970 Dunlop revived its take-over policy by resolving to buy control of a well-known Queensland company, the Intercolonial Boring Company. Originally formed in the fancifully-named town of Petrolia in Ontario in 1888, it soon migrated to Queensland. It had specialised in drilling for artesian water in the outback, but had also built up a chain of stores selling irrigation equipment, automotive parts, building supplies and hardware — including many Dunlop products.

Dunshea's bid for the Intercolonial Boring Company was another sign of his preference for friendly take-overs. It so happened that in 1970 many shares in the Brisbane firm were being quietly snapped up by a well-known corporate raider, Tjuringa Securities, whose aim, it was feared, was to strip the assets and close down the business. The jobs of the staff of the Intercolonial Boring Company were therefore in danger and the danger was heightened when one of the IBC's biggest shareholders, the Australian Mutual Provident Society (AMP), which had long run the company's superannuation fund, sold to Tjuringa its own holding of seven per cent of the IBC's capital. Shrewdly the chairman of the IBC, Jim McLennan, leaked the news of the likely take-over to Dunlop. Quickly Dunshea decided to bid, one of the few occasions in which he positively competed in an attempt to take over another firm: normally he acted quietly and was the sole bidder.

Dunshea offered roughly one dollar for each share in the Brisbane company. Tjuringa did not directly make an offer for the Brisbane company: it just continued to buy its shares at higher prices. Dunlop, however, had the money and the will-power. It was aided by the fact that the two big remaining shareholders, unlike the AMP, thought the IBC should not be stripped of its assets. In the end Dunlop controlled fifty-one per cent of the shares and was not satisfied until it held all.

On the purchase of IBC shares, Dunlop spent more than it could afford: $5.4 million in cash as well as 805 000 Dunlop shares. In the same twelve months Dunlop bought Gordon Plastics and a half interest in Kolotex Holdings, and the footwear interests of F and T Industries which was the old Felt and Textiles group. These four purchases, mostly made when Dunlop was acutely short of cash, were extravagant. They required a larger sum than Dunlop paid out in dividends in that financial year.

By the closing months of 1970, Dunshea was requesting that the heads of each corner of his empire should curb their spending and accumulate cash. The big spender was being forced, against his wishes, to become a miser. His plan for a grand new head office, on the corner site in Spring Street now occupied by the Shell building, had to be shelved and then abandoned. News that the federal government would reduce the import duty on rubber-soled footwear to forty-five per cent sent a chill through the Bankstown factory where many items of footwear could not withstand foreign competition if import duties were lowered. The outlook was not yet gloomy, but the company's prolonged Christmas was certainly over.

The work-force of more than 20 000 was called upon for a special effort. Slogans like 'teamwork' and 'productivity' were often on Dunshea's lips, but even the slogan of 'productivity' backfired. The president of the Australian Council of Trade Unions (ACTU), Bob Hawke, had led his unions into business ventures, including a middle-size retail store called Bourke's in Melbourne. Searching for goods to sell at bargain prices, Hawke personally approached Dunshea and expressed dissatisfaction with Dunlop's policy, common in peaceful periods in the rubber industry, of fixing the retail price at which goods could be sold to the public. Dunshea promised to deliver to Bourke's rubber goods which could be sold at less than normal prices, but several months passed, and no goods arrived. Dunshea, according to Mr Hawke, made a further promise but did not keep it. On 16 March 1971, Hawke denounced Dunshea, shrewdly pointing out how odd it was that the leader of the nation's productivity movement should indulge in a restrictive practice which was 'the antithesis of promoting productivity'. That Mr Hawke himself was a master of restrictive practices did not matter for the moment. After neatly scoring his point he banned deliveries to and from Dunlop factories in Victoria. Dunshea had to give in. He felt acutely the public humiliation. A friend who saw him on the evening of the defeat, dining with his wife in a city restaurant, thought that he seemed shattered. He was resilient, however, and breezed back into his office the next day.

He was now the defender more than the attacker. The spending spree had given way to a working bee, bent on cutting costs and collecting all possible cash. To change from one mood, one goal, to its opposite was not hard because nearly everything he did was enthusiastic. At the end of June 1971 he was even enthusiastic about the slight fall in the firm's net profit after tax. Such a small fall, he enthused, capped 'an extraordinarily difficult year'. Interviewed by Barrie Dunstan in the Melbourne *Herald* on Saturday 4 September, 'Mr Dunlop' sat back in his armchair of red leather and dismissed the doubters who had pulled the shares of his company down to $1.14 each. After his long spree of take-overs he maintained that Dunlop was in a stronger position than ever before to march into the future. He recalled the company's record in the year 1965–66 and pointed to a big improvement in every line of the scoreboard in the following five years. 'I nearly had to kill myself to pull this company around', he said defiantly. 'Remember I took over at the age of 60.'

In the privacy of the boardroom he reported eagerly that his calls for more productivity in the factories were meeting 'an enthusiastic and urgent response'. He was also heartened that many of the newly bought subsidiary companies were doing well. Even textiles, no longer glamorous in the face of imports, had a slightly higher rate of profit than tyres.

Dunshea's reputation remained high, for he could point to years of impressive results. The earning rate on Dunlop's ordinary shares had been only 8.1 per cent in the year ending June 1966, Blackwood's last year, a freakish year. Under Dunshea, however, the net earnings jumped in successive years to twelve per cent and seventeen per cent where they remained steady. Of all the five-year periods since 1900, Dunshea's initial five years ranked amongst the best: only three better periods could be found on record, he assured the board. He had carried through a remarkable expansion of the company, paid generously for the new businesses, but managed to achieve a high rate of earnings on the capital. The figures constantly before the board as late as the winter of 1971 were therefore cheering.

No longer depending so heavily on the cut-throat tyre industry, Dunlop seemed to gain a new stability in profits. About April 1971, in a report called 'The Dunlop Family Goal', Dunshea drew attention to the wonderful performance of the footwear division. Once a struggling part of the company, earning pitiful profits, it was now glamorous. The acquisition of the Grosby and Hollandia companies, along with alert management, gave the footwear group a remarkable yield of thirteen per cent on the gross assets it employed. Dunlop as a whole was now the biggest maker of footwear in Australia, and Dunshea hoped for even higher returns in 1972–3. Nothing in the company could now compete in profitability with shoes and boots. Dunshea was heartened too by pleasing yields in other groups and divisions that previously were not always profitable: Dunlopillo earning a return of 7.8 per cent on the gross assets employed, 'Other Rubber Products' with 7.6 per cent, Textile and Apparel with 6.4 per cent, and Sports Goods with 5.1 per cent. At the bottom of the list was the Automotive Division and even it had victories. Not long before, Dunlop was only the third-largest maker of tyres but now it was number one and earning, according to Dunshea, more profits than all the other tyre makers added together. That it returned a mere 5.2 per cent on gross assets employed made it the weakest of the Dunlop activities. To Dunshea this was proof of his good sense in persuading the directors to move away from undue dependence on tyres. But even tyres, like nearly everything else Dunlop made, would be far more profitable a year hence. So Eric Dunshea informed the directors in the last of his optimistic reports.

Much of the bright news on which he dwelt was true: so was the dour news which arrived in the second half of 1971. Australia's economy, under the new McMahon government, was less buoyant: unemployment was higher and ultimately affected the sales of clothing; industrial unrest was increasing; and foreign competition from East Asia was tougher. Many of Dunlop's factories, and especially the recent acquisitions in textiles, clothing and footwear, employed many women; and now equal pay for women was included in the Rubber Workers' Award in 1971 and would soon apply in textiles, thus making Dunlop factories even more vulnerable to foreign competition.

Meanwhile Dunlop needed cash for its expanded activities, more cash than it could find. The company had overreached itself. Tighter times — they were not yet lean times — exposed Dunshea's weakness. He began to borrow more and more. In November 1971, he told the directors that the Tricontinental Corporation had arranged a loan to Dunlop from overseas borrowers, but the first portion of this 'bridging finance' had to be repaid within six months and the final repayment was due within three years. A director, temporarily overseas but keenly following the company's financial affairs through the board minutes sent to him, would have been astonished to see the December minutes, without prior warning, revealing that Dunlop was urgently seeking loans amounting to thirty-six million American dollars.

Out of the blue, word came that Dunlop was urgently seeking even more money. At the board meeting in February 1972 Dunshea said he hoped to secure lines of credit totalling fifty million dollars largely through the Australian banks. That sum exceeded the net profits made in the entire Dunshea era. At the next meeting of the board, which proved to be Dunshea's last, agitated discussion centred on Dunlop's need to accumulate cash to repay all the loans falling due in the next two years. As if to load the dice, another overseas firm, General Tire and Rubber Co., had entered the crowded Australian tyre market.

For most of his term of office Dunshea could produce — and did — annual figures that showed the remarkable growth of Dunlop. Certain unfavourable figures he did not include in his series. The debt had jumped through the roof but even that seemed to be balanced by the impressive profits. Now, in the year 1971–2, the figures seemed to change direction. Nearly all Dunshea's statistics were running downhill. The overall impression of the four years of take-overs would have been sobering if a full and true set of figures had been assembled for the directors at the end of 1971, let alone the middle of 1972. In the four financial years between 1968 and 1972, Dunlop had issued the colossal total of 47 505 000 shares, mainly as part of the price of buying into other companies. Such a flood of new shares could not sustain the rate of earnings on each share, and since 1968 the rate had fallen from seventeen to eleven cents a share. Likewise the dividends paid on each share had fallen from eleven to seven and a half per cent.

Behind these figures of earnings and profits towered the debt. Dunlop's borrowings had increased by $65 573 000. Another set of figures did not appear in the balance sheet. The company's annual profits had been somewhat exaggerated by placing too high a valuation on the stocks unsold at the end of the year. The directors did not know what was happening. Perhaps Dunshea himself did not fully know the position. On some days he was erratic and provocative, unlike the old Dunshea. After a quarrel with a Sydney business man he did not visit Sydney, a vital field of operations and his old home town, for the best part of a year.

In retrospect, Dunshea was tripped up by the speed of his expansion. He was tripped by the enormous sum spent on his take-over adventure, by his own propaganda, by the economic clouds appearing in 1971 and 1972, and by the change of government policy towards the protection of Australian industry. If the economy had still been sunny and the government had still been highly protectionist, Dunshea might have been hobbling but not disabled. Instead his company was almost crippled by debt. The company's banker, the Commercial Bank of Australia, was carrying much of the weight. Apparently it did not know that Dunshea was planning to transfer Dunlop's main account to the Commercial Banking Company of Sydney, hoping thereby to cover more of the debt.

In the course of his business career Dunshea had come to the conclusion that an industrialist must not yield an inch to a powerful banker. In the battle of wills, the banker must be sat upon. Amidst all the financial pressures, Dunshea bluffed Dunlop's main creditor. He was willing to thump the table and go red in the face if a banker dared challenge his authority and his company's credit-worthiness. One day early in 1972 he and the secretary of the company travelled in the big Daimler just a few blocks from Flinders Street to Collins Street to call at the head office of the Commercial Bank of Australia. After eating a morning tea of hot buttered scones in the ornate office of the chief executive he commandeered the conversation as if he were the lender, not the borrower, and talked about Dunlop's plans for the future, the condition of the economy and everything but the exact state of Dunlop's finances, a state now bordering on peril. After a long conversation in which he did not once allow Dunlop's finances to be discussed he courteously took his leave and made his way with the company secretary to the waiting Daimler. 'Let that be a lesson to you', he said to the secretary.

Rumours were reaching the ears of financial journalists that Dunlop was at risk. By then Dunshea himself was weighed down. He had cancer, at first in the throat. He kept the news to himself, and when he had to visit the Peter MacCallum Clinic for treatment he asked his driver to let him out a block away so that he could enter the clinic unnoticed. He courageously continued to come to work, holding the reins tightly. Normally a stickler for board meetings, he did not come to the meeting on 7 April 1972. By now the directors knew of his illness. Sir Reay Geddes of English Dunlop, summoned at short notice from London for such an important meeting, came in time to discuss emergency plans. Sir Robert Blackwood agreed to act as chairman, and Ern Kellam took Dunshea's other post of chief general manager. No public announcement of the changes was made. 'A suitable expression of profound sorrow and condolence' was sent to Mrs Dunshea. Nine days later, he died.

FOURTEEN

The tightening noose
of debt

IN THE WEEKS of Eric Dunshea's final illness several of the senior executives were nervous about the company's future. They doubted whether most directors could even guess the full extent of Dunlop's vulnerability. Dollops of bad news about the company's accounts, items not previously mentioned, came to the board's attention; but none stood for a large sum. The board did not know that, in the words spoken privately by one executive, 'the profits of the last couple of years were substantially over-stated'. At the end of each financial year Dunshea seriously over-valued all the tyres, textiles, shoes and other items held in stock, thus inflating the result of the whole year.

Dunlop also was in debt, and that was no secret. By the standards of the early 1970s — but not by the spendthrift standards of the late 1980s — it was dangerously in debt. At least two of the directors of 1972 believed, and still believe, that the bankers were close to appointing receivers. Only the unlocking of the records of the main bank will reveal how perilous was Dunlop's position.

The heads of Dunlop, as the facts unfolded, did all they could to prevent the debt from rising further. For a few months their company was rather like a large ship at anchor, her engines being repaired too close to a rugged coast. The crucial gauge in the engine-room showed the debt–equity ratio. In effect it showed on one side the shareholders' funds in the business and on the other side the borrowings. In 1966, when Dunshea became chief general manager, the ratio of debt to equity was forty-six per cent. By 1969 it had soared to a dangerous ninety-four per cent, and a year later it was 125 per cent. Measured by this ratio the company had borrowed more than it owned.

Unfortunately this changing ratio, so far as is known, was not presented regularly to the board meetings as a topic of importance. Even if it had been presented, it probably would not have signified the true position. Dunshea had a tendency — and as an experienced accountant his word was accepted — to overvalue the equity. The implications of this for the ratio were alarming. For example in 1970 the debt–equity ratio of 125 per cent superficially meant that debt was 125, equity was 100, and total assets were 225 per cent. But what if the assets were over-valued? Several people prominent in the company at that time are of the view that the total assets were closer to 175. That would have signified, assuming the debt was 125, that the equity stood at only 50 in relative terms. Such a drastic revision would have represented a debt–equity ratio at the disturbing figure of 250 per cent.

For the next few years the task of the directors was to tug this ratio down. Dunshea, with herculean effort, pulled it down a little. After his death it stood at about 118 officially and far higher unofficially, and naturally was beginning to dominate financial discussions. To lower the official ratio to 100 called for the elimination of $21.4 million in debts — a forbidding sum. Even when it fell to 100 the ratio would be well above that of most companies with which Dunlop liked to be compared. Thus the ratio for Australian Paper Manufactures stood at 59, Australian Consolidated Industries stood at 63, Olympic stood at 67, Repco at 76, Myer at 82, Humes at 83, and British Tobacco at 96. They were better than Dunlop's official ratio and far better than its real but concealed ratio.

In August 1972 the board was handed the latest version of the problem. Even if profits increased during that financial year, and even if all kinds of pruning succeeded, and even if capital works were kept to the minimum, the ratio would still rise, probably to 119. The directors were told that the company was 'extremely vulnerable'. What if profits should fall? They were told that 'Dunlop cannot afford any significant decline in profitability for even one year without being in breach of financial commitments to creditors, shareholders or lenders'. In Sydney and Melbourne, indeed in every large city and scores of towns, employees of Dunlop were buying cars, saving for their marriage, paying off houses, or preparing for their first interstate or overseas holiday: all on the assumption that their financial future was safe. It was far from safe.

The task of rescuing the company was aided by the presence of new faces at the board table. They could see Dunlop and its difficulties with fresh eyes. Whereas the board had changed little during Dunshea's time as chief, it was almost transformed within a few months of his death. The two oldest directors — Sir Robert Knox who had been on the board for thirty-six years including sixteen as vice-chairman, and Sir Daniel McVey who had been a director for twenty-five years including twelve as chairman — stepped down. Three new executive directors were appointed: Ralph Grosby, who had come to Dunlop along with his own footwear firm and then revitalised Dunlop's footwear division; D. H. Kemp, who was director of development and research for Dunlop; and Leith Jarman who was newly appointed as general manager of

Dunlop. With the subsequent appointment to the board of the secretary and chief finance officer, Ian Clark, and the main textile executive, A. G. Eastwood, the majority of directors consisted of men whose careers were with Dunlop. Even after Ralph Grosby retired, the Dunlop executives and one former executive, Sir Robert Blackwood, outnumbered the other directors — M. L. Baillieu, J. B. Harper, Sir Brian Massy-Greene and Kenneth Wood, who acted as the alternate for Sir Reay Geddes of English Dunlop.

The reformed board was a first step towards the reform of the company. Eric Dunshea, combining the two chief posts, was not challenged often enough; he did not encourage challenge. In contrast Sir Robert Blackwood sat at the head of the table and smiled serenely on discussion. His seven years as chancellor of Monash University, especially during the thundery days when it was the hub of student radicalism, made him a patient pilot of discussion. In his quiet way he liked agreement to stem from the sheer merits of the proposition before the board. And if the proposition was not good enough? By all means let it be amended. At the same time he placed full confidence in his chief executive and rarely tried to interfere in administrative matters. When he did interfere he accepted the prompt rebuff.

Blackwood proved his worth when each year he had to face shareholders, many of whom were highly critical of the company's failure to fulfil the promises Mr Dunshea had made. At the annual general meeting of shareholders he spoke quietly about the company's problems. He did not bluster. He did not assert his superior knowledge. One advantage was his increasing deafness, and when some shareholders publicly asked pointed questions about the company's failings in recent years he misheard the questions and proceeded to give a rambling and irrelevant reply, delivered with such courtesy that shareholders found it too embarrassing to point out that he had misheard them.

While Ern Kellam was chief executive for the first two years after Dunshea's death, the reshaping of the troubled company fell on Kellam's ultimate successor, Leith Jarman. He had been a professional soldier: he worked quietly and believed battles should be won with the minimum of casualties and that victories should be accepted humbly. Educated at Williamstown High School and the Royal Military College, Duntroon, he fought against the Japanese in New Guinea and New Britain and was in the allied army occupying Japan after the war. Leaving the army in 1956 because he and his young family were being moved too often, Major Jarman joined Dunlop — in his own words — as an 'elderly cadet'. Working first at humdrum tyre jobs around Melbourne so that he could learn about the industry, he spent two weeks during the Olympic Games trying to sell tyres: he recalls that he sold none. Soon he was given responsibility in the loyal and slightly rheumatic company which Dunshea was steadily taking over. Placed in charge of the subsidiary companies that sold tyres through sixteen outlets in South Australia, Leith Jarman tried hard

Ern Kellam (left) aboard the Thomson steam car of the late 1890s. It was restored in the late 1950s.

to sell a poorish Dunlop tyre called Silent 90 against the competition of other brands which the Dunlop depots also stocked.

Jarman, without knowing it, was receiving the wide experience which would eventually enable him, when the company was in trouble, to dismantle the business and stitch the remnants together again. After a term at the Montague factory he was sent to footwear, serving as general manager in 1969–70. His special task was to sharpen the big Bankstown factory with its over-large staff in the offices and its impractical desire to make and stock innumerable kinds of boots and shoes, even items for which the total Australian market might be only one hundred pairs a year. The making of footwear was still fully protected by the tariff; and Jarman concluded that inefficiency was almost built into the industrial workshops around Australia. After short periods as head of the subsidiary, Universal Textiles, and of the Automotive Division, he came to the post of general manager and a seat on the board with unusually wide experience. He was soon using it. The company in the months after the death of Dunshea urgently needed tighter manage-ment. Whereas the Dunshea period could be summed up as 'disorderly diversification', the new period was one of orderly integration. Finance was

Leith Jarman.

the first area of chaos which Jarman tackled. One of Jarman's first acts was to insist that all requests for loans must come to head office for approval. Hitherto, despite the galloping debts, Dunshea had failed to curb the borrowings of the host of subsidiary companies.

Dunlop's troubles were increased by political uncertainty. A federal election was likely to be held late in 1972, and the first Labor victory since 1949 was possible, perhaps probable. Such a victory would alter the conditions of manufacturing: whether for better or worse, who could predict? Labor won, and Mr Whitlam became prime minister in December 1972, and for a time the economy seemed to improve. Dunlop and its hundreds of activities was half garden and half wilderness, and Leith Jarman pruned, spliced, sprayed, and replanted. The first full year since the death of Dunshea ended with the debt cut back by twenty-five million dollars. The second full year of pruning (1973–4) began promisingly but tariffs were cut, and equal pay for women was hastened. Following the brief war in the Middle East in 1973, the Organization of Petroleum Exporting Companies (OPEC) raised the price of oil; and all prices blew out like a balloon. The prices of raw materials soared, not only natural rubber but also synthetic rubber, the ingredients of which were made expensive by the price of oil. Wages jumped too. Foreign textiles, shoes and tyres poured in. Dunlop had difficulty in competing, and soon its warehouses were half full of unsold goods. Moreover with the rise in prices of almost everything, the cash needed for the daily business increased: the call for cash was now 'extraordinary'. Further, the various Dunlop managers, fearing that raw materials could remain scarce or become even dearer, ordered and ordered from overseas. Large numbers of managers had the right to order rubber, rayon and all kinds of raw materials: most used their right to the full. The sum outlaid was monstrous.

Jarman wrote,

> It is our own fault that we are not good cash planners but this must be viewed against the fact that only two years ago we did not plan at all. We narrowly avoided disaster then and our financial control has improved enormously since.

At the end of August 1974 he noted that creditors 'are as high as they could possibly be'. He reported that 'they are pressing for payment, and we are resisting'. The retailers who owed money to Dunlop for goods bought in recent months also felt the pinch and were tempted to be a few days late in paying their bills. If by chance all retailers were to be an average of seven days late in meeting their accounts, Dunlop would need another eleven million dollars in cash just to cope with that week's delay. The situation was unenviable.

Painful actions had already been taken to reduce the official debt–equity ratio to the safer figure of 100 at the end of 1973. That penny-pinching work was now futile. In the freak conditions of the following eleven months the ratio jumped back to 114. The debt could not be conquered. While the profits increased, so did the debts.

Rarely had Dunlop lived through such a chaotic year as 1973–4. Nothing seemed predictable. Some factories reported big losses, some reported big profits. The profits on footwear jumped thirty per cent. Textiles flourished until the last months of the financial year when suddenly orders for the summer season fell away. Moreover in the peak of prosperity so many shoes were ordered overseas that Melbourne and Sydney warehouses were crammed with them. Every factory seemed to offer a different story: the Warrnambool mill complained that its customers were slow to pay and that its employees were in a bout of absenteeism; nationally the sales of shoes with the newly-bought Adidas brand leaped by sixty-six per cent; conveyor belting earned profits for the first time in years; and the cost of batteries was so inflated by rising wages and raw materials that in the space of a couple of months the new Prices Justification Tribunal allowed successive increases of fourteen, seven and nine per cent in the price of batteries.

As unemployment in Australia increased in mid-1974, the public demand dropped for tyres, shoes, frocks and most of the goods the company made. At the end of the previous year Dunlop had employed 26 300 men and women — probably one of the five largest work-forces in the entire private sector. In the following ten months the work-force fell by 4700.

The debt remained a nightmare. Debt had originally soared largely because of Dunshea's over-eagerness to expand. The new surge in debt arose from factors beyond Dunlop's control and in part beyond Australia's. The inflation was world-wide, though Australia had its own disruptions because of dramatic changes and shifts in the Whitlam government's policy on wages, working conditions, tariffs, prices, the exchange rate, taxes, export incentives, and even import incentives. The market value of the ordinary share in Dunlop fell below that prevailing in the rumour-filled weeks after the death of Dunshea. Early in 1975 the dollar shares were worth a mere forty-nine cents.

Factories and depots had to be made more efficient, unprofitable business had to be pruned or sold. Latex foam was manufactured in three factories: it was cheaper to make it in one, and Mordialloc was chosen. The John Bull factory in Nowra (New South Wales) moulded rubber components but it was cheaper to centre that activity at Bayswater, leaving Nowra to make high-pressure hose until, in 1975, even that product was no longer made there. The old Perdriau rubber works at the Sydney suburb of Drummoyne were closed, section by section, and much of the valuable land was used for a shopping centre. The factories making cut rubber thread at Bairnsdale (Victoria) and weatherproof garments at Wagga Wagga (New South Wales) were closed. The woollen mill at Wendouree, on the outskirts of Ballarat, was closed, and its machines moved elsewhere. Each year in the mid-1970s factories were rearranged or closed, tyre depots were amalgamated, surplus offices and warehouses and factories were sold, and subsidiary companies were liquidated. In the year ending June 1974 more than one hundred fully-owned Dunlop companies were placed into liquidation, including thirty-nine Dunlop Tyre Service Companies, five companies making Marshall Batteries and companies as diverse as Clearlite Pools, Promenade Footwear, Garnetfoam, and the maker of men's suits, Anthony Squires Holdings.

Activities were abandoned. Dunlop ceased to build and install swimming-pools (on which over one million dollars was lost in one year), and ceased to manufacture the small-run rubber goods, and the lines of footwear and garments for which the Australian market was too small or tariff protection was too low. Jarman accepted the fact that a big company like Dunlop was unlikely to win any profit from certain small factories which, under the original owner, had been run with frugality and flair. Between 1972 and 1978,

Dunlop sold most of the numerous ventures conducted by Osti Holdings. Thus many employees of the Astoria Knitting Mills, Very Fine (Jersey) Knitters, Wines Knitting, Osti Fashions Dress, Osti Underwear, and John J. Hilton had three different employers in less than a decade: they were employed by Osti, Dunlop and now a new owner.

Dunlop withdrew from many textile and clothing activities which Dunshea had entered with such optimism. In the space of five years the capital Dunlop employed in these products fell by thirty million dollars. After its brief flirtation with women's clothes, Dunlop began to move away from women's hosiery, lingerie and frocks. For the most part it moved out of warp and weft knitting and general textured yarns. It closed one dye-works in New South Wales and ceased to weave and print textiles in Hobart. It moved out of men's shirts. In men's suits it sold to Stafford Ellison such brand names as Sax Altman, Ernest Hiller, and Anthony Squires.

Dunlop tended to move quickly out of industries depending heavily on a knowledge of fashion — the industries it should never have entered in the first place. At the height of its involvement with fashion industries it made numerous mistakes. In retrospect one persistent mistake was to use the name Dunlop. A famous name in tyres and rubber goods, it was an anachronism in fashion wear. To sell shoes designed by the famous Italian, Salvatore Ferragamo, under the name of 'Dunlop by Ferragamo' was to demean and devalue the shoes.

Whereas the company's expansion under Eric Dunshea signified faith in Australia and nearly all its manufacturing industries, the mood less than three years after his death was one of wariness towards many Australian industries. Mr Whitlam, who won the federal election for Labor soon after the death of Dunshea, gave less protection to Australian factories and increased their costs in various ways. The response of some companies was to think of manufacturing in Asia what they traditionally had made in Australia. In 1974 the scheme giving incentives to exporters was abandoned. They now had an incentive to serve their export markets by manufacturing outside Australia. By moving offshore they could make the same goods, pay low wages in their foreign factory and relatively low rates of taxation to the foreign government, and then send the goods to Australia where they would pay a relatively low import duty. Such goods would undercut any rival product made in Australia. The rapid rises in wages in Australia in the 1970s, as well as the federal policy of cutting import duties, was clearly pointing to a manufacturing industry that employed a smaller section of the work-force.

In 1977 Dunlop acquired a seventy per cent interest in a new footwear company, Grosby-Rubberworld (Philippines), and exported its machines to the factory compound in Manila for the making of shoes for export to Australia. In the same year Dunlop, having lost its export sales in tennis-balls in the USA, joined with English Dunlop in the manufacture of tennis-balls at Bataan in the Philippines for the Australian and other markets. In another Dunlop factory in the Philippines, golf-bags were now made under the popular Australian brand of Denzil Don. But the assumption that Asian factories, with their freedom from industrial trouble, were ever-reliable as suppliers was not always true. When earthquakes hit the city of Tientsin in China in 1976, Dunlop was deprived of thousands of football boots it was expecting for the Australian market.

In South-East Asia, Dunlop's major success of the post-war era was just beginning. The success rested on rubber, the commodity that Dunlop in the late 1960s had increasingly eschewed. Moreover the success was achieved by one of those companies originally taken over by Dunshea.

The Ansell Rubber Company seemed a stranger amongst Dunshea's long list of acquired textile, footwear and other firms. It was not listed on the stock exchanges and so it was a quiet addition to Dunlop. Nonetheless Ansell had such potential that it was one of the most expensive bids made by Dunshea. The price, not disclosed in the financial press in 1969, was the high sum of $5 549 000 in cash and three million Dunlop shares. In short Dunlop paid a sum equivalent to more than one year of its dividends, but the price was to be repaid many times over by Ansell's subsequent triumph in the markets of the world.

The Ansell family had originally made their name by making condoms. In their own factory in Melbourne they did not use that name: indeed few Australians knew the word 'condom'. In the Ansell factory they referred for decades to the condom machine as the 'A Machine' and to condoms as the 'A products'. Another name used in the factory was 'props' though the colloquial public name was French letters or Frenchies and the more formal name was usually contraceptives. At one time Australian laws and codes of behaviour effectively prevented the advertising of condoms, at least in the best dailies and weeklies, and it is said that for a time a law prevented their importation but not their manufacture. Many chemists, especially Catholic chemists, refused to stock them: those who did rarely displayed them inside the shop even in the 1920s. In most parts of the English-speaking world the silence and secrecy surrounding these widely-used bedroom products tended to obscure the history of the way they were manufactured and sold.

The rise of the remarkable Ansell business still suffers from this silence. Like small businesses it left behind few records, and myth and romance had to meet part of the deficiency in facts. Eric Ansell, born in London in 1878, is said to have worked as an operative in the rubber trade in London as a young man and then to have become assistant purser in one of the luxurious passenger liners on the England–Australia route. In 1902, while travelling to Australia in the orient liner *Omrah*, he fell in love with a young Australian, Daisy Jones, travelling first class with her aunt. Enamoured with her he deserted ship at Port Melbourne, walked a few miles to the Dunlop factory where he became a blue-collar worker for some three years, meanwhile marrying his girl, 'a charming, lively and beautifully educated person'. A few parts of this story are, on surface evidence, highly improbable. In the conspicuous social divisions around 1900, both in England and Australia, it was difficult and rare for a young man to move from blue-collar to genteel white-collar and back again. The next part of the story has more plausibility but still a film of doubt. In 1905, it is said, Dunlop decided to cease making condoms in the factory at Montague on the orders of Nicholas Fitzgerald, the chairman, who was a devout Catholic. According to the family story, young Ansell helped to dismantle the condom machine and move it to vacant ground nearby: 'Ansell, seeing an opportunity, approached the factory manager and offered to purchase the machine'. He began to make condoms and pack and sell them, and 'forthwith resigned from Dunlop'.

This last part of the tale about the history of Ansell, especially the Dunlop retreat from the condom business, has more the ring of truth; but even that truth cannot be confirmed. There is no record of Dunlop's board deciding to stop manufacturing condoms in 1905. Moreover such a decision, if it were made, would have been a decision of the essentially Protestant board and not just of the Catholic chairman, Fitzgerald. It is also reasonable to ask why Fitzgerald, if he held the strong Catholic view on the immorality of birth control, had allowed the manufacture in the first place, assuming it did occur. It is also reasonable to ask why, if he — alone of the directors — held such strong views, the other directors did not promptly call for the resumption of this profitable product in 1908, after his death.

There seems to be no surviving record actually proving that the Montague factory made condoms in its early years. The absence of a record, however, is not conclusive evidence. Such was the embarrassment then enveloping this product that it is conceivable that the manufacture of condoms was discussed by the Dunlop directors at various times but not considered a proper topic to be recorded in the minutes of their meeting. The story of Dunlop's decision about 1905 to abandon condoms and Ansell's decision to take them up may be the truth, but the circumstantial evidence does not yet support this story. For the time being, the origins of Ansell's business — now the world's leader in its field — is open to debate.

While it is not certain whether Dunlop made condoms, Eric Ansell certainly did. In Richmond, at his new address of 412 Swan Street, he made condoms. The business might not have been very profitable, because he worked full-time for the Zenith Rubber Company from 1912 to 1919. Devoting all his energies henceforth to his little factory he began to make the toy balloons that children blew at birthday parties. In a larger factory in Lyndhurst Street, Richmond, he tried his hand successfully at other rubber products — rubber gloves, mats, hot-water bottles, feeding teats, hoses, and various medical appliances. Working hard, he expected others to work hard, and by carefully cutting costs he produced cheap goods that retained their quality.

Nicholas Fitzgerald, chairman of Dunlop and devout Catholic, who was perhaps the unwitting founder of Ansell.

Ansell's business had many of the characteristics of the backyard factories except that he outgrew backyards. He gave his two sons a good education and they must have pleased him by entering the business. When he died in 1952 the Ansell factory was flourishing in River Street, Richmond, close to the Hawthorn bridge, and was the nation's best-known maker of household gloves. One reason why Australian women were becoming so addicted to household gloves was that Ansell made them skilfully and cheaply and publicised them with an advertising campaign centred on the attractive model, Bambi Shmith, now the Countess of Harewood. By 1960 the firm employed some five hundred, mainly women, and combined a large labour force with ingenious, automatic machines of its own design.

Eric's son, Harvey Ansell, something of a mechanical wizard, devised machines that saved labour at almost every main step of the process. The older son Lloyd knew how to keep the assembly line buzzing with energy. Ansell now produced so cheaply in high-cost Australia that it could export with ease: the export incentives devised in 1961 by the minister for trade, John McEwen, were a bonus. In 1964 Britain's biggest pharmacy chain, Boots, ordered over three million pairs of unlined gloves from Ansell. Greece and other lands began to import Ansell condoms.

In the factory, Harvey Ansell and his employee, Langham Dale, chipped away at another obstacle that was mechanically challenging. For decades Ansell had made the rubber gloves used by surgeons. The gloves were thick and heavy so that they could be worn again and again, after being washed and sterilised. With such thickness the gloves deprived the surgeon's fingers of some sensitivity; they were also hard on the hands. There were clear advantages in a lighter glove, thinner at the fingers but thicker towards the wrist. Above all a glove that could be sterilised in the process of manufacture and then used only once by the surgeon would save time and labour in the hospital. Such a glove, however, must be cheap and that called for an automatic manufacturing process of a novel kind. Ansell and Dale busied themselves for the best part of eighteen months in devising a 'two-coagulant' process that would produce a latex glove that was thick at the cuff and thin at the fingers. To make the one glove they successively used a strong coagulant or chemical compound and a weak one. 'Where the strong coagulant remained on the cuff', wrote Marjorie Johnston in *Ansell*, 'the latex formed a thick layer, with a thinner layer where the coagulant was weaker on the fingers and palms'.

Harvey Ansell set to work to design an automatic machine that employed this new method to mass-produce surgical gloves. Helped by a draftsman and his own engineers he designed the machine and supervised the building of it. Called the 4A, it could produce, each day, the impressive total of thirty thousand surgical gloves, each of which was tested for quality by an electronic machine. Soon the Gammex disposable gloves made by Ansell were being used by surgeons in the big Australian hospitals. While the smaller hospitals were to prefer the familiar thick reusable gloves, they were eventually persuaded to change over to the new throw-away gloves by the occasional outbreak of 'Golden Staph' in hospitals: the new Ansell glove was more hygienic. The victory of the Ansell glove in operating theatres in Australia and New Zealand was the slow prelude to the conquest of hospitals in cities across the world.

Most Australians knew nothing of this remarkable success. Ansell owned none of the big brand names in Australia. Moreover the surgeon's glove was not an item shoppers were likely to pick up in a pharmacy or see advertised in a coloured magazine. And yet the Ansell rubber gloves, whether designed for a surgeon or housewife or cannery worker, were quietly making profits at a rate which would have astounded the big makers of car tyres. For Ansell the household gloves remained the key product. In the year 1968–9 household gloves earned thirty-five per cent of its revenue, followed by fourteen per cent from surgical gloves. Lesser sales came from hot-water bags, rubber mats, balloons and condoms, each of which produced from seven to nine per cent of the revenue. Sixty nations were buying Ansell products, the chief customers being the United Kingdom, USA, Canada, Germany and Norway.

The extent of the profits now made by Ansell were not known within the rubber industry, and Dunlop was probably equally unaware of the annual profits made by this inventive firm. When Dunshea was looking for new areas of expansion that would lessen his firm's reliance on the automotive industry he did not think of Ansell. Curiously the Ansell brothers, then in their sixties, were looking for a buyer. They spent months in futile negotiation with the Abbott Laboratories of Chicago before they had their first talks with Ern Kellam, the deputy to Dunshea. Eventually Dunshea came into the final stage of the negotiations. On 6 June 1969, the Dunlop directors agreed to buy out Ansell. The valuation of Ansell's assets, mutually agreed to be twelve and a half million dollars, remained a secret. Friends of the Ansells would have been amazed had they learned that each brother and each wife was a multi-millionaire at a time when that word was still impressive. On the stock exchange the Dunlop purchase of Ansell was not seen as a major event, and yet it was to have a profound effect on Dunlop's future. The day would come when Ansell International would, in real terms, be as valuable as Dunlop was in 1969.

In its factory by the river bank at Richmond, Ansell continued to run itself for the new owners. Whereas Dunshea's reluctance to co-ordinate the firms he took over was to be a serious source of his ultimate financial difficulties, his hands-off policy was ideal for Ansell. It continued to work efficiently, to capture more markets overseas, and to earn increasing profits for Dunlop when profits were urgently needed. Lloyd and Harvey Ansell and their general manager Gordon More ran the business for another three years before Leith Jarman, with the full consent of the Ansells, began to place Dunlop men in several of the top positions. When Ian Dicker moved from Dunlop's battery factory at Sandringham to take over the running of Ansell in 1974, he was taking over one of the toddlers in the 'Dunlop family'. High in profits it was still small in output and sales.

A tough question facing Ansell was whether it should continue to make all its products in Australia or begin to build a big factory overseas. By 1974 the future of Australian manufacturing was uncertain: it was even cloudier for firms like Ansell which exported much of their product. When in 1974 the Whitlam government ended the export incentives which had encouraged Ansell and other firms to try to export as many products as possible, the decision that Ansell should go offshore became almost a certainty. Malaysia seemed to offer the soundest future. Its rubber plantations produced the latex which was Ansell's main raw material: an instant saving of twenty-five per cent was made by buying latex in Malaysia rather than in Melbourne. Wages in Malaysia were only seven and a half per cent of the ruling wages in Melbourne. Transport costs from Malaysia to the main export markets in Europe and the Americas were cheaper. A dozen pairs of surgical gloves, it was carefully calculated, could be made in Malaysia for 116 cents, whereas in Melbourne they would cost exactly double that to make. For household gloves the margin in favour of Malaysia was not so large, but still substantial.

While the Ansell brothers were cool towards Malaysia, a few of their senior staff were enthusiasts. In Dunlop nearly every senior manager faced with the choice favoured Malaysia. Dan McVey junior, managing director of Dunlopillo and soon to be head of the new General Products Group (embracing Dunlopillo, Slazenger and Ansell) had served as managing director of the Malaysian business of English Dunlop: he saw clear gains in making household and surgical gloves in Malaysia, using Ansell's own ingenious machines. The same conclusion was supported by Ian Dicker and by Leith Jarman.

For Dunlop to manufacture outside Australia had normally been illegal. In 1899 the Australian Dunlop and the English Dunlop pegged out their respective territories and usually were careful not to poach. The rigid defining of territories was one fact debarring Australian Dunlop from becoming a strong exporter. The Ansell family, suffering from no such legal prohibition, had exported energetically in the 1960s. In contrast, if Dunlop had been the expert in surgical gloves, it probably would not have entered the English market with such ease but rather it would have licensed English Dunlop to make and sell the gloves in the British Isles. By 1969, however, the old Dunlop division of territories was breaking down. Thus when the directors, meeting at head office in Flinders Street in Melbourne, held their brief discussion on the merits of buying out the Ansell family they wondered whether the soaring export of Ansell products to England and Europe, though probably allowable by the very fine print of the current agreement between the two Dunlops, might not be a breach of the spirit of the agreement. Dunshea replied firmly that he was sure, from numerous discussions with Sir Reay Geddes on other matters, that London would not feel annoyed. Presumably the English Dunlop did not itself make surgical and household gloves. Nor could it foresee the speed with which Dunlop-Ansell gloves would be stocked by European hospitals and shops.

So the factory was built near the west coast of Malaysia. The Malaysian Rubber Development Corporation was entitled to hold twenty per cent of the shares in a series of give-and-take arrangements, including Ansell's right to virtual freedom from income tax for the first nine years. The first gloves were produced in November 1976. Such was the demand for the surgical and household gloves that even the addition of more machines could not supply all the orders coming at the end of the decade from Japan, the USA and Britain. The Ansell products were a pointer to the future. Australia was pricing itself, indeed willing itself, out of the competitive market for manufactures; and the removal of Australian staff, machines and investment to

Malaysia, the Philippines, the USA and other nations was to be the next stage in the history of Dunlop. Indeed many of the goods manufactured abroad by Dunlop now returned to Australia, to be sold at prices far cheaper than the Dunlop factories in Australia could equal — if they had survived.

The company had emerged from the long storm. The directors were entitled to be proud of the figures placed before them in 1977. During the last five years Dunlop had reduced its debt by eighteen million dollars. It had increased its reserves by the remarkable sum of thirty-nine million dollars, partly through the sale of assets and investments. The earnings for each share had jumped from eleven to 19.7 cents — a higher rate of earnings than Dunshea had achieved in his finest year. Not one new share had been issued, though several companies had been bought, including Adidas and Garrard Shoes. Above all, the shareholders had the consolation that their dividend was returning to the old ten per cent.

Jarman warned that the ten per cent might be hard to maintain. Dunlop had made a remarkable recovery but he was not sure whether its new state of health was permanent: he thought it was likely to have a relapse. The truth was that Dunlop was still operating in unrewarding industries. The rewards which the federal government now prescribed or permitted in each area of manufacturing were changing more quickly than Dunlop itself. Dunlop's grimy factory at Montague, its dozens of textile and footwear factories, its chains of tyre depots, its various rubber works, its warehouses, its main areas of expertise, its skilled and loyal work-force, were like giant handcuffs that prevented the company from moving into more assured fields of activity. The rubber gloves alone had slipped out of the handcuffs.

Dunlop did not even possess a financial reputation which would enable it to raise more capital with ease. It was not one of the top twenty shares in Australia: it was not the kind of stock which most sharebrokers, bank managers and journalists said should be represented in every decent portfolio of shares. But the reputation of the Dunlop shares could be changed. An ingenious plan, rarely attempted in Australia, was now discussed in the boardroom. The plan was for Dunlop to return about one-quarter of its capital to the shareholders. In theory it sounded like an admission of defeat; but in effect it would throw off the handcuffs of the past.

In December 1977, Dunlop announced that it would seek permission to hand back, in one year's time, part of its own capital to shareholders. The Supreme Court of Victoria, the trustee for the debentures, and the shareholders themselves approved this step in turn. Accordingly Dunlop handed back the entire $1 860 000 embodied in its ten per cent preference shares, mainly held by life and general insurance companies. The dominant form of share when Dunlop was floated in 1899, the preference shares had long been outnumbered by the ordinary shares. Now the preference shares ceased to exist. At the same time the thousands of individuals and organisations who held the one-dollar ordinary shares received a cheque covering twenty-five cents on each share. This sum was believed to be not liable for tax. It served also as generous compensation for the second or final dividend normally paid at the end of each calendar year — usually six cents a share. Shareholders could not complain about such a payment, being far more than they had ever received as a final dividend. In theory each ordinary shareholder now held shares with a face value of seventy-five cents, but these were cancelled and, in exchange, each holder of two seventy-five cents' shares now received three shares each of fifty cents. It was the Melbourne broking firm, Capel Court, that had recommended the lower face value for the new Dunlop shares, especially pointing out that shareholders would feel a 'psychological' advantage if they held, say, three thousand Dunlop shares each of fifty cents rather than two thousand shares each of seventy-five cents. The whole transaction was largely an exercise in psychology, designed for a share market which supped on psychology at each meal.

In preparation for paying this grand sum of $23.5 million to shareholders, Dunlop had month by month accumulated the funds in a special bank account: most of the money came from the sale of assets accumulated in the take-over era and now redundant or best unloaded. Almost one year before the cheques were posted out to shareholders, the share market had accepted the carrot. Dunlop shares, selling at $1.14 on 1 December 1977, well before any rumour of the announcement could have been heard, climbed to $1.40 just before Christmas. Nor did they slide back to the old level. The 'return of capital' had a simple effect. It meant that even if Dunlop in the next financial year did not increase its profits, those profits would be measured against a reduced capital. The same annual profit could therefore finance a dividend which was measured as substantially larger in percentage terms. Even if profit fell a little, the company could, on the reduced capital, easily pay a twelve per cent annual dividend instead of a ten per cent dividend as in the recent past.

Here, in short, was a revived company. It now compared favourably with other large companies insofar as its dividend rate was higher and its earnings for each share were higher than in previous years. Such a company could more easily go to its shareholders or the public with a new share issue. Oddly, by paying back part of its capital Dunlop was in a position in the future to gain access to new capital. It could gain access to new loans that would actually dwarf the $23.5 million it returned to shareholders. It also had the great advantage of being able to issue new shares at a price attractive to investors. This was a vital aid in the crucial venture about to begin, of taking over an old rival in the rubber industry.

The first year showed the wisdom of the psychology. The crucial ratio of earnings per share, a ratio revered by many investors, was substantially improved, simply because of this new way of valuing each share. It was further improved by the rising profits. In the year ending June 1978, Dunlop earned 18.2 cents on each old one hundred cents share; and in the next year it earned

16.1 cents on each new fifty cents share; and thereby — according to the arithmetic of the share market — the earnings ratio was nearly doubled in the space of one year. Above all, the company could pay a higher dividend — not higher in money but higher in percentage — and still hold spare funds with which to help finance its own expansion. After the return of capital, Dunlop's first annual dividend was at the high rate of fourteen per cent. Here, sharebrokers proclaimed, was a company to invest in.

Most professions, industries and even sporting games have their own rule-of-thumb measurement of what is good. Dunlop had been advised to rearrange its capital so that it fitted the slide-rule used by most sharebrokers. Now it fitted. Just as important as the fitting of the rule was the fact that Dunlop, after a period of high debt, showed it was so far clear of danger that it could quickly save enough cash to pay big sums not only to banks but even to its own shareholders. Sir Robert Blackwood, the chairman, normally on the wave-length of engineers rather than stockbrokers, understood the requirement demanded of his company. With some pride he stated that Dunlop had now made 'the final step in the process of consolidation' which it began in the crisis of 1972. He was telling the public, in the language of the share market, that the rescue operation was complete. Moreover, Dunlop was now ready, fortified by its new capital structure, to launch into long-term ventures which Blackwood believed would be more profitable and secure than many of its traditional manufactures.

As if to throw away its best clothes, the company sold its head office at 108 Flinders Street. For eighty years — ever since the birth of the company — it had been the head office; and now it seemed stooped and unpretentious compared to the skyscrapers inhabited by big companies. Moreover a large part of the building was no longer used by the shrunken staff of head office, and so money would be saved by moving elsewhere. Dunlop moved to the twenty-third floor of the National Bank building at 500 Bourke Street, at the opposite end of the city. There the lease of one modern floor was far cheaper than the ownership of a whole building in Flinders Street.

On 2 November 1979, almost when the move was completed, Sir Robert Blackwood stepped down as chairman. He was now seventy-three, and had served on the board for twenty-eight years and been chairman for seven. Graciously, in his last words as chairman, he thanked the employees 'for the work they have done', his colleagues on the board for the way they had discharged their responsibilities, and the shareholders for their friendly attitude, especially in 'those first couple of years when my addresses to you contained little that could be called good news'. Jarman, soon after, retired as managing director but remained on the board. He had done more perhaps than anybody to rescue Dunlop, but his quiet, firm manner and his indifference to publicity prevented many who knew him from realising the extent of his achievement.

FIFTEEN

Beaurepaire's

THE HOARDINGS on the roadside and the neon signs on city buildings suggested that sales of tyres were booming. Half of the schoolchildren in Australia probably knew the names of at least three brands of tyres. In 1980 on late-night television a tyre salesman was bound to appear and proclaim, as if most of his viewers were hard of hearing, the merits of his cut-price tyres. While many sellers of Australian tyres were making money, the manufacturers were not; very large Australian factories now operated largely for the benefit of the employees and customers. One of the Australian tyre makers was bound to fall or surrender in the face of such absurd competition.

Six firms made tyres in Australia in the early 1970s. On their huge investment of about $120 million they averaged, after paying tax, a profit of a mere three per cent in 1971–2. Dunlop had reason to be pleased that Eric Dunshea had steered it away from too heavy a reliance on tyres, but it still had a big sum tied up in tyres. Even after closing its big harbour-side factory at Drummoyne in the mid-1970s, even after pouring money into modernising the old factory at Montague, it earned meagre profits from tyres. In June 1978 the Dunlop board was told that on a capital of sixty-five million dollars invested in making tyres, the year's loss was almost six million dollars.

Jarman even thought of abandoning tyres, but the calculations showed that for the time being it was easier to stick to them. Sale of the whole tyre business and its goodwill would earn little. Moreover, Dunlop's profits from batteries and other automotive products would fall if it ceased to sell tyres because the same chain of depots was used to sell all products, and each product aided the other. In 1979 the outlook for tyre making was further clouded when the federal government announced that it would cut the import duties on foreign tyres, temporarily at forty per cent, down to twenty-five per cent by January 1982.

Dunlop now looked for ways of regulating the competition. It thought of

Sir Frank Beaurepaire and his colleague Charlie Grainger at an Olympic dinner, talking to Laurie Pickard (centre), a toolmaker.

buying out the local interests of Firestone, an American company which had lost a small fortune in Australia. In the end such a buy-out was thought to be 'commercial lunacy'. There was discussion with Uniroyal, whose Adelaide factory specialised in steel tyres. Eventually, Dunlop and Uniroyal saved a little money by sharing their fourteen tyre outlets in Western Australia.

The thorny question was whether Dunlop should court its old rival, Olympic. The only other Australian-owned maker of tyres, Olympic, operated two Melbourne factories. Making the tubeless, steel truck tyres which Dunlop did not make, and even making tyres under the brand names of Goodrich and Uniroyal–Goodrich for those companies to sell, Olympic was the all-rounder of the tyre business. As Dunlop and Olympic each owned a chain of tyre depots around Australia, perhaps they could cut selling costs by sharing the depots and cut manufacturing costs by each specialising in certain tyres. In a confidential report for the Dunlop board, Leith Jarman noted that Olympic was now 'badly placed' in a troubled industry. 'For this reason business observers see Olympic as a takeover target', he added.

Olympic and Dunlop for so long had been competitors in the making and selling of tyres that the very thought of tightly co-operating did not come easily. Moreover Olympic was proud of its independence, and the older members of its blue-collar work-force were especially proud. Olympic was a public company but it was founded and still led by the Beaurepaires, one of the best-known families in Melbourne in the twentieth century, and the family bond seemed to deepen its regular employees' sense of distinctiveness. Even if both sides saw gains in merging, they would not at first ride easily on the same tandem bicycle for one simple reason: Frank Beaurepaire had founded Olympic partly to fight Dunlop.

The son of a London immigrant of French descent, Frank Beaurepaire had spent his childhood in Albert Park, in a street running down to the calm water of Port Phillip Bay. There he learned to swim in one of the fenced sea baths that dotted the waterfront. Before long he was swimming faster than most adults. No more than average in height but strongly built and remarkably determined, he was hailed, at Albert Park State School and then at Wesley College, as potentially one of the fastest swimmers Australia had seen. His father had little money — he was a grip man on the cable trams, a door-to-door grocer and later the manager of a hotel in China — and so young Frank depended on public donations and private help to pursue his swimming career. Selected in the Australian team (it was more a tiny cluster of individuals than a team) for the Olympic Games in London in 1908, this seventeen-year-old travelled to London in the steerage part of the ship. Training by himself in the River Thames and in London's swimming-baths, he finally won the Olympic silver medal for the 400 metres freestyle and the bronze for the 1500 metres freestyle.

Two years later he returned to Europe and proved that he was probably the best swimmer in the world. Everywhere his feats were marvelled at. He was his own coach and organiser, his energy was superhuman and he swam in competitions and championships so numerous that today no swimmer would think of attempting so much. Back in Melbourne he worked for Caldwell's Ink, his first commercial experience, before becoming an instructor in swimming for the Victorian Department of Education. Thereby classed as a professional, he missed the 1912 Olympic Games. Next he missed the 1916 Games which were cancelled by war. An operation for acute appendicitis prevented him from going overseas as a lieutenant in the 7th Battalion but later he went to the front line in France as a recreation officer for the Young Men's Christian Association.

The most famous swimmer Australia had produced, in that era before the nation was a world leader in swimming, Beaurepaire became a household name. That was the first secret of his subsequent success in business: anything called Beaurepaire was almost certain to sell, especially in Victoria. He showed it was true by selling real estate in Melbourne with ease. In 1921, with a Canadian named Russell Taylor, he made the decision to retread car tyres. This dive into the rubber industry at the very shallow end did not instantly succeed.

In America and England after the First World War many small firms were springing up to retread car tyres. As the tyre was very expensive, anything that could prolong its life was a money-earner. Originally the tread of the car tyre lasted longer than the fragile side-walls, but with the coming of the new cord tyre the carcase was much stronger and the walls usually outlasted the tread. Thus in the early 1920s tradesmen began to fix a new tread to the cord tyres: they were like resolers of shoes but more expensive. Working in backyards and little workshops up city lanes, they did not please the big tyre firms which saw the retreaders as reducing the demand for new tyres. Later Dunlop and other manufacturers would be forced to enter the retread business. Beaurepaire did it the other way round, becoming that world rarity, a retreader who eventually manufactured his own new tyres; but that was a decade into the future.

In downtown Sydney, at 49 William Street, Frank Beaurepaire and his Canadian partner set to work. Dressed in dungarees, Frank operated the equipment in the steamy basement of a building and learned how to make a secondhand tyre appear to be new again. He was also the salesman, the advertiser. He did not need to pay for advertisements: his surname was his advertisement, a wonderfully apt name for a repairer of tyres. To drum up business he hit on the idea of making a quick note of the number plate of any car which he noticed was travelling on bald tyres. Finding out the car owner's address from the official records, he then wrote to him and offered to retread the bald tyre at a low price.

In his spare time he was still a swimmer, and his swimming fame brought him new opportunities. On Coogee Beach on 4 February 1922 he was prominent in the brave rescue of a young swimmer whose forearm had been torn off by a shark. A large subscription fund was raised to reward the rescuers, and Frank's share of that reward financed another venture. He had married a friend from a Presbyterian Sunday school, Myra McKay, who was the niece of Hugh Victor McKay, the maker of the Sunshine Harvester; now she was pregnant and felt homesick for Melbourne. Perhaps this was the time to return to the city where his name was even greater as a business asset. He spoke with Myra's brother, Oscar, and he agreed to become the partner in a new retreading workshop in Melbourne.

It was opened in November 1922 at 264 La Trobe Street, only four minutes' walk from the General Post Office. Normally, motorists wanted a retread for their own tyre rather than to buy someone else's tyre that had been freshly retrod, and so they drove their car to the retread shop and left it there for the day. So many cars arrived each morning that much of the work of removing the tyres from the cars was done on the footpath. The crowded footpaths and the noise and smell of the bluestone workshop cannot have pleased all of the neighbouring shops and offices.

The building contained two gas boilers, the moulds in which the tyres were heated for retreading, the buffer which imposed the tread, and the air compressor for the quick inflating of tyres. The equipment was worked for long hours on every day except Sunday but this was a generation which had grown up with horse stables in dozens of city lanes, and with noisy blacksmiths, metalworkers, farriers and tinsmiths operating in city streets. For them the car was simply a successor to the horse. They saw nothing odd in the tyre retreader and the petrol bowser occupying the kerbside and footpath of a busy city street.

Compared to firms like Dunlop and Barnet Glass, the Beaurepaire Tyre Service was an infant amongst giants. Even so, Beaurepaire had two of the characteristics sometimes seen in the tyre giants of the British Empire. Like Perdriau in Sydney and the du Cros family in the United Kingdom, he was of French ancestry: indeed he mostly was known as Frank de Beaurepaire until his marriage in 1915. He also displayed that sporting prowess which marked many of the early Dunlop leaders in Dublin and Melbourne and the Perdriau family in Sydney. To be admired by the sporting fraternity was an asset in the motoring as well as the bicycle industry, and a typical motorist treated a car as an advanced form of bicycle or horse buggy, to be used more for pleasure at the weekend than for business on weekdays. As motoring was a sport, motorists were pleased to identify themselves with a sporting champion like Beaurepaire and bring their frayed tyres to him for retreading. Beaurepaire's workshop soon became a landmark. More and more motorists were pleased to drive there, and have their car jacked up on the footpath or kerb, while they exchanged a word with the celebrated swimmer.

Though he was aged thirty-three in 1924 his fame as a swimmer was still growing. In the last half century there is probably no swimmer in the world who has had the prolonged international career that Frank Beaurepaire sustained. Though he could now spare little time for swimming, he still swam with success. The tyre-man was still one of the world's great swimmers. After he competed in the 1920 Olympic Games his serious swimming days were assumed to be over, but four years later he took time from work to travel in an ocean liner to Europe where he competed in the 1924 Olympic Games in Paris. There he swam third in the final of the 1500 metres, freestyle: he had won the same Olympic bronze medal four years previously in Antwerp and sixteen years previously in London.

When he returned to Melbourne, his fame even higher, he attracted more customers. He increased the range of his products. Erecting petrol bowsers on the kerb-side his employees worked the pumps and sold the Baurol brand of petrol, imported in large drums. He also resolved to sell brand-new tyres after buying a cheap consignment of three thousand American tyres shipped to Melbourne in error. Ordering three thousand inner tubes to be specially made at the Barnet Glass factory at Footscray, he launched a grand sale of cut-price tyres and tubes to match. The agent for that American brand, impressed with his ingenuity, gave him attractive discounts if he could sell more tyres. Frank Beaurepaire could sell almost anything. After all, he was still on the sporting pages, swimming the old trudgen style in his singlet-top bathing costume. He was to compete in first-class championships until the age of thirty-seven, by which time his seat on the Melbourne City Council gave him more publicity.

In manner Frank Beaurepaire could be abrupt: occasionally he was pigheaded. When his mood was tempestuous he was a sight to behold, but normally he was calm, courteous and completely in control. Charm he possessed in plenty. As he grew older his dark face sometimes gave the hint that he came from some ancient Celtic cave but his dark solemnity made his sudden smile all the more captivating. Always he worked at rapid pace. Willing to lend a hand and dirty it when the work was not quite meeting the deadline, he won the respect of all his employees. His name helped him to borrow money to finance the growing business, but he was careful not to borrow too much. In the 1920s Mr and Mrs Beaurepaire moved house often, usually moving half a step up the property ladder, from Caulfield to Garden Vale, to Elwood and Kew where at the corner of Edwards Street and Cotham Road they lived in a Californian bungalow: they were one of the few two-car households in Kew. The young barrister and politician, Robert Menzies, lived only a few doors away. The two men became friendly; and when Beaurepaire made the momentous decision to manufacture his own tyres, he persuaded Menzies to become one of his first twenty-seven shareholders. Menzies was simply a small shareholder showing his personal loyalty to Beaurepaire.

Just before the world depression Frank's partner, Oscar McKay, went to Western Australia to become a farmer. Frank stayed on. Business became difficult, but adversity was the kind of handicap race in which he thrived. His decision to begin to manufacture tyres was really made in the depression year of 1932. An act of bravery, it was made partly through the fear that he might be left with no tyres to sell if Dunlop became more powerful.

Dunlop, following its mergers with Perdriau and Barnet Glass, dominated the selling of tyres in Australia. Now its only remaining competitors were Goodyear in Sydney and the Rapson tyre factory by the river bank at Launceston. Dunlop wished for orderly marketing and an end to discounting; but Beaurepaire, like any shrewd retailer, liked to play manufacturers off one against the other, buying his goods at the cheapest price. He now relied on Rapson to sell him bargain tyres, and in 1932 he could buy them at handsome prices. Rapson, however, was on the edge of collapse. Where then would Beaurepaire buy the bargain tyres that were the secret of his success? Nearly all the evidence suggested that he should take the plunge and try to make his own tyres.

Visiting America in 1932 for the Olympic Games in Los Angeles, Beaurepaire travelled by railway to the world's tyre centre, Akron in Ohio, to investigate the manufacturing processes and the costs. His decision was virtually made. At West Footscray, just beyond the football ground, he bought six acres of land on which he would make tyres. Early in 1933 he hired Jack Cameron, a capable Scottish tyre designer from the closed Rapson factory. For his works manager and chief engineer he signed Charles Grainger from Barnet Glass. The tyre factory of Barnet Glass stood at the opposite end of Footscray, and proved an endless source of skilled labour.

The world's worst depression might seem a poor time to open a factory, but the costs of building and equipping were cheap, and furthermore the economy was likely to be reviving by the time the factory was ready. The land for the factory was especially cheap, costing only five hundred pounds an acre after the Bank of New Zealand had foreclosed on the mortgage of the previous owner. The machinery was cheap because Australian firms were eager for any contract. A secondhand boiler was bought for the engine-room. Thompsons of Castlemaine made the vulcanising pans or autoclaves, Goninans of Newcastle made the cracking, mixing and seaming mills, and Ruwolts of Richmond made the machinery for moulding and heating the tyres. Of the expensive items only the calender was imported from across the world. The raw rubber of course was imported, and the cotton cord fabric and additives were bought cheaply from the Lancashire cities of Preston and Manchester.

Beaurepaire's first made a truck tyre. Moulded by Bill Reed and Jack Carmody, it emerged from the autoclave on 12 February 1934. The factory was almost ready for continuous production. Men were hired; not too many, for the factory began on a humble scale. 'I remember', said Frank Beaurepaire, 'when the first eighty-seven fellows turned up to work for us on opening day, and I went round to meet them all with Charlie Grainger'. It was a happy day for all: 'they were delighted even to have a job'.

The recovery from the depression was under way. Dunlop and Goodyear welcomed Olympic to the boxing ring with a sudden cut of ten per cent in their prices. Olympic had no alternative but to cut its own prices. It was to become an expert in cutting prices.

To identify his new tyres with his swimming career Beaurepaire named his company the Olympic Tyre and Rubber Co. — the Olympic name was everyone's property in those days. As times were hungry the first shareholders were permitted to buy their shares on time-payment, paying in instalments of half a crown for each share over a period of more than six months. The first head office was at the Union Bank on the corner of Elizabeth and La Trobe Streets but it was soon moved out to the factory at Footscray. Beaurepaire himself was chairman and managing director, giving most of his attention to sales, and his colleagues on the board were Charles Grainger; W. J. Orr, who was sales manager, and J. T. Vinton Smith, the only outsider on the board. Beaurepaire's first lieutenant, Charles Butt, was engaged as director and general manager in August 1934. Dunlop's chief accountant, Butt had earlier served as a senior official with Rapson in Tasmania — a handy source of recruits for Olympic — and so knew how to manage a tyre firm that had to count every halfpenny spent.

The way Butt was hired shows how Beaurepaire operated in those hustling years. After taking his wife home from an evening at the theatre he called at Butt's house to talk with him and look him over. Butt later described the episode:

> So, round about 11.30 p.m., he turned up and we had a chat, a long chat. He opened his heart to me, telling me how he was having to face keen competition, and all about the tricks being used to prevent the company selling its tyres. He said: 'It is a case of sink or swim, but I think we will swim'.

Beaurepaire was skilled in selecting his technical men. They had to be practical, they had to display drive and flair, and they had to 'get along with me'. To get along with Frank sometimes called for a little patience and forbearance. Those who gave him loyal service he repaid with loyalty. Of the large employers in Melbourne he was eventually to be one of the more generous, setting up superannuation and share-participation schemes well ahead of his era. At that time there was no holiday pay, but his firm, after the normal closing of the factory at Christmas 1934, paid a bonus of one day's wages to employees who resumed work when the factory was reopened in the new year. In the following year an issue of 120 000 shares was arranged, and fifty thousand of them were set aside for employees. A financial bonus was paid to employees who had been working for Olympic for half a year or more. Frank did not encourage unions but accepted them. Mick Kennedy of the Rubber Workers' Union was to become one of his closer friends.

Dunlop's chiefs, knowing how the Rapson tyres had finally succumbed to competition, were inclined to predict that the Olympic tyre factory would be a one-year wonder. They doubted whether Beaurepaire even had the capital to mount a selling campaign. He had been slow to pay his bills for tyres and other items he bought from Dunlop and Goodyear, and in June 1933 the Dunlop directors had been told that 'this dealer' already owed large sums. It was planned that Dunlop and Goodyear and others should launch 'simultaneous legal action', but of course he paid. They suggested that financially he was skating on thin ice as a retreader and seller of tyres, let alone in his new, more difficult role as a manufacturer of tyres.

To the surprise of Dunlop's chief officers, Olympic produced good tyres and managed to sell them. War was now waged. In almost every second month Dunlop devised ways of cutting down Olympic's sales of tyres. It cut prices again, it tied up dealers in new contracts, it ran advertising stunts and entered into temporary alliances with Goodyear. Nothing succeeded. After Bartlett arrived from England as the new-broom general manager of Dunlop Perdriau, and after he spent a few weeks inspecting the tyre trade in Australia and talking privately with car manufacturers and his rival tyre maker, Goodyear of Sydney, he wrote early in February 1936 a confidential report which would have delighted Frank Beaurepaire if it had come before his eyes: 'I am of the opinion that we and the Goodyear Company have very seriously underestimated Olympic competition. Olympic are, I understand, working twenty–four hours a day, whereas we and Goodyear are reducing production.' While Dunlop's machinery was idle for part of the daylight hours, Olympic was working every machine in the daytime and some at night in order to meet the demand for its tyres.

The car manufacturers were actually barracking for Olympic. L. J. Hartnett, the head of General Motors, which assembled cars at Port Melbourne, told Bartlett that he wanted Olympic to succeed. He thought that tense competition between the tyre-makers would provide cheaper tyres for his new cars. Likewise at Geelong, the Ford executives told Bartlett that they were now giving some of their orders for new tyres to Olympic. As Ford traditionally was a big buyer of Dunlop tyres this was bad news for Bartlett. Moreover he received the clear hint that unless Dunlop supplied, at cheaper prices, the 'other rubber parts which go toward the manufacture of a car, the Ford orders for Dunlop tyres might suffer further. Clearly, Olympic was not on the way out: it was on the way in.

Like the firm of Barnet Glass in earlier years, Olympic showed what could be achieved by a smaller company with strong leadership and team-work. Beginning with car and truck tyres Olympic moved in the space of seven years to bicycle tyres, moulded products, rubber-insulated cables and hoses, selling them with the aid of skilled advertising. In the last year before the outbreak of the Second World War, Olympic's dividend was fourteen and a half per cent.

The separate Beaurepaire Tyre Service, with its sales of petrol and its retreading, continued to flourish through a network of branches. During the depression an increased number of motorists decided to retread their old tyres rather than buy new. Such was the fashion for retreading that in 1936 Dunlop itself was considering setting up workshops where it could retread car tyres. Some motorists who called at Beaurepaire's were advised that the tyre was too frail to carry a retread. The Beaurepaire salesman had just the tyre for them — a brand new Olympic tyre.

Whereas most tyre makers started with a factory and then opened shops and depots in order to promote sales, Beaurepaire already knew how to sell. He was bubbling with ideas for increasing sales. One of his schemes was to change the law so that sixteen-year-olds could ride light motor cycles. When war broke out he increased his business by supplying the defence department.

Sir Frank Beaurepaire — he was knighted during a second term as Lord Mayor of Melbourne — was now a leading industrialist. In the post-war boom he continued to expand. He did not know the meaning of standing still. By the mid-1950s he employed more than four thousand people, and controlled an impressive share of the tyre market in Victoria. Full of energy, he was no longer active in politics and municipal affairs but was absorbed in other public issues. He did more than probably most to win for Melbourne the right to stage the Olympic Games. Diverting part of his wealth to the promoting of amateur sport he gave to the University of Melbourne a physical education centre, swimming-pool and running track that had no rival in an Australian educational institute. It was opened just when the overseas athletes reached Melbourne to compete in the 1956 Olympic Games.

Sir Frank did not enter the completed building. On 29 May 1956 he called for a haircut at a shop in Spring Street, Melbourne. After some laughing banter with the barber he suffered a fatal heart attack. Rarely in Australian history had the death of an industrialist aroused so many expressions of regret. The prime minister, Sir Robert Menzies, travelling in the liner *Arcadia*, radioed a message of sadness and praise. Olympic's main factories halted work so that employees could hear a memorial address in honour of their founder.

The death of such a founder, so single-minded about his business, sometimes ushers in a period of danger. Olympic Consolidated Industries, as it was now called, seemed to pass easily through the danger. Charles Butt became chairman, while Ian Beaurepaire, the only son, became the vice-chairman, succeeding Butt three years later.

Ian was not a replica of his father, and that probably helped the business adjust to a new era. Born in the suburb of Sunshine, which was virtually founded as a farm-machinery town by his mother's family, the McKays, Ian went to Carey and then Scotch, by which time his parents were building their Spanish-mission house close to that school's side gates. Ian wanted to study economics but his father, with Olympic tyres in mind, suggested chemical engineering. It was made clear that the chemistry of tyre-making was a more teachable art than economics, an impression which events of the last decade have partly confirmed. Studying in the daytime at what is now the Royal Melbourne Institute of Technology (RMIT), Ian worked three nights a week at Footscray, partly in the machine shop.

After Japan entered the war, Ian applied to join the air force, enlisting at the recruiting depot at the Melbourne town hall, his father being the lord mayor. In 1942 as a fitter-armourer he went to Milne Bay in New Guinea where he worked on Beaufort aircraft. Very young airmen could join air crew only with their parents' consent, and as Sir Frank would not consent, Ian waited until he turned twenty-one then promptly joined an air crew: 'I thwarted the old man'. In the last weeks of the war he flew missions as the pilot of a Kittyhawk. Discharged in November 1945, he returned to Olympic and went through every department from tyres to cables. He found it easier to model himself on Charles Butt than on his father. From Butt, he recalled, he learned accuracy — Butt admired precision — and the importance of writing clear letters. In 1951 he became a director of Olympic and soon was the managing director of the allied Beaurepaire Tyre Service. When he replaced Butt as chairman he already possessed the loyalty of a very large part of the work-force for whom Beaurepaire was a special name.

Ian Beaurepaire.

Olympic flourished by moving into such fields as the making of electrical cables, car batteries and the polyurethane foams used in insulation. It continued to sell tyres through its own Beaurepaire Tyre Service, which eventually ran more than 150 depots. Its big factory at Cross Street in Footscray, employing more people than any other tyre factory in Australia, seemed to have the edge on Dunlop. Olympic expanded in 1975, buying for a mere nine million dollars the modern factory which the Ohio firm of Goodrich operated at little profit beside the Hume Highway at Somerton, on the northern edge of Melbourne. There, Olympic made tyres carrying its own and other brands, making them with such efficiency that its Geebung factory near Brisbane became redundant.

By the late 1970s Olympic and Dunlop were in the same fix. They were efficiently making tyres, but more than ever before, the federal government was warning that too many companies were making tyres. It was one of the first

Beaurepaire tyre service, Bendigo, about 1929, with petrol pumps on the kerb and stocks of tyres and batteries inside.

major manufacturing industries to be affected by the radical policy of lower tariffs.

Poor profits from tyres were almost inevitable. In the first half of 1978, big investors began to sell large holdings of Olympic shares. The life assurance offices — AMP, National Mutual and Colonial Mutual — sold hundreds of thousands of shares in Olympic. The price of Olympic shares was disturbingly low. As the assets were three times the value of the shares, Olympic was now a prime target for a take-over. Ian Beaurepaire was told by John Dahlsen of Corr and Corr, the solicitors, that his company was vulnerable to any rich take-over-man who bought up companies, pulled them to pieces, and sold everything worth selling at handsome profits.

Bernie Hendel was said to be such a man. Experienced in textiles, the head of La Monde Industries and a director of Bradmill, he soon acquired close to ten per cent of Olympic's issued capital; many of his shares he bought from the big life assurance companies. He did not yet know Ian Beaur paire but he passed on the message that, as one of the biggest shareholders in Olympic, he wanted a seat on the Olympic board. A seat was not forthcoming. That was the last thing Ian Beaurepaire, as chairman and chief executive, had in mind. Olympic's new managing director, John Hall, was even less welcoming towards Hendel. An engineer by profession, Hall called a tyre a tyre and left few of his associates in doubt that he thought Hendel was a menace to the existence of Olympic and the jobs of its employees. Hall, a champion oarsman in his youth, could in his forthright manner almost imitate the captain of a galley. He possessed human warmth and kindness in abundance but it was sometimes hidden.

Beaurepaire and Hall had not yet met Hendel. Eventually contact had to be made with a man who was moving towards ownership of fifteen per cent of Olympic's shares. At the first meeting the rapport was not noticeable. Hendel, however, was too powerful to be ignored. Receiving the seat he requested on the board, he moved into Olympic's head office and occupied a large room near the chairman's. It seemed only a question of time before he would occupy the chairman's room. At his own request he was made vice-chairman and chief executive, effectively demoting Hall: indeed he called for the sacking of Hall.

Hendel was astute and quick to learn, but what he knew about the rubber and plastics business was not always apparent. Nonetheless he held close to thirty per cent of the shares in Olympic, and was beginning to speak of Olympic as 'we'. The fact that he was personally involved did help to dilute the strong impression that he was just an asset-stripper, and he told Olympic's employees that he was 'part of a team' and that his large shareholding would prevent a hostile take-over: 'We need no longer look over our shoulders', he announced. The evidence suggests that Hendel was interested, temporarily at least, in keeping Olympic alive, and in the hope of finding ways of co-operating with Dunlop he had twice invited a Dunlop executive, John Gough, to a snack-lunch in the office of his small textiles factory in Collingwood.

While John Hall fought Hendel all the way, Ian tried tactfully to hold Hendel at bay. As Derek Beaurepaire wrote of his kinsman: 'While he must have felt depression, despair and great anger, he continued to remain calm and polite. He knew he had to live with Bernie Hendel and he knew that some of the things Bernie was saying were right — and some were terribly wrong'.

On 25 May 1979, after a quarrel with John Hall about the advisability of selling off the company's land near Brisbane, Bernard Hendel walked out of the office. Lean, energetic and quick moving, he made 'a point of saying that he did his best thinking when jogging'. After storming out of the office, he had travelled home and taken his evening jog, after which he collapsed. When he was not at the office next morning Ian Beaurepaire rang his home and learned that he had died. The first attempted take-over of Olympic had ended.

The solicitor Arnold Bloch took the vacant seat on the board, in effect representing the Hendel family, while the other Olympic directors wondered whether the Hendels would continue to buy shares through their private company, Jacobin, or would begin to sell them. Olympic was like a raft at the head of a waterfall, about to fall over or — maybe — be rescued. Most of the Olympic directors and managers had had enough of being rescued against their wishes. To their relief the Hendels' shares were sold to a wide range of institutions and individuals for a net return of $16.4 million. Olympic's future seemed safe again. Olympic then decided, in imitation of Jarman's recent brainwave at Dunlop, to make its credentials more appealing by arranging a return of capital totalling $13.9 million. It made the announcement in March 1980 and was widely congratulated. Profits were also rising, and for the year ending 30 June they were sixty-five per cent higher than in the previous year.

Just when Ian could breathe calmly, having saved the business his father had founded, he received almost out of the blue a request that a deputation be permitted to call on him. The deputation consisted of the chairman and managing director of Dunlop. After years of shunning the taking over of large companies, Dunlop was returning to the chase.

Only a few months before Dunlop began to pursue Olympic, it was thinking of moving well away from its reliance on tyres. Canberra's new tariff policy condemned tyres as a long-term investment. Indeed at the end of the previous year, a new direction for the company was being sought. A strategy paper, prepared by John Gough as the incoming managing director, argued that Dunlop needed a new activity 'which will be its main avenue of growth in the years ahead'. The new activity must not depend on the tariff wall. If it was a ready-made business, bought by Dunlop, it should contribute immediately to the company's earnings. If it was purchased it should cost no more than one hundred million dollars. While a manufacturing activity was not ruled out, another line of business was to be preferred.

If, in the course of these discussions in Dunlop's boardroom at the end of 1979, a director had proposed that Dunlop should think of buying Olympic, he might have been told that Olympic was too much like the hot frying pan out of which Dunlop itself was now trying to jump. A few months later Dunlop did its sums. Olympic itself was the new business.

Olympic, Olex and the Pulsar

J OHN GOUGH became managing director of Dunlop just when its plans to buy out Olympic were almost in place. It did not seem quite the time for a new chief executive to take charge, and yet in retrospect the time was right. Leith Jarman had rescued the company from the brink of collapse in the early 1970s and organised all the painful pruning and lopping. He had proved outstanding in those thankless tasks which rarely attract the kind of praise given to a business leader who expands but are as important as expansion itself. It was largely Jarman's idea that Dunlop should resume its expansion by trying to buy out the business. John Gough had done the homework which justified on paper such a purchase. Now he and the chairman had to carry through the purchase and, more importantly, make it pay at a time when the future for Australian-made tyres was uncertain.

While Gough seemed a world removed from the grimy ceilings of Montague he had an ancestry in manufacturing such as no previous Dunlop executive could match. The Gough family had worked in textile factories for at least three generations. His father, Leslie Gough, born in the Derbyshire mill town of Belper, had reached Melbourne with his young wife in 1927. Joining the hosiery firm of Prestige in Brunswick, he was to become its managing director two decades later, when it had close to two thousand employees. His son, John, also decided to go into textiles and after leaving Melbourne Grammar School he embarked in the *Dominion Monarch*, with ten bunks to a cabin, and voyaged to post-war England where he studied textiles at Leeds University and worked in mills and factories in vacations.

In the next four years John Gough gained experience with firms still performing capably in the industry where England had led the world. He also saw the backside of industrial England. As he recalled some forty years later:

When you lived in a place like Leeds with its back-to-back houses and soot and smoke, and when you went outside in winter and saw your white collars turn black, and when you saw the long queues outside the doctor's, you could see why they turned to socialism. Whether socialism was the solution was another thing, but you could see why they looked for a solution.

England gave him some feeling for the importance of industrial relations.

Back in Australia, Gough worked for short periods in textiles and in the advertising firm of USP Benson, before going to the hosiery firm of Kayser where he began as advertising manager and ended as a director. After Kayser was taken over by the English firm of Courtaulds he became dissatisfied. 'In management', he once said, 'you learn more by being involved with people you see making mistakes'. He learned a lot from Courtaulds.

Accepting an offer in 1970 to become general manager of Dunlop's footwear division, he went to Sydney to manage the Bankstown factory. This was the year when Dunlop was almost buried in footwear and textiles as a result of the Dunshea take-overs. Gough's success — with Ralph Grosby — in trying to keep the worthwhile products and discard the profitless lines was such that in 1976 he was invited to join the main board of Dunlop. He was soon seen as the likely successor to Leith Jarman as managing director. His work in selling the unprofitable subsidiaries in textiles and footwear, and those which, though profitable, were not in Dunlop's line of expertise, helped to put together the nest egg which financed the vital return of capital to the shareholders, itself the prerequisite for the rise in price of Dunlop shares and thus the prelude to any future take-over.

John Gough was fifty-two when he became managing director. Unlike most of his predecessors he was fascinated with the selling of goods. He must have known more than the earlier chief executives about the unpredictable swings in fashion and the way they affected sales. He was unusually interested in words and images — he had worked in a major advertising agency. As he was the main promoter of the idea that Dunlop should expand into a new line of business, one not protected by tariff walls, it must have been a slight anticlimax in his first important task as chief executive to negotiate the taking over of a tyre company, Olympic, which at first sight would anchor Dunlop to its old moorings.

Dunlop, at this turning-point in its history, also had a new chairman of the board. Sir Brian Massy-Greene, a director for eleven years, succeeded Blackwood. In mood he was more an expansionist, though he combined caution with optimism; he had been perhaps the only director to be worried by the sight of Dunshea riding in the clouds a decade earlier. Now in his early sixties, he had spent much of his later career as the chief executive of Consolidated Gold Fields which, in his time, became one of the largest mining firms with interests extending from iron ore and mineral sands to coal and

Sir Brian Massy-Greene visiting Ansell's factory at Richmond.

copper. Experienced in finance, he had sat on the board of the Common-wealth Banking Corporation for twenty years in all, twelve of them as deputy chairman: later he was to be chairman. Mt Goldsworthy Mining and the Mt Lyell Mining and Railway Company were amongst companies he had ably chaired. In business practices he held strong views about what was right and wrong. In the demarcation of responsibilities at the top, he had clear ideas about the respective duties of the chairman and chief executive. He was no sooner the chairman of Dunlop than the board made a decision with implications that extended much further than could have been predicted.

The decision — to buy Olympic — was to be a turning-point in Dunlop's history. As Sir Brian later realised: 'It sharpened everyone's wits. Suddenly they found they had been taken into a completely new environment'.

At half past two on the afternoon of Tuesday 6 May 1980, the company's new leaders, John Gough and Sir Brian Massy-Greene, called by arrangement at Olympic's head office in Swanston Street, the building which later became the head office of the ACTU. Escorted into the chairman's office, they sat down with Ian Beaurepaire and John Hall. Amidst the subdued tension and curiosity that such meetings usually generate, Sir Brian Massy-Greene announced that his company wished to buy out Olympic. He explained that Australia had too many tyre makers and that if the two firms came together they could save money and retain their competitive place in a cut-throat market. He added that Dunlop Australia was willing to pay $2 each for the small number of preference shares and $1.20 in cash (or a mix of shares and cash) for each of the ordinary fifty-cent shares. The offer did not represent a very generous valuation of Olympic, as the hosts must have quickly realised.

The Dunlop board papers contain a record of that afternoon's conference which evokes the atmosphere:

> At no stage during the meeting did Mr Beaurepaire adopt a difficult attitude. His stance was friendly and rational but at the same time protective of the Olympic position. Mr Hall on the other hand was more aggressive, at times provocative. He appeared to have more influence than was anticipated.

The news of the proposed take-over, perhaps the largest in the industrial history of Australia, was publicly announced next morning. Olympic issued a page-long statement urging its shareholders not to sell. The price offered them was said to be too low. Olympic claimed to be entering a period of prosperity: why then should it surrender? Then followed a silence. Olympic for its part had no intention of resuming the negotiations begun in the meeting at its head office.

After some days John Gough decided to break the silence and ring Ian Beaurepaire. They were not friends in the real meaning of that word but they were friendly acquaintances, for their families had owned adjacent beach houses at Mount Eliza. On the phone Gough said, 'Ian, I do want to see you. I'd like to see you by yourself'. The response of Ian was that the meeting should be more formal, with someone else from his company also present. Gough disagreed but later Beaurepaire rang with his ever-present courtesy and said with reluctance that he would meet him alone. At Gough's suggestion, Beaurepaire's family house in East Melbourne was chosen as the meeting place, at eight o'clock one evening.

'I was hepped up by all this', recalled Gough, 'and, I hasten to add, nervous'. On the stroke of eight he knocked at the door of the house and could hear someone coming down the passage with a couple of dogs and telling them to 'go away'. They went into a sitting-room, the dogs were removed, and Gough made a short speech about the importance of the take-over or merger and the need to satisfy both parties. Beaurepaire listened and then said words to this effect: 'I want to tell you something; I can never sell Olympic to Dunlop; my father would turn in his grave.' Gough had no knowledge of the relations between Sir Frank Beaurepaire, the founder, and the Dunlop people. Ian Beaurepaire explained it all, how his dad had started as a humble retreader, then a seller of tyres, how he struggled, how he fell out completely with Dunlop and its desire for orderly marketing arrangements, how its head would sometimes summon him for discussions and berate him, and how he went into the manufacture of tyres to secure supplies for which he could not rely on Dunlop. 'He hated Dunlop,' said Ian fervently.

About nine o'clock he offered Gough a whisky. Being courteous he offered him a second. The atmosphere thawed, they talked freely, and Gough went out the front door at about a quarter past eleven. Discussions at last were under way but the way was still rough. A prominent Melbourne accountant, Ken Holder, soon to join the board of Dunlop, began to act as the middleman between Gough and Beaurepaire. His task he carried out firmly and sensitively, talking to one and then carrying his words to the other and so going backwards and forwards again. Within a fortnight Beaurepaire and Gough were edging towards a compromise that would offer the holders of the Olympic ordinary shares an additional payment of one-sixth, or a total of $1.40 a share.

Ian was becoming more sympathetic to the take-over if somehow the old names and identity could be preserved. He was very agreeable to the suggestion that the name Olympic should be in the official title of the enlarged company. As Dunlop, half a century ago, had renamed itself 'Dunlop Perdriau' to satisfy the second party in a similar take-over, the new name of Dunlop Olympic Limited could hardly be seen as a break with tradition. For English Dunlop, however, the new combined name was a disappointment, a dilution.

Ian was eager that his own work-force should be protected and that if any major tyre factory were to be closed it should not be Olympic. His insistence was not a problem. It was already realised on both sides that the Olympic factory at Footscray was superior to Dunlop's black rabbit-warren of factories at Montague. It was also agreed that Ian Beaurepaire should sit on the Dunlop board. In the same spirit the Olympic brand name and the Beaurepaire Tyre Service should retain their 'competitive identity' and be allowed to compete with Dunlop brands within a dovetailed organisation.

These concessions were accepted at a meeting of leaders of the two companies on the evening of Monday 26 May 1980. Then the Olympic board recommended the revised offer to all of its shareholders. The merger was soon complete. On 1 August, Ian Beaurepaire attended his first meeting as a director of Dunlop Olympic, remaining on the board for a dozen years. His old company, Olympic Consolidated, continued to operate, but became a subsidiary of Dunlop; the Olympic factories continued to operate under their own name, though under the ultimate control of Dunlop; and Olympic tyres were still sold under their own name. Even in 1993 the Olympic neon signs still light up at night.

Dunlop had paid, in shares and cash, about ninety-eight million dollars for all the shares in Olympic. Of that sum two-thirds represented payment for the tyre business. In the last fifteen years, tyres had been more important to Olympic than to Dunlop; and in 1980 the tyre business of Olympic was privately valued at 120 million dollars compared to 101 million dollars for Dunlop's tyre business. In all other parts of the combined business, except cables, Olympic was smaller. Indeed at 30 June 1980 the total assets of Dunlop's empire in the single area of clothing, textiles and footwear were worth more than all of Olympic's assets added together.

The united company, with its 168 shops and depots, and the Dunlop Tyre Service shops and Intercolonial Boring Company shops, had 365 commercial outlets selling tyres, batteries and other products. Some depots stood on opposite corners of the same intersection. The task of making the new organisation effective, the task of removing pointless competition, had barely begun when the new company itself was in the firing-line.

The year 1980, one of the most momentous in the history of the company, was not quite over when a take-over offer suddenly appeared. Just as Olympic, back in May, was attacked from an unexpected quarter, now in December the directors of the new Dunlop Olympic were flabbergasted by the source of the attack on them. The bidder was a close and long-time 'friend of the family' and its personal links with Dunlop went back seventy-five years.

The mining and investment firm, North Broken Hill, was bidding for Dunlop. The new chairman of North Broken Hill was Leith Jarman who had just stepped down as managing director of Dunlop after helping to rescue it from deep water. Now North Broken Hill was formally making a bid for a company of which he was still a director. The deputy chairman of North Broken Hill, J. B. Harper, was also a director of Dunlop. M. L. Baillieu, who recently had retired as chairman of North Broken Hill and now held the courtesy title of president, had long been on the board of Dunlop; and in the history of Dunlop he was one of the ten directors of longest standing. The Baillieus, the main family in the history of North Broken Hill, were probably the most important family in the financial history of Dunlop. In nearly every year since 1905, when W. L. Baillieu joined the board after negotiating the sale of Barnet Glass to Dunlop, a Baillieu had been a member of the board of Dunlop.

In the financial history of Australia it is unlikely that two major companies linked so fraternally for so many years, had collided in such a way. The confrontation, in the eyes of Dunlop, was hostile. For Leith Jarman it was embarrassing. It was not his plan to try to take over his old company.

The plan came largely from Lawrence Baillieu who, as executive director of North Broken Hill, saw merit in diversifying his mining company. Dunlop, with its wide range of manufacturing interests, was an obvious choice. Moreover the innate strength of Dunlop was well known to the Baillieu family because Lawrence Baillieu's own father, M. L. Baillieu, had long sat on the Dunlop board. Nor would Leith Jarman have been invited to become chairman of North Broken Hill but for his work in restoring Dunlop. In other words, North Broken Hill, in eyeing Dunlop, knew exactly what it was bidding for. Moreover it probably sensed that the long and friendly relations between the two companies would smooth their coming together, if the take-over bid were successful.

Jarman was actually in a private aircraft travelling from Broken Hill to Melbourne when he first heard of the take-over idea. It was raised by Lawrence Baillieu, who was flying the plane. After Jarman recovered from the surprise and after he heard the reasons why North Broken Hill should pursue Dunlop, he promptly rejected the scheme. The idea would not go away, however, just because it entangled him in the most awkward way. He became acutely aware of his own conflict of interest. As chairman of North Broken Hill it was his responsibility to promote its best interests. Therefore he wondered whether he was correct in trying to dissuade Lawrence Baillieu from at least raising the scheme with the other directors. At the same time he sat on the board of Dunlop and therefore had to promote its best interests.

A few weeks later Jarman told Lawrence Baillieu that he should feel free, if he so wished, to raise with the other directors of North Broken Hill the question of taking over Dunlop. At the same time Jarman, and his colleague Harper were meticulous in emphasising their own conflict of interest. Their solution was to stand completely aside from the topic. They took no part in the subsequent North Broken Hill discussion and later, on the advice of the Dunlop chairman, they took leave of absence from the Dunlop board until the difficult question was resolved.

North Broken Hill's directors met. The case in their eyes was strong. They should bid for Dunlop Olympic. So they decided to approach Dunlop in the same formal way as, seven months earlier, Dunlop had approached Olympic. The matter would be kept secret until Lawrence Baillieu could call on his opposite number at Dunlop, John Gough. The appointment was arranged, Baillieu was ushered into Gough's office on the twenty-third floor of 500 Bourke Street, and after the usual pleasantries he announced that his company wished to buy effective control of Dunlop. Gough was taken by surprise. Absorbed in all the decisions involved in Dunlop's take-over of Olympic, he had not for one moment imagined that the new Dunlop Olympic would itself be the target for a take-over. Moreover he was astonished that the bid should come from North Broken Hill. He had regarded it as 'a white knight', more likely to defend than to pursue Dunlop. At the same time he realised that his Dunlop colleagues on the North board were strictly neutral and were not party to the plan.

North Broken Hill did not offer cash in return for Dunlop shares. It simply offered one of its own shares for every three Dunlop shares. As one North share was worth about $3.75 and as three Dunlop shares were together worth less than $3, the offer was — on the surface at least — attractive to Dunlop shareholders. North did not wish to buy a majority of shares. Indeed it hoped for an arrangement that would be satisfactory to both boards. It did not wish to touch the valuable name of Dunlop nor dismantle the new organisation now being welded together after the absorption of Olympic. North, moreover, was happy for Dunlop to continue in its own right. North simply wished to buy effective control of Dunlop and let it operate much as it was.

The offer was made when the stock exchanges were slack and their members were preparing for Christmas. Dunlop therefore had time on its side. Its first response on 17 December was to say it was 'dismayed with the basis, value and the timing of the proposal'. The new year arrived and North Broken Hill did not apply pressure. It did not vigorously buy Dunlop shares on the market. For its part Dunlop, wary about the take-over, played for time. It did not even formally reply to the offer made by North Broken Hill.

Meanwhile the prices of minerals fell on the world markets, and the price of North Broken Hill shares fell too. The bargain offered to Dunlop shareholders slowly ceased to be a bargain. Each North share offered to them was now worth little more than the price of three Dunlop shares. Finally, North Broken Hill withdrew its bid after it had acquired less than twenty per cent of the shares in Dunlop. In retrospect, the bid would have succeeded but for the timing. If North Broken Hill had made its decision three months earlier and pressed home the offer, it would have gained the advantage of the high price of its own shares. Most shareholders in Dunlop would then have accepted the offer. As it was, North Broken Hill made a substantial profit on the transaction, because later it sold its Dunlop shares to institutions that were acceptable to Dunlop.

The failure to buy Dunlop was to be only a minor setback to North Broken Hill's plan to widen its base. In 1982 it took over the Associated Pulp and Paper Mills, with a big paper mill at Burnie and its vast expanse of forests. In 1984 it took over Electrolytic Zinc Industries with its zinc refinery at Hobart and its mines on the west coast. In 1988 it merged with Peko Wallsend Limited, thus acquiring valuable interests in coal, scheelite, mineral sands, uranium and the Robe River iron ore. Under the name of North Broken Hill Peko Limited it became one of Australia's biggest mining companies.

The threat of take-over had postponed many of Dunlop's plans to reap the advantages of the recent take-over of Olympic. The staff of these two tyre organisations were still rivals as much as partners. Though under common ownership, each still manufactured similar tyres, and sold them in rival depots and service stations, many of which stood on opposite sides of the same street. Big savings were available if the overlap could be cut. Whereas half a century ago the big tyre merger between Dunlop and Perdriau and Barnet Glass had provided few of the expected advantages because the three organisations were virtually allowed to continue, year after year, as semi-independent rivals, the duplication in Dunlop and Olympic was now tackled with vigour.

It was soon realised that in making tyres, Olympic had the edge on the bigger firm, Dunlop. The morale on its shop floor was a little better, its management was a little leaner. Maybe Olympic's identification with a well-known sporting family, the Beaurepaires, and that family's pride in the Olympic work-force, gave it a certain unity and self-esteem. In contrast the Dunlop tyre factory was divided into ethnic pockets each with its own leaders and demands and traditions. When the decision was made to close one of the two tyre factories, the Dunlop factory was likely to be the loser.

The decision to sell Montague, the most famous rubber works in Australia, was aided by the fact that it was crowded and cramped. In an era when the automated techniques of making tyres called for a factory that was on the one level, Montague was an oddity, a smoky relic of the age of steam and small machines. One director privately called it 'Dark Ages Montague'. Fifteen of its buildings were two or more storeys in height and incapable of the latest layout and methods, let alone of housing the latest heavy machinery. Three of the buildings were massive brick structures of four storeys, resembling old Lancashire cotton mills rather than a modern tyre factory. The Montague factory was a warren divided by streets, several of them busy. It was possible to walk from the Dunlop buildings nearest the city of Port Melbourne to those nearest the Yarra River and all the time be walking under a Dunlop roof except for the five streets that had to be crossed. Such a network of buildings, some on private and some on leased land, offered no future for a factory. Moreover they were less than two kilometres from the General Post Office and the heart of the city, in an age when industrial smoke and odours were more and more the subject of protest.

Dunlop Olympic prepared to sell a total of 21.9 acres of land at Montague. It was called in the coloured brochure 'the greatest urban development opportunity in Australia', though it was not seen so glowingly by the developers. The last tyre — made for a Mirage fighter aircraft — was completed there on 10 September 1982, and all was ready for the sale. Many of the machines were moved to other factories, and the employees were paid off or transferred to other Dunlop workingplaces. Part of the Montague land, though sold and cleared of buildings, lay unused nearly ten years later. The only Dunlop activity carried on there today is the retreading of truck tyres.

Olympic's original factory at Footscray became the company's main tyre works. Fortunately it had been laid out in the era of the car, whereas Dunlop's was originally planned in the days of cycling. The Olympic works straggled across twenty-three acres of land at West Footscray, most buildings were of one storey, and they were more suited for a modern production line, though much of the machinery was old. As many as 1700 people had worked there in the busiest years of the 1970s and now its output — and that of the similar Somerton tyre works — increased to cope with the loss of Montague. Its 'victory' over Montague, a source of enormous pride to many of the Olympic employees who had been there for thirty or forty years, did not always make for harmony. Old Montague employees and many sellers of Dunlop tyres likewise retained their old loyalties. Olympic had been a rival for too long to become instantly an ally. In some quarters the 'infighting' went on for years after the merger. For decades both of the competing companies had emphasised that their employees must be loyal to their product; the message could not be wiped off the memory in a day.

In the long term Olympic's special asset was not the tyre factories but Olex Cables. Since 1940 Olympic had manufactured electrical cables. Bringing in Nylex as equal partner in 1970 the new company borrowed two letters of the alphabet from the name of each owner and called itself Olex. With a reputation for making efficient cables in Australia, Olex Cables even joined with A. D. Zayani in building a factory to make aluminium cables at Bahrain in the Persian Gulf. Ian Beaurepaire, realising that Olex was a special asset, urged the new owner, Dunlop Olympic, not to sell its share for at least a year. His advice was sensibly followed. Olex continued to flourish in the early 1980s under the leadership of Michael Derham and Bob Cruickshanks. When the chance arose to buy out Nylex, Dunlop became the sole owner. By June 1982 Olex had 1600 employees, was the sole Australian maker of coaxial cables, and its annual sales totalled 155 million dollars — or not far short of the Dunlop sales in clothing and textiles.

In another burst of expansion Olex in 1984 moved into one of the wonder products of the decade. In alliance with the Sumitomo Electric Industries of Japan and Pirelli Cables Australia, Olex began to manufacture optical fibres and optical cables in a new factory in the western Melbourne suburb of Tottenham. Using the optical fibre, messages could be despatched — with bursts or pulses of light — at the speed of lightning. Compared to any previous method of transmission it was cheap because a huge number of messages could be sent along a single line in an hour. Optical fibres used less space. A fault, too, was easily tracked down. Through these bundles of optical fibres, the computer data, television programmes and telephone messages could travel long distances. Telecom Australia favoured this form of communications, and so the market grew quickly. This bonanza could not have been confidently predicted when Olympic sold out to Dunlop in 1980.

Dunlop's new interest in the electrical industry persuaded it to analyse a large electrical wholesaling business which came on the market in June 1982. It proved one of the important decisions of the decade, though at the time it

Lawrence & Hanson sold electrical appliances at 33 York Street, Sydney, in the mid-1890s.

seemed only of middling importance. The firm of Lawrence and Hanson was the oldest electrical business in Australia. It was begun in Sydney in 1886 by a new English immigrant, Alfred Lawrence, just when the electric light was beginning to challenge gas. In Wynward Street he set up a warehouse for imports and a repair shop for electrical equipment, and three years later he was joined by another new immigrant, Arthur Hanson, who gave drive to the firm.

Early in this century Lawrence and Hanson opened branches in other states. In the 1920s, when the wireless was the latest novelty, they became famous for their portable radio set, sold at a price equal to two months' wages for the average worker. In the 1930s they provided lighting for many of the biggest buildings and also designed and built the early traffic lights. In the consumer boom after the war they organised the manufacture and sale of a host of products ranging from electric shavers to 'electric wool blankets from Linda'. In 1968, by now a public company, they were taken over by Andrew Grimwade's fast-rising company, Kempthorne–Mistral, later called Kemtron. Whatever was new they sold on a large scale, whether coloured televisions or freezers. They were not always profitable and when Neville Moffatt arrived as managing director in 1976 they were losing money from imported and local electrical products. Within a short time the firm was again making money. It was clearly a potential prize for anybody interested in expanding in the national electrical market.

Dunlop, with its new stake in electrical cables as a result of the Olympic merger, decided to buy shares in this old firm with its 150 wholesale branches and outlets. In 1982 it bought fifty per cent of the shares from Kemtron and in March 1985 bought the remainder. Under the name of Auslec Lawrence and Hanson it grew rapidly, becoming the fastest horse in the Dunlop stable. Within four years it was selling some forty thousand products — mostly 'the same old switches and wires' but also the lighting to big shopping centres and other projects.

By 1986 Dunlop had seven business groups, and the most profitable — the electrical group — had not existed at the start of the decade. For the year ending June 1986 the electrical group earned a profit of $78 million (before tax and interest), which was well ahead of the $47 million profit of the next group, the Consumer Products which specialised in footwear, clothing, bedding and sporting goods. Tyre Manufacture came third with $32 million, followed by Latex and Medical Products with $30 million, Industrial Products such as hose and foam and plastics with $25 million, and tyre retailing with $10 million.

No matter how hard the company tried to reduce its dependence on the automotive industry, it was occasionally tempted to expand again within that industry. After concentrating less on tyres, it had suddenly increased its reliance on tyres by buying out Olympic in 1980. Likewise Dunlop had long been a manufacturer of storage batteries for motor vehicles, but by the early 1980s — with too many competing factories in Australia — it was ceasing to make satisfactory profits from its large plant at Sandringham (Victoria) and at one time seemed likely to move out of batteries. Then again it changed gear. The excitement of the new Pulsar battery lured Dunlop further into the battery industry.

The Pulsar battery was largely an invention of the Dunlop staff in Australia — the flowering of a seed sown back in the early 1970s when the technical director, Harold Kemp, and the company's physicist Bill McDowell looked afresh at the strengths and weaknesses of the traditional battery. After experiments and the spending of three million dollars, Dunlop developed a Pulsar battery which was cheaper to make than the orthodox battery. It required no maintenance, lasted longer, was relatively free from corrosion, and its cranking power was impressive. An additional advantage was that it was more compact and lighter than the normal battery. It was valuable not only for cars and trucks but had gains for helicopters, self-propelled wheel-chairs and golf carts, ride-on grass mowers, and for the starting of pumps and generators. At the end of 1983 John Gough felt he could safely announce 'that a product developed by our own people here in Australia will lead the world into the next generation of battery technology'. At Breakwater, near Geelong, Dunlop Olympic built the first Pulsar plant with a capacity to manufacture 320 000 batteries annually on the basis that employees would work around the clock in three shifts. Senator John Button, minister for industry, technology and commerce, opened the factory in 1985, and a year later the Pulsar received the Australian Design Award.

9 out of 10

CHAMPIONSHIPS

are won with

DUNLOP

Polished Ebonite BOWLS

It is no mere coincidence that DUNLOP
BOWLS are successful in so many important championships throughout Australia. Their even density ensures greater
accuracy under all conditions, and they
will not chip, crack, shrink or vary in
weight. Every Dunlop Bowl is tested
before it leaves the factory by an Official
Tester of the Australian Bowling Council.

PRODUCT OF DUNLOP PERDRIAU

*'For much of its history Dunlop had been mainly a manufacturer'. The
bowls used on bowling greens were an early product.*

The Pulsar battery had many advantages. As there was increasing concern about pollution in cities and as a battery-driven car would reduce air pollution, the battery seemed to be the power cell of the future. As Japan depended almost entirely on imported energy it had an incentive to sponsor the use of battery-driven cars or anything that reduced her reliance on oil imported from the Middle East. The Pulsar seemed ripe for the world market.

Dunlop first had to find an international launching pad for the battery. In January 1985 it bought 14.9 per cent of the shares in the English company, Chloride Group PLC, for sixty-nine million dollars Australian. In July it announced that it had made a more decisive entry into overseas markets by buying out Chloride's interests in five nations, including its battery factories in Canada and Mexico, in eight states in the USA scattered between Oregon and Florida, and in Elizabeth (South Australia) and Wellington (New Zealand). Dunlop at once became the biggest maker of batteries both in Australia and New Zealand, while in North America it possessed outlets for launching the Pulsar battery. The factory planned for Columbus, Georgia, was to produce its first Pulsar batteries in 1988, selling them under the name of Pacific Chloride.

Dunlop was expanding rapidly into other foreign markets, both as manufacturer and seller. Its ventures of the mid-1970s — in Ansell's latex products in Malaysia and in footwear and tennis-balls in the Philippines — were followed in the first half of the 1980s by similar projects in other lands. Ansell entered America as a manufacturer by taking over Akwell Industries with its two factories in Alabama, and then by buying Pacific Polymers with its techniques for manufacturing 'super-clean gloves' for the silicon chip industry in the United States. In 1985 Ansell also opened a factory for making household gloves and balloons in Thailand. Its export markets were widening, and it was selling more household gloves to West Germany than to its home market of Australia. Of the rubber gloves used for medical examinations it was now the world's largest manufacturer.

Enlarging its interests in footwear, Dunlop bought three-quarters of the capital of Winestock Footwear, a Sydney firm which was Australia's largest importer of footwear from China, and in 1984 bought the Hamilton Shoe Co., based in Missouri, which sold some forty million dollars American of Penaljo footwear a year. The aim was to use these outlets for China-made footwear. Amongst a host of smaller overseas transactions was the supplying of heavy tyres to the huge Ok Tedi open cut in the mountains of Papua New Guinea and the purchase of Apair, a glove company in the United Kingdom.

The take-over of Olympic had been central to the expansion in the first half of the 1980s. At first sight it seemed a backward step because it involved Dunlop more heavily in tyres — the product whose future was now clouded by Canberra's policy of lower tariffs. In the hands of the company it became a constructive step. The tyre industry was made more efficient but not unwisely expanded. Olympic's share in foam and polyurethane was a boon. Its Olex cable factory became a basis of rapid growth, especially into the relatively high-technology area of optical fibres — a step which Olympic as a smaller company could not have made to the same extent. Olex and its cables and optical fibres gave the company by the mid 1980s a big cash flow. Above all it had given Dunlop for the first time a major place in the electrical industry, with the purchase of the big distributors of electrical goods, Lawrence and Hanson. In the fevered building and construction boom of the second half of the 1980s, Dunlop was to be the main supplier to electrical contractors in Australia.

For much of its history Dunlop in Australia had been mainly a manufacturer but it was moving quickly under John Gough's ideas to distribution as a major activity in its own right. The purchase of Olympic in 1980 helped to make these changes possible but the changes also reflected a new set of aims for the company — aims being debated in the boardroom at the very time when the purchase of Olympic seemed temporarily to contradict those aims.

The first half of the 1980s was one of the most successful half decades in the company's history. Faced with pinched conditions for tyres, the company had reshaped its factories. It had moved with much success into the electrical industry, as a manufacturer and distributor. It had gained toeholds and then footholds in many nations, and powerful positions for some products in the USA, West Germany, and other large markets. Its overseas employees, counted only in the hundreds in 1980, climbed to seven thousand in the following five years. The value of overseas sales was multiplied by four in that half decade, providing the company with one-sixth of its total revenue in the year ending June 1985.

Jarman's vigorous pruning of Dunlop during the late 1970s and Gough's successful planting in the first half of the 1980s had given the company a new vigour. Those who analysed the balance sheets of big public companies now found plums in a Dunlop pudding that previously had tasted bland. They noted that the money earned on shareholders' funds increased dramatically from nine per cent in the year ending June 1978 to nineteen per cent in the typical year of the mid-1980s. In June 1985 an investor who had bought one thousand dollars of shares in the company ten years ago now owned shares worth seven thousand dollars, and that gain did not include the dividends received. The company had a glamour not seen since Dunshea's day, and solidity as well.

SEVENTEEN

The end of Father Dunlop

I N AUSTRALIA the Dunlop company for more than forty years had possessed a protector. In a normal year, it had been in little danger of being taken over by another Australian company simply because in the last resort it could invoke the aid of its powerful ally and protector. The protector was English Dunlop. But in 1980, for the first time, it could not confidently be called upon for help. During the dangerous skirmish with North Broken Hill, Australian Dunlop really needed the help of English Dunlop, but by then the English company was absorbed in its own illness.

Father Dunlop in London could not offer vigorous help because he was hobbling along and was himself a potential item of prey to commercial raiders. The initial cause of the decline of English Dunlop was its seizing of an opportunity. Sir Reay Geddes, as chairman of Father Dunlop, had decided in the late 1960s that his company should improve its ranking in the tyre world. He was partly inspired, it seems, by the miracle-like expansion of Dunshea's Dunlop on the far side of the world. Sir Reay, as one of the directors of Dunlop Australia, saw Dunshea's star becoming brighter every month, and was sometimes conscious of the slower progress of his own London-based Dunlop. His company's profits merely kept pace with inflation: he was running energetically on the same spot. Moreover, his company was not as influential in the global rubber industry as it had been before the Second World War. It had lost most of its market in Japan where before the war it sold one in every four tyres, and it was not a force in booming east Asia, having made the mistaken decision that the future lay more in Latin America. Father Dunlop was not even so powerful in England and continental Europe because his strength was in the traditional cross-ply tyres whereas Michelin of France was beginning to capture Europe with its steel radial tyre — long-lasting and revolutionary in design.

Accordingly in 1969, Geddes looked for a strong partner on whose shoulders he might climb. He flirted briefly with Rio Tinto Zinc, the big mining house which operated in Australia through Conzinc Riotinto of Australia, but his eyes were soon fixed on Europe. Believing rightly that Britain would soon enter the European common market, and believing that in such an event the big English firms should each find working partners in Europe, Sir Reay Geddes proposed confidentially to the Italian tyre maker, Pirelli, that the two firms should form an alliance or union. Geddes thought that by working together, by sharing the results of their research and by each specialising in certain territories, Dunlop and Pirelli could improve their success in the tyre-glutted markets of Europe and in major export markets.

An alliance would make Dunlop-Pirelli one of the largest tyre firms in the world, second only to Goodyear Tire and Rubber of the USA. As Dunlop was larger than its proposed ally it had no fear that it would be submerged by Pirelli. Indeed the unusual plan allowed for each company to remain relatively independent while sharing in profits and while co-ordinating their two-pronged attack on tyre markets in different nations.

Pirelli, the older company, had been founded in Milan in 1872. One of Italy's largest, it employed about 35 000 people in its homeland and another ten thousand in British footwear, tyre and cable factories spread between Hampshire and the Scottish border. Pirelli could sense advantages in a union with another big tyre company because, unknown to Dunlop, it was drifting towards the financial rocks. Negotiations between Milan and London, spread over some twenty months, were helped by Edward Heath's victory in the British general election in June 1970. Heath was a strong supporter of Britain joining the European Economic Community, and it was right to assume that when it joined Europe a new era of competition in tyres would begin. A pact between the Italian and English rubber giants seemed sensible. Here was possibly the biggest coalition of companies in the history of western Europe. It was definitely not a merger, for each company remained independent though it was the main shareholder in the other. On 1 January 1971 the union or coalition came into effect.

The union was to resemble John Boyd Dunlop's brand-new bicycle tyre of the 1890s: exciting to ride on but liable to puncture. Weeks after the union started, Pirelli revealed that its contribution to profit for the year would be far smaller than anticipated. The kindest interpretation to be placed on this news was that its accountants had been incompetent or that Pirelli's forecasts had, almost overnight, been falsified by the onset of grave weaknesses in Italy's economy and rubber industry. The profit expected from Pirelli turned out to be the huge loss of eighteen million pounds for the first year. Fortunately for Pirelli it could share in Dunlop's own profits.

English Dunlop, now ranked amongst the world's top sixty companies, was not as strong in reality as it was on paper. England's economy was not competitive, and unemployment grew and industrial relations were stormy. Tyres, the mainstay of Dunlop, were hit by cheap imports from eastern Europe and by the unexpected success of Michelin's new tyre. On English roads the Michelin steel-belted tyre was the winner, for its lower rolling resistance led to savings in petrol during the oil scarcity of 1973–4 and the following era of dear petrol. Dunlop had been slow to appreciate one of the rare revolutions in tyre-making, a French revolution. Indeed if Dunlop had formed a pact with the French rather than the Italian company its future would have been enhanced.

The union of Dunlop and Pirelli became a disaster. Part of the explanation, wrote the London journalist and historian James McMillan in *The Dunlop Story*, lay in the 'Anglo-Saxon and Latin temperaments'. As seen by Australian eyes, another cause of failure lay in the personality of Sir Reay Geddes. He had entered the arrangement, his eyes squinting in the bright sun of European harmony. An able and personable man he was inclined to have great visions. Occasionally he came to Melbourne as a full director of Dunlop Australia and was dined in business circles where he sometimes gave the impression that his head was in the clouds, way above the Italian Alps.

At first the union had little effect on the Dunlop company in Australia. Pirelli did not manufacture tyres in Australia though it shared an interest with English Dunlop in New Zealand. The same English directors or their alternates continued to sit on the board in Melbourne, no Italian taking their place. The Australian market for tyres remained free from Dunlop-Pirelli competition except in those categories of tyres not made in Australia. In only one matter did Australian Dunlop lose through the European union. The technical agreement whereby English Dunlop had given the benefits of its research to Australian Dunlop was rewritten. Under new terms the cost of the latest European research was expensive.

In 1978, after Sir Reay Geddes retired, the steps were taken to dissolve the Dunlop-Pirelli marriage. Both parties now were wiser and weaker. Dunlop was much weaker. It was not even ahead of Michelin on its own home market. Dunlop reported heavy losses in 1979 and 1980. It withdrew from sponsorship of motor-racing, a sport in which it was famous. Closing down several of its largest tyre factories, Dunlop cut its work-force in the United Kingdom from 43 000 to 22 000 in the space of three years. Profits continued to fall but it was observed later that the salaries of directors leaped higher and higher. Directors and executives from Melbourne still called at Dunlop's head office when visiting England, but felt that the old firm had lost its way.

The tyre industry changes so quickly, new ideas sweeping all before them, that a weaker tyre-maker can fall far behind in the race. Father Dunlop, ageing rapidly, was stumbling. He was now a target for the commercial raiders. From Malaysia a group of investors bought into Dunlop, and by April 1980 it owned about twenty per cent of the shares, mostly through nominee companies, and was the biggest single holder with more than twice as many shares as the next-biggest, Prudential Insurance. When two Malaysian investors, Ghafar Baba and C. A. Eng, were given seats on the Dunlop board in London, the sense of siege did not diminish: the board was dangerously split into two. The division deepened when the company's Malaysian rubber plantations, for long the glory of Dunlop, were sold to Chinese-Malay investors and not to Malays. The disharmony on the board was increased by the belief of the British directors that the Malays were simply raiders eager to gain control of Dunlop and strip its assets and the belief of the Malays that, in the company's current lethargy, there would soon be few assets worth selling.

English Dunlop was a very powerful influence on the Melbourne company from 1927, when it bought its large holding of shares, until the late 1970s when it became enmeshed in its own troubles. For half a century it was a major source of new techniques, new products and marketing ideas. At the board-room of Dunlop in Melbourne it exercised influence on all major financial decisions, especially issues of capital, new borrowings, and ventures in manufacturing. Its holdings in Australian Dunlop fluctuated from year to year, but usually it held from ten to twenty per cent of the total capital. In the late 1960s, during the Dunshea spree, the rapid expansion of Dunlop Australia's capital meant that the proportion held by English Dunlop declined. By September 1977 the three big shareholders in Dunlop were English Dunlop with 9.2 million ordinary shares, the AMP Society of Sydney and the State Superannuation Board of New South Wales each with over three million shares, and North Broken Hill with 1.6 million shares. Within a few years English Dunlop held well under ten per cent of the capital but was still entitled to appoint its three directors. As in the past the English directors were normally represented on the board in Melbourne by alternate directors who were always Australian residents. Indeed most of the members of the board even in the late 1970s were either alternates for English Dunlop or had originally joined the board as alternates, later accepting an invitation to become permanent directors in their own right when a vacancy occurred.

The link with England, once so valuable, was now worthless: the name Dunlop was no longer the leader in English tyre-making. Fort Dunlop was no longer a fertile source of ideas and techniques in other rubber products; the association with Fort Dunlop was no longer a warning to any Australian company that thought of trying to take over Australian Dunlop. That North Broken Hill made its bid for Dunlop Olympic in 1980 was a sure sign that English Dunlop could no longer be taken seriously. Twenty years earlier, a similar bid would have rallied English Dunlop to the front line.

As Father Dunlop became feeble and impecunious he began to sell more overseas assets. Australian Dunlop, having sold its early interests in New Zealand to English Dunlop just before the world depression, now thought of trying to buy them back. Those assets, small when they were bought from

Australian Dunlop back in 1929, were now large. Under Philip Proctor, the young English engineer who arrived in Wellington in January 1937, the firm responded to the demands of the new Labor government that New Zealand build up its factories. After the war, in a thoughtless gesture, the government gave licences for three tyre factories when there probably should only have been one. Firestone made its first tyres at Christchurch in 1948 and the local Reid NZ Rubber made its first tyres at Auckland in the following year. At Upper Hutt, near Wellington, Dunlop NZ produced its first local tyres — the words 'Made in New Zealand' engraved on the wall of each tyre — on 11 March 1949.

Dunlop NZ, a public company in which English Dunlop usually held just over fifty-one per cent of the shares, had an increasing output of tyres, including tyres labelled Goodyear as well as Dunlop. By the 1970s it was one of New Zealand's larger private employers. Its scattered factories manufactured a variety of sporting goods ranging from billiard tables to underwater fishing suits and golf balls, while its old Barnet Glass Perdriau factory near Christchurch was the maker of Dunlopillo.

In all these years Dunlop NZ had few connections with Melbourne and countless connections with London. Its managing directors came from England. Its new techniques and products and most of its ideas for advertisements arrived from England. The career path of its staff was unlike the path open to officers in Dunlop Australia. Thus Don Smith, who was sales director in New Zealand from 1961 to 1974, had begun his career at Fort Dunlop near Birmingham in 1937 before migrating with his parents to New Zealand where he joined the New Zealand Loan and Mercantile Co., which then distributed Dunlop tyres mostly imported from England. After serving as a pilot in the European war — he was the only survivor after his Lancaster bomber exploded over German-occupied territory — Don Smith was given a rehabilitation course with English Dunlop before returning home to become the sales representative for Palmerston North. In 1959 he did an administration course with English Dunlop, worked for Dunlop in Rhodesia and returned to New Zealand to take charge of sales in a period when his firm won close to half of the local market for tyres. His career path, with two toes in England and eight in New Zealand was inconceivable for an employee of the Australian company.

By the early 1980s the governments of New Zealand and Australia were already moving towards their trans-Tasman common market, but the Dunlop company in Wellington had few links with the Dunlop company in Melbourne. Accordingly, when in 1984 the directors of Australian Dunlop decided to make a bid for the New Zealand company, they were in effect bidding for a stranger. Their bid succeeded. Already Australian Dunlop owned the Holeproof and Prestige textiles and clothing works in Auckland, to which it added — by virtue of its latest acquisitions from Father Dunlop —

factories making tyres, batteries, flexible hoses, industrial products and sporting goods in other New Zealand cities. In 1985 the purchase of Canzac Cables, the second-largest maker of electrical cables, improved Australian Dunlop's position as a major manufacturer in New Zealand.

The position of Father Dunlop was now precarious. His empire was dissolving. New Zealand was gone: Australia was next. The crucial question was whether he would retain his interest in the Australian business and his right, under the agreement made half a century earlier, to appoint three directors. In Melbourne, Sir Brian Massy-Greene as chairman thought Father Dunlop was now a passenger, not even paying his fare. English Dunlop's research and development, through a lack of money, were falling behind; and in Melbourne the Dunlop executives realised — once they had taken over the Olympic tyre business — how effectively that company, though lacking overseas connections, managed to obtain the best overseas techniques and ideas. In short the link to English Dunlop was no longer an asset. Indeed it was becoming a liability because the English firm was now out of favour with bankers, and that could indirectly but illogically affect the credit rating of the Australian company carrying the Dunlop name.

The practice, since 1899, of dividing the world into Dunlop territories, with English Dunlop monopolising the name of Dunlop in most of the world, now posed difficulties for the Australian company, in view of its determination to trade world-wide. John Gough said privately in the early 1980s that if his company were ever to progress, it had to 'break free from this barnacle'. In England the old barnacle was losing its grip. Hoping to regain strength, it borrowed from banks. By 1983 the loans from banks exceeded three hundred million pounds sterling, and the payment of interest was painful.

An amputation could perhaps save Father Dunlop. An attempt was made to sell the tyre business in England and continental Europe, but the tyre market was fiercely competitive and now Dunlop's tyre factories had more a nuisance value to their rivals than a great value in their own right. In September 1983 the tyre factories and trademarks in Europe and much of the world were sold to Sumitomo Rubber Industries, part of a Japanese combine. In the British Isles the Dunlop tyre factories were now owned by Japan.

English Dunlop still held a variety of interests in Britain, the USA and the more important parts of the former British Empire. Many of these overseas assets were sold for ready cash. Now some of the shares in Dunlop Olympic, being valuable, had to be sold, parcel after parcel. Curiously no word of this plan formally reached the board in Australia. John Gough first heard of it when he was entertaining in his Melbourne home the chief executive of English Dunlop, Alan Lord, formerly a high official in the treasury, who was visiting Melbourne for a meeting of the board of Dunlop Olympic. The phone rang: it was a sharebroker keen to tell Gough the news that a large block of shares in Dunlop Olympic had changed hands in London. Who was selling?

The broker made enquiries. Such was the magnitude of the transaction that it could only be part of the holding hitherto held by Dunlop of England. 'I can't believe it', said John Gough to the broker at the other end of the phone. 'The managing director of English Dunlop is in my home having dinner.' The sales continued, mainly to English institutions buying Australian shares as an investment.

Alan Lord was the last of the many English directors to sit on the board in Melbourne. Soon after the annual meeting of Dunlop Olympic shareholders, held in Melbourne in November 1984, he resigned. English Dunlop sold its final shares in the Australian company, thus ending a link that had lasted for ninety-one years. There was no farewell speech, no vote of thanks from England or Australia. The parting was accepted as inevitable before it finally happened.

Father Dunlop could not even be saved by the amputation of limbs. In 1985 the remaining interests of Dunlop, embraced by the English company Dunlop Holdings, were bought by BTR. Known formally as British Thermoplastics and Rubber, the giant English company had a longer history than Dunlop. Beginning in 1823 as Stephen Silver's waterproof clothing factory, its home from 1852 was a big factory site at Silvertown, in east London. There the company — long known by the grand name of Silver's India Rubber Works and Telegraphic Cable Co. Limited — specialised in coating underwater telegraph cables with the rubbery substance, gutta percha. As bicycles and then motor cars boomed, it was a competitor of English Dunlop and sold its Palmer tyres in Australia in the early 1900s. After many ups and downs, including a period when it was controlled by Goodrich of Akron, BTR dropped out of tyre-making in 1956 and did not look back.

Whereas English Dunlop clung to tyres when they were no longer buoyant, BTR concentrated on more profitable industries, especially plastics and electrical products. Eager to keep on expanding, it grew partly by take-overs. In 1983, in perhaps the largest take-over in British industrial history, it bought Thomas Tilling for £637 and in 1984 it bought control of the Nylex Corporation of Australia. Now in March 1985 it bought Dunlop Holdings, continuing to retain the name in many of its subsidiaries ranging from Dunlop Aerospace to Dunlop Nigerian Industries. Though sections of the old English Dunlop thrived under new owners, it was a sad end to a remarkable industrial triumph.

In Australia the death of Father Dunlop aroused nostalgia in many old employees. For the head office it was the end of a relationship which, once vital, was now more an encumbrance than a strength. The cutting of the English link soon made some of the Melbourne directors ask the question, 'Who are we?' Australian Dunlop, no matter what its formal name as a public company, was widely seen as an outpost of English Dunlop.

The name of Dunlop Olympic seemed to maintain the public's impression that somehow England controlled the Australian company. This impression, however, was no longer true. Not only was the company in Australia detached from England, but increasingly it was becoming global in its activities. For long confined to one corner of the world by its 1899 agreement with English Dunlop, the Melbourne company was becoming more an international company. Perhaps it was time to adopt a name that reflected the change?

The managing director, John Gough, was inclined to think that a new name was becoming a necessity. The company's latest name, Dunlop Olympic, partly reflected the politics of the merger of 1980. By satisfying the loyalists, it had helped to cement the merger. But in the five years since the merger the company had travelled far. It was no longer so absorbed in the manufacture of tyres, and yet the two names Dunlop and Olympic largely carried the image of tyres to the average Australian. By the 1980s the car tyre was definitely not glamorous. A humdrum product, it was taken for granted because it was far more reliable than the old tyres with their frequent punctures and their short motoring life. Accordingly it was reasonable to suggest that a company which was now a world leader in certain products but not a world leader in tyres should seek a new name.

Even the name of Dunlop, in the eyes of several high officials of the company, was no longer a sure advantage. The company did not use the name Dunlop in its field of fastest growth, the latex products which were manufactured in Australia and overseas under the name of Ansell. Furthermore, the international name of 'Dunlop' had become tarnished. In its final decade the parent company was no longer the leader in tyre technology, and the financial troubles that led to its demise further clouded the name of Dunlop.

Leaders of Dunlop Olympic, meeting overseas financiers, found that a visiting card bearing the name Dunlop did not open financial doors quite as readily as in the past. If it did open those doors, the first question to be asked was: 'What is your relationship to the Dunlop in Europe?' Directors and high officials from Melbourne found themselves explaining, with some sense of relief, that they were no longer connected to Fort Dunlop in England and the once-mighty London house of Dunlop. All these influences made the renaming of the company a topic of complexity. Moreover, nothing will capture the attention of directors more than a boardroom discussion about the exact wording of an important sentence, slogan or symbol in a company report. Everyone can understand such a discussion; everyone can contribute to it; and no two board members think exactly alike about the meaning and emotional impact of the key words.

John Gough, having worked in advertising as a young man, went to an advertising firm to discuss a new name for his company. The suggestion made to him was OZCO. It was certainly Australian but to the point of being ockerish. Gough then called on another advertising leader, Peter Clemenger. He eventually suggested Pacific Dunlop. He pointed out that it would be foolish, after more than ninety years, to walk completely away from the name

Dunlop. Why abandon a name when, over the years, millions of dollars had been spent in promoting it? At the same time the addition of Pacific would define the Australian company's main area of operations. The word Pacific was glamorous and clean and blue: its freshness contrasted with Dunlop and its black-tyre image and its smell of rubber. At the annual general meeting of shareholders at the Southern Cross Hotel in November 1985, the new name was sold to the shareholders with the aid of film shown on a large screen. The new name, shareholders were informed, 'most suitably describes the company's growing position in world markets'. Outside Australia the company had employed only 2400 people in 1981 and now it employed seven thousand. In the present financial year international sales were expected to be one-quarter of total sales. The shareholders agreed that the company should change its name, yet again. On New Year's Day 1986 the name of Dunlop Olympic was replaced by Pacific Dunlop.

With the demise of English Dunlop, and the resurgence of Australian Dunlop, Australia was becoming the global flagship of that name which in the English-speaking world was synonymous with rubber.

Pace-makers and ice-cream

As PACIFIC DUNLOP manufactured in more lands and traded in hundreds of new products, the opportunities for expansion were multiplied. The take-overs of existing firms became so frequent that they were sidelights rather than highlights of the year. Thus in the year 1986–7, Pacific Dunlop bought eighty-one footwear shops in New York and New Jersey, partly as outlets for the shoes purchased in China — Pacific Dunlop was now the world's biggest customer of leather footwear from the huge Chinese shoe industry. In the same year a German and a French company were bought as distributors of Ansell products, a foam manufacturer was bought in the USA, a tyre retailer in New Zealand and the Hyco works for compounding polyvinyl chloride and the Hallmark fibre products were bought in Australia. In addition the company bought in Australia a total of six businesses that distributed electrical and industrial products. That was actually one of the lighter years for acquisitions.

In July 1987, Pacific Dunlop became the largest manufacturer of clothing in Australia, following the purchase of the wide-ranging Bonds business. George Bond, a Kentucky man, emigrated to Sydney in 1906 and began to make hosiery in the wartime year of 1917. Long before his brand name of 'Chesty Bond' became part of Australian folklore, the firm earned a reputation for its salesmanship. By the late 1920s it grew its own cotton, operated two mills in Sydney and one in New Zealand, and advertised its products — ranging from hosiery to underwear and towels — with flair. When Kingsford Smith and Ulm made the first flight across the Pacific they wore, of course, Bond's singlets and underwear. In the 1960s Bonds became the main maker of baby-wear and in 1970 it merged with the Australian textile interests of the big British firm of Coats Patons under the name of Bonds Coats Patons Limited. On the recommendation of Robert Hershan of Pacific Dunlop it was

George Bond, founder of Bonds Industries, and his travelling salesmen, 1925.

acquired in 1987. It owned Chesty Bond, Grand Slam, Gotcha, Dri-Glo, Cotton-tails and other strong 'readily identifiable brand names' — a formula on which Pacific Dunlop now pinned its faith. Overall, Bonds were strong in some of those branches of textiles — for instance towels and outerwear and cotton spinning — where the main Dunlop textile brands of Holeproof and Rio were weak. Though under common ownership, many of the separate apparel sections within Pacific Dunlop continued to compete intensely with each other for shelf space in shops.

Robert Hershan had the task of fitting Bonds into his section of Pacific Dunlop. He had hardly begun the reorganising when he acquired Niblick, which led the market in shoes for golf, bowls and casual walking. Already Grosby, long owned by Pacific Dunlop, was Australia's largest supplier of shoes in general. Hershan allowed many of the distinct clothing and footwear sections to vie with each other for a place on the shelves of retailers. 'Our business', he explained simply, 'is managing outstanding brands with high public awareness'.

Pacific Dunlop was making or distributing so many products in so many nations by 1987 — it owned 166 factories and more than one thousand retail outlets — that the managing of them raised problems. Moreover the international spread of business was likely to continue. As the new chairman, Sir Leslie Froggatt, explained to shareholders late in 1987, the firm had such a big percentage of the Australian market in many of its products that 'future

Kingsford-Smith and Ulm wore Bond's woollen singlets and underpants during their epic flight across the Pacific in 1928. Bond's made full use of the airmen's letter of praise.

growth of a substantial nature is therefore more likely to come from outside Australia'. In managing that growth, Pacific Dunlop did not set up London or New York or Malaysian offices to control the variety of activities in each nation. The links were all to Melbourne, and so the footwear and battery and latex products in the USA for example had more contacts with Melbourne than with one another.

The company developed its own pattern of control and management. At 500 Bourke Street in Melbourne was its small head office, occupying only a couple of floors. The head office was small because the management and most of the decision-making was delegated to groups, subsidiary companies, and factories. John Gough believed that a managing director must delegate but know what is happening. While he gave maximum responsibility to each head, allowing him to use his own methods of achieving the agreed targets of production and profit, he expected to be kept informed: he did not wish 'to be caught flat-footed' by news of important changes in his own organisation.

Gough thought the crucial task for the managing director was the selecting of the right people for the important jobs. He had to keep the outstanding people in the company, he had to develop them and encourage them. It did not matter whether they had been to university. 'Good men can come from anywhere, absolutely anywhere', he said. A rising manager should relate to people and should not be over-ambitious: indeed he should encourage ambition in others. One weakness he noted of certain capable executives was that they 'didn't want good people around them'. Thereby they helped to drive away the individuals on whom the company might well depend, a decade hence. A firm as big and expansive as Pacific Dunlop needed many talented individuals.

Another belief of John Gough was that top managers should be intensely interested in the products they made. They might be moved from tyres to footwear and then to cables, but each time they should fall in love with the new product. Thus Michael Derham of Olex Cables was said, when driving his car, to be always looking at new buildings to see what brand of cables was being installed. A first-class footwear man like Ralph Grosby would glance at the shoes of every person he met. In that way managers learned what products were coming into vogue and what types of people were wearing them or shunning them. 'Great business men', Gough sometimes said, 'are people in love with their product'.

One hallmark of the firm in the 1980s was its insistence that products as different as rubber tyres and cotton singlets had more in common than had hitherto been realised. Products that were very different still needed the same skills in control of quality, in packaging and promoting, and in research into markets and into customers' preferences. Moreover they required similar skills in the art of distributing them to wholesalers and retailers. But while products needed these common skills they were all different: the good managers had to be obsessed by their particular products.

Pacific Dunlop now resembled a federation of companies, each company or division receiving a high measure of independence so long as it was successful, and some companies even competing with each other. For finance, however, each of the main organisations depended on head office. As each group had its own needs for new funds, and its own priority in suggesting which firm should be taken over or which new factory should be built, the demands for capital were heavy. Financial decisions, and the deciding of priorities, were ultimately the responsibility of the board. The directors had to watch the rise of debt as new companies were bought out, and they had to judge the financial implications of expanding into new areas. A company expanding rapidly in a relatively unorthodox way had to debate what it was doing: it had to be its own critic. That called for a strong board, including individuals who knew the company's traditional business and others who followed closely the new lines of business.

By the late 1980s the structure of the board was different from that of any other period in the company's history. Whereas for more than forty years it had a minority of English directors, it was now entirely Australian. Whereas in its first quarter of a century none of its own salaried executives or former executives sat on the board, and whereas in the early 1970s the board was dominated by such men, it was now more a board of independent outsiders. Of the thirteen directors in 1987, only three (Philip Brass, Bill Beischer and Ian Clark) were still executives. Another two (John Gough and Leith Jarman) were former full-time executives of Dunlop but now directors of a variety of leading companies in addition to Pacific Dunlop, while Ian Beaurepaire was a former chief executive and chairman of Olympic. The policy, when taking over another company, was to allow none of its directors a seat on the board of Pacific Dunlop: Beaurepaire was the exception, sitting on the board from 1980 until 1992.

There had been a long period, from about the 1930s to the early 1970s, when the main group of outside or part-time directors were from the same stable: they directed many of the big mining companies in the Collins House group. By the late 1980s there was no sign of a powerful outside stable. Two of the outside directors, Kenneth Holder and James Kennedy, were prominent chartered accountants, and Charles Goode was a leading stockbroker and chairman of Potter Partners Group. The remaining four of the outside directors — Sir Leslie Froggatt of Shell in Australia, Leslie Newby of Humes, Bruce Redpath of Mayne Nickless and Alan Coates of the AMP Society — had been chief executives of powerful companies operating in industries with no strong parallel to Pacific Dunlop. After Redpath retired from the board, a vacant seat was to be filled in 1991 by Ian Webber of Mayne Nickless. At the same time, the tradition of appointing the chief executives of well-known companies and other institutions was extended with the election of Professor David Penington, vice-chancellor of the University of Melbourne. In 1992,

Film star John Wayne was persuaded to advertise a Grosby shoe in the early 1970s.

within the same tradition, Margaret Jackson became a director. A director of Qantas and a former partner in the accountancy firm of KPMG Peat Marwick, she was the first woman to sit on the board.

The company had gone further than most of the big Australian companies of recent decades in trying to establish a balance of power in which the decisions or recommendations of the main salaried executives of the company could, if necessary, be easily scrutinised and even challenged. Memories had not yet faded of the Dunshea era, that hazardous time when the dazzling ascent and stunning descent of the chief executive was not challenged until it was almost too late. It was still the rule to avoid at all costs the Dunshea concentration of power — he had been both chairman and chief executive — and so in 1986 Sir Brian Massy-Greene was succeeded by Sir Leslie Froggatt as chairman. Froggatt likewise had never been an employee of Dunlop: his whole career had been with oil, working in places as far apart as Egypt and Indonesia before becoming, in 1969, the chairman and chief executive of the

Shell group in Australia — positions he held until 1980, by which time he was beginning to accept seats on the boards of many public companies and government corporations. Froggatt as deputy chairman and then as chairman of Dunlop brought a long experience of international trade and clear views on the dangers facing a company expanding into many new fields. He supported expansion, so long as enough people in the company had the foundation of skills and knowledge for a venture into new territory. That was one lesson, he said, taught emphatically by the Dunshea era.

Just as the directors now represented a wide range of business experience, so too did the chief executives. Whereas they were traditionally tyre men, the two chief executives of the 1980s had not been reared in the rubber industry. When Gough ceased to be managing director late in 1987 he was succeeded by Philip Brass who, like Gough, had no background in tyres and the automotive industry. Brass was originally a shoeman. Brought up in Melbourne by his grandparents — 'very humble people' he called them — he worked on Saturday mornings at his uncle's shoe stall in the street markets. There he began to inhale the excitement of selling. Winning a scholarship to study commerce at the University of Melbourne, he worked in vacations for another distant relative who owned Hollandia Shoes. Philip Brass gained experience in the Hollandia factory at Lilydale, and then learned cost accounting and purchasing with the same company.

A year 'on the road' in Gippsland, driving from town to town in order to sell to the boot-and-shoe shops, increased his love of selling. So much was he absorbed in the contest of selling that when Hollandia was largely bought out by Dunlop in 1968 he thought of going to New York as a shoe salesman. He stayed with the new firm, however, and rose quickly, becoming general manager of Grosby Footwear at the age of twenty-six: as managing director of Pacific Dunlop in 1991 he was to move the whole Grosby operation to China.

He once confided that in his footwear years he thought his group 'did some great things'. He brought John Wayne to Australia to promote its shoes — promoting products was one of Brass's abilities — and he set up a factory in the Philippines and shipped the shoes to Australia, one of Dunlop's first overseas ventures. Brass was in his early thirties when, as manager of all Dunlop's footwear, clothing and textiles activities, he also became a member of the main board. His policy in clothes was to move the company out of high fashion, out of men's suits and jackets, manchester and almost everything that was expensive and, instead, manufacture clothes with brand names, low prices and big sales volumes. Fond of selling and promoting goods, he was strongly behind the emphasis on consumer products. Curiously his first important investment decision was on upmarket products that were more costly than nearly everything that Pacific Dunlop made. It was simply an opportunity that came to Brass's door.

Paul Trainor, the creator of the opportunity, was a Sydney boy, educated

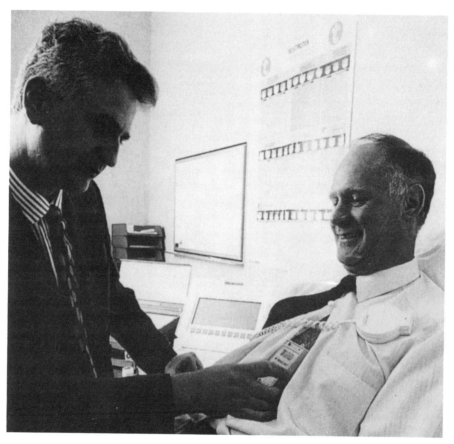

Bill McDowall, inventor of the Pulsar battery, received a pacemaker implant in 1979.

at a Marist Brothers College and at St Ignatius. As a teenager during the war he went to work with his father who was originally an optician and later skilled in the field of X-rays and microscopic analysis. Paul gained a wide experience with medical suppliers, then at the age of thirty-eight, with a wife and three children to support, he suddenly decided to take a risk. Mortgaging his house to raise capital he rented an office in Willoughby and set up his own small organisation called Nucleus. From eight to six on each working day he serviced scientific equipment in hospitals and other places on six-month contracts. After six each evening he and a few chosen members busied themselves on research and development. His exuberance and mental energy made light of the long working week.

He tried to select people who, irrespective of their qualifications, were top grade. He hoped they would work thirteen or fourteen hours a day and sometimes at weekends, and he hoped that their spouses would eventually see the merit of this dedication when the financial rewards finally arrived. He

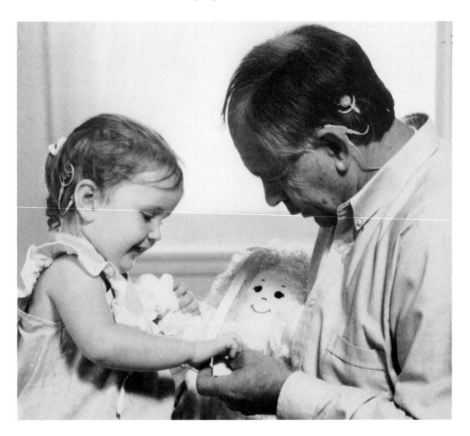

That sophisticated hearing device, the Cochlear, can be seen near the ear of all except the doll.

favoured employees with a strong ethical sense and strong character. An individualist, he was tolerant of other individualists. Preferring people who, like him, responded to challenge he set up a scheme of profit-sharing: 'I was a socialist', he recently said, 'and I still am', by which he meant that he believed in sharing profits as well as striving for them. He was delighted when, the business growing in great leaps, some of his staff received more in annual bonus than in annual salary. In 1970 his firm, though barely in its fifth year, had three hundred employees.

As a sideline his firm entered one of the glamour fields of medicine, the pace-maker, and helped to make it glamorous. The Nucleus pace-makers were electronic devices worked by a battery, generating an electric pulse which made the heart beat regularly. The technical standards of Nucleus were high: they had to be, because their product was the difference between life and death.

As the main market for pace-makers was overseas, Trainor tried to sell his product first in New Zealand and then in India and England. An English cardiac surgeon had faith and began to implant the Nucleus pace-maker in his patients. Sales grew, right across Europe. When in the early 1970s Nucleus decided to open a French factory, at Chatellerault just south of Tours, it already possessed about twenty per cent of the European market for this wonderful device. In Milwaukee, Trainor's firm bought out the General Electric factory: in Sao Paulo in Brazil it opened its own factory. It was a remarkable campaign by a little Sydney company that had started with a lot of brains and very little capital.

After Professor Graeme Clark of Melbourne University developed a bionic ear, Nucleus joined in the project, eventually forming in 1984 a firm called Cochlear to make and sell the product. Their work on this sophisticated hearing device led the world. With an implant of the bionic ear, old people who were 'profoundly deaf' could begin to hear. Once the new product was seen to confer no hazardous side-effects, young people for the first time were permitted to have a Cochlear implant. In the year 1990–1 a total of 1448 deaf people were to receive a Cochlear implant. Some were two-year-olds who had hardly heard a sound until their day of days miraculously arrived. The implant provided an electrical stimulus to the nerve fibres surviving in the inner ear. It gave to the very deaf an improved ability to identify sounds, to read the lips of others, and even to identify some spoken words.

Nucleus's main field was the pace-maker, and its main market in the mid 1980s was in the USA. Nucleus Limited also owned fifty-three per cent of the shares in another public company, Telectronics Holdings, which was the world leader in the kind of pace-maker which controlled heart spasms and so reduced the risk of heart attack. Constant research was essential, and twenty-five million dollars in a year was spent on some one hundred different investigations. To place the best product in the market was no assurance that it would be the best in two years' time.

The latest research in physiology or a new way of cutting the weight of the tiny pace-makers quickly gave one product an advantage over another. At the same time a new product was often copied with ease — to possess the world patents was not always a complete protection. Moreover the products could be the subject of frequent litigation. One faulty product ran the risk of losing, through lawsuits, the profits of the previous couple of years. The legal side of the business was vital. In the end Nucleus held more world patents than were held in every field by the CSIRO.

Paul Trainor, having built up this unique business in medical aids so that nearly two thousand people were employed, thought it was time to ensure the employee's long-term future. In 1988 he was ready to sell. He was emphatic that the buyer had to be an Australian company. Selecting ten such companies, he studied them and commissioned outside reports on them, finally whittling the list to three. The new owner of Nucleus must be capable of exporting. It must be eager to promote technical development. He finally chose Pacific Dunlop because it was a strong exporter and because, he said later, it displayed 'the work ethic'.

Knowing John Gough, he rang him, explaining that Nucleus was looking for a new owner. He flew from Sydney to Melbourne with his finance chief, Bill Thomas, to sound out the possibility of a deal. The first conversations were carried on with such secrecy by Nucleus that Gough had to seek permission for Brass to be brought into the discussions and take them over: Brass as the new managing director would have to carry any deal through and so he and Gough flew to Sydney to continue discussions. Trainor deliberately had no part in further negotiations. The terms of the take-over were for others to decide.

It was obvious that if Pacific Dunlop gained control, a large amount of power would be delegated to Nucleus. This conformed to Pacific Dunlop's current mode of management. It made special sense in view of the unusual technology of the Nucleus products. Brass was increasingly impressed with the Nucleus staff's enthusiasm, knowledge and desire to make the best possible product. 'Many were scientific dreamers', he confided later. They were utterly absorbed in the technology of their products. They did not want profit for profit's sake; they wanted profits only to survive. And yet their skill in inventing, in manufacturing and in selling had earned them remarkable success. In agreeing to buy Nucleus, Brass was making his first major decision. The offer, however, indirectly had a deadline: he had only about three weeks to decide. Every day he learned all he could about an industry that was utterly new to him. The main question was whether the company was worth buying. A second question was: did Pacific Dunlop have the managerial and technical skills to make the most of its purchase? The first question was easily answered. Nucleus was a bargain. It was hopelessly undervalued by the share market. Even if Pacific Dunlop paid about $190 million in cash and shares, being about double its market price, Nucleus was still an excellent purchase by world standards.

The transaction was completed at a gallop. A special meeting of the board of Pacific Dunlop was called for lunch-time on 28 July 1988. The only business was to consider whether to make the offer to Nucleus shareholders. Risks could be seen. The line of business was quite new to Dunlop and therefore outside the guideline for expansion. Here the brand names were not impor- tant. The acquisition of Nucleus would not easily lend itself to the company's internal circuit of transfers whereby talented administrators moved to a new product and soon felt at home. At the same time it was in the medical field where Pacific Dunlop, by virtue of Ansell, was a famous name.

At that lunch-time meeting the decision was made to buy the Nucleus group. In the following months Paul Trainor expressed his pleasure with the deal by giving away half of his share of the proceeds to his employees, to charities and to relatives. Pacific Dunlop had no reason to regret its side of the bargain. By its standards the business was small; and in Nucleus's first year as part of Pacific Dunlop it contributed only about four per cent of the total profit. It was already viewed, however, as 'a new core business of the future'. Sales of its pace-makers soared, as predicted, and 40 000 were implanted in the one year. In the year ending June 1991 one of every eight pace-makers implanted in patients throughout the world was made by Pacific Dunlop, under the name of Telectronics.

Part of the company's enthusiasm for medical products had come from the bounding success of Ansell. Fully owned by Pacific Dunlop, Ansell continued to grow like a hothouse plant. Its surgical gloves became more popular in the French and German markets through the take-over of local firms. It acquired, in June 1989, an American company that had made most of the innovations in industrial gloves, the Edmont Glove Co., with its factories in Ohio, North Carolina and Louisiana. With that purchase Ansell became the largest producer in the world of industrial gloves. At the same time Ansell won twenty per cent of the British market for condoms, partly by the take-over in 1988 of the Richard Bronson charity, the Healthcare Foundation. In the year 1988–9 it supplied 3.55 million gross of condoms to the United States government which in turn sent them to Third World countries as part of its programme for controlling the world's population. At the same time its new factory at Lat Krabang near Bangkok produced one in every ten of the children's balloons made in the world. That was not the only balloon factory, for Ansell found it cheaper to supply balloons to children in the USA from a factory at Juarez in Mexico.

All of the Ansell products were based on latex. Six of the factories, the latest in Colombo in Sri Lanka, stood close to the rubber plantations that were the source of the latex. By the start of the 1990s Harry Boon, the head of Ansell International, was proud to announce that his firm was consuming ten per cent of the world's annual output of latex.

This remarkable venture, begun in the Melbourne suburb of Richmond, had expanded in southern Asia partly to save the cost of shipping the raw materials from Asia to Melbourne. Increasingly the Asian factories cut the ground from under the old Australian factory, which could not even profitably serve the Australian market. The fall in import duties, the increasing demands for the factory to meet environmental standards which South Asian factories did not have to meet, and the expense of shipping containers of raw latex to Melbourne — these facts closed the factory by the river at Richmond in August 1989. It was cheaper to import gloves and condoms to Australia. If in Canberra the federal ministers and advisers were wondering why Australia was facing a crisis in the balance of payments, and why in essence it was so busy as an importer and so sluggish as an exporter, a visit to the deserted factory at Richmond would have illuminated their thinking. Here was one of the most successful factories in Australian history, moving its machinery to Asia and locking its doors, largely because governments did not understand what made a factory profitable.

Pacific Dunlop, owning wide interests outside Australia, was attracted to a broader mixture of products than ever before. It was becoming an international company, though it believed it must do well in a business in Australia before venturing into the same line of business overseas. It also argued that it should expand only in a line of product which the public and the share market believed Pacific Dunlop could handle. John Gough argued that the company, in everything of importance it sold, must be a market-leader. The products it sold should have a brand name that meant something to the consumer. Dunlop and Adidas, Olympic and Ansell were amongst such names. It was pointless to have the best factory and the best product under the sun if the product did not strongly attract buyers. More than ever before, efficient selling was becoming central to the company's vision of its business.

John Gough set out these views in the winter of 1988 when he addressed the Australian Institute of Management after receiving, for his services to management, the John Storey medal. His views explain why in that same year Pacific Dunlop was eager to acquire the business which, curiously, Sir John Storey himself once controlled. The company being pursued was Repco, one of Australia's best-known brands.

Repco was short for Replacement Parts, the company's earlier name. Repco had been founded in Collingwood in 1922 by George Russell, who had served as an ambulance driver in the First World War and then resumed his peacetime trade of motor mechanic. Skilled at reconditioning engines, Russell also became a capable businessmen, alert for chances to sell spare parts. With his new partner of 1926, Bill Ryan, he imported spare parts for all kinds of cars, sometimes altering the parts so that they suited rough Australian roads and driving conditions. When the American-made pistons on Ford cars did not suit Australian conditions his firm made new piston rings.

In 1937 Repco Limited became a public company with that rarity, a female company secretary, Miss Maud Terdich. After the war Repco shared in the profits of the boom in motoring. It manufactured brakes, cables, gaskets, propeller shafts, oil seals, clutch assemblies and a variety of other parts for the most popular car, the Holden. When its founder, George Russell, died of a brain tumour he was succeeded in 1946 by that fine administrator Sir John Storey and then Sir Charles McGrath, who first caught the boss's notice when he was that red-headed boy delivering goods for Repco on a bicycle. Repco grew year after year. By the 1960s it was a name in world motoring. It exported spare parts to the numerous lands where the Holden was sold, and in England it was a manufacturer of clutches and wheel-balancers. Above all it began to make the engine for a famous racing car. In 1966, the Repco–Brabham car won the World Championship Grand Prix events in France, Britain, Germany and Holland. One of the few celebrated names in Australian manufacturing, Repco's employees exceeded ten thousand. In 1971, of the Australian companies ranked highest in market value, Repco was number twenty-three.

Sir Jack Brabham driving the Repco–Brabham racing car in which he won the 1966 world championship.

The long birthday party for Australian manufacturing was almost over. In the 1970s, wages were rising faster than productivity, import duties were beginning to fall away, and export incentives were ended. Australian goods lost their favoured position in British and Commonwealth markets. By 1981 the Australian content in the grand total of cars sold in Australia was less than half. At the same time Repco's bold adventures in other lands were faltering. Its big factory set up in Singapore to manufacture universal joints was hit by dearer electricity — a result of expensive oil — and by the motorists' new preference for front-wheel drive vehicles. The Repco factory in Singapore was sold. A venture in spare parts in America was closed as 'a management disaster'. In 1981 the purchase of Lucas, manufacturer of lead-acid batteries, turned Repco into Australia's biggest maker of car and tractor batteries; but that industry was not a profit-mine. In the Australian slump of 1982–3, Repco had to dismiss or retire employees not in hundreds but in thousands. In little over one year its employees declined from about 15 000 to 12 000. Neil Walford as chairman tried to spring-clean the organisation in every corner but the odds were against him. Repco's shares were underpriced: it was ripe for a raid. In the mid 1980s it slipped into the hands of Ariadne Australia, a busy raider of that period.

A few years later, Pacific Dunlop could see gains in buying Repco. That firm held around forty per cent of the Australian market in its typical products. Moreover its morale during the Ariadne period had been kept high, partly through the efforts of Tony Smeaton, its head. The receivers who now controlled Ariadne were inclined to sell a large part of the Repco business, if the price was favourable, but the negotiations conducted by Philip Brass were slow and delicate. At first he hoped to pay only 165 million dollars but the final price announced in September 1988 was higher. In all, 232 automotive stores and 110 outlets in the brake and clutch division were taken over by Pacific Dunlop. A year later the New Zealand business of Repco, owned by Renouf under the name of Repco Merchants Limited, was also bought.

A hallmark of Pacific Dunlop's business in the 1980s was an intense interest in distribution. It came to regard the efficient distributing of products as an art in itself and not the tail-end of manufacturing. Another advantage of the distribution business was that, compared to manufacturing, it required a relatively small amount of capital to earn a good profit. Neville Moffat was vital in building up the firm's skill in distribution. A country boy from Albury — he called it 'a New South Wales country town situated in Victoria' — he had worked for Sir Arthur Warner's Electronic Industries in Victoria, for Sandovers in Perth, and later for the electrical retailer, Homecraft, in Melbourne before moving to Lawrence and Hanson. A specialist in electrical goods, he came to Pacific Dunlop with that take-over.

When Philip Brass saw how well Moffat handled the wholesaling of electrical goods, he thought Moffat might also consider taking over the distribution of the industrial rubber products made at the Bayswater factory. Moffat was about to drive from his office in South Melbourne to Tullamarine to catch a plane to Sydney when he was asked by Brass to call at head office at 500 Bourke Street for a few minutes. Out of the blue he was invited to take over the distribution of products about which he knew nothing. He began to protest. Brass replied: 'You're not in the electrical wholesale business — you're in the distribution business'. Moffat was so surprised by the proposal that, driving along the freeway to the airport, he missed the turnoff. By the time his aircraft reached Sydney he knew Brass was right. After he took over the distribution of Industrial Products, it was considered easy for him to take over Repco's distribution business — except the bicycles, which were to go to the sporting goods section. Nonetheless when he heard that Repco was coming his way, he confessed that 'I steeled myself'. He found no difficulties in taking it over. The Repco business in spare parts was sound, and so too was the staff.

By 1990, the distribution business under Moffat held close to six hundred branches and other outlets, and more than six thousand employees. In South Melbourne he did not sit in a grand central office to co-ordinate the selling of electrical goods, industrial rubber goods and automotive parts. Instead each organisation in each state was self-contained. Thus in Perth his section had three specialised businesses, doing their own work in their own way, arranging their own transport for all the goods they brought from the eastern states. Often Pacific Dunlop goods would pass each other in the night, travelling in separate trucks across the Nullarbor Plain. In this nation-wide distribution business, the six hundred buildings were leased on the short term, the capital tied up in the business was relatively small, and with the aid of computers and a full flow of information, the lowest possible stocks were kept on hand. The margin of profit on each item sold was small but that mattered little because by 1991 the annual sales exceeded one billion dollars.

The take-over of Repco had widened the company's interest in auto parts in Australia and New Zealand. Wider effects came from the penetration deep into the battery industry in the United States. Already making car, truck and other batteries in North America, Pacific Dunlop made the plunge in October 1987. It bought one of America's best-known battery companies, GNB Holdings of Minnesota, and with the purchase package came a quarter interest in the company which held more than thirty per cent of the French market and sold the famous Steco pink battery, 'la batterie rose'. In an unusual step Pacific Dunlop recruited an outside executive specifically to guide the expansion in batteries. Graham Spurling, who had been head of Mitsubishi Motors Australia, was recruited two months before the take-over of GNB was completed. Usually Pacific Dunlop did not recruit outsiders for high posts, preferring to promote people already working in the company or employ the experienced executives who arrived with a take-over.

Batteries, only a minor activity at the start of the 1980s, employed some five thousand people in the last years of the decade and provided close to twenty per cent of total sales in their best years. North America was the heart of the battery group, and Spurling himself lived in Minnesota, presiding over more than twenty factories which produced batteries for new Ford, Toyota and other models, as well as replacement batteries sold through major chains from the Pacific to the Atlantic. GNB was also strong in batteries for pleasure boats, holding nearly one-quarter of the marine market in the United States, producing a variety of batteries including the super crank or battery that started the boat's engine. For those Americans who regularly went fishing, GNB was a household name, being the sponsor of the fishing programme compered by Bill Dance and attracting four million viewers in 1990. Amongst engineers in the United States' navy the GNB brand was familiar, for it supplied auxiliary power to the nuclear submarines.

In Australia, Pacific Dunlop was more prominent in batteries than ever before. The heart of the battery operations was now in South Australia, following the closing of the Sandringham (Victoria) factory in 1988. At Elizabeth (South Australia) a factory acquired as part of the Chloride take-over was modernised to become the supplier of ninety per cent of the batteries fitted to new cars in Australia and some sixty per cent of the batteries fitted to replace batteries in cars already on the road. South Australia was also the site of the company's joint project, with the German firm Varta Batterie AG, to make the huge batteries for the new fleet of Australian submarines. Opened at Port Adelaide in 1991, the factory was building huge batteries, covering about the area of a tennis court, for the submarines. Half of each battery was built into the stem and half into the stern of the submarine, and had to be built into position before the submarine was welded together.

In each new avenue of expansion there had been a visible logic. Each venture had a close relation to one of Pacific Dunlop's earlier ventures. Thus the tyre, the original product, had led to the making of other rubber products or other automotive products; or the making of rubber boots had led into leather or plastic footwear; or the acquiring of a firm for one particular product had given the company interests in other allied products, like electrical goods. In 1991 the pattern seemed to be altered. For the first time in its history Pacific Dunlop toyed with venturing into foodstuffs. The more it examined that industry, the more it was tempted to bid for a group of firms which all the oldtime heads — Proctor or Bartlett or Blackwood — would have shunned as utterly outside their expertise. Even Dunshea, the everyman of business, might well have said an emphatic *no*.

Pacific Dunlop decided to try to buy out Petersville Sleigh and so become one of the largest makers and distributors of foods in Australia. In effect it was bidding for the nation's largest maker and distributor of ice-cream with its own brands of Peters and Pauls and its agency for Mars Bar Ice Cream. It was also bidding in the same package to gain control of a leading group of frozen foods under the brands of Edgell – Birds Eye, a major brand of microwave meals, leading makers of meat pies including Four 'N Twenty, and nation-wide brands of cakes and pastries, the distributor of a range of products extending from Golden Crust flour to Robur and Twinings teas. With the food business would come a half interest in the big shipping agency of Patrick Sleigh, and full ownership of Banbury Engineering which sold heavy earth-moving equipment. In the same purchase would come ownership of sawmills along Australia's east coast, a Tasmanian woodchip plant at Long Reach, the Tasmanian Board Mills in Launceston, and two chains of stores (Hardy's and Robb and Brown) selling building supplies in eastern Australia. The total sales of this unusual organisation, the outcome of a variety of mergers and take-overs, exceeded one billion dollars a year.

The name of this organisation, now targeted by Pacific Dunlop, reflected its zigzag history. Ice-cream and petrol were not normally partners, but the business known as Petersville Sleigh had an abnormal history.

Frederick A. B. Peters came from Michigan to Sydney in 1907, carrying with him a book of recipes for making what he said was top-grade ice-cream. He first made it at Manly by the sea before moving to Redfern, where his emphasis on quality gave him access to the small summer market for ice-cream. To him, quality was everything, and that included nutrition. Ultimately he argued that he was making not a luxury food but a necessity. Before he called his Peters ice-cream 'The Health Food of a Nation', he first had to spread across the nation. In Queensland he provided his formula, brand name and capital to a company acquiring the exotic name of Peters–Arctic Delicacy Co., and three factories in Townsville, Rockhampton and Brisbane. In Victoria he established a public company on similar terms. Under the name of the Peters American Delicacy Company (Victoria) Limited his company made ice-creams in a lane at the back of the Windsor Hotel. The first annual report lamented that the summer of 1929–30 was the coldest for one-third of a century and that business was poor. Ice-cream was still seen as a delicacy for hot days, and the Melbourne factory normally ceased to make ice-cream at about Easter, resuming when the warm months returned.

The coming of the American soldiers in 1942 did more than any other event to persuade milk bars to stock ice-cream throughout the year, and increasingly it was stored in cans in shop refrigerators made by Peters in their Burnley factory and leased out for a peppercorn rental to milk bars and lolly shops in Victoria and Tasmania. The suburban grocer — the grocery supermarket belonged to the future — did not sell ice-cream.

The ice-cream business in the 1940s had some of the hallmarks of Dunlop's tyre business, far apart as the two products were. Both products depended on efficient distribution. Both relied on rigid adherence to secret formulas. Long after Mr Peters died his book of ice-cream instruction was sealed with a lock, just like the early rubber-making recipes at Montague. In Melbourne the enthusiastic head of the business, Emil Christensen, an industrial chemist of Danish descent, was a martinet for adhering to the old recipes brought out from Michigan. For years he was emphatic that fresh strawberries should be injected into strawberry ice-cream, just as the older Dunlop technicians had long preferred natural rubber to the synthetic rubber. The ice-cream and the tyre trades had initially shared another practice, both being intensely seasonal, with summer the peak season for selling bicycle tyres as well as for selling ice-cream. Both Dunlop and Peters were proud to be Australian and their advertisements used that point of pride in fending off severe foreign competition.

Peters, like Pacific Dunlop, had acquired new businesses by virtue of personal contacts. Thus in Bendigo, Les McLure was a milkman who ladled out his fresh milk to people at their back doors, then opened a milk bar and sold Peters ice-cream, and finally moved to Ascot Vale in Melbourne and made his own brand of meat pie, Four 'n Twenty, which he sold largely to milk bars. When he decided to retire he approached his supplier from his milk-bar days, Christensen, and offered to sell the meat-pie business. On behalf of Peters, Christensen gladly bought the business because Peters were already

*A Four 'n Twenty Pie displayed high above the crowd at the Royal Melbourne
Agricultural Show.*

busy suppliers of the milk bars which in those days were the main vendors of
hot meat pies.

So Peters and Dunlop had many similarities. Both were manufacturers,
both were Australian owned, both were heavy advertisers and both were
traditionally keen to tie up their retailers. Peters had this advantage, that it
was never forced to follow in the steps of Dunlop and open its own specialised
shops selling direct to the public. In comparing the two industries in 1991,
Philip Brass quickly sensed that they had more in common than was generally
realised.

Ultimately the big asset of the Peters organisation was Edgell–Birds Eye,
which specialised in canning and freezing foods. One of the quiet triumphs of
country-town enterprise, the cannery had been founded in Bathurst, New
South Wales, in 1926 mainly to preserve the asparagus which Gordon Edgell's
nearby farm was producing in larger quantities than the Sydney produce
market could handle. At the time Edgell himself was relatively old to be
thinking of risking money in a completely new business. Aged sixty, an
engineer before he became an orchardist and farmer, he had enough drive to
start another career. His son, Maxwell Edgell, visited California to learn about

the canning of food, and the Bathurst cannery with its handmade cans expanded from asparagus to carrots, apples, green peas and other rural produce. It soon turned to soups, just at the time when canned soups were beginning to compete with the home-made soup cooked on the stoves of a million Australian kitchens. Edgell's wartime cannery, built in 1943 at Cowra, New South Wales, was a success.

Edgells turned to frozen foods, eventually buying from Unilever the brand name of Birds Eye. In 1959 at Bathurst, in the presence of Prime Minister Menzies, and with the vague and distant blessing of Dr Spock and his views on child-rearing, Edgells made the now fashionable tins of baby food under the brand name of Edgell–Gerber. Its purchase of the large H. J. Heinz cannery in Devonport in 1955 made it prominent in Tasmania, but six years later the Peters Ice Cream (Vic) Limited acquired a large food-processing plant at Ulverstone, only half an hour by car from the Edgell factory at Devonport. The Edgells were perhaps nervous of the new competitor and its product Hy-Peak. They were also short of money in that sharp economic downswing and 'credit squeeze' which lifted Australia's rate of unemployment to more than two per cent and almost deprived Menzies of victory in the federal election of 1961. So the three Edgell brothers approached Peters and successfully offered to sell out. Not one of the brothers was given a seat on the Peters board but the Edgell brand lived on in the supermarkets that were becoming common in the 1960s.

The diverse and large Peters business, with Jim Shaw as managing director, flourished. Though Peters was a household name and one of the strenuous advertisers at children's time on television (a host of children belonged to Peters Pals), its canned and frozen foods became more important than the ice-cream. Peters was now the largest of the Australian-owned food firms. Profitable to the shareholders, nationally known for its products, it was increasingly a target for take-over bids, especially from overseas firms including big Swiss internationals. At cocktail parties Jim Shaw became suspicious of the friendly hand on the shoulder and the tempting question: 'Wouldn't you be better off as part of a larger company?'. He was careful to X-ray the invitations to special lunches where 'merger' was likely to be the topic of discussion.

Peters became the target for two Australian firms which had no interest in foods. In 1981 it succumbed, choosing what it saw as the lesser evil. It sold out to H. C. Sleigh Limited, a many-sided Australian firm which had become a public company in 1948. For decades, Sleigh's main business had been in shipping and petrol. It owned oil tankers and the chain of Golden Fleece petrol stations. It was even a competitor with Dunlop in tyres, buying out the Hardie Tyre and Rubber Company in 1960 and selling seventy per cent of its shares to the American tyre firm of Firestone in 1966. Sleigh was also an exporter, shipping the first post-war cargo of coal to Japan and winning the Indonesian army's contract for full-cream milk-powder. In 1981, Sleigh was able to make the offer for the Petersville food business because it had cash in hand from the sale of its Golden Fleece petrol business to Caltex.

H. C. Sleigh knew something about the Peters empire because its late chairman, Sir Hamilton Sleigh, had sat on the Peters board for some seventeen years. Indeed the take-over by Sleigh was a shock. The heads of Peters had long thought that Sleigh — to use the advertising jingle — was one of Peters Pals. The only consolation for Peters was that before long its portion of the business was deemed more promising than the Sleigh portion with its ships, travel agencies, its three-tenths interest in a New South Wales coal-mine, contracts for aerial surveillance of the coast, and a list of other interests. The new firm came to be called Petersville Sleigh.

It did not survive long. In 1982 it was the target of a bid. John Spalvins, rising to fame as one of the corporate raiders in the era of incessant raiding, used the brewing firm of Tooth to buy forty-nine per cent of Petersville Sleigh for his high-borrowing organisation. So the old Peters, Edgell and Sleigh businesses became part of a tangled ownership under Spalvins. The winner of many duels in the corporate take-over tournaments of the 1980s, Spalvins was finally lanced by its own debts. And that was when Philip Brass of Pacific Dunlop became interested.

The old Adelaide Steamship Co., now called Adsteam, was the core of the Spalvins group. Of the shares in Petersville it specifically held nineteen per cent. One of its allies, Tooth the brewing firm, held thirty-nine per cent, and another, David Jones the retailer, held four per cent. These three firms were part of the same marriage. In effect, this group owned more than sixty-two per cent of the shares in Petersville Sleigh.

In the 1980s the accumulation of high debts was often the springboard to corporate greatness. By 1991, debt was the trapdoor to extinction. Petersville Sleigh and its sister companies, under new control, were in financial trouble. The whole structure of interlocked companies was weighed down by debt. Its future was in the hands of foreign and Australian banks — at least twenty-four of them. But for that debt, Philip Brass would have ignored Petersville Sleigh. Its plight, however, gave him an opportunity of entering the foodstuffs business at a reasonable price.

He investigated Petersville Sleigh on and off for several years without giving any indication that he was interested. There were considerable risks in entering a new line of business. He wanted to know as many as possible of the risks in advance. Maybe four or five other companies could be interested in buying Petersville Sleigh. Brass waited to see if they moved. When they did not move, he hastened his own company's assessment. Then he wrote down a plan of action with meticulous attention to the timetable.

His confidential plan was the main item of business when the board met in Melbourne at a quarter to nine on the morning of Friday 12 July 1991. Each director had before him a high pile of papers on a company called 'Santa' but

Right: After Frank Beaurepaire, a former swimming champion, founded his firm for retreading and manufacturing tyres, he shrewdly decided to capture Olympic as a brand name.

Below: Peters ice-cream had its own show in the late 1950s, the first years of television, and even then, clowns Zig and Zag were promoting Peters.

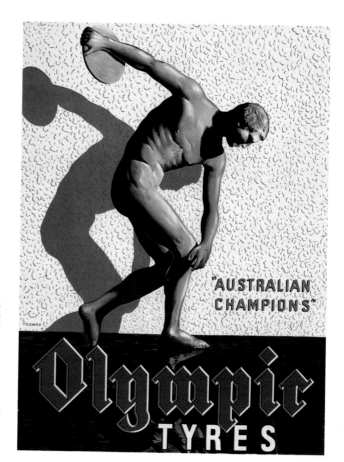

IT'S GOTTA BE **BONDS**

Left: Chesty Bond and his singlet was one of the older advertising symbols of the nation when in 1993 the actor Paul Mercurio, fresh from Strictly Ballroom, was invited to join him in promoting Bonds.

Below left: In 1937 ice-cream was still overwhelmingly a summer delicacy but Peters tried to make 'the health food of a nation' an all-seasons food.

Below: Peters ice-cream in the days when threepence was a lot of money.

"THE HEALTH OF THE PEOPLE IS THE HIGHEST LAW" *Cicero*

For "goodness" sake eat Peters!

Peters ICE CREAM

Phone J5221 (7 lines)

THE HEALTH FOOD OF A NATION

PETERS

"THERE'S NOTHING NICER UNDER THE SUN"

PETERS ICE CREAM

3D

3D

MADE & GUARANTEED UNDER THE HEALTH ACT OF VICTORIA 1919 BY PETERS AMERICAN DELICACY Co (VICTORIA) LTD MELBOURNE.

The company set up a Western Pacific Rim advisory board which met in Tianjin, China, in 1993. Directors Philip Brass and John Gough with Dr Narongchair Akrasanee, Tang I-Fang, Jing Shuping, Tan Sri Zain Azraai and Washington SyCip.

The Olex cable factory was opened at Tianjin, northern China, in 1992.

The board of directors in 1988. Standing from left are William Beischer, James Kennedy, Alan Coates, Ian Clark and Ian Beaurepaire. Seated are Bruce Redpath, Kenneth Holder, Philip Brass, Sir Leslie Froggatt, John Gough, Charles Goode and Leith Jarman. J. Leslie Newby was absent.

John Gough, Sir Leslie Froggatt and Philip Brass.

Ansell's factory in Sri Lanka manufactures gloves and condoms.

The main factory of South Pacific Tyres at Somerton, just north of Melbourne.

*Overleaf: By the early 1990s, Pacific Dunlop had
probably the widest collection of popular brand-names
ever held by one Australian company.*

Consumer Products

Healthcare

PACIFIC·DUNLOP

Automotive

STOWAWAY

DUNLOP

GOOD YEAR

Beaurepaires

McLEOD TYRES

Building & Construction

Dunlopillo

Simmons

Kimpton

Distribution

Repco

The Flying D arrived as the company's logo in 1967 and though later superseded, is still used in various ways.

unmistakably Petersville Sleigh. Brass summed up the proposal to make a bid
for Santa on the share market. It had a 'strong stable of brands operating in
predictable, rationalised markets'. The food industry itself was believed to be
'profitable', and was not really vulnerable to a recession: people must eat.
Moreover about three-quarters of the firm's sales were to four major retailers,
with which Pacific Dunlop already had close relations.

The core of the Petersville Sleigh business was Edgell–Birds Eye. It supplied
about forty per cent of the company's total revenue, being one of Australia's
major canners of vegetables, a leader in frozen foods, and the supplier of potato
chips to McDonalds and a wide range of caterers. Edgell–Birds Eye alone
employed about three thousand people. The key question was whether this
part of the business was strong enough to justify the entire package? Brass went
through the arguments set out in the papers now before the directors. Edgell
– Birds Eye was meeting fierce competition from imported vegetables,
especially tomatoes and asparagus, where low-cost countries had an advantage because those two crops had a high labour content. Generally, however,
the firm could hope to withstand foreign competition because the cost of
transporting foreign cans and frozen foods to Australia ate up too much of the
profit. Moreover, Brass thought there was a chance of making this vital part
of Petersville more efficient — a year later he was to close three of the Edgell
–Birds Eye canneries in country towns.

How much should Pacific Dunlop offer? The figure suggested was $1.15 for
each Petersville share, a sum that was well above the market price. It could
therefore be seen as generous to the Petersville shareholders. On the other
hand there was a chance that another large firm — eager to buy Petersville or
eager to keep Pacific Dunlop out of the food business — might offer a few
additional cents for each share. Perhaps Pacific Dunlop, it was privately
thought, might have to increase its bid a little, as a last resort. And how should
the payment be made to Petersville shareholders? There was only one way of
paying — in cash. The bankers who virtually controlled Petersville would
want cash. In any event, Pacific Dunlop, if it were to pay with shares instead
of cash, would have to draw up a prospectus to meet the requirements of
company law. That task would take up time, but Brass knew that time was not
on his side. How much cash was needed? About 374 million dollars was
needed — only a fraction of Pacific Dunlop's total assets — and the company's
depleted cash could be restored by a new issue of shares if the purchase
succeeded.

The directors agreed with his plan to bid for the food firm. It was announced
the following Monday, and Brass began to negotiate all the main items with
Bob Cumberlidge, managing director of Petersville Sleigh. The news instantly pushed up the sagging Petersville shares from 88 cents to $1.20.
Eventually Pacific Dunlop agreed to pay exactly that price for each share.

Meanwhile the bid puzzled some investors and indeed a few manufacturers

Producing french fries at the Edgell–Birds Eye plant at Ulverstone, Northern Tasmania. The plant, opened on 13 May 1993, is designed to process 400,000 tonnes of potatoes per year.

of food. Dunlop had been operating in Australia for ninety-eight years and had not previously produced something that was licked, let alone eaten; and now it was trying to woo the food buyers. And yet it was fair to say that the purchase of the Nucleus business and its pace-makers and other medical products in 1988 had been a riskier leap than the leap into foodstuffs. Sophisticated medical products were far removed from the company's existing skills and interests. On the other hand a food business with famous brand names in everything from baby food to prawn crackers had clear similarities to the socks, singlets, jogging shoes, household gloves, pillows, golf and tennis-balls, bicycles, and even tyres and batteries which the firm had long made and sold.

Philip Brass maintained that the Pacific Dunlop businesses were all based on efficient, low-cost manufacturing, effective distributing, and the imaginative promoting of well-known brands. 'The offer for Petersville Sleigh', he said, 'was made because it fits our criteria and skills so well'. A witty financier, on the day the offer was announced, had another way of explaining it. Here is a fine example of lateral thinking by a public company, said Nestor Hinzack: 'Anyone who doesn't buy condoms will want to buy baby food'.

The offer was soon accepted by a majority of shareholders. On 30 August, Petersville Sleigh became a division of Pacific Dunlop. Renamed the Pacific Brands Food Group, it was operated as a self-contained part of the organisation with Grant Latta as managing director. In effect Pacific Dunlop was becoming an aircraft carrier providing a mobile base for a variety of aircraft which largely flew on their own.

Significantly, most of the food business acquired did not depend on tariffs. Pacific Dunlop's policy was to avoid industries that were protected by tariffs, though in tyres it still had to depend on protection. Amidst all the novel products the tyre remained an important part of the business. To the average Australian, the word Dunlop was most likely to signify a car tyre. Of the Australian-made products familiar to most people, a Dunlop tyre was, as they say, almost 'the daddy of them all'. It had been on the market in one form or other for almost a century: it was older than Vegemite, Foster's beer and BHP steel and perhaps every other long-time, national household name except CSR sugar. And yet the future of the Dunlop tyre was not safe in the face of imports of cheap foreign tyres from some of the world's biggest factories.

After the closing down of the old Montague factories in 1982, tyre-making was concentrated in the less-cramped Olympic factories in the Melbourne suburbs of Footscray and Somerton. They became more competitive, but under Canberra's policy of lower tariffs the imported tyres continued to roll in. Bill Beischer, who as general manager headed the tyre business, was convinced that Dunlop's role in the industry would cease unless it found an ally with the latest techniques for making tyres. In 1987 the executives of Pacific Dunlop did what would have been unimaginable in earlier years. They negotiated with a long-time overseas competitor in Australia, the American firm of Goodyear, to combine the tyre operations of the two firms in Australia and New Zealand. They also agreed to combine in Papua New Guinea where Dunlop, since 1969, had operated a busy retreading and tyre service industry under the name of Dunlop Papua and New Guinea Pty Ltd.

In 1987 South Pacific Tyres was formed, with Goodyear and Pacific Dunlop each owning half of the company. This had big advantages in Gough's eyes. The two big Australian tyre-makers, instead of competing with each other, would co-operate in competing against imported tyres. Moreover, the firm would have access to the latest American techniques and innovations in tyres. From 1987 Australia had only one major manufacturer of tyres operating in an industry where, less than two decades previously, half a dozen tyre firms manufactured. Three years later, with the closing of the old Goodyear factory at the Sydney suburb of Granville, the tyre industry was largely confined to Melbourne. Back in the 1960s, however, five Australian cities had their own tyre factories.

In the year of the company's centenary, South Pacific Tyres was manufacturing tyres at three Melbourne factories and at the old Dunlop NZ factory near Wellington, from which consignments were shipped to Australia. The four main brands of tyres in production — Dunlop, Goodyear, Olympic and Kelly — were sold to motorists through the Beaurepaire, Goodyear and McLeod Tyre Stores in Australia, and the Beaurepaire, Goodyear and Frank Allen Tyre Stores in New Zealand.

The showplace of South Pacific Tyres was a factory making steel radial truck tyres at Somerton, on the plains just north of Melbourne. A few old hands from Montague visited the new factory and could not quite believe it: some said they would be ill at ease working in such a tidy factory. And where, they thought, were the time-blackened ceilings that were the hallmark of any decent rubber works. Whereas Montague had been cramped and grimy, hot in summer, crowded with people at the changing of the shift, and the scene of so much manual work, the Somerton factory was vast, high and well lit with conditioned air and automatic machinery. Employees who stood at one of the factory doors in the twilight might see the occasional rabbit and even a fox, for the Somerton factory stood on the edge of rocky grazing land. In contrast a 'tyre-builder' standing at night by one of the countless doorways at Montague might have seen a rat scurrying up a lane. Employing relatively few people to make a large output of heavy tyres, the new Somerton factory was highly competitive and capable of winning export markets.

By the start of the 1990s less than ten per cent of the sales revenue of Pacific Dunlop came from tyres, although nearly seven thousand people were employed in tyres. For the company, tyres were much less important as a source of revenue than were Ansell's latex products. Clothes and footwear and sporting goods earned three times the total profit earned by tyres, but slowly tyres were to become more profitable. Their manufacture, under Rodney

Chadwick, became more efficient than ever before. With the co-operation of the trade unions, Somerton's work practices were soon in advance of nearly all other factories in the automotive industry. The twelve-hour shift was worked so that maximum use would be made of expensive machinery. Tyres had turned the corner.

As Pacific Dunlop engaged in more overseas ventures, its methods of finance had to be reshaped. In January 1987 its shares were listed for the first time on the London Stock Exchange. A month later its shares were listed in Tokyo, and before long its annual report was appearing in the Japanese language as well as English. In July 1987 it was listed in New York, thus becoming probably the first Australian company to be listed in the big three overseas financial markets. While more and more of the shareholders had international addresses, another large contingent of shareholders were the rank-and-file employees. The tradition, strong in the 1920s, of encouraging employees to buy shares in the company for which they worked was revived in the 1980s, and by the end of the decade more than five thousand employees owned shares which they bought with interest-free loans.

In the decision to manufacture and trade in whatever part of the world provided opportunities, the company was influenced partly by the Australian government's reluctance to support manufacturing within Australia. The decision was also aided by Australia's removal of foreign exchange controls in the early years of the Hawke government and the subsequent ease with which capital and profits could be transferred around the world. To move offshore was the trend of the decade for many big Australian companies. In October 1989, thirteen of the top fifteen Australian companies had substantial assets abroad and they gained an important part of their sales and profit from those overseas operations. Thus Pacific Dunlop had 41 per cent of its assets abroad (earning 25 per cent of its profit abroad); and yet it ranked only in the middle of the top companies in terms of its overseas involvement.

The overseas ventures called for more capital. The company now tended to finance overseas ventures by borrowing in the same currency. 'If we invest in America, we borrow US dollars to finance it', said Ian Clark. Thus in the United States sixty-five million American dollars was raised from a convertible note issue in 1986 and another seventy-five million dollars in 1987. Funds were borrowed overseas at lower rates than those available in Australia in the high-interest years of the decade. Even so, the memory of the deeds of that exuberant borrower, Eric Dunshea, lived on in the minds of directors and executives. In what proved to be an over-optimistic period in Australian finance, they remembered Dunshea and were careful not to allow their burden of annual interest payments to become too heavy.

In the way it organised itself, the company was unusually decentralised. In its centenary year, 1993, the managing director, Philip Brass, controlled nine operating groups, each of which had its own managing director: Ansell

International (Harry Boon); GNB Batteries (Graham Spurling); Cables (Ian Campbell); Distribution (Barry Saunders); Industrial, Foam and Fibre (Philip Gay); Medical Group (William Thomas); Pacific Brands which consisted of Clothing, Textiles, Footwear and Sporting goods (Robert Hershan); Pacific Brands Food Group (Grant Latta); and South Pacific Tyres (Rodney Chadwick). Along with Brass, two of these managing directors, Chadwick and Spurling, had seats on the board of Pacific Dunlop. The head office was leanly staffed. Responsibility rested with each group, each factory and depot, each working-place. In handling money, however, Pacific Dunlop was a centraliser. The head office was becoming a mini-bank in its own right. All the operations in several hundred factories and in thousands of offices and sales outlets in many lands, all the financial risks involved in borrowing and lending and transferring funds and in exchanging them from one currency to another, were concentrated in what was called a treasury, housed in head office in Melbourne. For the year 1991 this mini-bank handled about twenty-six billion dollars. About one-seventh of the company's pre-tax profit was coming from this mini-bank and, in smaller part, the insuring and leasing arrangements it conducted for the company.

Ian Clark as finance director supervised the company's finances for seventeen years, the last of them in an emerging era sometimes described as 'financial globalisation'. When he retired in 1991, at the mere age of fifty-five, he had seen the collapse of many international walls of finance and the erosion of many monetary borders. He saw the increasing role of overseas investors in Pacific Dunlop. In effect it was foreign capital returning after the retreat of English Dunlop but it was on a larger scale than ever before. In the late 1980s, in the space of about four years, the US, European and Japanese investors came to own some thirty-five per cent of the shares in Pacific Dunlop. They had mostly bought their shares in the open market; barely one in ten had come from the global issue of shares made by Pacific Dunlop in May 1989. American investors especially saw a future in Pacific Dunlop. Their feeling was that a company leading the market in medical-examination gloves and condoms was likely to prosper in the face of the AIDS scare.

The main reason why overseas institutions and individuals bought shares was simply the company's recent run of successes. Between 1984 and 1990 its after-tax profit rose from $66 million to $301 million. Earnings for each share were twenty-five cents in 1984 and six years later they were forty-two cents. And employees increased from 19 500 to nearly 45 000 in the space of five years declining in 1990 to 41 000. In the same six years sales almost trebled, and one-third of total sales were now outside Australia. The world's economic slump of the early 1990s was to test the solidity of that period of growth but at the start of 1993 there was no sign of brittleness.

Epilogue

THE COMPANY had begun in a Melbourne lane in 1893, making one product — a bicycle tyre that resembled a fat sausage of tropical rubber. By the time the company was fifty years old it was making many products but they were primarily of rubber: the truck and car tyres, bicycle tyres, aircraft tyres, rubber boots, hot-water bottles, rubber mats, the rubber parts of milking machines, pillows and seats and other rubber cushioning products as well as all those rubber parts that acted as cushions or buffers in a variety of products and industrial processes. In a typical year far more than half of the revenue came from tyres.

The first rush to diversify began under Eric Dunshea when the company was about to celebrate its seventy-fifth birthday, but his rush almost ended in rout. After much lopping and pruning the move towards diversity began again about 1980. It has not been halted. Nowadays Pacific Dunlop handles so many products that not one employee can know the name of all the products it makes or sells in scores of countries. If samples of each of the products the company makes or distributes were to be displayed side by side, they would call for a supermarket with sections ranging from foodstuffs and medical supplies, tyres and other motor accessories, to electrical goods and sporting goods, footwear and clothes. And in some sections would be many versions of the same item, all made by Pacific Dunlop under different brands, whether bicycles under such names as the Malvern Star, Speedwell, Repco, Raleigh and Cyclops, or clothing under such names as Cottontails, Red Robin, Holeproof, Rio, No Knickers, Heroes, Berlei, Jockey, Chesty Bond, Gotcha, Explorers, Underdaks, Computer Socks, Grand Slam and Antz Pantz.

Pacific Dunlop had begun simply as an *Australasian* company — to use a word much favoured at the turn of the century. It operated only in Australian and New Zealand territories. While it imported many goods from England it never exported outside its territories — unless a major war dislocated the normal supply routes. Its first name affirmed its geographical boundaries: it was the Dunlop Pneumatic Tyre Company of Australasia from 1899 and the Dunlop Rubber Company of Australasia from 1905. It did not drop the word 'Australasia' from its title until the mergers of 1929. Twelve years later the word Australia appeared for the first time in the company's title, remaining there until 1980 when the Olympic company was taken over. Indeed for some forty-five years the company did not even manufacture in New Zealand, having sold back that territory to English Dunlop.

For long the firm was Australasian or Australian partly because its main patents and brand names had authority only in this corner of the world. While legally it could not trade under the name of Dunlop outside Australia and New Zealand, it remained primarily Australian for another reason. The incentives to concentrate on Australia were so strong: a fast-growing population in most decades, and a high-spending people who took to the motor car and therefore to rubber tyres ahead of nearly all other peoples. Moreover, the federal government built a high tariff wall around Australia, providing sure profits for factories that were only moderately efficient.

The company's main decision, in its recent history, was to break out of Australia. That began in the 1970s, when Mr Whitlam was prime minister. Dunlop's decision to build factories for latex gloves and condoms in Malaysia and for shoes in the Philippines was a defensive but positive response to the federal government's new policy towards manufacturing. No longer was the Australian factory to be so protected as of old. Even incentives to export factory goods were abolished by Mr Whitlam's government. The lower tariff imposed against imports encouraged a few Australian firms to build factories outside Australia and to bring back the goods. If those factories were efficient they could also export to other lands. Ansell was the first great success; it succeeded in its new overseas home even before its products were boosted by the AIDS epidemic.

Another change early in the 1980s reflected an emphasis on attack rather than defence. The company no longer expanded overseas to cope with Australian obstacles and to meet Australian needs. It expanded overseas because that was where the huge markets lay and that was where the big firms operated: that was the international league where only the efficient and fast-changing firms could survive. The United States market, which dwarfed Australia's, especially became the company's goal. In a variety of products, ranging from batteries and latex products, pace-makers, Cochlear implants and shoes, Pacific Dunlop became a force in the United States as well as other major markets. In several products it was one of the two or three leaders in the United States; in several it led the world. These achievements were possible only by leaving Australia and by facing the strongest competition the world could offer.

Even in Australia more of the factories and products faced competition from foreign imports, some of them from Dunlop-owned factories in foreign lands. Thus in 1960 close to one hundred per cent of the company's profits had come from tyres and other products that depended on tariff protection. By 1985 about thirty-five per cent of the company's profits still came from Australian-made products that depended on tariff protection. By 1991 the proportion had fallen to sixteen per cent. After the announcement in March 1991 by the prime minister, Mr Hawke, that the level of protection would come down further, Pacific Dunlop was likely to enter an era when it earned only ten per cent of its profit from goods made in Australia behind a tariff wall — or to be exact, a low fence. If the government's policy was maintained, import duties on footwear, clothing and textiles would be low by 1995 and duties on motor vehicles would be low by the year 2000, thus reducing the production of cars and the need for new-car tyres.

In one important part of its Australian operations, the company did not have to rely on the protective tariff. Foam and fibre products and such rubber products as conveyor belts were bulky and not so easily imported. Beds and quilts and pillows (whether rubber or filled with down or feathers) and sofas could not be shipped to Australia cheaply. In the early 1990s the company in Australia and New Zealand was expanding its manufacturing of many rubber and plastic products. In one year the company took over The Roberts Company, Vita Pacific and their consumer products, and the extrusion operations of Hunter Douglas in Queensland. In New Zealand it bought out Servitor which made polyurethane products, and Barnes Plastics which was the main moulder of expanded polystyrene used in packaging cheese, taps, and an endless number of products. In pillows and quilts it bought out Kimpton and Northern Feather. After nearly sixty years Dunlopillo remained a big name in Australia — one of the few innovations of English Dunlop still prominent.

By 1992 the company manufactured goods in many nations stretching from Germany and France, Mexico, the USA and China in the northern hemisphere to such equatorial lands as Malaysia, Sri Lanka and Thailand and such southern lands as Brazil, Papua New Guinea and New Zealand. The tendency to open new factories overseas rather than in Australia was strong. Thus in the year 1990–1, the making of pacemakers was concentrated in Miami, Florida; the production of balloons was being transferred from the high-cost USA to Sri Lanka; and a new Olex plant at Shenzhen in southern China began to make cables while a sister plant was being built in northern China. In the same year another Grosby footwear factory was being built in China, as were underwear factories for Bonds, Holeproof and Berlei. In Beijing an endless line of Holeproof socks, at the rate of twelve million pairs a year, came from another factory. Soon there would be thirteen Pacific Dunlop factories in East and South-East Asia. In December 1991 the company set up an Asian advisory board, probably the first such board to advise a major Australian company. Called the Western Pacific Rim Advisory Board, it consisted of five well-known businessmen in East Asia: Dr Narongchai Akrasanee of Bangkok, Tan Sri Zain Azraai of Kuala Lumpur, Jing Shuping of Beijing, Washington Sycip of Manila, and Tang I-Fang of Singapore.

Within Australia the company was growing more by acquiring existing factories than by building new. Of course a few new factories arose each year, and older factories were transformed or enlarged. Thus in 1992, at Somerton in Victoria, there stood a new factory capable of recycling one-third of all the tyres discarded in Australia each year (three and a-half million tyres), while at Ulverstone in north–west Tasmania an upgraded factory was capable of converting 150 000 tonnes of potatoes a year into frozen french fries. Most of the large factories were being built in Asia. Between 1987 and 1992 the number of the company's employees in Australia increased by only 7000 but those working in other lands increased by 11 000. In June 1992 the company employed a total of 48 000 women and men, with almost 28 000 in Australia, almost 7000 in the USA, almost 4000 in Malaysia and almost 3000 in China, over 2000 in both Sri Lanka and New Zealand, and 1500 in Thailand.

Dunlop had begun in Melbourne by making only one product, largely by hand. It continued to make that product, the bicycle tyre, until 1972. Meanwhile it added a host of new products, becoming the largest supplier of consumer goods in Australia. By June 1992 it was making thousands of different products in nearly 200 factories in thirteen different lands. Its revenue was close to six billion dollars, of which only one dollar in every seven came from the new Petersville. It employed far more people in overseas lands than it had employed everywhere on the eve of taking over Olympic in 1980. No other manufacturing company in the history of Australia had become so global. No other company had ever involved itself in such a wide span of products in such a variety of industries.

Notes on sources
of information

Reminiscences

Part of the material in the history came from the recollections of directors, executives and many other employees. Only a fraction of the information they provided could be used in the book, but some of the most revealing episodes and observations came from the recollections of the following people:

Present and past directors: John Gough, Philip Brass, Rodney Chadwick, Sir Leslie Froggatt, Ian Clark, Ian Beaurepaire, D. H. Kemp and Leith Jarman.

Senior executives: John Rennie and Mohammad Elzanaty.

Retired employees: Bert Wittig, Neville Moffatt, Stan Johnston, Bill Jacobs, Ted Benbow, Len Knight, Bill Appleby, Jack Burnes, Wal Best, Ted Faggeter, Marjorie Williams, Stan Marshall, Alan Clayton, Ivan Stevens, Laurie Daggard, Frank Perry, Phil Appleyard, Cam Wilson, Col Dawson, David Staley, Bill Waterson, Syd Neath, Stan Orton, Saul Ziven, Harold Christensen, Len Knight, Bruce Mitchell, Phil Manton, John Creswell, Bill Pask, Alby Taylor, Bill Matthews, Stan Mather, Fred Rohrer, Claude McFarlane, Robert Hurst, Jackie Center, Georgie Lilley, Clarrie Penhall, Orm Burton, Ross Dodson, Fred Wickham, Dick Dowling and Jim Mercer.

Special thanks go to Peter McGough for collecting old Dunlop posters, signs and products, to John McLean for finding so many photographs, and to Julie Gibbs of Allen & Unwin for supervising the production of the book.

In New Zealand I gained much from Peter Scott, Michael Phelan, Don Smith, the staff at the Upper Hutt tyre factory, and Julian Proctor, who is a son of Sir Philip Proctor. I express my thanks to Jim Shaw and Paul Trainor for answering my queries on businesses taken over by Pacific Dunlop and to the late Geoff Garland, who spoke on his father's business career.

Thanks go to Peter Darvell of Darvell & Associates, London, for providing information on Ernest Terah Hooley.

Company records

Most of the evidence on which this history is based comes from the private archives of Pacific Dunlop. Generally the evidence for the last sixty-five years is far more detailed than for the first thirty-five years. Thus the board's minute books, beginning in 1899, are relatively brief. Moreover the directors meeting regularly in Melbourne received verbal information rather than written papers to guide their decisions.

The board papers, perhaps the most valuable source of all, begin in the late 1920s after English Dunlop bought back an interest and wished to be informed more closely of the reasons behind the decisions. These papers became voluminous. Even the papers presented to each board member in the last twenty years would run to many thousands of pages — reports on specific activities of the company, background papers to take-overs, reports of overseas visits, outlines of new products, statistics on the growth or shrinkage of markets.

The published annual reports of the company, from 1899, are lean on information for perhaps the first forty years. The thin leaflet slowly gave way to the annual reports of seventy to ninety pages published in recent years. The chairman's addresses at the annual meetings of shareholders, sometimes a useful guide, have not always been found for the first three decades. Early prospectuses and share registers have been kept.

The letters passing from Melbourne to London between 1893 and say 1980 — and they must have numbered many thousands — have vanished, with the exception of the few preserved in board papers. For the 1890s when there was no separate Australian company, almost the only official source is the two volumes of private ledgers which list early balance sheets, the expenditure on advertisements, travels and promotions. There are several secret books, beginning in 1908–9, in which the pre-1914 formulas for various rubber products were set down. Share registers have been kept.

In the first company magazine, the monthly *Dunlop Gazette*, Harry B. James began a series of entertaining articles, 'Looking Back', in November 1938. He recalled his career with Dunlop and especially the cycling races he promoted from the mid 1890s. Later 'house magazines' are useful in a variety of ways. In the Noel Butlin Archives Centre of the Australian National University were deposited, between 1957 and 1960, much material on promotion and advertising including price lists of early products, and several of the early bicycle photographs published in this book.

In the incidental material in the company archives are valuable papers and clippings. They include D. Harold Kemp's typewritten 'notes on the news' written for ABC radio on rubber-related topics, mainly from 1949 to 1956; John Edwards's long interview with Eric Dunshea in the *Australian Financial Review* on 29 April 1971; and Barrie Dunstan's interview with Dunshea in the Melbourne *Herald* on 4 September 1971.

English Dunlop's Papers

The early minute books of the English company, with their references to setting up the bicycle–tyre factory in Melbourne in 1893, have not come to light. Mr D. S. Hunt, manager of secretarial administration for BTR in Vincent Square, London, tried to locate them in 1991–2, his company having taken over the largest part of the English Dunlop. Nevertheless, much information on the English company is in the Australian records, including occasional reports by the English chairmen.

Other rubber companies

The archives of the rubber companies taken over by Pacific Dunlop and its predecessors are patchy. On the two Barnet Glass firms acquired, the internal records are few. The records of the Perdriau Rubber Co. are better: they include the Memorandum and Articles of Association of 1904, the printed directors' reports and balance sheets presented to shareholders; various letters and items kindly lent by Kelvin Perdriau of Sydney; the reminiscences of Henry Perdriau, recorded in September 1929 and recalling the start of the business in 1881; and various advertisements and price catalogues.

For Olympic the minute books have survived. A valuable and painstaking typescript history of the firm, 'Alpha and Omega: the History of Olympic', was compiled by Derek Beaurepaire. Observations about Sir Frank Beaurepaire and Olympic, as seen from the eyes of a rival, appear from time to time in the Dunlop archives. The volumes of the house magazine, *Olympic News*, run to 1980. On Dunlop New Zealand there is much material in Pacific Dunlop's own archives. A valuable unpublished, unsigned typescript of seventy-nine pages, 'History of Dunlop Co. in New Zealand', was written by Sir Philip Proctor who came out from English Dunlop in 1937.

Other companies taken over by Pacific Dunlop

On the clusters of companies bought out by Pacific Dunlop, especially since 1968, the surviving records vary from almost nothing to riches — sometimes the riches had to be condensed into two sentences, during the writing of this book. On Petersville Sleigh, interesting records were collected by Jim Shaw. Bruce Hillsmith of Bateau Bay, New South Wales, kindly sent a cassette and notes on the history of Edgell – Birds Eye. There is a useful, unsigned typescript on the history of Repco, taking the story to about 1988.

Books, journals and other printed records

On the history of the rubber industry in the British Isles and the world: H. L. Terry, *India–rubber and Its Manufacture* (London, 1907); A. G. Donnithorne, *British Rubber Manufacturing: An Economic Study of Innovations* (London, 1958); P. Schidrowitz and T. R. Dawson, *History of the Rubber Industry*

(Cambridge, 1952); James McMillan, *The Dunlop Story: The Life, Death and Re–birth of a Multi– national* (London, 1989); Geoffrey Jones, 'The Expansion of British Multinational Manufacturing, 1890–1939', ed. Akio Okochi and Tadakatsu Inoue, *International Conference on Business History*, (University of Tokyo, 1984, vol. 9, pp. 125 ff.); Geoffrey Jones, 'The Growth and Performance of British Multinational Firms Before 1939: The Case of Dunlop', *Economic History Review* (1984, pp. 35–53); Eric Tompkins, *The History of the Pneumatic Tyre* (Dunlop Limited, London, 1981); J. H. Dunning and R. D. Pearce, *The World's Largest Industrial Enterprises 1962–1983* (Aldershot, UK, 1985, pp. 171 ff.); Austin Coates, *The Commerce in Rubber: The First 250 Years* (Singapore, 1987). On the early history of cycling and motoring, especially in Australia: G. G. C. Hanslow, *The Australian Cycling Annual* (Sydney, 1897, a copy in the New South Wales Public Library) which tells much about the early history of Australian cycling; Jim Fitzpatrick, *The Bicycle and the Bush: Man and Machine in Rural Australia* (Melbourne, 1980), an outstanding work on early cycling; S. A. Cheney, *From Horse Power to Horsepower* (Adelaide, 1965); Susan Priestley, *The Crown of the Road: The Story of the RACV* (Melbourne, 1983); Keith Winser, *Story of Australian Motoring* (Melbourne, 1955); Peter Collier and David Horowitz, *The Fords: An American Epic* (New York, 1987); Robert Haldane, *The People's Force: A History of the Victoria Police* (Melbourne, 1986); A. E. Harrison, 'The Competitiveness of the British Cycle Industry, 1890–1914', *Economic History Review* (vol. 22, 1969).

On companies competing with or associated with Dunlop: Graham Lomas, *The Will to Win: The Story of Sir Frank Beaurepaire* (Melbourne, 1960); Marjorie Johnston with John Wippell, *Ansell: Portrait of an International Company* (Glen Waverley, 1990), a valuable record of a company that became crucial to Pacific Dunlop; Tim Hewat, *The Plastics Revolution: The Story of Nylex* (Melbourne, 1983); George G. Foletta, *Woven Threads* and *The Foletta Family* (privately published, 1969 and 1975); Guyon W. Crozier: *Para, 75 Years: 1910–1985* (Christchurch, 1985) for George Skellerup's early career with Dunlop in Australia; and Michael Hast, *100 Years of Power: the Lawrence & Hanson Story* (Hawthorn, 1986).

On other facets of Australia's commercial and industrial history: Michael Cannon, *Land Boom and Bust* (Melbourne, 1972); D. P. Mellor, *The Role of Science and Industry* (Canberra, 1958) for synthetic rubber and for the pilot's anti–blackout suit; Brian Carroll, *Australian Made* (Melbourne, 1987); *Victoria and its Metropolis* (Melbourne, 1888, vol. 2, pp. 604), on Bernard Glass; *Cyclopedia of Victoria* (Melbourne, 1903, vol. 1, p. 533–4, 541), on Barnet Glass and W. J. Proctor; articles in *Australian Dictionary of Biography* on W. L. Baillieu by J. R. Poynter in vol. 7 and on W. A. Watt by Geoffrey Serle in vol. 12; entries in the English *Dictionary of Business Biography* (London, 1984, vol. 2) on William Harvey du Cros, Sir Arthur du Cros, and Sir Eric Geddes.

Newspapers and magazines

On the first years of the Dunlop pneumatic tyre in Australia, the cycling magazines are more useful than the company's own records. The best source is the *Australian Cyclist*, especially from 1893 to 1905. It includes an interview with W. J. Proctor on 29 August 1895 and a report on 1 May 1902 of the lawsuit, Dunlop's car versus Bloomfield's horse. Another valuable source is the *Austral Wheel* and its interviews with E. W. Rudd in March 1898 and W. J. Proctor in November 1898. Other newspapers were consulted on specific issues: the *Australasian*, 2 October 1897, p. 718, for the story of the 1886 ride to Geelong; the *Economist* of London, 1898–1900, for the ups and downs of the English Dunlop company; the *Lyttelton Times* (New Zealand), 20 April 1906, for the fire at Dunlop's building in Christchurch; the Adelaide *Register*, 2 August 1913, for the opening of Dunlop's building; the *Australian Motorist* for 1916–18; the *Argus*, Melbourne, for a variety of reports including the lawsuit on the Dunlop automobile and Bloomfield horse on 23 April 1902 and V. J. Saddler's obituary on 5 August 1924; the South Melbourne *Record*, August 1908 and February 1909, on the smoke nuisance at Montague; *Industrial Australian and Mining Standard* (Melbourne) on secondary industry in the 1920s; *Stock Exchange Record* (Melbourne) for comments on the Perdriau and Barnet Glass rubber companies and the Rapson Tyre and Rubber Co. (Aust.) Limited in the late 1920s and early 1930s.

Government publications

An investigation into rubber goods was conducted by the Interstate Commission of Australia, *Commonwealth Parliamentary Papers*, 1914–17, vol. 7, part 2. The best source on the early history of Barnet Glass is the court case, Glass V. The Pioneer Rubber Works of Australia Limited, in the *Victorian Law Reports*, 1906, pp. 754–77, and in *The Argus Law Reports*, 1906, pp. 529 ff.

Other archives

Minutes of the Rubber Trade Board, 1909–13, which fixed wages and working conditions, are in the Public Records Office of Victoria. Papers on Barnet Glass (1900, 1904, 1907) and Dunlop Pneumatic Tyre Co. of Australasia (1899 and later) are in the archives of Victoria's Corporate Affairs Office, Melbourne. The first minute book of the Royal Automobile Club of Victoria, in the founding of which Dunlop men were prominent, is held at the RACV, Melbourne.

Pacific Dunlop officials

Chairman
Fitzgerald	The Hon. Nicholas	1899–1907
Riley	James H.	1907–11
Grice	Sir John	1911–29
Watt	The Rt Hon. William A.	1929–46
Bartlett	Wallace A.	1946–7
Stewart	Sir Alexander	1947–56
McVey	Sir Daniel	1956–68
Dunshea	Eric E.	1968–72
Blackwood	Sir Robert R.	1972–9
Massy–Greene	Sir Brian	1979–86
Froggatt	Sir Leslie	1986–90
Gough	John B.	1990–

Chief Executive Officer
Proctor	William J.	1899–1904
Garland	Richard	1904–19
Snodgrass	Donald G.	1928–9
Ormiston	Frederic S.	1929–35
Fenton	Albert	1929–35
Bartlett	Wallace A.	1935–47
Blackwood	Sir Robert R.	1947–66
Dunshea	Eric E.	1966–72
Kellam	Ernest A.	1972–4
Jarman	Leith M.	1974–80
Gough	John B.	1980–7
Brass	Philip	1988–

Usually the chief executive officer was called general manager, but from 1928 to 1935 and from 1972 onwards his title was managing director.

Directors

Fitzgerald	Hon. Nicholas	1899–1907
Hughes	Frederic G., Major–General	1899–1944
Grice	Sir John	1899–1935
Saddler	Valentine J.	1899–1924
Rennie	Z. C.	1899–1900
Garland	Richard	1900–19
Riley	James H.	1905–29
Baillieu	William L.	1905–33
Stewart	Sir Alexander	1924–56
Beharrell	Sir George, DSO (Dunlop UK)	1927–49
Fraser	Sir Colin (Alternate 1927–38)	
Geddes	Sir Eric (Dunlop UK)	1927–37
Smith	Frederick J. (Alternate 1927–36)	
Snodgrass	Donald G	1927–9
Watt	The Hon. William A.	1929–46
Ormiston	Frederick S.	1929–35
Fenton	Albert	1929–35
Perdriau	Edgar M.	1929–34
Perdriau	Henry	1929–35
Storey	David A., Colonel	1934–64
Cross	Charles C. B.	1934–6
Daniell	Harold	1934–58
Baillieu	The Rt Hon. Lord (Dunlop UK)	1933–8
Proctor	Charles A. (Dunlop UK)	1937–45
Massy–Greene	Sir Walter (Alternate 1934–52)	
Smith	Frederick J.	1936–46
Fraser	Sir Colin	1938–44
Bartlett	Wallace A.	1944–7
McVey	Sir Daniel	1947–72
Beharrell	Sir George E. (Dunlop UK)	1949–68
Blackwood	Sir Robert R.	1951–79
Dunshea	Eric E.	1951–72
Simkin	Roy H.	1951–60
Baillieu	Marshall L.	1952–79
Priestley	Donald H.	1955–61
Knox	Sir Robert (Alternate 1936–56)	
Chippindall	Sir Giles	1959–69
Kellam	Ernest A.	1961–79
Stewart	James Cuming	1964–70
Geddes	Sir Reay (Dunlop UK)	1967–79
Guest	James C.	1968–70
	(Alternate 1953–68)	
Holt	Eric (Dunlop UK)	1968–71

Fraser	Sir Campbell (Dunlop UK)	1968–83
Baillieu	John M. (Alternate 1971–9)	
Grosby	Ralph	1972–3
Kemp	D. Harold	1972–6
Massy Greene	Sir Brian	1972–86
	(Alternate 1968–72)	
Jarman	Leith M.	1972–92
Clark	Ian H.	1973–91
Eastwood	A. G.	1973–6
Beischer	William R.	1975–89
Scott	J. R. (Dunlop UK)	1975–6
Gough	John B.	1976–
Harper	John B.	1977–81
	(Alternate 1957–74)	
	(Substitute 1975–7)	
Froggatt	Sir Leslie T.	1978–90
Wood	Kenneth	1979–85
	(Alternate 1973–4)	
	(Substitute 1975–9)	
Newby	J. Leslie	1979–92
	(Substitute 1977–9)	
Harvey	A. T. (Dunlop UK)	1979–82
Beaurepaire	Ian F.	1980–92
Holder	KennethB.	1980–
Brass	Philip	1980–
Barnet	Peter C.	1982–4
Lord	Alan (Dunlop UK)	1982–4
Kennedy	James J.	1984
	(Substitute 1980–4)	
Redpath	Bruce R.	1984–9
	(Substitute 1979–84)	
Coates	Alan W.	1987–
Goode	Charles B.	1987–
Chadwick	Rodney L.	1990–
Spurling	Graham G.	1990–
Penington	Professor David G.	1991–
Webber	Ian E.	1991–
Jackson	Margaret A.	1992–
Burgess	Ian G.	1993–

Company Secretary

Proctor	Charles A.	1900–10
Sherwood	C. O.	1910–11

MacKirdy	Henry	1911–37
Kellam	Ernest A. (Acting 1937–9)	1939–42
Dunshea	Eric E.	1942–66
Clark	Ian H.	1966–74
Stevenson	David L.	1974–5
Hewitt	Trevor	1975–82
Anderson	Alan W.	1982–3
Horton	Kerry W.	1983–4
Rennie	John C.	1984–

Executive Committee at 30 April 1993

Philip Brass	Managing Director Pacific Dunlop
Michael J. Bolton	Group Chief Accountant Pacific Dunlop
Harry Boon	Managing Dierctor Ansell International
Ian A. Campbell	Managing Director Olex Cables
Rodney L. Chadwick	Chief Executive South Pacific Tyres
Roger A. Eustace	Group Executive — Corporate Pacific Dunlop
Philip R. Gay	Managing Director Pacific Dunlop Industrial, Foam & Fibre Group
David M. Graham	Treasurer Pacific Dunlop
Robert B. Hershan	Managing Director Pacific Brands
Grant F. Latta	Managing Director Pacific Brands Food Group
Howard J. McDonald	Executive General Manager — Corporate Affairs Pacific Dunlop
John C. Rennie	Company Sercretary Pacific Dunlop
Barry A. E. Saunders	Managing Director ALH Australia

Graham G. Spurling	Managing Director GNB International Battery Group
William G.M. Thomas	Chief Executive Officer Nucleus Group
Ian D. Veal	Executive General Manager — Finance Pacific Dunlop

Index